# Cull of the Wild

## *A Contemporary Analysis of Wildlife Trapping in the United States*

**Animal Protection Institute**
**Sacramento, California**

*Edited by*
Camilla H. Fox and Christopher M. Papouchis, MS

*With special thanks for their contributions to*
Barbara Lawrie, Dena Jones, MS, Karen Hirsch, Gil Lamont,
Nicole Paquette, Esq., Jim Bringle, Monica Engebretson, Debbie Giles,
Jean C. Hofve, DVM, Elizabeth Colleran, DVM, and Martin Ring.

*Funded in part by*
Edith J. Goode Residuary Trust
The William H. & Mattie Wattis Harris Foundation
The Norcross Wildlife Foundation

Founded in 1968, the Animal Protection Institute is a national nonprofit organization dedicated to advocating for the protection of animals from cruelty and exploitation.

Copyright © 2004 Animal Protection Institute

Cover and interior design © TLC Graphics, www.TLCGraphics.com

Indexing Services: Carolyn Acheson

Cover photo: © Jeremy Woodhouse/Photodisc Green

For further information about the Animal Protection Institute and its programs, contact:

Animal Protection Institute
P.O. Box 22505
Sacramento, CA 95822
Phone: (916) 447-3085
Fax:    (916) 447-3070
Email: info@api4animals.org
Web: www.api4animals.org

Printed by Bang Publishing, Brainerd, Minnesota, USA

ISBN 0-9709322-0-0

Library of Congress ©2004

# TABLE OF CONTENTS

# FOREWORD

Trapping advocates want us to believe that trapping can be humane and that there are no alternatives to this barbaric and timeworn practice. Regardless of how "humane" one tries to be, however, trapping is extremely inhumane and too often results in serious physical and psychological damage to the victim. The very thought that many of our animal kin experience serious lifelong psychological harm should they survive being trapped is foreign to many people. Nonetheless, animals can suffer psychological damage as painful to them as it is to humans. I often wonder how those who trap animals would like being trapped themselves? I doubt they'd like it very much. Well, neither do other animals.

*Cull of the Wild* is a timely and timeless contribution. It is loaded with useful and hard-to-find data concerning all aspects of trapping. While such activities as commercial fur trapping are indeed dying industries, unfortunately, they aren't yet dead. Trapping is also used in other venues as human interests continue to widely and wantonly trump those of other animals. We seem to have a strong urge to dominate nature — to redecorate it — to move animals around from place to place, to control populations, and to kill animals when they become nuisances, impediments to building new homes, shopping malls, and parking lots. *Cull of the Wild* dispels many of the myths used to justify trapping, be it for fur or "nuisance" or predator control and makes a compelling case that use of body-gripping traps is not only unnecessary, it is increasingly unjustifiable in a society that calls itself civilized.

So, my suggestion is a simple one — read this wonderful book, share it with others, and use it as a guide for improving how we go about interacting with other animals. Many thanks to the Animal Protection Institute for undertaking this time-consuming project. It will certainly be an extremely valuable contribution. I wish this book were available when I studied coyotes. At the end of my time studying coyotes, I vowed never to trap another coyote. I remember, and am continually haunted by, the eyes of each and every coyote staring up at me, pleading to be released, crying (if they could) to be freed, because of their fear and psychological trauma and perhaps hidden physical injuries. I also came to realize that until different and more humane methods were available, I just might not be able to conduct a particular study. Trading off new knowledge for coyote trauma wasn't an acceptable road to travel. Given our big brains and collective wisdom, I know that we could develop more humane alternatives rapidly when we have to interfere in the lives of other animals, when it is in the best interests of an individual. If there was a moratorium on leghold traps today, I have no doubt that trappers would quickly develop humane alternatives. It's amazing what we can do when we're pressured to do it.

Historical precedence and convenience have to be put aside for more humane practices and love for other animals. As a result, the world will have less cruelty, and I doubt that anyone would disagree with the fact that a world with less cruelty and more compassion would be a better world in which to live and to raise children.

*Marc Bekoff*
*Professor of Biology,*
*University of Colorado, Boulder*
*Editor,* The Encyclopedia of Animal Behavior

# PREFACE

In 1863, Charles Darwin called the leghold trap one of the cruelest devices ever invented by man, stating, "Few men could endure to watch for five minutes an animal struggling in a trap with a torn limb ... Some ... will wonder how such cruelty can have been permitted to continue in these days of civilization."[1]

Despite Darwin's admonitions almost 140 years ago, the steel-jaw leghold trap remains one of the most commonly used traps in the United States. While 80 countries have recognized the cruelty of the leghold trap and banned its use, including the member countries of the European Union, the U.S. continues to promote its use. Private and government trappers set hundreds of leghold and other body-gripping traps on public and private lands for profit, recreation, and for "wildlife management" purposes.

Few people who witness the brutality of body-gripping traps in action can endure the sight for long. I was 17 when I first saw a leghold trap up close. While attending the World Society for the Protection of Animals international conference in Luxembourg, I was moved to tears by a heart-wrenching film that showed trapped animals writhing in pain and terror. I watched in mesmerized shock as animals frantically struggled for freedom, ripping tendons and severing limbs in a vain attempt to free themselves from the trap's vice-like grip. I saw the power with which a leghold trap could maim an animal, and later, when trying to set one myself, nearly crushed my finger as I accidentally triggered the trap's jaws. Little did I know that a decade later I would be exposing the cruelty of trapping to audiences as blissfully ignorant as I was at that age.

Since then, I have set hundreds of leghold traps, snares, and Conibear kill-traps to educate the public about the horrors of trapping and the painful truth behind fur. In advocating for the protection of furbearing animals and an end to commercial fur trapping, I have learned two important lessons. First, most people don't know that trapping is still legal in the United States; and second, most people are deeply disturbed by the pain and suffering trapped animals are forced to endure. When shown a picture of an animal mangled by a body-gripping trap, people generally react with a mixture of revulsion and empathy. Some turn away at the sight of such graphic cruelty. Others are so moved that they feel compelled to help. It is the job of animal advocates to channel this compassion into action.

National public opinion polls show that the majority of Americans oppose the use of body-gripping traps and the killing of animals for their fur. When given the opportunity to ban such practices at the ballot box, the public has supported trapping prohibitions. From 1994 to 2000, voters in Arizona, California, Colorado, Massachusetts, and Washington passed state ballot initiatives that banned or severely restricted certain traps and trapping practices.

Such public opposition has led to a dramatic decline in trapping. Today, less than 150,000 Americans (less than 1/10 of 1% of the population) trap and kill animals for profit or recreation, compared to more than 800,000 who trapped wildlife in the early 1980s. Still, these remaining commercial and recreational fur trappers trap and kill more than 4 million animals each year. Millions more are trapped and killed in predator and "nuisance" wildlife control programs.

State and federal wildlife agencies must acknowledge that a growing majority of Americans who oppose the use of cruel traps are demanding that "management" of wildlife be humane, selective, and, preferably, non-lethal. These agencies have two choices: They can either change with the times and alter their management techniques, or face increasing public condemnation and legislative efforts aimed at banning traps deemed inhumane and non-selective.

In the time it has taken you to read this page, hundreds of animals have stepped into the jaws of body-gripping traps throughout North America. Many of these animals have families and young. And like us, they feel pain and fear.

As Darwin espoused more than a century ago, an important part of society's progress lies in questioning and ultimately outgrowing some of its most cruel and barbaric practices. Trapping is one such practice. Apart from its blatant cruelty, the trapping and killing of wildlife for profit and pleasure reinforces a lack of compassion toward nonhuman animals, entrenches humankind's perceived feelings of separateness from, and domination over, the natural world, and stifles human evolution toward a more just and peaceful society.

My deepest hope is that this book will inform and empower its readers, be they animal advocates, legislators, researchers, students, wildlife managers, or concerned citizens, to help make this world a kinder, gentler, and more civilized place for the nonhuman animals with whom we share this planet.

*Camilla H. Fox*
*Animal Protection Institute*
*December 2004*

NOTES

1. Charles Darwin. "Trapping Agony." *Gardeners' Chronicle and Agricultural Gazette* (August 1863).

# INTRODUCTION

The trapping of wildlife remains at the center of a sharp philosophical debate over the management of wild animals in North America. Interested stakeholders represent a broad range of perspectives, from those who view wildlife as commodities and/or "pests" that need to be controlled, to those who believe that wild animals possess inherent rights and intrinsic value. Public opinion surveys have consistently shown that a majority of Americans oppose the practice of trapping wildlife for recreation and profit as well as the use of body-gripping devices.

Since the first state bill banning leghold traps was introduced in the New Hampshire legislature in 1901, animal and environmental advocates have sought to stop cruel and indiscriminate trapping practices through administrative, legislative, and public initiatives. While a few states have passed legislation banning specific trapping devices and methods, most reforms at the state and federal level have been blocked by the powerful consumptive wildlife use lobby, which has sought to convince legislators and the public that trapping is humane, selective, and an important economic industry. Further, state and federal wildlife agencies contend that trapping is necessary for wildlife management, a self-serving argument that has facilitated the continued use of cruel devices under the guise of wildlife conservation.

In this book, the Animal Protection Institute has endeavored to provide a broad array of information on trapping to counter the arguments made by trapping proponents and state wildlife management agencies. This book is intended to be used both as a primer on trapping and as a reference tool providing specific information on trapping devices, practices, and regulations as well as statistics on the species and numbers of animals captured in the United States.

Chapter One provides an overview of trapping in North America, including a brief history of fur trapping, statistics on species and numbers of animals trapped, and a discussion of public attitudes toward trapping and fur. The arguments used to justify and legitimize trapping as put forth by trapping proponents are discussed and refuted in Chapter Two. Chapter Three describes the trapping devices used to capture wildlife, and reviews the scientific research on trapping and the use of injury scales in assessing trap-related injuries.

Chapter Four reviews the history of trap research and the development of trapping standards, providing information on federally-funded trap-testing programs and efforts in the European Union to ban the import of furs from countries still using leghold traps. Chapter Five details trapping regulations in all 50 U.S. states, including legal traps, methods, trap check time requirements, etc. U.S. Fish and Wildlife Service trapping programs on National Wildlife Refuges are documented and discussed in Chapter Six. In Chapter Seven, the different approaches to changing trapping policies through the legislative, administrative, and initiative processes are described, along with a review of federal, state, and local public policy initiatives.

We hope you find this book useful. Please contact the Animal Protection Institute for current trapping statistics, information about the latest efforts to ban trapping, and assistance with organizing a campaign.

# CHAPTER ONE

# Trapping in North America: A Historical Overview

*Camilla H. Fox*

*Few men could endure to watch for five minutes an animal struggling in a trap with a torn limb ... Some will wonder how such cruelty can have been permitted to continue in these days of civilization.*

— Charles Darwin

American history is filled with glorified images of adventurous trappers braving the wilds of colonial North America and paving the way for settlement of the continent. These images persist, invoking idealized notions of the pioneer spirit. The legacy of the fur trade, however, tells quite a different story.

## THE EARLY FUR TRADE

Commercial trapping for wildlife in North America began during the initial occupation by European explorers and colonists, although it wasn't until 1581 that the first ship arrived on the continent with the purpose of delivering animal furs to Europe. Profits from that voyage were staggering, and fur traders recognized the potential wealth to be made from trapping wildlife and selling furs. The ethics of exploiting wildlife for economic gain were not considered, much less debated: Profit was the motivating factor.

By 1620, nearly 100 fur traders operated around Chesapeake Bay. Fur trading had become one of the most lucrative industries of the New World, and North American furbearers were being trapped in unprecedented numbers to satisfy the whims of European fashion.

The quest for fur led to the exploration of the western United States in the seventeenth and eighteenth centuries, and was the impetus behind the Lewis and Clark expedition of 1803. Trappers, called "mountain men," replaced the Native American trappers with whom earlier explorers had bartered. Men such as Jim Bridger, Kit Carson, and Jedediah Smith blazed into fame, along with fur companies known as the American, Missouri, and Northwest. These trappers and traders traveled to western Canada and southern California in search of fur. Generations of settlers followed the trappers' land and water routes and colonized the West. During this period, millions of buffalo, antelope, bear, otter, beaver, fox, and wolf were slaughtered for their fur, hides, other body parts, or for no reason at all. Rotting carcasses remained, littering the prairies and plains.

In the eighteenth and nineteenth centuries, the continent's teeming populations of beaver, otter, fox, and other furbearing animals seemed inexhaustible, and trapping "seasons" and "bag limits" did not exist. Never in U.S. history had animals been slaughtered in such astonishing numbers.

In some areas, beaver, wolverine, pine marten, fisher, kit fox, and otter were trapped to the verge of extinction. Wolves and grizzly bears were virtually exterminated south of Canada, while the North Pacific sea otter population inhabiting the waters between Baja California and Japan was almost wiped out by the end of the nineteenth century — all to feed the growing fur trade. The invention of the steel-jaw leghold trap in 1823 by Sewell Newhouse gave trappers a potent weapon that helped to increase the killing. By 1830, when silk top hats replaced beaver pelt hats as the reigning fashion, the beaver population in the U.S. had already been decimated. It would be almost a century before beavers began to recover.

By the beginning of the twentieth century, the fur trade had ebbed, many wildlife populations were depleted, and a new consciousness emerged regarding the necessity for wildlife conservation and the ethical treatment of animals. Concerned citizens began pushing for legislative controls of consumptive wildlife uses. Protective laws regulating hunting and trapping of certain species, albeit minimal, were passed and state wildlife agencies were established with the mandate of "managing" state wildlife populations.

The birth of the conservation movement and the establishment of laws and regulations limiting hunting and trapping were controlled largely by trapping/hunting interest groups. They filled the positions of power on commissions established to adopt and enforce wildlife laws. Although the numbers of hunters and trappers have declined precipitously and are now far outnumbered by non-consumptive wildlife enthusiasts, they still dominate state fish and wildlife agencies. While hunters and trappers played a significant role in wildlife conservation 75 years ago, the bias toward consumptive wildlife use today is unjustified and has taken a heavy toll.

## Trapping in the 1990s

Although many people think fur trapping went the way of the buffalo hunter, the worldwide fur trade persists. The U.S. and Canada remain two of the largest trapped-fur–producing countries in the world (see Tables 1.1 and 1.2), along with Russia.* In 1997, more than five million animals were trapped in the U.S. for their fur, according to state wildlife agency estimates. This figure considers only target animals, however: At least as many unreported non-target animals may fall victim to body-gripping traps every year.

The United States lags far behind the rest of the world with regard to trapping reforms. More than 80 countries have banned the leghold trap,[†] a device condemned as inhumane by four national and international veterinary associations.[‡] In 1995, member countries of the European Union[§] banned leghold traps and sought to ban the import of furs from countries still using these traps. However, the United States — the world's

---

*Canada trapped approximately 1.5 million animals while Russia trapped an estimated 3–4 million animals in 1997.

[†] Countries banning the leghold trap: Austria, Bahrain, Bangladesh, Belgium, Belize, Benin, Botswana, Brazil, British West Indies, Bulgaria, Burkina Faso, Burundi, Cameroon, Cayman Islands, Chile, Colombia, Costa Rica, Cuba, Cyprus, Czech Republic, Denmark, Dominican Republic, El Salvador, England, Equatorial Guinea, Finland, France, Gabon, Gambia, Germany, Ghana, Greece, Greenland, Guinea, Guyana, Hong Kong, Hungary, India, Israel, Ireland, Italy, Ivory Coast, Jamaica, Jordan, Kenya, Korea (Republic of), Lebanon, Liberia, Liechtenstein, Luxembourg, Mali, Malawi, Malaysia, Maldives, Mauritania, Mexico, Moldavia, Monaco, Morocco, Mozambique, Netherlands, Nicaragua, Niger, Nigeria, Norway, Pakistan, Panama, Philippines, Poland, Portugal, Russia, Scotland, Senegal, Seychelles, Singapore, Spain, Sri Lanka, Swaziland, Sweden, Switzerland, Tanzania, Thailand, Togo, Trinidad & Tobago, Tunisia, Uganda, United Arab Emirates, United Kingdom, Wales, Zaire, Zambia, Zimbabwe.

[‡] The American Veterinary Medical Association, the American Animal Hospital Association, the World Veterinary Association, and the National Animal Control Association have all deemed the steel-jaw leghold trap "inhumane."

[§] Countries that comprise the European Union (as of 2004): Austria, Belgium, Cyprus, Czech Republic, Denmark, Estonia, Finland, France, Germany, Greece, Hungary, Ireland, Italy, Latvia, Lithuania, Luxembourg, Malta, Netherlands, Poland, Portugal, Slovakia, Slovenia, Spain, Sweden, United Kingdom.

## TABLE 1.1

### Number of animals trapped in U.S. by species, 1986–1999.*

| Species | 1986–87 | 1987–88 | 1988–89 | 1989–90 | 1990–91 | 1991–92 | 1992–93 | 1993–94 | 1994–95 | 1995–96 | 1996–97 | 1997–98 | 1998–99 | Total |
|---|---|---|---|---|---|---|---|---|---|---|---|---|---|---|
| Badger | 26,822 | 30,591 | 16,102 | 7,155 | 6,296 | 10,275 | 8,425 | 7,865 | 9,976 | 6,978 | 12,080 | 16,099 | 6,750 | 165,414 |
| Beaver | 556,050 | 473,994 | 309,581 | 270,637 | 176,586 | 205,074 | 197,647 | 275,485 | 469,570 | 273,073 | 428,629 | 466,319 | 333,132 | 4,435,777 |
| Black Bear | 0 | 77 | 75 | 55 | 50 | 40 | 32 | 35 | 45 | 25 | 41 | 56 | 59 | 590 |
| Bobcat | 79,778 | 84,226 | 48,719 | 28,661 | 14,458 | 22,521 | 20,956 | 25,176 | 29,106 | 19,714 | 35,712 | 35,955 | 24,070 | 469,052 |
| Coyote | 327,724 | 333,129 | 171,366 | 122,023 | 102,840 | 154,282 | 186,120 | 201,479 | 195,601 | 147,465 | 179,533 | 193,627 | 154,660 | 2,469,847 |
| Fisher | 5,480 | 6,751 | 4,871 | 4,085 | 3,607 | 3,588 | 5,340 | 6,316 | 7,771 | 6,266 | 8,102 | 14,957 | 8,441 | 85,575 |
| Fox, Arctic | 165 | 612 | 361 | 73 | 0 | 42 | 252 | 144 | 149 | 43 | 135 | 51 | 208 | 2,235 |
| Fox, Gray | 278,047 | 311,232 | 146,112 | 111,618 | 69,504 | 88,855 | 72,865 | 76,819 | 92,470 | 69,306 | 88,900 | 76,711 | 77,344 | 1,559,783 |
| Fox, Red | 399,869 | 390,797 | 277,639 | 170,541 | 158,211 | 168,319 | 146,616 | 148,309 | 160,273 | 146,026 | 167,587 | 171,495 | 130,082 | 2,635,764 |
| Fox, Kit/Swift | 8,633 | 5,998 | 3,702 | 1,918 | 907 | 1,616 | 1,782 | 1,969 | 1,903 | 609 | 2,776 | 727 | 444 | 32,983 |
| Lynx | 1,257 | 1,053 | 1,222 | 1,336 | 1,275 | 2,077 | 1,325 | 1,228 | 793 | 576 | 1,771 | 2,916 | 2,785 | 19,614 |
| Marten | 39,807 | 44,480 | 45,941 | 34,363 | 10,585 | 12,199 | 7,853 | 11,131 | 13,002 | 12,977 | 9,986 | 14,546 | 9,013 | 265,883 |
| Mink | 374,374 | 406,841 | 250,549 | 133,222 | 95,967 | 128,695 | 127,211 | 147,034 | 177,472 | 122,938 | 168,635 | 203,521 | 147,598 | 2,484,058 |
| Muskrat | 6,040,768 | 6,185,105 | 2,488,010 | 1,290,119 | 946,251 | 1,411,060 | 1,378,950 | 1,901,390 | 2,396,924 | 1,395,718 | 1,840,267 | 2,627,155 | 1,426,857 | 31,328,574 |
| Nutria | 1,026,557 | 662,427 | 234,528 | 306,161 | 143,366 | 251,606 | 142,088 | 237,136 | 190,319 | 204,266 | 353,447 | 398,623 | 131,271 | 4,281,795 |
| Opossum | 856,361 | 911,492 | 378,140 | 178,035 | 112,235 | 168,652 | 136,846 | 147,730 | 192,578 | 163,269 | 288,244 | 328,926 | 227,365 | 4,089,872 |
| Otter | 23,238 | 24,335 | 13,067 | 12,906 | 9,018 | 12,129 | 12,592 | 18,900 | 26,243 | 23,553 | 31,314 | 28,167 | 17,614 | 253,076 |
| Raccoon | 3,364,039 | 3,621,523 | 1,651,126 | 1,072,777 | 776,903 | 1,204,347 | 1,030,666 | 1,295,472 | 1,808,663 | 1,537,501 | 2,327,039 | 2,389,163 | 1,846,649 | 23,925,868 |
| Ringtail | 55,937 | 56,379 | 23,027 | 10,886 | 5,698 | 5,370 | 7,743 | 7,435 | 7,580 | 6,818 | 19,955 | 15,111 | 4,174 | 226,113 |
| Skunk | 236,411 | 232,805 | 127,287 | 69,764 | 45,806 | 58,956 | 53,797 | 60,213 | 77,063 | 60,168 | 97,258 | 124,833 | 77,624 | 1,321,985 |
| Weasel | 11,252 | 18,051 | 11,295 | 5,557 | 3,863 | 3,863 | 3,754 | 9,335 | 24,345 | 9,874 | 10,035 | 11,744 | 7,941 | 130,909 |
| Wolf, Gray | 801 | 1,101 | 860 | 1,082 | 1,089 | 1,162 | 1,043 | 1,600 | 1,483 | 1,251 | 1,448 | 1,229 | 1,495 | 15,644 |
| Wolverine | 646 | 578 | 473 | 503 | 534 | 600 | 387 | 505 | 638 | 401 | 661 | 604 | 505 | 7,035 |
| Total | 13,714,016 | 13,803,577 | 6,204,053 | 3,833,477 | 2,685,049 | 3,915,328 | 3,544,289 | 4,582,705 | 5,883,968 | 4,208,814 | 6,073,555 | 7,122,535 | 4,636,081 | 80,207,447 |

Data Source: Data obtained from state fish and game departments and/or from the International Association of Fish and Wildlife Agencies.

Data Accuracy: Some data may be missing for some species years and/or species. API does not claim totals are exact or complete. "0" may indicate either an absence of information for that year for that particular species or that no animals were trapped during that year.

* Trapped: Some figures may include animals killed by means other than trapping. Refer to individual species' page for details.

For current trapping data, see API's websites www.api4animals.org and www.BanCruelTraps.com.

## TABLE 1.2

*Number of animals trapped in Canada by province, 1992–2003\**

| Province | 1992–93 | 1993–94 | 1994–95 | 1995–96 | 1996–97 | 1997–98 | 1998–99 | 1999-00 | 2000-01 | 2001-02 | 2002-03 |
|---|---|---|---|---|---|---|---|---|---|---|---|
| Newfoundland | 11,328 | 12,712 | 19,011 | 16,558 | 16,558 | 20,966 | 20,825 | 22,868 | 18,673 | 24,215 | 20,385 |
| PEI | 5,119 | 6,353 | 6,950 | 6,078 | 8,293 | 8,150 | 6,839 | 3,616 | 5,088 | 6,624 | 4,953 |
| Nova Scotia | 27,077 | 29,275 | 48,613 | 49,611 | 67,129 | 55,360 | 50,700 | 30,586 | 27,112 | 39,138 | 35,195 |
| New Brunswick | 32,467 | 36,698 | 51,016 | 46,092 | 57,449 | 65,638 | 51,275 | 40,957 | 37,123 | 51,509 | 44,288 |
| Quebec | 165,288 | 204,607 | 275,006 | 239,947 | 248,931 | 306,256 | 234,860 | 216,952 | 210,118 | 263,561 | 176,803 |
| Ontario | 241,800 | 293,035 | 382,608 | 278,315 | 396,852 | 371,165 | 307,970 | 353,200 | 207,806 | 298,236 | 239,360 |
| Manitoba | 81,102 | 124,250 | 145,920 | 129,828 | 201,277 | 208,766 | 98,619 | 95,371 | 99,514 | 109,603 | 85,427 |
| Saskatchewan | 63,600 | 92,651 | 131,469 | 135,474 | 203,403 | 169,014 | 82,139 | 87,886 | 86,967 | 98,056 | 85,530 |
| Alberta | 115,059 | 181,540 | 187,626 | 140,525 | 167,242 | 217,754 | 135,748 | 120,034 | 116,210 | 100,198 | 106,791 |
| B.C. | 42,080 | 36,283 | 50,245 | 42,947 | 43,990 | 45,651 | 35,573 | 38,165 | 35,930 | 32,546 | 39,424 |
| NWT | 26,668 | 37,808 | 38,212 | 33,800 | 46,801 | 42,856 | 14,183 | 36,791 | 13,076 | 17,080 | 31,184 |
| Yukon | 4,885 | 5,450 | 7,288 | 9,072 | 9,527 | 9,179 | 7,195 | 7,419 | 6,406 | 3,260 | 8,263 |
| Nanavut | N/D | N/D | N/D | N/D | N/D | 12,573 | 3,438 | 3,460 | 5,056 | 6,452 | 2,355 |
| Private total trapped | 816,473 | 1,060,662 | 1,198,190 | 1,128,247 | 1,467,452 | 1,533,328 | 1,049,364 | 1,057,305 | 869,079 | 1,050,478 | 879,958 |
| Private total pelt value | $14.50 | $23.10 | $25.90 | $25.40 | $34.50 | $28.03 | $16.64 | $18.00 | $19.95 | $23.70 | $22.50 |

(in millions of $ Canadian)

\* Statistics from Statistics Canada. Data may include both trapped and hunted furbearers.
For current trapping data, see API's websites www.api4animals.org and www.BanCruelTraps.com

largest fur producing and consuming nation — continues to defend commercial fur trapping and the use of the leghold trap, and even threatened the EU with a trade war over the issue. Despite increased public opposition to the use of cruel traps and decades of redundant research, leghold traps and other primitive trapping devices remain legal in most U.S. states and public land systems.\*

In the U.S., commercial trapping steadily decreased during the 1990s due to reduced domestic demand for fur, plummeting pelt prices, and increased public awareness. Accordingly, sales of trapping licenses have declined in many states (see Table 1.3). Millions of animals, however, continue to be trapped for the growing overseas luxury fur trade, and trapping for "nuisance" and "damage control" has increased dramatically.

Animal advocates have had some success banning or limiting certain traps and/or trapping practices at the local and state levels through the administrative and public ballot-initiative processes (see Chapter Seven). From 1994 through 2000, voters in five states (Arizona, California, Colorado, Massachusetts, Washington) passed ballot initiatives restricting the use of body-gripping traps for commercial and recreational trapping. These successes reflect a growing public perception that trapping is cruel, unnecessary, and unjustifiable. With such heightened controversy and increased public awareness, efforts to restrict trapping will inevitably continue.

## The Status of Fur
## at the Turn of the Century

It was hard not to notice the return of fur trim, collars, and novelty items in fashion magazines and New York runways in 1999 and 2000. Conspicuous consumption was "in," fashion

---

\* For example, as of December 1, 2000, trapping was legal on more than half of all National Wildlife Refuges in the U.S. — areas specifically set aside to *protect* wildlife. In July 1999, the U.S. House of Representatives voted 259–166 to restrict trapping (and ban leghold traps and neck snares) on the refuge system for commercial and recreational purposes. But pro-trapping and fur-interest lobby groups pressured the Senate to kill the amendment by a 64–32 vote.

## TABLE 1.3

*Number of trapping licenses sold in the U.S., 1992–2002.*

| State | 1992–93 | 1993–94 | 1994–95 | 1995–96 | 1996–97 | 1997–98 | 1998–99 | 1999–00 | 2000–01 | 2001–02 |
|---|---|---|---|---|---|---|---|---|---|---|
| Alabama | 445 | 441 | 519 | 413 | 619 | 574 | 474 | 557 | 416 | 429 |
| Alaska[1] | 1,856 | 1,514 | 1,581 | 2,305 | 2,634 | 2,856 | 1,808 | 1,457 | 1,613 | N/D |
| Arizona | 234 | 194 | 109 | 34 | 84 | 86 | 88 | 83 | 73 | 66 |
| Arkansas[2] | 173 | 72 | 68 | 68 | 94 | 42 | 33 | 30 | 25 | N/D |
| California | 338 | 300 | 313 | 257 | 282 | 292 | 170 | 79 | 76 | 211 |
| Colorado | 1,033 | 1,072 | 1,089 | 1,046 | 878 | 669 | 672 | 786 | 1,076 | 1,355 |
| Connecticut | 509 | 417 | 396 | 390 | 371 | 401 | 388 | 372 | 375 | 364 |
| Delaware | 213 | 225 | 232 | 175 | 216 | 234 | 199 | 150 | 168 | 185 |
| Florida | 227 | 225 | 232 | 228 | 217 | 288 | 224 | 191 | 207 | 192 |
| Georgia | 351 | 346 | 376 | 392 | 477 | 433 | 427 | 479 | 487 | 410 |
| Idaho | 673 | 596 | 748 | 638 | 779 | 7ł2 | 626 | 558 | 607 | 647 |
| Illinois | 2,914 | 2,824 | 3,267 | 2,704 | 3,814 | 4,440 | 3,739 | 2,347 | 2,130 | 2,680 |
| Indiana | 2,621 | 3,045 | 3,501 | 3,042 | 3,985 | 4,336 | 3,920 | 2,451 | 2,420 | 2,900 |
| Iowa[3] | 7,635 | 7,488 | 8,429 | 7,387 | 8,091 | 9,299 | 9,045 | 16,772 | 14,940 | N/D |
| Kansas | 3,757 | 3,467 | 3,959 | 4,267 | 4,582 | 5,331 | 5,069 | 4,244 | 3,916 | 3,875 |
| Kentucky | 403 | 515 | 638 | 529 | 914 | 1,064 | 849 | 618 | 628 | 691 |
| Louisiana | 1,189 | 1,274 | 1,686 | 1,700 | 2,691 | 2,442 | 1,578 | 1,024 | 987 | 871 |
| Maine | 2,846 | 2,624 | 2,660 | 2,507 | 2,701 | 2,854 | 2,871 | 2,682 | 2,658 | N/D |
| Maryland[4] | 1,665 | 1,402 | 1,374 | 1,926 | 1,971 | 1,032 | 1,601 | 1,379 | 1,177 | N/D |
| Massachusetts | 426 | 291 | 449 | 305 | 328 | 248 | 211 | 255 | 324 | 287 |
| Michigan | 11,210 | 9,831 | 10387 | 11,052 | 13,445 | 18,289 | 18,520 | 17,169 | 17,519 | 19,082 |
| Minnesota | 5,763 | 5,601 | 6,895 | 5,630 | 6,675 | 6,996 | 6,652 | 4,936 | 5,337 | N/D |
| Mississippi | 312 | 229 | 245 | 201 | 417 | 395 | 331 | 330 | N/D | N/D |
| Missouri | 3,376 | 3,096 | 3,554 | 4,023 | 4,608 | 5,072 | 4,388 | 2,842 | 2,120 | 2,922 |
| Montana | 1,898 | 1,884 | 2,197 | 2,004 | 2,244 | 2,616 | 2,588 | 2,686 | 2,665 | 2,846 |
| Nebraska | 4,029 | 4,143 | 5,255 | 5,132 | 6,767 | 8,216 | 7,544 | 5,497 | 4,564 | 4,662 |
| Nevada | 488 | 510 | 524 | 373 | 420 | 482 | 320 | 382 | 408 | N/D |
| New Hampshire | 418 | 380 | 439 | 393 | 403 | 411 | 400 | 397 | 389 | 419 |
| New Jersey | 500 | 461 | 483 | 558 | 487 | 626 | 588 | 461 | 454 | 509 |
| New Mexico[5] | 1,086 | 1,140 | 1,206 | 1,007 | 1,063 | 1,189 | 1,046 | 1,273 | 1,506 | 1,482 |
| New York | 7,559 | 6,958 | 7,783 | 7,446 | 9,055 | 9,405 | 9,632 | 8,412 | 7,917 | 8,000 |
| North Carolina | 706 | 709 | 899 | 845 | 1,038 | 963 | 750 | 648 | 733 | 818 |
| North Dakota[6] | 28,081 | 27,075 | 25,634 | N/D | 23,202 | 19,839 | 19,476 | 18,381 | 16,706 | N/D |
| Ohio[7] | 4,716 | 4,257 | 5,586 | 20,057 | 23,151 | 24,597 | 22,229 | 20,403 | 30,854 | N/D |
| Oklahoma | 497 | 650 | 532 | 579 | 771 | 1,434 | 896 | 632 | 529 | 747 |
| Oregon | 906 | 775 | 863 | 759 | 826 | 937 | 847 | 807 | 1,450 | N/D |
| Pennsylvania | 20,345 | 19,526 | 22,376 | 21,840 | 25,636 | 27,413 | 25,877 | 17,604 | 18,551 | 19,410 |
| Rhode Island | 40 | 75 | 52 | 50 | 43 | 47 | 50 | 51 | 51 | 50 |
| South Carolina | 429 | 451 | 470 | 471 | 458 | 477 | 479 | 567 | 563 | N/D |
| South Dakota | 881 | 898 | 1,184 | 993 | 1,262 | 1,376 | 1,305 | 716 | 565 | 649 |
| Tennessee | 218 | 165 | 228 | 173 | 249 | 275 | 300 | 185 | N/D | N/D |
| Texas | 6,648 | 6,148 | 6,682 | 6,121 | 8,807 | 7,350 | 4,830 | 3,309 | 3,246 | 2,847 |
| Utah | 1,320 | 1,315 | 1,287 | 1,248 | 1,131 | 1,190 | 1,191 | N/D | N/D | N/D |
| Vermont | 635 | 535 | 484 | 476 | 458 | 548 | 543 | 538 | 499 | N/D |
| Virginia | 894 | 709 | 966 | 829 | 1,360 | 1,407 | 1,048 | 1,146 | 1,175 | 1,196 |
| Washington | 435 | 531 | 595 | 504 | 588 | 646 | 608 | 505 | 323 | 181 |
| West Virginia[8] | 2,500 | 2,500 | 2,500 | 2,500 | 2,500 | 2,500 | 2,500 | 2,500 | 2,500 | 2,500 |
| Wisconsin | 5,284 | 4,692 | 4,992 | 4,054 | 4,475 | 4,649 | 4,308 | 2,962 | 2,729 | 2,949 |
| Wyoming | 868 | 891 | 968 | 941 | 932 | 958 | 974 | 976 | 1,084 | 1,128 |
| Total | 141,550 | 134,467 | 146,892 | 130,572 | 178,199 | 187,976 | 174,212 | 152,820 | 158,740 | 87,560 |

**Note:** Most figures include resident and non-resident trapping license sales. **N/D** indicates data not provided by state agency. **AK[1]:** Does not separate hunting/trapping licenses. The figure used includes license figures for "non-resident hunting/trapping," "resident hunting/trapping," and "resident trapping" license sales. **AR[2]:** Does not separate hunting/trapping licenses beginning in 1994/95 season. Figures represent only non-resident trappers. Does not maintain statistics on how many resident hunters trap under the all-inclusive "sportsmans" license sold to both hunters and trappers. **IA[3]:** Licenses are sold for the calendar year, not the season. Also sells a combination license, which includes hunting. **MD[4]:** Does not separate hunting/trapping licenses beginning in 1994/95 season. Figures after the 1993/94 season are based upon the 1993/94 figure and are included for representational purposes only. **NM[5]:** Figure includes license sales for furbearer trapping and hunting. More furbearers are killed from hunting (predator calling) than from trapping. **ND[6]:** Does not separate hunting/trapping licenses. **OH[7]:** Beginning in 1995, a "furtaker's permit" was issued, replacing the standard trapping license. Both furbearer hunters and trappers are included in license totals since 1995. **WV[8]:** Does not separate hunting/trapping licenses. Figures in chart provided by James Evans of the WV Division of Natural Resources (pers. conversation 7/21/03) and are a general estimate of the total number of resident and non-resident trappers.

For current trapping data, see API's websites www.api4animals.org and www.BanCruelTraps.com

## TABLE 1.4

### Average pelt prices in U.S., $ per pelt, 1988–2002*

| State | 1988-89 | 1989-90 | 1990-91 | 1991-92 | 1992-93 | 1993-94 | 1994-95 | 1995-96 | 1996-97 | 1997-98 | 1998-99 | 1999-00 | 2000-01 | 2001-02 |
|---|---|---|---|---|---|---|---|---|---|---|---|---|---|---|
| Badger | $2.00 | $2.29 | $3.90 | $5.10 | $4.50 | $8.09 | $6.50 | $3.50 | $4.20 | $6.04 | $6.04 | $15.52 | $0.00 | $8.00 |
| Beaver | 7.47 | 7.20 | 4.90 | 5.14 | 4.92 | 7.78 | 8.67 | 15.88 | 25.12 | 29.77 | 17.09 | 18.35 | 12.22 | 14.01 |
| Bobcat | 38.13 | 26.13 | 15.88 | 11.82 | 8.90 | 19.12 | 19.24 | 20.45 | 24.31 | 28.00 | 39.40 | 25.00 | 25.00 | 19.22 |
| Coyote | 2.89 | 3.94 | 5.00 | 10.74 | 13.45 | 9.95 | 5.20 | 22.22 | 19.75 | 14.75 | 11.63 | 18.66 | 11.60 | 12.72 |
| Fisher | 109.65 | 66.86 | 40.81 | 31.26 | 26.87 | 25.86 | 25.78 | 21.73 | 28.51 | 32.50 | 27.01 | 19.43 | 17.62 | 18.70 |
| Fox, Gray | 14.62 | 6.20 | 4.19 | 6.84 | 8.00 | 9.76 | 8.48 | 9.77 | 10.73 | 10.20 | 7.15 | 7.00 | 7.13 | 9.31 |
| Fox, Red | 13.16 | 9.44 | 6.05 | 11.52 | 9.15 | 11.18 | 12.97 | 18.94 | 20.26 | 20.80 | 16.50 | 17.16 | 11.91 | 15.71 |
| Marten | 42.81 | 36.34 | 32.60 | 37.84 | 25.83 | 31.56 | 31.15 | 35.40 | 33.41 | 40.50 | 13.37 | 27.53 | 28.29 | 18.33 |
| Mink | 29.69 | 18.01 | 16.08 | 20.55 | 10.20 | 15.35 | 10.52 | 14.08 | 17.03 | 15.95 | 12.99 | 12.00 | 8.33 | 7.45 |
| Muskrat | 2.04 | 0.92 | 0.83 | 1.51 | 1.31 | 1.64 | 1.58 | 2.21 | 3.12 | 3.60 | 1.87 | 2.27 | 2.16 | 2.85 |
| Opossum | 1.04 | 0.95 | 1.65 | 1.60 | 1.75 | 1.45 | 1.58 | 1.52 | 3.80 | 2.87 | 0.70 | 0.75 | 1.00 | 1.55 |
| Otter, River | 17.81 | 18.71 | 18.95 | 22.99 | 30.27 | 48.61 | 48.38 | 37.71 | 53.02 | 48.57 | 35.25 | 64.41 | 52.73 | 44.97 |
| Raccoon | 7.80 | 4.64 | 2.74 | 5.65 | 5.14 | 6.79 | 5.88 | 13.61 | 15.61 | 17.72 | 15.73 | 9.06 | 5.27 | 8.78 |
| Skunk | 1.03 | 0.90 | 2.41 | 1.36 | 1.21 | 1.87 | 1.61 | 2.91 | 2.65 | 2.88 | 4.88 | 2.25 | 1.17 | 4.09 |
| Weasel | 0.25 | 0.87 | 1.39 | 0.99 | 1.40 | 2.03 | 1.00 | 2.07 | 2.36 | 2.55 | 2.00 | 2.75 | 2.50 | 0.00 |

* **Prices based on national fur auction sales.** (Note: 1995–2000 pelt prices are based on top auction averages and may reflect higher pelt prices when compared to local or state auction sales.)
For current trapping data, see API's websites www.api4animals.org and www.BanCruelTraps.com

## NUMBER OF ANIMAL SKINS NEEDED FOR A 40-INCH FUR COAT

| | | | |
|---|---|---|---|
| Mink ..............60 | Muskrat .............50 | Red Fox ...............42 | Raccoon............40 |
| Badger ...........20 | Lynx ...................18 | Coyote ................16 | Beaver...............15 |

magazines told us, political correctness "out." Fur could even be seen in the J. Crew, Banana Republic, and Hammacher Schlemmer Fall/Winter 2000 catalogs.

According to the Fur Information Council of America, fur sales in 1999 increased by 15% from the previous year, bringing fur salon sales to a total of $1.4 billion. Imports of fur apparel from countries such as Hong Kong and China increased by 63% between January and July 2000 when compared to the same seven-month period in 1999, according to U.S. Commerce Department data.

Is it accurate to say, "Fur is back"? Yes and no. When inflation is factored in, the $1.4 billion in fur sales in 1999 is still 30% less than in 1988. Further, Adriana Furs and Evans Inc., two of the largest U.S.-based fur retailers, both filed for bankruptcy in the late 1990s after failing to pay their major creditors, indicating how badly the fur industry fared during that decade.

Despite increased fur sales in 1999, trappers were lying low with stockpiles of low-grade furs in their freezers that wouldn't sell at auction. While demand for fur-farmed species such as mink has increased worldwide, interest in full-length "flashy" fur coats made from wild-caught species such as coyote, lynx, and red fox has not. "All agree the trapping season for 2000–01 will most likely see the shortest harvest ever," according to fur market analyst Parker Dozhier's report in the November 2000 issue of *Trapper & Predator Caller*. "Lower fur prices, high employment rates (particularly in the rural sectors) and the increasing price of gasoline are sighted [sic] as reasons for an anticipated lack of trapping pressure." Trappers who received $16 for a raccoon pelt in 1996 made less than half that in 1999/2000; a female fisher that once sold for more than $120 brought under $20 at auction in 1999/2000 (see Table 1.4). State and national trapper surveys consistently show that trapping is

more of a "hobby" than a significant income-generating activity. According to a 1992 national Gallup survey of trappers, approximately 30% of all trappers in 1991 reported no household income from trapping, suggesting "that motives other than monetary gain are also important to trappers," including "outdoor experience, recreation, challenge and a variety of other personal rewards that are largely nonmonetary."[1]

In response to volatile fur markets in the U.S., the North American fur industry has sought to open markets in Asia and Eastern Europe, where fur has only recently become a symbol of status and affluence, and where the animal protection movement has been largely absent. In 1997, Russia, Korea, and China consumed approximately 50% of the world's fur. However, instability in the Russian and Asian economies in 1998 and 1999 sent fur sales plummeting in these countries, leaving fur auction houses with large stockpiles of leftover furs. U.S. fur interests hope China will fill the void with its "60 million potential customers," according to *Fur World* magazine.

Increased worldwide interest in fur-trimmed and -lined items also threatens to increase trapping pressure. An estimated 90% of the foxes killed globally for their pelts are used as fur trim on designer clothing and accessories. Consumers appear less concerned about the social stigma associated with wearing fur if it is discreetly used as trim or lining. Animal advocates have historically been less inclined to target wearers of fur-trimmed garments than those wearing conspicuous full-length fur coats.

## Public Attitudes Toward Trapping and Fur

Most Americans are unfamiliar with traps and trapping practices, and this lack of knowledge and the misinformation disseminated by trapping proponents can lead to an inconsistent public opinion on trapping. In 1977, pre-campaign polling showed 66% of Ohio voters supported a proposed statewide trapping ban. Before the vote, opponents of the ballot measure conducted an intensive media campaign delivering the message that trapping is essential to wildlife management and the protection of public health and safety. Six weeks after the first poll, 63% of voters cast ballots *against* the ban.

Despite limited public awareness of trapping, opposition to the use of leghold traps has remained constant over the past 20 years. In a 1978 national survey commissioned by the U.S. Fish and Wildlife Service and conducted by Yale University professor Stephen Kellert, 78% of respondents opposed the use of steel-jaw leghold traps.[2] Eighteen years later, a national poll commissioned by the Animal Welfare Institute showed that 74% of Americans opposed the use of leghold traps.[3] Several statewide polls conducted in the 1990s during anti-trapping initiative campaigns supported these findings.

In a 1986 survey of veterinarians conducted by the Animal Welfare Institute, 79.3% of all surveyed veterinarians opposed the use of the steel jaw leghold trap.[4]

More people are opposed to leghold traps in particular than to trapping in general or to killing animals for fur. While 78% of respondents to Kellert's survey opposed the use of leghold traps, only 57% disapproved of killing furbearers for clothing. A 1995 Associated Press poll reported that 60% of respondents agreed it was "always wrong to kill an animal for its fur," and 64% approved of "most of the protests being made by animal rights groups against using animals to make fur coats."

Attitudes toward trapping, as with other animal-related subjects, depend on the species of animal involved, whether pain and suffering are present, and the stated purpose of the activity. In a 1997 statewide survey of California voters, 81%

opposed "allowing animals to be trapped and killed for the commercial sale of their fur." There was less opposition, however, to trapping for private property damage control (60%), for flood damage control (58%), and for protection of public safety (44%).

Wearing or selling fur products is somewhat less objectionable to the public than the killing of animals for their fur. Although 50% of respondents to a 1993 *Los Angeles Times* poll indicated they "generally oppose" the wearing of clothes made of animal furs, only 32% of those surveyed by ABC News in 1989 said seeing someone wearing a fur bothered them because animals were killed to make it.[5] And only 20% of those sampled for a 1990 *USA Today* poll thought fur sales should be banned.[6]

## Trapping for Damage Control

In addition to the animals killed for profit and recreation, millions more animals are trapped for "damage control" purposes each year by state and federal agencies, private nuisance wildlife control operators (NWCOs), and individual landowners. The U.S. Department of Agriculture's Wildlife Services agency traps tens of thousands of predators, including coyotes, bobcats, bears, mountain lions and foxes annually in the name of "livestock protection." This program, funded by U.S. tax dollars to benefit a small number of ranchers, relies heavily on leghold traps, strangulation neck snares, and other indiscriminate devices.

With increased urbanization, conflicts between humans and wildlife have grown dramatically over the past thirty years, creating a growing industry focused on lethal control of suburban and urban wildlife. Countless raccoons, opossums, squirrels, skunks, and gophers are trapped and killed by NWCOs with almost no state or federal oversight. Because most states do not require that animals trapped for "damage" or "nuisance" control be reported, the total number of animals killed for these purposes is unknown.

# TABLE 1.5

## Animals trapped in the U.S. by state, 1986–1999. *

| State | 1986-87 | 1987-88 | 1988-89 | 1989-90 | 1990-91 | 1991-92 | 1992-93 | 1993-94 | 1994-95 | 1995-96 | 1996-97 | 1997-98 | 1998-99 | Total |
|---|---|---|---|---|---|---|---|---|---|---|---|---|---|---|
| Alabama | 102,822 | 97,925 | 23,545 | 5,631 | 1,618 | 4,106 | 861 | 1,784 | 4,555 | 2,769 | 11,221 | 6,254 | 1,235 | 264,326 |
| Alaska | 49,435 | 49,606 | 43,885 | 33,316 | 11,963 | 17,038 | 8,905 | 13,473 | 13,877 | 12,997 | 17,605 | 15,756 | 12,772 | 300,628 |
| Arizona | 49,631 | 50,697 | 27,937 | 11,765 | 3,720 | 6,982 | 7,225 | 10,130 | 2,857 | 443 | 2,453 | 2,609 | 2,602 | 179,051 |
| Arkansas | 282,905 | 226,907 | 96,006 | 39,698 | 31,930 | 44,080 | 34,037 | 41,722 | 62,569 | 87,937 | 127,917 | 75,907 | 43,577 | 1,195,192 |
| California | 72,736 | 70,713 | 43,488 | 21,432 | 15,216 | 16,490 | 13,361 | 16,694 | 14,545 | 15,011 | 24,136 | 19,199 | 9,500 | 352,521 |
| Colorado | 57,781 | 60,565 | 33,994 | 25,846 | 17,903 | 9,776 | 24,632 | 22,933 | 39,672 | 12,069 | 12,268 | N/D | 57 | 317,496 |
| Connecticut | 18,601 | 19,410 | 9,944 | 6,710 | 7,163 | 6,450 | 5,550 | 4,724 | 7,775 | 5,320 | 6,424 | 7,657 | 4,338 | 110,066 |
| Delaware | 32,574 | 19,634 | 41,661 | 38,617 | 18,266 | 38,595 | 35,483 | 31,639 | 42,489 | 25,234 | 52,898 | 43,581 | 19,009 | 439,680 |
| Florida | 33,452 | 44,011 | 9,962 | 4,054 | 434 | 1,659 | 1,498 | 1,760 | 2,556 | 2,947 | 3,954 | 3,146 | 714 | 110,147 |
| Georgia | 89,781 | 120,766 | 46,827 | 26,865 | 15,119 | 21,556 | 16,944 | 19,724 | 23,248 | 25,751 | 29,350 | 26,102 | 24,121 | 486,154 |
| Hawaii | 0 | 0 | 0 | 0 | 0 | 0 | 0 | 0 | 0 | 0 | 0 | 0 | 0 | 0 |
| Idaho | 103,360 | 94,729 | 51,871 | 37,994 | 28,194 | 47,184 | 20,926 | 24,134 | 21,150 | 20,999 | 36,069 | 33,431 | 22,886 | 542,927 |
| Illinois | 753,384 | 638,032 | 282,420 | 164,724 | 129,997 | 259,429 | 166,972 | 224,339 | 312,159 | 230,324 | 305,842 | 378,427 | 215,250 | 4,061,299 |
| Indiana | 385,609 | 363,707 | 120,764 | 89,431 | 62,145 | 109,682 | 80,799 | 117,367 | 126,625 | 88,203 | 96,413 | 297,367 | 199,432 | 2,137,544 |
| Iowa | 763,489 | 752,325 | 350,419 | 148,340 | 140,718 | 170,348 | 222,492 | 256,401 | 342,643 | 342,174 | 306,035 | 319,180 | 247,978 | 4,362,542 |
| Kansas | 282,782 | 281,922 | 171,384 | 86,475 | 58,065 | 88,809 | 69,870 | 92,916 | 132,263 | 108,937 | 177,116 | 213,748 | 138,851 | 1,903,138 |
| Kentucky | 144,496 | 159,048 | 71,301 | 45,717 | 20,744 | 42,920 | 26,085 | 16,459 | 25,511 | 18,708 | 48,277 | 53,057 | 26,431 | 698,754 |
| Louisiana | 1,438,394 | 1,009,428 | 311,595 | 347,902 | 156,692 | 296,294 | 172,396 | 271,921 | 264,119 | 280,654 | 486,471 | 468,454 | 140,759 | 5,645,079 |
| Maine | 84,456 | 93,990 | 65,254 | 20,389 | 17,169 | 21,715 | 19,170 | 18,984 | 25,885 | 19,303 | 26,716 | 25,397 | 20,991 | 459,419 |
| Maryland | 129,832 | 118,249 | 46,860 | 31,875 | 41,673 | 64,656 | 48,023 | N/D | N/D | N/D | N/D | N/D | N/D | 481,168 |
| Massachusetts | 37,906 | 38,272 | 19,651 | 27,752 | 18,642 | 17,934 | 13,892 | 13,217 | 16,136 | 10,944 | 9,867 | 2,156 | 2,276 | 228,645 |
| Michigan | 802,330 | 799,597 | 371,178 | 1,292 | 1,182 | 1,352 | 1,479 | 315,384 | 451,649 | 1,870 | 423,253 | 588,328 | 370,306 | 4,129,200 |
| Minnesota | 1,289,803 | 1,563,605 | 478,159 | 341,785 | 222,067 | 197,145 | 261,916 | 401,257 | 627,981 | 388,511 | 444,840 | 430,526 | 369,043 | 7,016,638 |
| Mississippi | 113,616 | 103,308 | 59,554 | 30,776 | 15,650 | 19,542 | 21,693 | 23,639 | 20,601 | 16,264 | 37,868 | 30,345 | 30,169 | 523,025 |
| Missouri | 423,530 | 351,531 | 184,900 | 111,267 | 91,192 | 151,139 | 108,250 | 144,000 | 202,802 | 170,290 | 276,986 | 237,536 | 130,719 | 2,584,142 |

* Some figures may include animals caught/killed by means other than trapping. Refer to individual species' page for details.

N/D = No data provided by state wildlife agency.

For current trapping data, see API's websites www.api4animals.org and www.BanCruelTraps.com

## TABLE 1.5 (CONTINUED)

### Animals trapped in the U.S. by state, 1986–1999.[a]

| State | 1986–87 | 1987–88 | 1988–89 | 1989–90 | 1990–91 | 1991–92 | 1992–93 | 1993–94 | 1994–95 | 1995–96 | 1996–97 | 1997–98 | 1998–99 | Total |
|---|---|---|---|---|---|---|---|---|---|---|---|---|---|---|
| Montana | 100,115 | 109,527 | 67,916 | 39,534 | 30,321 | 42,010 | 35,920 | 47,731 | 55,854 | 39,280 | 66,876 | 62,434 | 41,340 | 738,858 |
| Nebraska | 320,266 | 357,527 | 176,910 | 111,063 | 78,477 | 121,261 | 110,087 | 169,021 | 253,783 | 214,857 | 405,665 | 417,289 | 302,700 | 3,038,906 |
| Nevada | 28,837 | 23,568 | 8,694 | 6,917 | 3,473 | 9,348 | 6,203 | 8,574 | 7,069 | 5,050 | 13,032 | 15,438 | 6,361 | 142,564 |
| New Hampshire | 17,687 | 19,906 | 14,433 | 9,826 | 7,595 | 10,393 | 7,417 | 9,253 | 14,173 | 9,734 | 11,010 | 11,335 | 10,390 | 153,152 |
| New Jersey | 231,464 | 230,196 | 205,479 | 143,872 | 78,178 | 84,543 | 90,701 | 49,512 | 66,883 | 91,315 | 89,143 | 93,904 | 76,182 | 1,531,372 |
| New Mexico | 48,570 | 20,050 | N/D | 8,001 | 7,461 | 9,491 | 14,195 | 19,108 | 17,898 | 3,845 | 3,511 | 3,896 | 301 | 156,327 |
| New York | 542,113 | 615,881 | 343,194 | 192,091 | 175,797 | 202,986 | 185,357 | 188,648 | 281,394 | 172,931 | 296,404 | 316,722 | 211,158 | 3,724,676 |
| North Carolina | 108,145 | 98,502 | 34,013 | 27,975 | 13,893 | 21,693 | 10,679 | 19,937 | 20,579 | 15,059 | 29,263 | 18,753 | 10,349 | 428,840 |
| North Dakota | 144,747 | 220,103 | 70,062 | 25,310 | 23,024 | 31,960 | 32,687 | 29,708 | 38,889 | 76,283 | 104,636 | 536,029 | 37,581 | 1,371,019 |
| Ohio | 705,529 | 626,683 | 290,281 | 262,461 | 188,164 | 384,103 | 269,567 | 285,525 | 347,568 | 273,291 | 257,947 | 361,221 | 185,086 | 4,437,426 |
| Oklahoma | 122,881 | 68,184 | 37,049 | 11,436 | 5,423 | 13,826 | 8,253 | 8,792 | 15,208 | 12,479 | 32,928 | 29,885 | 9,821 | 376,165 |
| Oregon | 90,420 | 89,514 | 42,864 | 34,238 | 25,354 | 32,058 | 23,166 | 31,641 | 34,834 | 26,839 | 48,158 | 51,171 | 29,464 | 559,721 |
| Pennsylvania | 1,280,519 | 1,204,213 | 670,579 | 485,847 | 342,125 | 410,272 | 366,326 | 342,150 | 498,808 | 367,620 | 501,671 | 581,337 | 524,192 | 7,575,659 |
| Rhode Island | 1,944 | 1,867 | 1,015 | 450 | 688 | 673 | 988 | 859 | 1,028 | 976 | 875 | 1,073 | 1,312 | 13,748 |
| South Carolina | 45,642 | 51,158 | 19,060 | 8,674 | 7,742 | 10,708 | 7,070 | 6,913 | 7,012 | 10,132 | 13,277 | 10,672 | 9,486 | 207,546 |
| South Dakota | 324,124 | 334,924 | 75,231 | 17,952 | 19,650 | 31,253 | 27,534 | 37,120 | 72,950 | 77,954 | 68,371 | 92,307 | 35,511 | 1,214,881 |
| Tennessee | 125,942 | 96,667 | 27,217 | 14,994 | 4,847 | 20,450 | 5,764 | 5,408 | 13,406 | 9,223 | 17,236 | 13,328 | N/D | 365,403 |
| Texas | 410,246 | 866,105 | 325,060 | 156,439 | 104,519 | 129,648 | 122,671 | 128,766 | 170,615 | 120,673 | 315,669 | 258,034 | 127,154 | 3,235,599 |
| Utah | 80,298 | 82,984 | 50,160 | 33,661 | 16,402 | 33,581 | 24,472 | 41,239 | 48,435 | 44,127 | 40,862 | 47,066 | 49,738 | 593,025 |
| Vermont | 34,040 | 26,414 | 12,731 | 6,717 | 10,085 | 7,399 | 7,656 | 6,772 | 8,267 | 3,727 | 8,592 | 11,774 | 6,704 | 150,878 |
| Virginia | 169,800 | 161,837 | N/D | 28,022 | 24,987 | 37,068 | 20,671 | 22,685 | 42,321 | 24,690 | 65,451 | 51,963 | 12,904 | 662,399 |
| Washington | 52,587 | 42,008 | 22,803 | 18,745 | 12,408 | 19,140 | 12,364 | 17,234 | 19,439 | 15,802 | 23,909 | 25,082 | 12,402 | 293,923 |
| West Virginia | 99,774 | 104,362 | 39,857 | 19,261 | 13,313 | 25,228 | 15,185 | 11,465 | 23,465 | 14,566 | 41,355 | 32,548 | 18,253 | 458,632 |
| Wisconsin | 1,038,668 | 1,159,356 | 666,183 | 445,680 | 342,854 | 540,783 | 732,766 | 995,781 | 1,028,405 | 685,582 | 640,086 | 778,187 | 861,635 | 9,915,966 |
| Wyoming | 46,953 | 64,064 | 40,703 | 24,658 | 20,785 | 30,538 | 24,106 | 14,233 | 11,986 | 5,084 | 13,614 | 22,879 | 12,085 | 331,688 |
| Total | 13,714,016 | 13,803,577 | 6,204,053 | 3,833,477 | 2,685,049 | 3,915,328 | 3,544,289 | 4,582,705 | 5,883,968 | 4,208,814 | 6,073,555 | 7,122,535 | 4,636,081 | 80,207,447 |

* Some figures may include animals caught/killed by means other than trapping. Refer to individual species' page for details.

N/D = No data provided by state wildlife agency.

For current trapping data, see API's websites www.api4animals.org and www.BanCruelTraps.com

---

# FACTS ABOUT FUR TRAPPING IN THE U.S.

- 81% of trappers learned their skills by "trial and error."

- Most frequently trapped species in the U.S.: muskrat, raccoon, beaver, opossum, red and gray fox, coyote, mink, skunk, weasel, fisher, otter, marten, and bobcat.

- "For the regional sample as a whole, respondents reportedly owned an average of 98 foothold and 47 body gripping (Conibear) traps. It would appear that the padded foothold trap has yet to be extensively adopted by northeastern trappers. The average number of padded foothold traps owned is two, while the average number used during the most recent trapping season was one."

- Average annual income derived from trapping-related activities for trappers trapping in the 1992/93 and 1993/94 seasons was $434.

- Nearly all respondents for the combined six-state sample were male (98%) and white (98%); the average age was 45 years.

Source: Muth, Robert M., Rodney R. Zwick, John J. Daigle, et al. *The Sociocultural and Economic Value of Furbearer Resources: A Study of Trapping in Six Northeastern States*. Final technical report, 1996.

---

Trapping and other indiscriminate control methods have failed to solve human/wildlife conflicts because they generally ignore the underlying systemic problems and provide at most only a temporary remedy to the perceived problem. Public education, as well as the implementation of effective and humane wildlife management methods, is necessary to resolve human/wildlife conflicts over the long term.

## Trapping for Wildlife Management

Wildlife management, as currently practiced by state and federal agencies, revolves largely around the utility of wildlife to humans. Consumptive uses of wildlife in the form of trapping or hunting are often favored, even to the detriment of wildlife species. Economics strongly dictate when, where, and how animals are trapped, even when necessary biological data are lacking. When pelt prices rise, pressure on furbearers increases (see Figures 1.1–1.15) and in some situations, the size of a furbearer population can fluctuate depending on its economic worth. Allowing economics and the interests of consumptive-wildlife users to dictate wildlife management has depleted populations of some species, and created unnatural increases in others.

Over the last century, there has been a paradigm shift in the public's perception of wildlife. The majority of Americans no longer view wildlife as a resource to be stocked, managed, and killed for profit. Instead, there is growing awareness that wild animals have intrinsic worth and should therefore be managed in a way that is ethical, humane, non-invasive, and environmentally sound. State and federal wildlife agencies must take heed and alter their management approaches to reflect the needs of wildlife and the opinions of the majority of Americans who are non-consumptive wildlife users. In addition, sound wildlife management must aim to conserve and restore native ecosystems, while maintaining respect for all species.

## Conclusion

Advocates have helped reduce the number of animals trapped commercially in the U.S. from nearly 14 million in 1987 to less than 5.5 million in 1997 (see Table 1.5). If pelt prices remain low, the future of the commercial fur trade looks bleak. However, potential overseas fur markets and the increasing popularity of fur trim could reverse this trend.

Efforts to target trapping for purposes other than commerce and recreation pose a more difficult task for advocates. Many former fur trappers, unable to profit from their trade, have switched to "nuisance" or "damage control" trapping, a fast-growing, highly unregulated industry capitalizing on increased urban/suburban conflicts with wildlife.

Ultimately, the public will determine the future of trapping in North America. Enhanced public education and strategic policy efforts can bring an end to commercial fur trapping and ensure that humane treatment and co-existence, not lethal control, become the guiding principles of wildlife management.

NOTES

[1] International Association of Fish and Wildlife Agencies Fur Resources Technical Committee. "Ownership and Use of Traps by Trappers in the United States in 1992." Fur Resources Technical Committee of the International Fish and Wildlife Agencies and the Gallup Organization, Washington, D.C. (1993).

[2] Stephen R. Kellert. "American Attitudes and Knowledge of Animals." *Transactions of the Forty-fifth North American Wildlife and Natural Resources Conference* 45 (1980): 111–23.

[3] Animal Welfare Institute. "Opposition to Steel Jaw Leghold Traps is Overwhelming." Press Release, 2 December 1996.

[4] Animal Welfare Institute. *Animals and Their Legal Rights*. 4th ed. Washington, D.C.: Animal Welfare Institute, 1990.

[5] John Balzar. "Creatures Great and Equal." *Los Angeles Times*, 25 December 1993, p. 1.

[6] *USA Today*, 8 February 1990, p. 1A.

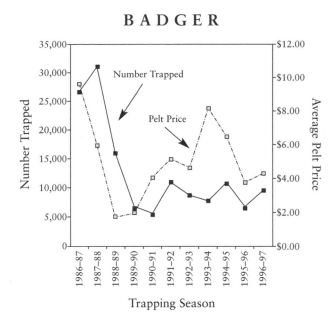

Figure 1.1 *Number of badgers trapped in the U.S. and average pelt prices, 1986-1997.*

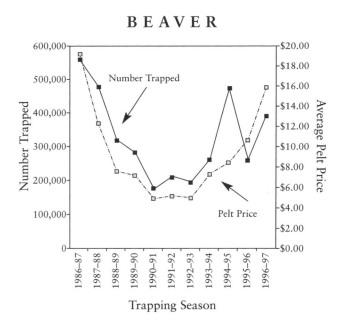

Figure 1.2 *Number of beavers trapped in the U.S. and average pelt prices, 1986-1997.*

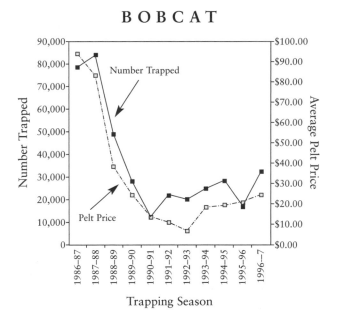

Figure 1.3 *Number of bobcats trapped in the U.S. and average pelt prices, 1986-1997.*

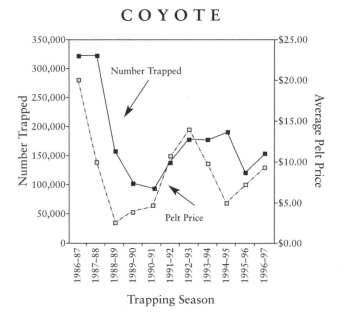

Figure 1.4 *Number of coyotes trapped in the U.S. and average pelt prices, 1986-1997.*

Note: Most U.S. states do not separate hunted and trapped animals, so totals may include hunted animals.

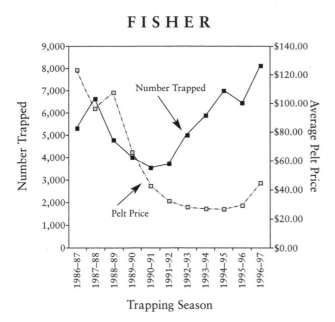

**FISHER**

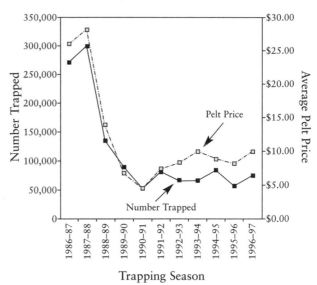

**GRAY FOX**

*Figure 1.5 Number of fishers trapped in the U.S. and average pelt prices, 1986-1997.*

*Figure 1.6 Number of gray foxes trapped in the U.S. and average pelt prices, 1986-1997.*

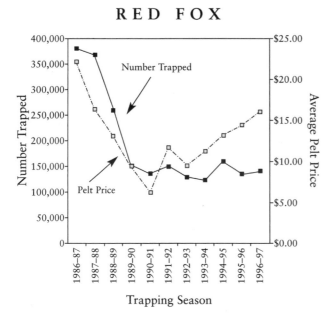

**RED FOX**

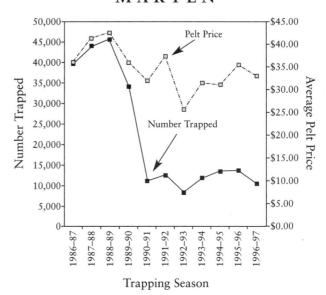

**MARTEN**

*Figure 1.7 Number of red foxes trapped in the U.S. and average pelt prices, 1986-1997.*

*Figure 1.8 Number of martens trapped in the U.S. and average pelt prices, 1986-1997.*

Note: Most U.S. states do not separate hunted and trapped animals, so totals may include hunted animals.

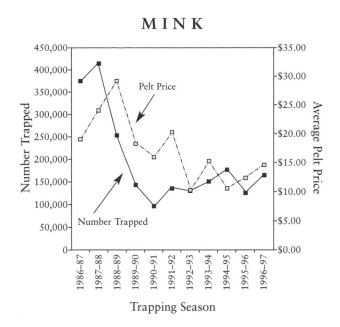

Figure 1.9 *Number of minks trapped in the U.S. and average pelt prices, 1986-1997.*

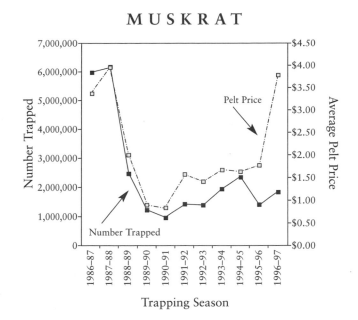

Figure 1.10 *Number of muskrats trapped in the U.S. and average pelt prices, 1986-1997.*

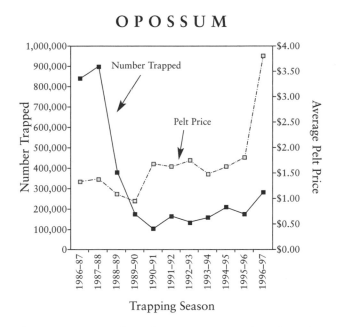

Figure 1.11 *Number of opossums trapped in the U.S. and average pelt prices, 1986-1997.*

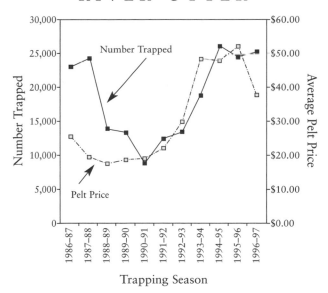

Figure 1.12 *Number of otters trapped in the U.S. and average pelt prices, 1986-1997.*

Note: Most U.S. states do not separate hunted and trapped animals, so totals may include hunted animals.

## RACCOON

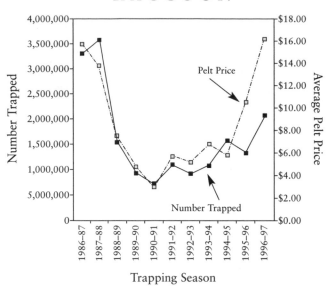

*Figure 1.13 Number of raccoons trapped in the U.S. and average pelt prices, 1986-1997.*

## SPOTTED AND STRIPED SKUNK

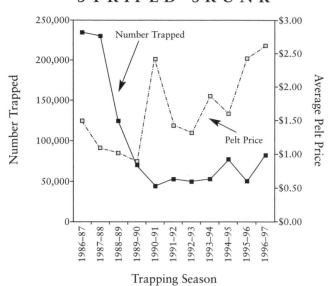

*Figure 1.14 Number of skunks trapped in the U.S. and average pelt prices, 1986-1997.*

## WEASEL

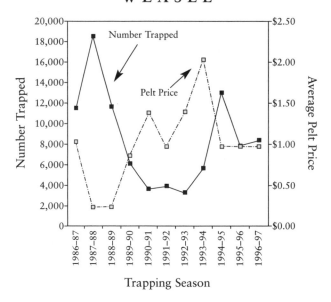

*Figure 1.15 Number of weasels trapped in the U.S. and average pelt prices, 1986-1997.*

Note: Most U.S. states do not separate hunted and trapped animals, so totals may include hunted animals.

# MOST COMMONLY TRAPPED FURBEARERS IN THE U.S.

### Badger (Taxidae taxus)
### Order: Carnivora
### Family: Mustelidae

- Approximately 17,000 trapped in 1997/98 (~31,000 in 1987/88)*

- Top three badger trapping states (1986–97)*: North Dakota, Nebraska, Minnesota

- Average pelt price (1999/2000): ~$16

- Major fur markets: Flat market; some pelts sold to North America, Europe, Asia

*Primary traps used:* Mid-sized body-gripping traps; Nos. 1³⁄₄, 2, and 3 leghold traps

### Beaver (Castor canadensis)
### Order: Rodentia
### Family: Castoridae

- Approximately 300,000 trapped in 1997/98 (~470,000 in 1987/88)*

- Top three beaver trapping states (1986–99)*: Minnesota, Wisconsin, New York

- Average pelt price (1999/2000) = ~$18

- Major fur markets: North America, Western Europe

*Primary traps used:* Large-sized body-gripping traps; No. 4 leghold traps; underwater snares

### Bobcat (Felis rufus)
### Order: Carnivora
### Family: Felidae

- Approximately 27,000 trapped in 1997/98 (~84,000 in 1987/88)*

- Top three bobcat trapping states (1986–99)*: Texas, Kansas, California

- Average pelt price (1999/2000) = ~$25

- Major fur markets: Asia, Hong Kong, Japan

*Primary traps used:* Nos. 1¹⁄₂, 1³⁄₄, 2, and 3 leghold traps

*Trap totals are based upon statistics provided by state wildlife agencies. Information may not be complete or entirely accurate as some states failed to provide information, while other states may not record all target species trapped. In addition, figures provided may include both trapped and hunted animals as some states do not separate killing methods. Figures do not include those animals killed for "nuisance" or predator control.

### Coyote (Canis latrans)
### Order: Carnivora
### Family: Canidae

- Approximately 110,000 trapped in 1997/98 (~320,000 in 1987/88)*

- Top three coyote trapping states (1986–99)*: Texas, Nebraska, Kansas

- Average pelt price (1999/2000): ~$19

- Major fur markets: Flat market; trim trade/Korea, Italy

*Primary traps used:* Nos. $1\frac{1}{2}$, 2, 3, and 4 leghold traps; neck and foot snares

### Fisher (Martes pennanti)
### Order: Carnivora
### Family: Mustelidae

- Approximately 8,300 trapped in 1997/98 (~6,800 in 1987/88)*

- Top three fisher trapping states (1986–99)*: Maine, Minnesota, New York

- Average pelt price (1999/2000): ~$19

- Major fur markets: Flat market

*Primary traps used:* Mid-sized body-gripping traps; Nos. $1\frac{1}{2}$ and 2 leghold traps

### Gray Fox (Urocyon cinereoargenteus)
### Order: Carnivora
### Family: Canidae

- Approximately 53,000 trapped in 1997/98 (~300,000 in 1987/88)*

- Top three gray fox trapping states (1986–99)*: Pennsylvania, Texas, Arizona

- Average pelt price (1999/2000): ~$7

- Major fur markets: North America, China

*Primary traps used:* Nos. $1\frac{1}{2}$ and 2 leghold traps

*Trap totals are based upon statistics provided by state wildlife agencies. Information may not be complete or entirely accurate as some states failed to provide information, while other states may not record all target species trapped. In addition, figures provided may include both trapped and hunted animals as some states do not separate killing methods. Figures do not include those animals killed for "nuisance" or predator control.

### Lynx (Felis lynx)
### Order: Carnivora
### Family: Felidae

- Approximately 2,700 trapped in 1997/98 (~1,000 in 1987/88)*

- Only state that allows lynx trapping: Alaska

- Average pelt price (1999/2000): ~$30

- Major fur markets: Hong Kong, Japan

*Primary traps used:* Large-sized body-gripping traps; Nos. 2, 3, and 4 leghold traps; snares

### Marten (Martes americana)
### Order: Carnivora
### Family: Mustelidae

- Approximately 14,000 trapped in 1997/98 (~40,000 in 1987/88)*

- Top three marten trapping states (1986–99)*: Alaska, Maine, Minnesota

- Average pelt price (1999/2000): ~$28

- Major fur markets: North America, Japan, Europe

*Primary traps used:* Small-sized body-gripping traps; Nos. 1 and 1½ leghold traps

### Mink (Mustela vison)
### Order: Carnivora
### Family: Mustelidae

- Approximately 144,000 trapped in 1997/98 (~417,000 in 1987/88)*

- Top three mink trapping states (1986–99)*: Minnesota, Wisconsin, Iowa

- Average pelt price (1999/2000): ~$12 (for wild mink, not ranch mink)

- Major fur markets: Europe, Russia, South Korea

*Primary traps used:* Small-sized body gripping traps; Nos. 1 and 1½ leghold traps (including stop-loss)

*Trap totals are based upon statistics provided by state wildlife agencies. Information may not be complete or entirely accurate as some states failed to provide information, while other states may not record all target species trapped. In addition, figures provided may include both trapped and hunted animals as some states do not separate killing methods. Figures do not include those animals killed for "nuisance" or predator control.

### Muskrat (Ondatra zibethicus)
### Order: Rodentia
### Family: Cricetidae

- Approximately 2 million trapped in 1997/98 (~6 million in 1987/88)*

- Top three muskrat trapping states (1986–99)*: Wisconsin, Minnesota, Pennsylvania

- Average pelt price (1999/2000): ~$2

- Major fur markets: China, North America**

*Primary traps used:* Small-sized body-gripping traps; Nos. 1 and 1½ leghold traps (including stop-loss); drowning cage traps (also known as "colony" or "submersion" traps)

### Nutria (Myocastor coypus)
### Order: Rodentia
### Family: Myocastoridae

- Approximately 400,000 trapped in 1997/98 (~660,000 in 1987/88)*

- Top three nutria trapping states (1986–99)*: Louisiana, Texas, Oregon

- Average pelt price (1999/2000): ~$5

- Major fur market: China**

*Primary traps used:* Mid-sized body-gripping traps; Nos. 2 and 3 leghold traps; snares

### Opossum (Didelphis marsupialis)
### Order: Marsupialia
### Family: Didelphidae

- Approximately 230,000 trapped in 1997/98 (~910,000 in 1987/88)*

- Top three opossum trapping states (1986–99)*: Pennsylvania, Texas, Missouri

- Average pelt price (1999/2000): ~$0.75

- Major fur markets: Flat market

*Primary traps used:* No. 1 leghold traps; cage traps

*Trap totals are based upon statistics provided by state wildlife agencies. Information may not be complete or entirely accurate as some states failed to provide information, while other states may not record all target species trapped. In addition, figures provided may include both trapped and hunted animals as some states do not separate killing methods. Figures do not include those animals killed for "nuisance" or predator control.

**With the economic upheavals in Russia and Asia, fur markets have crashed in these countries. Many of the fur species heavily consumed by these countries, such as raccoon and muskrat, were withdrawn at fur auctions in 1999 because of lack of demand and the absence of these markets.

### Raccoon (Procyon lotor)
### Order: Carnivora
### Family: Procyonidae

- Approximately 2.1 million trapped in 1997/98 (~3.6 million in 1987/88)*

- Top three raccoon trapping states (1986–99)*: Pennsylvania, Illinois, Ohio

- Average pelt price (1999/2000): ~$9

- Major fur markets: Eastern Europe, Turkey, Russia, Greece**

*Primary traps used:* Mid-sized body-gripping traps; Nos. 1 and $1\frac{1}{2}$ leghold traps; cage traps (primarily used by nuisance wildlife control operators)

### Red Fox (Vulpes vulpes)
### Order: Carnivora
### Family: Canidae

- Approximately 120,000 trapped in 1997/98 (~373,000 in 1987/88)*

- Top three red fox trapping states (1986–99)*: Pennsylvania, Minnesota, North Dakota

- Average pelt price (1999/2000): ~$17

- Major fur markets: Trim trade/ China, Hong Kong, Korea, Western Europe

*Primary traps used:* Nos. $1\frac{1}{2}$, $1\frac{3}{4}$, and 2 leghold traps; snares

### River Otter (Lutra canadensis)
### Order: Carnivora
### Family: Mustelidae

- Approximately 25,000 trapped in 1997/98 (~24,000 in 1987/88)*

- Top three river otter trapping states (1986–99)* = Louisiana, Arkansas, Minnesota

- Average pelt price (1999/2000) = ~$64

- Major fur market: China

*Primary traps used:* Mid- and large-sized body-gripping traps; Nos. 3 and 4 leghold traps; underwater snares

*Trap totals are based upon statistics provided by state wildlife agencies. Information may not be complete or entirely accurate as some states failed to provide information, while other states may not record all target species trapped. In addition, figures provided may include both trapped and hunted animals as some states do not separate killing methods. Figures do not include those animals killed for "nuisance" or predator control.

**With the economic upheavals in Russia and Asia, fur markets have crashed in these countries. Many of the fur species heavily consumed by these countries, such as raccoon and muskrat, were withdrawn at fur auctions in 1999 because of lack of demand and the absence of these markets.

*Striped Skunk (Mephitis mephitis)*
*Spotted Skunk (Spilogale, Putoris)*
*Order: Carnivora*
*Family: Mephitidae*

- Approximately 230,000 trapped in 1997/98 (~288,000 in 1987/88)* (note: figures may include striped, hog-nosed, and spotted skunks)

- Top three skunk trapping states (1986–99)*: Texas, Minnesota, Pennsylvania

- Average pelt price (1999/2000) = ~$2

- Major fur markets = Flat market; some pelts sold to North America, Europe, Asia

*Primary traps used:* Nos. 1 and 1½, leghold traps; cage traps

*Weasel*
*(Long-tailed, Mustela frenata)*
*(Short-tailed, Mustela erminea)*
*Order: Carnivora*
*Family: Mustelidae*

- Approximately 14,000 trapped in 1997/98 (~18,000 in 1987/88)*

- Top three weasel trapping states (1986–99)*: Minnesota, Wisconsin, Michigan

- Average pelt price (1999/2000): Flat market

- Major fur markets: Flat market

*Primary traps used:* Small-sized body gripping traps; Nos. 1 and 1½ leghold traps

*Trap totals are based upon statistics provided by state wildlife agencies. Information may not be complete or entirely accurate as some states failed to provide information, while other states may not record all target species trapped. In addition, figures provided may include both trapped and hunted animals as some states do not separate killing methods. Figures do not include those animals killed for "nuisance" or predator control.

**With the economic upheavals in Russia and Asia, fur markets have crashed in these countries. Many of the fur species heavily consumed by these countries, such as raccoon and muskrat, were withdrawn at fur auctions in 1999 because of lack of demand and the absence of these markets.

# CHAPTER TWO

# Refuting the Myths

*Camilla H. Fox and Christopher M. Papouchis*

*A society which can allow animals to innocently get caught in steel traps and die an agonizing death under the desert sun, attempting to chew their way out of a trap, crying out in a nonresponsive universe, a society that can allow that to happen can't possibly have the spiritual strength to deal with all the issues of habitat and biodiversity and living thoughtfully and lightly on the land.*

— BRUCE BABBITT, *U.S. SECRETARY OF THE INTERIOR* (1993–2001)

## MYTH: Trapping is humane and causes little pain and suffering to animals.

Trapped animals break legs, dislocate shoulders, sustain lacerations, tear muscles, and cut their mouths and gums attempting to free themselves. An animal trapped on land may starve, become dehydrated, or be attacked by other animals if left in the trap too long. Animals caught in aquatic trap sets may struggle desperately before drowning; beavers can take up to 24 minutes to drown, mink up to 18 minutes, and muskrat up to 5 minutes.[1]

Trappers assert that captured animals are sometimes found "resting" or "sleeping." For animals that instinctually try to flee when caught or confined, however, the absence of activity indicates extreme anxiety and exhaustion, a state more commonly referred to as shock. Most trapped animals attempt to free themselves and struggle violently against the trap, sometimes for hours, before fatigue and shock set in. In one study, raccoons captured in padded leghold or EGG traps for 12 hours fought against the trap and/or against the trap's surroundings for about 7 hours.[2] Few trappers actually witness the moment an animal is trapped or the ensuing struggle. When traps are checked daily or every 48, 72, or 96 hours, depending upon state laws, trappers most often find a terrified animal, exhausted from struggle, in shock and most likely hungry and dehydrated. It is grossly inaccurate to say such an animal is "resting peacefully."

Traps used today are notorious for their cruelty. Leghold traps have been banned or severely restricted in 88 countries and in eight U.S. states (AZ, CA, CO, FL, MA, NJ, RI, WA). The American Veterinary Medical Association, the American Animal Hospital Association, and the National Animal Control Association have all declared the steel-jaw leghold trap inhumane.

Nevertheless, it remains the most commonly used trap in the U.S.

The padded leghold trap (also called the Soft Catch trap), touted by the trapping community as the humane alternative to the steel-jaw version, can still cause significant injuries to trapped animals. A 1995 study in New York, conducted by the U.S. Department of Agriculture Wildlife Services (formerly Animal Damage Control) agency, found that nearly all (97%) of animals trapped in padded traps experienced severe swelling of the trapped limb and 26% had lacerations and fractures.[3] Despite such findings, and even though trap-use surveys indicate that fewer than 2% of U.S. trappers even own padded traps, trapping proponents claim that padded traps have made trapping "humane."[4]

Strangulation neck snares, popular with many trappers, especially in the western U.S., are perhaps the cruelest of all trapping devices. Made of a light wire cable looped through a locking device, this snare is designed to tighten around an animal's neck as she or he struggles. Animals trapped in neck snares may suffer for days, and their heads and necks are frequently swollen with thick and bloody lymph fluid, a condition called "jellyhead" by trappers. Death is often slow and painful. Strangulation neck snares are commonly used by Wildlife Services for killing predators deemed a threat to livestock. The Canadian Federal Provincial Committee for Humane Trapping concluded, after years of study, that snares "do not have the potential to consistently produce a quick death."[5]

Conibear traps are supposed to kill animals instantly by snapping the spinal column at the base of the neck. This is *only* possible, however, if the "right"-sized animal enters the "right"-sized Conibear at just the "right" speed so that the striking bars hit the animal correctly. A 1973 report found Conibear traps generally kill less than 15% of trapped animals instantly, and more than 40% usually die slow, painful deaths as their abdomens, heads, or other body parts are squeezed between the trap bars.[6] While later research and development has produced more efficient Conibear traps,[7] the traps evaluated in the 1973 report are still widely used throughout North America (see Chapter Three).

## MYTH: Death by trapping is more humane than death in nature.

Trappers argue that trapping provides a quick, humane death for animals that would otherwise suffer a cruel death from starvation, disease, or predation. This argument falsely presumes, however, that all animals will die in this manner. Further, the natural cycle of life and death helps maintain genetic diversity and a strong gene pool.

How "humane" is death for a trapped animal? A trapped animal unfortunate enough to be alive after spending hours or days struggling for freedom, fending off predators, suffering without water or food, and often freezing will be clubbed to death and suffocated. Trappers seldom shoot trapped animals since bullet holes and blood damage the pelt and reduce the value of the fur. The terror and pain a trapped animal must endure before being put out of its misery can hardly be called "humane" or kinder than a natural death.

*Get Set to Trap*, a trapper education manual published by the California Department of Fish and Game (DFG), recommends clubbing trapped animals twice with a "heavy iron pipe about 18–24 inches long, or an axe handle … once to render it unconscious and again to render it either dead or comatose." Trappers are advised to "pin the head with one foot and stand on the chest (area near the heart) of the animal with the other foot for several minutes" until the animal suffocates.

The December 1996 issue of *The Trapper and Predator Caller*, a trapping trade magazine, instructs how to kill a trapped fox: "There are several ways used by experienced trappers. I prefer to stun a fox by tapping it on the nose, hard, but not hard enough to draw blood. Quickly put one foot on its neck, to hold it down, and with the other foot press down hard on the chest area. Remain standing on the fox until it is dead, which only takes a few minutes."

Many states sometimes allow private nuisance wildlife control operators (NWCOs) to trap and kill so-called "pest" animals, including raccoons, skunks, squirrels, and opossums, in almost any manner. Common killing methods include drowning, poisoning, and clubbing. Some states do not even require NWCOs to have a trapping license or define acceptable methods for killing animals.

## MYTH: Trapping is selective.

Despite numerous modifications, most traps remain notoriously indiscriminate. Each year, millions of non-target animals are caught in traps set for other animals.

A 1990 New York State Department of Agriculture study examined the effectiveness and selectivity of coyote depredation control techniques and found that 10.8 non-target animals were trapped for every coyote captured.[8] Dick Randall, a former government-employed trapper, testified before Congress in 1975 that for every target animal trapped, at least two non-target animals are trapped.[9]

From 1980–1989, leghold traps injured 23.6% of all bald eagles admitted to The Minnesota Raptor Center, the second most common identified source of injury after shooting.[10] Mark Martell, field biologist with the Raptor Center, described the dangers of leghold traps to bald eagles and other raptors in a September 12, 1989, letter to a wildlife advocacy organization:

> Since our clinic began receiving birds in 1972 we have admitted over 5,000 raptors. Of that number 338 (through the end of 1988) had injuries caused by leg hold traps. Pole trapping (which is now illegal in Minnesota and Wisconsin) caused some of these injuries, while others were the result of incidental catches in traps set for furbearers. Of the 569 Bald Eagles admitted through the end of 1988, 95 had leghold trap caused injuries. Almost all of these are caused by eagles stepping into traps set for fur bearing mammals. These figures represent only those birds which are sent to us and do not reflect the birds that die in the traps or are let go or escape from the traps and die later. Our veterinary staff feels very strongly that the vast majority of birds caught in traps die from the injuries unless treated.

In one study of foxes trapped in padded leghold traps, so many raccoons were captured (in spite of the researchers' conscious efforts to avoid raccoons) that the study had to be redesigned to *include* raccoons as a target species (and presumably to justify their capture for the purposes of the study).[11] In another study, 39% of animals trapped in leghold traps and leg snares were "non-target animals," including four dogs and one domestic cat. All small mammals and birds caught sustained severe injuries, and were found dead in the traps.[12]

Conibear traps are indiscriminate and have been shown to capture up to two non-target animals per target animal when used in standard sets.[13] A field study of the Conibear 120 Magnum (an "advanced" Conibear trap used to trap marten, mink, and other small furbearing mammals) found non-target species comprised more than 73% of all captures.[14]

Neck snares are also highly non-selective, including the breakaway neck snare designed to allow large non-target animals such as deer or livestock to escape. This, however, has done little to reduce non-target capture rates. In a two-year field study in South Dakota, the Denver Wildlife Research Center prototype, Gregerson, and Kelley breakaway snares caught deer or domestic livestock in 26%, 20%, and 11% of all captures, respectively. Fifty-six percent of the 91 deer were unable to escape; all but four died (see Chapter Three).[15]

## MYTH: Trapping is a necessary management tool to control wildlife populations.

Trappers and many wildlife managers claim that trapping removes "surplus" animals from the wild, thereby preventing species from overpopulating and destroying their habitat. In nature, however, animals regulate their own populations based on available food and habitat: There is no such thing as a "surplus" animal. Moreover, trappers attempt to target the healthiest animals with the best fur, not the ill, aged, infirm, or very young animals typically subject to natural selection.

Some species, such as coyotes and foxes, can compensate for population reductions caused by trapping. For example, trapping coyotes causes the remaining pack members to disperse, which results in more coyotes reproducing in the absence of the pack hierarchy. Also, pups born into exploited populations are more likely to survive past their first year because of the reduced competition for food. Coyote populations are thereby able to replenish their numbers and recolonize vacated territories, effectively negating the impacts of trapping.

Trapping can severely impact species that cannot naturally compensate for externally caused population reductions. Several states allow the trapping of sensitive species including wolverine, lynx, fisher, marten, kit fox, and river otter. Heavy trapping pressure nearly wiped out sea otters, beavers, and several species of spotted cats.

The lynx is very vulnerable to external population reductions because of its low reproductive rate. A 1997 lawsuit forced the U.S. Fish and Wildlife Service to consider listing the lynx under the Endangered Species Act (ESA), citing studies that 86% of lynx mortalities were directly attributable to trapping. A 1999 U.S. Department of Agriculture Forest Service report concluded: "Trapping for other large furbearers in areas occupied by lynx may pose a risk. Lynx appear to be extremely susceptible to trapping, and where trapping is permitted it can be (and has been) a significant source of mortality."[16] Despite the clear cause for concern, Montana still allowed lynx to be trapped for commerce and recreation in 1998 and 1999. Finally, in August 1999, wildlife advocates and the threat of a lawsuit pressured the Montana Fish, Parks and Wildlife Commission to finally close the lynx season.

Trapping is anything but an effective "management tool."

## MYTH: Trapping is necessary to protect livestock.

Livestock producers have trapped predators for centuries, in the belief that trapping is necessary to protect their sheep or cattle. These attempts, however, have been largely unsuccessful in solving conflicts between livestock and predators.

As discussed in the previous myth, coyotes are able to compensate for lethal control. In addition, lethal control techniques have ensured that only the most resilient coyotes survive, resulting in what some researchers call a "super coyote." Those coyotes predisposed to take carrion are selected against, while the more predatory individuals who go for live prey are favored.

Despite the increasing number of coyotes killed in the name of "livestock protection" by the U.S. Department of Agriculture's Wildlife Services program, the coyote's range and population continue to expand. In 1995, Wildlife Services killed 40,632 coyotes; in 1997, that number more than doubled to 82,394.

Trapping and other lethal methods are not a viable solution to conflicts between predators and livestock. Improved non-lethal methods including better animal husbandry, sheltering animals at night, aversion techniques, fencing, and guard animals (e.g., dogs, llamas, and burros) can be used to protect livestock while allowing predators to continue their important roles in the ecosystem.

## MYTH: Trapping helps control the spread of disease.

Trappers and wildlife managers play on the fear of rabies and other diseases by claiming that trapping controls the spread of disease. However, according to the Centers for Disease Control (CDC), the National Academy of Sciences (NAS), and the World Health Organization, as well as numerous other scientific, public health, and veterinary organizations, no scientific evidence supports this claim. In 1973, the NAS subcommittee on rabies concluded:

> Persistent trapping or poisoning campaigns as a means to rabies control should be abolished. There is no evidence that these costly and politically attractive programs reduce either wildlife reservoirs or rabies incidence. The money can be better spent on research, vaccination, compensation to stockmen for losses, education and warning systems.[17]

In fact, researchers have discovered that trapping actually *increases* the spread of disease. The CDC and other authorities attributed a raccoon rabies epidemic on the East Coast to the translocation of more than 3,000 raccoons from Florida to West Virginia in 1977 by trappers and hunters to boost local populations.[18] At that time, the particular strain of raccoon rabies was restricted to Florida, but some of the animals translocated to West Virginia were infected. The epizootic has spread across much of the northeast and to the Canadian border. Potential costs associated with prevention and control activities of the disease have been estimated in the hundreds of millions of dollars.[19]

By removing mature, immune animals, trappers reduce competition for habitat and make room for newcomers who may not be immune. Larger raccoon litters also result in young who are more susceptible to the disease.[20] In addition, animals infected with rabies do not eat during the latter stages of the disease and thus do not respond to baited traps. Hence, traps set will more often capture healthy animals than infected animals.

Despite all of the evidence to the contrary, state and federal agencies continue to encourage fur trappers to trap and kill animals in the name of disease control. However, the most successful attempts to control rabies in wildlife have utilized bait containing oral rabies vaccine. Public funds currently spent on trapping programs would be better used on such proven successes, along with public education emphasizing prevention of rabies through pet vaccinations, securing garbage cans, not feeding wildlife, etc.

## MYTH: A fur coat is more environmentally friendly than a synthetic coat.

In the late 1990s, the fur industry tried to "green" its image by claiming that real fur garments were more environmentally friendly than fake furs. It takes nearly three times more energy, however, to produce a fur coat from trapped animals as it does to produce a synthetic fur, according to a study by Gregory H. Smith, a transportation research engineer at the University of Michigan.[21] Included in Smith's calculations were the energy costs of skinning, pelt drying, transportation, processing, and manufacture of real trapped-fur garments. Much of this energy is derived from petroleum products. Environmentally harmful chemicals, including chromium and formaldehyde, are used in the processing of real fur garments to keep them from rotting. In 1991, six New Jersey fur processors were fined more than $2 million for releasing toxic waste into the environment.[22] Far from being "natural, renewable resources," real fur products consume more of our precious irreplaceable energy resources than do those made from synthetic materials.

## MYTH: Trapping provides significant income and employment opportunities for many Americans.

Trapping proponents claim trapping provides jobs and a viable income for many Americans. Yet in their own trade publications, trappers complain that trapping hardly pays for itself. In the June/July 1996 issue of *The Trapper and Predator Caller*, one trapper admits, "I have caught a lot of fur for an old geezer, but if I had counted all my … expenses, I doubt if I made a dollar an hour. I could have made more money picking manure with the chickens."

In the spring of 1997, the Animal Protection Institute conducted a national survey to determine the average annual income of trappers in each state. State wildlife agencies indicated that income from trapping was either extremely low or non-existent. The head Furbearer Research Biologist with the Kansas Department of Wildlife & Parks wrote, "Variability among trappers is too great to provide any form of estimate of income. The time and expenses incurred while trapping would need to be accounted for (equipment, vehicle use and gas, time invested, etc.) to provide a reliable estimate of a trapper's expenses. Income derived from these calculations have indicated that trappers lose money."

A 1992 national Gallup survey of trappers found that "approximately 30% of all trappers in 1991 reported no household income from trapping ... [and] only 5% of trappers in this survey reported obtaining at least 20% of their total household income from trapping. Most trappers reported earning small incomes from trapping. This suggests that motives other than monetary gain are also important to trappers. The average cost of trapping per day was $30.67."[23]

The manufacturing of fur products takes place mainly in countries outside the U.S. where labor is cheap (the U.S. is one of the largest suppliers of raw fur to countries that manufacture fur garments). The fur garments are then imported into the United States for retail sale. Clearly, the U.S. fur industry is more concerned with finding cheap labor than providing employment opportunities for Americans, despite its claims to the contrary.

## MYTH: Trapping is tightly regulated.

Although most states regulate trapping and set bag and season limits, these regulations are often extremely lax, poorly defined, and loosely enforced. Many states allow the use of traps known to be non-selective and to cause severe injuries or death to both target and non-target species. Four states (Alaska, Michigan, Montana, North Dakota) do not require trappers to check their traps at all, and twenty states allow animals to languish in traps for two to four days. Forty-eight states allow animals to be killed in whatever method the trapper

*"I probably set my first leghold trap when I was in my early teens ... If I had continued down that path, I have no doubt that today I would be happily employed by some state wildlife agency ... performing my duties of promoting annual furbearing harvesting and unquestionably accepting the principles of wildlife management — those laid-in-stone beliefs that I had subscribed to for so many years — were not really proven biological facts at all. In fact, when subjected to scientific scrutiny, and deprived of both the economic and political arguments, they began to deteriorate. Suddenly, without ever knowing it, I was one of those who had changed."* [25]

chooses. (Georgia is the only state to mandate that trappers "... carry a weapon of .22 cal. rimfire while tending traps and to use that weapon to dispatch any furbearing animal to be taken.") Very few states tightly monitor the number of animals trapped each year. Some rely on voluntary or mandatory "fur dealer/buyer reports" to estimate annual trap kill totals. Others obtain their data through random telephone or mail surveys, with response rates from 10% to 60%. State wildlife agencies then estimate the total numbers of animals trapped each year from these partial reports. Most states do not require trappers to report the number of non-target animals trapped.

Few states require or even offer trapper education courses. Rather, 81% of trappers reported that they had learned their skills by "trial-and-error," according to a 1996 survey.[24] The 1992 Gallup survey of trappers revealed that only 17% of trappers nationwide had taken a formal trapper education course.

Also largely unregulated are private nuisance wildlife control operators (NWCOs) who trap, remove, and most often kill animals deemed "pests"; few have any biological knowledge about wildlife.

## Conclusion

Trappers and state and federal agencies frequently use these myths to convince the public that trapping is not only humane, but also necessary to protect human health and safety and to manage wildlife populations. However, these arguments fly in the face of a large body of scientific evidence showing that the trapping of wildlife is both inhumane and biologically unsound. Historically, trapping has led to the decline of a number of species, including the lynx, river otter, gray wolf, beaver, and kit fox. Today, fur trapping is carried out less as a commercial, moneymaking enterprise than as a recreational "hobby." The continued exploitation of wildlife and the use of cruel traps cannot be justified in a society increasingly concerned about animals, the environment, and our role as stewards of a finite planet.

## NOTES

1. F. F. Gilbert and N. Gofton. "Terminal Dives in Mink, Muskrat and Beaver." *Physiology & Behavior* 28 (1982): 835–840.

2. G. Proulx, et al. "Injuries and Behavior of Raccoons (Procyon lotor) Captured in the Soft Catch, and the EGG™ Traps in Simulated Natural Environments." *Journal of Wildlife Diseases* 29 (1993): 447–452.

3. R. L. Phillips, et al. "Leg Injuries to Coyotes in Three Types of Foothold Traps." *Wildlife Society Bulletin* 24 (1996): 260–263.

4. International Association of Fish and Wildlife Agencies Fur Resources Technical Committee. "Ownership and Use of Traps by Trappers in the United States in 1992." Fur Resources Technical Committee of the International Fish and Wildlife Agencies and The Gallup Organization, Washington, D.C. 1993.

5. The Federal Provincial Committee on Humane Trapping, "Findings and Recommendations." Federal Provincial Wildlife Conference. Canada. 1983.

6. H. C. Lunn. "The Conibear Trap – Recommendations for Its Improvement." Humane Trap Development Committee of Canada, Canadian Federation of Humane Societies. 1973.

7. G. Proulx, et al. "Assessment and Preliminary Development of the Rotating-Jaw Conibear 120™ Trap to Effectively Kill Marten (Martes americana)." *Canadian Journal of Zoology* 67 (1989): 1074–1079; G. Proulx, et al. "The C120 Magnum with Pan Trigger: A Humane Trap for Mink (Mustela vison)." *Journal of Wildlife Diseases* 26 (1990): 511–517; G. Proulx and M. W. Barrett. "Evaluation of Mechanically Improved Conibear 220™ Traps to Quickly Kill Fisher (Martes pennanti) in Simulated Natural Environments." *Journal of Wildlife Diseases* 29 (1993): 317–323; G. Proulx, et al. "A Humane Killing Trap for Lynx (Felis lynx): the Conibear 330™ with Clamping Bars." *Journal of Wildlife Diseases* 31 (1995): 57–61.

8. T. N. Tomsa and J. E. Forbes. "Coyote Depredation Control in New York — An Integrated Approach." USDA-APHIS-ADC. 1990.

9. D. Randall. "Hearings before the Ninety-Fourth Congress to Discourage the Use of Painful Devices in the Trapping of Animals and Birds." U.S. Govt. Printing Office, Washington, D.C. 1975.

10. P. T. Redig and G. E. Duke. "The Effect and Value of Raptor Rehabilitation in North America." Transaction of the 60th North American Wildlife & Natural Resources Conference. Wildlife Management Institute, Washington, D.C. 1995.

11. B. F. Tullar. "Evaluation of a Padded Leg-Hold Trap for Capturing Foxes and Raccoons." *NY Fish and Game Journal* 31 (1984): 97–103.

12. D. K. Onderka, et al. "Injuries to Coyotes and Other Species Caused by Four Models of Footholding Devices." *Wildlife Society Bulletin* 16 (1990): 303–307.

13. M. Novak. "Traps and Trap Research." in M. Novak, et al., eds. Wild Furbearer Management and Conservation in North America. Ontario Trappers Association, North Bay, Ontario, Canada, 1987. 365 pages.

14. G. Proulx and M. W. Barrett. "Field Testing the C120 Magnum for Mink" *Wildlife Society Bulletin* 21 (1993): 421–426.

15. R. L. Phillips. "Evaluation of 3 Types of Snares for Capturing Coyotes." *Wildlife Society Bulletin* 24 (1996): 107–110.

16. L. F. Ruggiero, et al. "The Scientific Basis for Lynx Conservation: Qualified Insights." The Scientific Basis for Lynx Conservation. USDA Forest Service Gen. Tech. Rep. RMRS-GTR-30. 1999.

17. "Control of Rabies." National Research Council, Subcommittee on Rabies, National Academy of Sciences, Washington, D.C. 1973.

18. S. R. Jenkins and W. G. Winkler. "Descriptive Epidemiology from an Epizootic of Raccoon Rabies in the Middle Atlantic States, 1982-1983." *American Journal of Epidemiology* 126 (1987): 429–437.

19. "Extension of the Raccoon Rabies Epizootic-1992." *Journal of the American Medical Association* 268, No. 13 (October 7, 1992): 1646–1647.

20. "Controlling Wildlife Rabies through Population Reduction: An Ineffective Method." *The Rabies Monitor* 4 (1) (Spring 1996).

21. G. H. Smith. "Energy Study of Real vs. Synthetic Furs." University of Michigan. 1979.

22. "EPA Seeks $2.2 Million in Penalties from Six NJ Firms in the Fur Industry for Hazardous Waste Violations." U.S. Environmental Protection Agency News Release, New York: 8 October, 1991.

23. International Association of Fish and Wildlife Agencies Fur Resources Technical Committee. "Ownership and Use of Traps by Trappers in the United States in 1992." Fur Resources Technical Committee of the International Fish and Wildlife Agencies and the Gallup Organization, Washington, D.C. 1993.

24. R. M. Muth, et al. "The Sociocultural and Economic Value of Furbearer Resources: A study of Trapping in Six Northeastern States." Final Technical Report, U.S. Fish and Wildlife Service, Division of Federal Aid, Region 5, Hadley, Massachusetts, 111. 1996.

25. Thomas Eveland. *Jaws of Steel.* Silver Spring: The Fund for Animals, 1991.

# Trapping Devices, Methods, and Research

*Depending on how hard the animal has struggled, the leg will be lacerated, often dislocated at the shoulder, sometimes twisted off above the paw so that only the leg sinews bind the limb to the trap.*

— DICK RANDALL, *FORMER U.S.–GOVERNMENT–EMPLOYED TRAPPER*

## PRIMARY TYPES OF TRAPS USED IN THE UNITED STATES

*Camilla H. Fox and Christopher M. Papouchis*

### Leghold Traps

The steel-jaw leghold trap (hereafter called the leghold trap) is a spring-powered device employing two metal jaws that clamp onto an animal's leg when it steps on the trigger, which is called a pan. Leghold traps come in two general designs: longspring and coil-spring, named for the type of spring mechanism used to produce the trap's clamping force. Trappers  generally prefer coil-spring leghold traps to longspring traps because of their stronger clamping force, which reduces an animal's ability to escape or "pull out" from a trap. In addition, coil-spring traps allow the addition of "beefer springs" to augment the trap's clamping force.

Leghold traps are produced in a variety of sizes for different target species, from No. 1 (used to catch muskrats, weasels, and other small furbearers) to No. 6 (not commonly used, but may be used to trap bear and other large mammals). On land, leghold traps are most frequently set for coyote (Nos. 1½–4), bobcat (Nos. 1½–3), fox (Nos. 1½–2), raccoon (Nos. 1–1½), skunk (Nos. 1–1½), and other furbearing animals. Leghold traps are often set in aquatic environs for muskrat, otter, mink, and beaver, usually with the intent of drowning the animal.

An archaic device that has changed little in fundamental design since its invention more than 150 years ago, the leghold trap is the type most commonly used by fur trappers in the U.S. (see Table 3.1). Leghold traps are used to capture an estimated 80% of the animals trapped in the U.S., according to the National Trappers Association.[1]

Most animals caught in leghold traps react to the instant pain and restraint by frantically struggling in an attempt to free themselves, often enduring fractures, ripped tendons, severe swelling (edema), blood loss, amputations, and/or tooth and mouth damage from biting the trap. Some animals even chew or twist off their trapped limb trying to escape. Termed "wring-off" by trappers, this self-mutilation means the loss of a marketable pelt for the trapper and probable death for the trapped animal from starvation, gangrene, or attack from predators. For animals trapped in water, death comes by drowning as they attempt to either surface for air or drag the trap underwater to reach land. Drowning is a slow, agonizing death that can take up to 20 minutes for some species.[2] Death by drowning has been deemed inhumane by the American Veterinary Medical Association (AVMA).[3]

Leghold traps will capture *any* animal that steps into the trap's jaws, although animals too large for the trap will not be held. Each year, an unknown number of non-target animals fall victim to these indiscriminate devices, including threatened and endangered species, birds, and domestic animals. Dick Randall, a former government-employed trapper and an expert in his field, became a vocal opponent of the use of indiscriminate traps. In 1975, Randall testified before Congress about the non-selective nature of leghold traps, noting that:

Even though I was an experienced, professional trapper, my trap victims included non-target species such as bald eagles and golden eagles, a variety of hawks and other birds, rabbits, sage grouse, pet dogs, deer, antelope, porcupines, sheep and calves ... My trapping records show that for each target animal I trapped, about 2 unwanted individuals were caught. Because of trap injuries, these non-target species had to be destroyed.[4]

Several scientific studies document the high rate of non-target captures.[5] Though advances in trigger design appear to have decreased this rate,[6] recreational and commercial trappers may not be using the new technology because such design modifications have been shown to decrease the capture rates of target species as well.[7] The cost of new traps or modifications is also a deterrent for many trappers, who may use dozens of traps at a time on their traplines.

More than 80 countries have banned leghold traps,* including all 15 member nations of the European Union. In Canada, restrictions have been placed on the use of leghold traps used on land and are only legal for trapping fox, coyote, lynx, bobcat, and wolf; however, leghold traps are still legal for trapping mink, muskrat, otter and beaver in underwater drowning sets. In the U.S., eight states have either banned or severely restricted leghold traps.† Public opposition to the use of leghold traps is growing within the U.S., as evidenced in a number of polls over the last two decades (see Chapter One) and by the recent passage of five state ballot initiatives banning the use of leghold traps for commercial or recreational trapping (see Chapter Seven). A Caravan Opinion Research poll commissioned by the Animal Welfare Institute, conducted in November 1996, showed that 74% of Americans believe leghold traps should be banned.

---

* Countries banning the leghold trap: Austria, Bahrain, Bangladesh, Belgium, Belize, Benin, Botswana, Brazil, British West Indies, Bulgaria, Burkina Faso, Burundi, Cameroon, Cayman Islands, Chile, Colombia, Costa Rica, Cuba, Cyprus, Czeck Republic, Denmark, Dominican Republic, El Salvador, England, Equatorial Guinea, Finland, France, Gabon, Gambia, Germany, Ghana, Greece, Greenland, Guinea, Guyana, Hong Kong, Hungary, India, Israel, Ireland, Italy, Ivory Coast, Jamaica, Jordan, Kenya, Korea (Republic Of), Lebanon, Liberia, Liechtenstein, Luxembourg, Mali, Malawi, Malaysia, Maldives, Mauritania, Mexico, Moldavia, Monaco, Morocco, Mozambique, Netherlands, Nicaragua, Niger, Nigeria, Norway, Pakistan, Panama, Philippines, Poland, Portugal, Russia, Scotland, Senegal, Seychelles, Singapore, Spain, Sri Lanka, Swaziland, Sweden, Switzerland, Tanzania, Thailand, Togo, Trinidad & Tobago, Tunisia, Uganda, United Arab Emirates, United Kingdom, Wales, Zaire, Zambia, Zimbabwe.

† States banning or severely restricting leghold traps: Arizona (on public lands only, 1994), California (1998), Colorado (1996), Florida (1973), Massachusetts (1996), New Jersey (1986), Rhode Island (1971), and Washington (2000).

Many animal care–related associations, including the World Veterinary Association, the American Animal Hospital Association and the National Animal Control Association have policy statements opposing the use of steel-jaw leghold traps. In 1993, the Executive Board of the American Veterinary Medical Association (AVMA) declared, "The AVMA considers the steel-jaw leghold trap to be inhumane."

## Other Types/Modifications of Leghold Traps

### Padded Leghold Trap

Designed to reduce injuries in captured animals, padded leghold traps have thin strips of rubber attached to the trap's jaws. Trapping proponents

tout the padded leghold trap as a humane alternative to the traditional steel-jaw version because a number of studies have shown that padded traps can reduce the incidence of severe injuries in several species.[8] However, most of these studies also report that padded traps do not eliminate significant injuries to animals, and for some species, including raccoons, padded traps may actually cause more severe injuries than the standard steel-jaw version. Moreover, most trappers will not use these traps because they suspect them to be less efficient than unpadded traps. Surveys indicate that less than 2% of traps owned by U.S. trappers are padded leghold traps.[9] Trappers have admitted that padded leghold traps are not a panacea and can cause significant and sometimes life-threatening injuries to some species:

> Padded traps should be an alternative available to trappers, but not required for animals such as raccoons which appear to suffer more injury when caught in padded traps. (*American Trapper*, September/October 1995)

> We learned that these padded traps do not restrain the animal for very long, and in many cases they do as much damage to the

animals as regular jawed traps. (*The Trapper & Predator Caller*, April 1994)

### EGG Trap

The EGG trap is a leghold trap encased in an egg-shaped plastic cover to prevent self-mutilation by raccoons and other small furbearing species. The EGG trap was found to reduce injuries to raccoons in a laboratory setting[10] but still had unacceptably high injury scores in field trials.[11] In a field study on opossums, the researchers

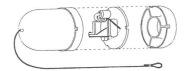

concluded that the EGG trap caused less severe injuries than unpadded No. 2 coil-spring leghold traps; however, the EGG trap still caused excessive swelling, lacerations, and fractures.[12]

### Stop-loss Leghold Trap

The stop-loss leghold trap is a traditional longspring leghold trap with an auxiliary spring-activated steel bar that slams shut on the animal's body to prevent the animal from twisting or chewing off its trapped appendage. Tom Garrett, trap expert and

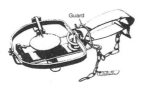

author of *Alternative Traps*, said of the stop-loss: "The stop-loss is undoubtedly one of the cruelest traps ever made. It appears, depending on ambient conditions, to kill from half to three-quarters of its victims within 24 hours and 90% within 48 hours. Mink caught in these traps can continue to struggle, if not retrieved, for several days."[13] Though banned in Canada, the stop-loss is legal in most U.S. states.

### Jump Leghold Trap

The jump trap is a standard leghold trap with extra spring force designed to "jump" up when triggered so that the jaws close higher on the leg. Like the stop-loss, the jump trap was designed to prevent pull-outs and "wring-offs." Smaller

animals captured in jump traps can incur greater injuries because of the trap's ability to catch the animal higher on the leg (or body if the animal is rodent-sized). Jump traps are made in four sizes and are used primarily for trapping coyote, fox, marten, river otter, muskrat, skunk, and beaver.

### Offset Leghold Trap

The offset trap is a traditional leghold trap with a small gap between the closed jaws, which ostensibly allows small non-target animals to escape and reduces trap injuries in larger animals. Offset leghold traps frequently have stronger springs and, therefore, added clamping force. Small animals with short legs are most often unable to escape and are maimed when the offset trap catches them on the shoulder or body. Larger animals still experience severe trap injuries to the paw and leg, as the gap between the trap jaws is usually smaller than the actual width of the trapped animal's paw. Studies of offset leghold traps are equivocal with regard to injuries.[14]

### Laminated Leghold Trap (or "Laminated Jaws")

The laminated leghold trap is a standard leghold trap with a strip of rolled steel attached to the trap jaws. Theoretically, the wider jaws spread out the initial impact and then disperse the clamping force, resulting in decreased limb injuries. While some studies suggest that laminated traps reduce injuries when compared to standard steel-jaw leghold traps,[15] these reductions were less than those of padded-jaw leghold traps.[16]

### Pan Tension Devices

Pan tension (PTDs) devices replace the standard pan trigger of leghold traps and allow adjustment of the weight required to spring the trap. Studies show that PTDs can be efficient at excluding smaller "non-target" species, but species similar in weight or larger than the target species are still captured.[17]

### Toothed or Serrated Leghold Trap (or "Toothed-Jaw")

The toothed-jaw trap is a standard leghold trap with teeth or serrations on the jaws. Ostensibly designed to reduce trap "pull-outs," toothed leghold traps can cause severe injuries to captured animals. Nineteen states allow their use for land sets and 26 states allow their use for water sets.

## Conibear/Kill-Type Traps

Although there are several different models of so-called "quick kill" traps, they tend to be known collectively as Conibears, after the developer of the

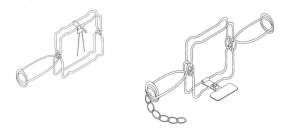

prototype, Frank Conibear. Conibear traps consist of two metal frames hinged at the center point and powered by two torsion springs to create a scissor-like action. One jaw has a trigger that can be baited. The opposite jaw has a catch, or "dog," that holds the trap open. Intended to be an "instant killing" device, the Conibear trap is designed to snap shut on an animal's spinal column at the base of the skull, causing a fatal blow.

Manufactured in a variety of sizes, Conibear traps are frequently used in water sets to trap muskrat (model 110/ 5 in.), nutria (220/ 7 in.), river otter (220 or 330), and beaver (330/ 9–12 in.). They are also used on land to trap raccoon (220), pine marten (110 or 220), badger (220), weasel (110), and other furbearers. Killer traps similar to the Conibear have been manufactured and used by trappers, but most appear to exhibit problems similar to the Conibear.

Many problems exist with Conibear and similar kill-type traps, most notably their inability to consistently cause instant death and their inherent danger to non-target species. As noted in the 1999 *Final Environmental Document Regarding Furbearing and Nongame Mammal Hunting and Trapping* published by the California Department of Fish and Game, Conibears suffer from a variety of trigger-aversion and design flaws. "Several factors keep this trap from killing consistently and quickly, including the size of the animal, the species involved, the position of the animal at trap closure, and the impact and clamping levels of the trap. The most significant flaw is the trigger system that performs erratically, preventing a fatal blow to the animal's body."[18] A 1973 report found Conibear traps generally kill less than 15% of trapped animals instantly, and more than 40%

## TABLE 3.1

*Leghold trap and Conibear trap use in the U.S. by species\**

| SPECIES | PERCENT OF TRAP USE | | NO. OF ANIMALS |
|---|---|---|---|
| | LEGHOLD | CONIBEAR | |
| *Carnivores* | | | |
| Bobcat | 97.5 | 2.5 | 2,893 |
| Coyote | 99.7 | 0.3 | 7,215 |
| Fisher | 26.2 | 73.8 | 1,175 |
| Fox, Gray | 100.0 | 0.0 | 6,164 |
| Fox, Red | 99.8 | 0.2 | 12,016 |
| Lynx | 100.0 | 0.0 | 439 |
| Marten | 56.0 | 44.0 | 1,476 |
| Mink | 86.6 | 13.4 | 11,753 |
| Raccoon | 84.5 | 15.5 | 12,785 |
| Skunk | 80.0 | 20.0 | 1,082 |
| Weasels | 97.1 | 2.9 | 415 |
| Wolf | 100.0 | 0.0 | 57 |
| *Rodents* | | | |
| Beaver | 33.1 | 66.9 | 5,070 |
| Muskrat | 55.6 | 44.4 | 17,627 |
| Nutria | 56.8 | 43.2 | 132 |

\* "National Trap Use Survey." National Trappers Association. Bloomington, Ill. 1990.

usually die slow, painful deaths as their abdomens, heads, or other body parts are squeezed between the trap bars.[19] While later research and development has produced more efficient Conibear traps,[20] the traps originally examined in the 1973 report are still widely used. Even Tom Krause, former president of the American Trappers Association and current editor of *The American Trapper*, notes, "Traps of the standard Conibear design exhibit trigger aversion problems, and do not acceptably position sufficient numbers of animals for killing blows."[21]

## Other Types and Modifications of Conibear/Kill-Type Traps

### Bionic Trap

The Bionic trap is a 27 x 15 cm mousetrap type device with a 13.4 x 16 cm jaw powered by a coil-spring, which closes 180° on a fixed base. A plastic cone mounted on the trap is designed to funnel an animal toward the baited trigger. Different-sized cones are used to select for different-sized target

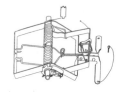

species. The Bionic trap is generally used to trap small- to medium-sized furbearers including mink and marten.

### Kania Trap

The Kania trap is a narrow mousetrap with a 14 cm long striking bar powered by a coil-spring. The trap is set perpendicular to a running pole and an animal that steps on the trigger is struck by a bar. The sensitivity of the trigger varies, firing under weights ranging from 10 to 55 g. The Kania trap is used to trap small furbearer species, such as squirrels.

# SURVEY: OWNERSHIP AND USE OF TRAPS BY TRAPPERS IN THE UNITED STATES IN 1992

This telephone survey of 2,474 trappers in the United States [Northeast (627), South (533), Midwest (673), West (536), Alaska (105)] was carried out by The Fur Resources Committee of the International Association of Fish and Wildlife Agencies and The Gallup Organization, Inc., September–December 1992.

## General Findings

- Average age of trapper in the U.S. = 45 (trappers 19 years of age or younger accounted for less than 2% of the total surveyed; only 17% of trappers in the survey were younger than 30 years).

- More than 98% of trappers are male.

- Average household income = $30,750

- Average annual trap-related expenses = $1,126

- Average cost of trapping per day = $30.67

- Approximately 29% of all active trappers in 1991 reported no household income came from trapping. Approximately 5% of trappers in the survey report at least 20% of their total household income came from trapping.

- Average number of traps owned = 205 (of which 59% were leghold traps; 22% body-gripping traps; 11% snares; 2% padded leghold traps; 1% cage traps; and 5% other traps.)

- "Very few trappers own or use padded traps … Padded traps cost approximately 70% more than the standard foothold traps."

- In the U.S., the most popular traps owned by trappers are No. 110 body-gripping traps, No. 1-½ coil-spring leghold traps, owned by 65% and 61% of the trappers respectively.

Snares were the third most popular trap style noted in that survey, although they were not specifically counted.

- "Western trappers tended to own large traps and relied more heavily on snares than did others. Trappers in the West depended largely on No. 3 long spring foothold traps and snares … only a few trappers owned padded footholds …"

  - In Alaska, "Snares were the most popular device, and those that had them had over 114 … The No. 330 body-gripper is more popular in Alaska than in other regions … As in other regions, padded footholds were rarely owned."

- "Almost half of all trappers modified or changed their traps when they were purchased."

- "Half of the trappers (52%) in our survey trapped exclusively on private land, 12% trapped exclusively on public lands, and 36% trapped on both."

- "Nuisance wildlife removal appears to be a significant activity among trappers that we interviewed … Nationwide, 63% of trappers we interviewed said they had been contacted to trap problem animals, and an average of 26% of those trappers' activities involved removal of nuisance wildlife … It is important to note that in some states, nuisance animal control trappers are not required to be licensed as are fur trappers and thus were not surveyed."

- Snares were legal for approximately half of all trappers in the survey. Snare use was high in Alaska, where trappers frequently used them in both water sets (67%) and land sets (87%).

- "We asked those trappers who primarily used snares for primary target species if their snares were normally used as a killing device or as a live-restraining device. Trappers using snares to capture coyotes mostly used them as a kill-trap, as did over half of those snaring other species. However, use as a live-restraint device was not uncommon, and half of those using snares for raccoons reported them to be used as a live-restraint trap."

- Primary target species for trappers in 1992 in order of importance: raccoon, mink, muskrat, red fox, beaver, coyote, gray fox, bobcat, pine marten, river otter, opossum, fisher, lynx, wolverine, striped skunk, wolf, badger, nutria.

- Primary target species in Midwest and Northeast, in order of importance: raccoons, muskrats, mink and red fox; most common traps used are No. 1, No. 1½ , No. 2 coil-spring, No. 110 Conibear.

- Primary target species in the West: coyotes and bobcats; most common traps used are snares, No. 3 longspring, No. 3 coil.

- Primary target species in South: raccoon, gray fox, red fox, mink, and coyote; (10% of trappers also live trapped foxes and coyotes to sell for use in hound-running pens).

- "Very few trappers in our survey had taken a formal trapper's education course taught by agencies. Nationwide only 17% had taken such a course."

- "Trapper incentives are apparently changing, especially in the South, where trappers report the lowest average percent of income from trapping. Here, it appears that a growing number of trappers are either focusing on nuisance animal control or are providing live animals to the coursing pen industry. This increased nuisance control work in the United States is likely due to both the quantity of nuisance problems, but also the lack of traditional fur trapping due to extremely low pelt values, especially in the South. During the time of this survey, the pelts of some furbearer species were completely unmarketable from much of the Southern region."

## C120 Magnum

The C120 Magnum trap consists of a Conibear 120 frame equipped with two Conibear 220 springs, a flat metal bar welded to each striking bar, and a four-pronged trigger. These modifications to the traditional C120 were designed to promote double strikes and additional force. The C120 Magnum was developed to target small- to medium-sized furbearers, including mink and marten.

## C120 Mark IV

The C120 Mark IV is a C120 with heavier wire springs and the addition of two rectangular bars welded onto the opposite jaws of the C120 frame. When the trap is sprung, only one bar comes in contact with the animal and, depending on how the trap is set, it can strike the animal from either the top or the bottom. This trap has most often been studied on marten.

## Sauvageau 2000

The Sauvageau 2000 series killing trap (Conibear style) is similar to the C120 Magnum in that it has additional striking bars welded to the frame to

increase striking force. This trap comes in different models; the Sauvageau 2001-8 is used for arctic fox.

## Snares

A snare is a primitive wire noose, simple in design and vicious in action. Snares are generally categorized as "neck," "body," or "leg" (also called "foot") snares, depending upon which area of the animal's body the trap is designed to target. Snares can be set on land or in water to capture a variety of species. As with other body-gripping devices, however, snares are indiscriminate. Because they are cheap and easy to set, trappers often saturate an area with dozens of snares to catch as many animals as possible.

A standard snare used by fur trappers generally consists of a light wire cable looped through a locking device and is designed to tighten as the animal pulls against it. These types of snares are known as "manual snares" because the animal provides the energy necessary to tighten the snare. ("Power snares" that use one or more springs to provide the killing energy are less commonly used by trappers in the U.S.). The more a snared animal struggles, the tighter the noose becomes; the tighter the noose, the greater the animal's struggle and suffering. "Snare locks" are sometimes added to neck or body snares to stop the snare from tightening past a certain loop size.

## Neck Snare

A neck snare is a snare set vertically (above ground) to target the neck of an animal. Neck snares are most often used to catch canids (coyotes, foxes, and wolves), but may also be used to trap bobcats, lynx, and other species. Neck snares are generally set as killing devices. Some smaller animals lose consciousness in about six minutes when neck-snared; larger animals can suffer for days. Trappers even have a term, "jellyhead," to refer to the thick, bloody lymph fluid that swells the heads and necks of neck-snared canids. Snares frequently have to be replaced after each capture due to twisting and strain on the snare cable that results from animals' struggling to free themselves.

## Body Snare

The body snare is designed to kill animals by strangulation, crushing vital organs, or drowning if used underwater. Body snares are often set underwater to target beaver or otter. Snares do not discriminate, however, and will capture any animal around any body part. Even the Canadian Federal Provincial Committee for Humane Trapping (a committee set up to improve the

acceptability of trapping methods in Canada, with government support) has deemed neck and body snares not to be "quick killing devices."[22]

## Leg (or Foot) Snare

Distinct from neck and body snares is the leg (or foot) snare. Leg snares are generally set horizontally and are designed to close upon an animal's leg in order to restrain, but not kill, the animal. Some models may be more humane and/or efficient than leghold traps for capturing certain species, according to recently published scientific studies.

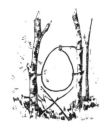

Leg snares differ in complexity, efficacy, and humaneness. Spring-activated leg snares employ a spring-powered mechanism that cinches the noose on an animal's leg when it steps onto the pan (a trigger mechanism that is weight-sensitive). The Aldrich leg snare, invented by Jack Aldrich, is most commonly used for capturing bear and appears to cause fewer injuries than leghold traps. According to Tom Garrett, author of *Alternative Traps*, the Novak leg snare appeared on the market in the 1980s and was "withdrawn from the market after it inflicted almost six times as much injury to coyotes in the 1986–87 Alberta field tests as did the competing Fremont leg snare."[23] The Fremont leg snare, developed by Al Fremont in the 1980s, is similar to the Aldrich leg snare in design but is made to capture smaller animals. One study found that Fremont snares caused fewer injuries to coyote than leghold traps.[24] Injury reduction and efficiency, however, is often a function of trapper knowledge and skill. Because leghold traps are still legal in much of the U.S., trappers have little incentive to try alternative traps, such as leg snares. Leg snares are more commonly used in Canada and in European countries, including France, where leghold traps are prohibited.

## Live-Holding Traps

There are many types of live-holding devices, some more humane than others. The most familiar live trap is the Havahart cage trap, used primarily to capture "nuisance" animals in suburban and urban areas. Bait is placed inside, and once the animal has entered and jarred the trigger, the door slams shut. Though live-holding devices are often considered humane, the degree of humaneness is entirely dependent upon how frequently the traps are checked. Leaving a raccoon in a cage trap for days is far from humane and may lead to self-mutilation, tooth and mouth injuries, and, depending upon the length of time, death.

### Bailey Trap

This is a live-holding trap resembling a wire mesh clam shell and comprised of two open sections, joined together by spring-powered hinges. Designed to be set in  water and to target beaver, the trap is activated when an animal enters the trap and jars the trigger, forcing the two open sections to snap together around the animal.

### Cage Trap

Cage traps come in a few different styles, but all are oblong wire mesh cages with doors that swing from hinges at the top of the cage. A pan trigger is attached to the floor of the trap and linked to the door so an animal stepping upon it will close the cage. Two common cage traps are the Tomahawk and Havahart.

### Hancock Trap

Similar to the Bailey trap in its spring-powered hinged design, the Hancock trap resembles a wire trunk and is used primarily for capturing beaver and otter.

### Log Trap

The log trap is a live-holding capture device, invented by former trapper Ed Cesar, made out of native materials secured on the spot. Log traps are labor intensive and are more commonly used in Canada where trappers have registered trap lines on vast tracts of land. The boxes are about 4 x 1 x 1½ feet and are generally made to trap lynx, wolverine, bobcat, fox, and other forest

carnivores. Considered more humane and efficient than other standard trapping devices, log traps can last more than 20 years if regularly maintained.

## Other Traps

### Colony Trap (also known as "Submarine Trap")

Colony traps are cage or box traps set in water to capture and drown multiple animals. Also known as "submarine traps," these types of cage traps are frequently used in Western Europe to catch muskrats. Colony traps are legal in a number of states (see Chapter Five).

### Deadfall Trap

Primitive in design, a deadfall trap is any trap that consists of a baited trigger attached to a heavy object, such as a rock or tree limb, designed to crush any animal pulling on the trigger. This trapping method is not very common today in

North America, but is still used illegally by poachers in tropical countries and by some indigenous peoples, primarily to  catch animals for food. Fur trappers prefer other traps because use of deadfalls frequently damages the animal's pelt.

## Pitfall Trap

Not commonly used today, pitfall traps, like deadfalls, are a primitive form of capturing device used by indigenous cultures prior to the development of mechanically-activated traps. Simple in design, the pitfall consists of a concealed pit or dug-out hole large enough to contain an animal. Animals are lured to the area by the bait and fall into the hole, where they are unable to escape.

## Pole Trap

Pole traps (often called "running poles," "tree sets," or "spring poles") were made with the same intent as stop-loss and jump traps — to reduce an animal's chances of escaping the trap by gnawing or twisting off its trapped appendage. Pole traps consist of body-gripping traps set on a log, tree branch, or pole so that when an animal is caught it will dangle by its crushed paw, unable to escape. In addition to reducing twist or chew-off, trappers favor pole traps because they reduce the likelihood that predators will attack the trapped animal, thereby reducing pelt damage.

## NOTES

1. "National Trap Use Survey." National Trappers Association. Bloomington, Ill. 1990.

2. F. F. Gilbert, and N. Gofton. "Terminal Dives in Mink, Muskrat and Beaver." *Physiology & Behavior* 28 (1982): 835–840.

3. E. J. Andrews, et al. "Report of the AVMA panel on euthanasia." *Journal of the American Veterinary Medical Association* 202 (1993): 229–249.

4. D. Randall. *Hearings before the Ninety-Fourth Congress to Discourage the Use of Painful Devices in the Trapping of Animals and Birds.* Washington: U.S. Govt. Printing Office, 1975.

5. S. L. Beasom. "Selectivity of Predator Control Techniques in South Texas." *Journal of Wildlife Management* 38 (1974): 837–844; M.

Novak. "The Foot-snare and the Leg-hold Traps: a Comparison." *Proc. Worldwide Furbearer Conference* 3 (1981): 1671–1685.

6. E. J. Turkowski, A. R. Armistead, and S. B. Linhart. "Selectivity and Effectiveness of Pan Tension Devices for Coyote Foothold Traps." *Journal of Wildlife Management* 48 (1984): 700–708; R. L. Phillips and K. S. Gruver. "Performance of the Paws-I-Trip™ Pan Tension Device on 3 Types of Traps." *Wildlife Society Bulletin* 24 (1996):119–122.

7. Phillips and Gruver. "Performance."

8. B. E. Tullar. "Evaluation of a Padded Leg-hold Trap for Capturing Foxes and Raccoons." *NY Fish and Game Journal* 31 (1984): 97-103; G. H. Olsen, et al. "Injuries to Coyotes Caught in Padded and Unpadded Steel Foothold Traps." *Wildlife Society Bulletin* 14 (1986): 219–223; S. B. Linhart, et al. "Field evaluation of Padded Jaw Coyote Traps: Effectiveness and Foot Injury." *Proceeding of the Vertebrate Pest Conference* 13 (1988): 226–229; G. H. Olsen, et al. "Reducing Injuries to Terrestrial Furbearers by Using Padded Foothold Traps." *Wildlife Society Bulletin* (1988): 303–307; T.J. Kreeger, et al. "Pathological Responses of Red Foxes to Foothold Traps." *Journal of Wildlife Management* 54 (1990):147-160; R. L. Phillips, et al. "Field Evaluation of Three Types of Coyote Traps." *Proceedings of the Vertebrate Pest Conference* 15 (1992): 393–395; J. W. Kern, et al. "Field Evaluation and Comparison of Four Foothold Traps for Terrestrial Furbearers in Wyoming." Technical report for Furbearers Unlimited, Bloomington Ill. 1994: 28 pp.; R. L. Phillips, et al. "Leg Injuries to Coyotes Captured in Three Types of Foothold Traps." *Wildlife Society Bulletin* 24 (1996): 260-263.

9. International Association of Fish and Wildlife Agencies Fur Resources Technical Committee. "Ownership and Use of Traps by Trappers in the United States in 1992." Fur Resources Technical Committee of the International Fish and Wildlife Agencies and the Gallup Organization, Washington, D.C. 1993.

10. G. Proulx, et al. "Injuries and behavior of raccoons (Procyon lotor) captured in the Soft Catch™ and the EGG™ traps in simulated natural environments." *Journal of Wildlife Diseases* 29 (1993): 447–452.

11. G.F. Hubert, et al. "Evaluation of two restraining traps to capture raccoons." *Wildlife Society Bulletin* 24 (1996): 699–708.

12. G. F. Hubert, et al. "Evaluation of Injuries to Virginia Opossums Captured in the EGG Trap™." *Wildlife Society Bulletin* 27 (1999): 301–305.

13. T. Garrett. *Alternative Traps: The Role of Spring Powered Killing Traps in Modern Trapping, the Role of Cage and Box Traps in Modern Trapping, and the Role of Legsnares in Modern Trapping.* Washington: Animal Welfare Institute, 1996 (revised 1999).

14. D. W. Kuehn, et al. "Trap-related Injuries to Gray Wolves in Minnesota." *Journal of Wildlife Management* 50 (1986): 90–91; J. M. Houben, et al. "An Evaluation of Laminated Offset Jawed Traps for Reducing Injuries to Coyotes." *Proceedings of the Great Plains Wildlife Damage Control Conference* 11 (1993): 148–153; Phillips. "Leg injuries."; G. F. Hubert, et al. "Injuries to Coyotes Captured in Modified Foothold Traps." *Wildlife Society Bulletin* 25 (1997): 858–863.

15. J. M. Houben, et al. "An Evaluation of Laminated Offset Jawed Traps for Reducing Injuries to Coyotes." *Proceedings of the Great Plains Wildlife Damage Control Conference* 11 (1993): 148–153; Phillips. "Leg Injuries."; Hubert. "Injuries to Coyotes."

16. Phillips. "Leg Injuries."; Hubert. "Injuries to Coyotes."

17. F. J. Turkowski, et al. "Selectivity and Effectiveness of Pan Tension Devices for Coyote Foothold Traps." *Journal of Wildlife Management* 48 (1984): 700–708; Phillips and Gruver. "Performance."

18. *California Department of Fish and Game Final Environmental Document Regarding Furbearing and Nongame Mammal Hunting and Trapping.* California Department of Fish and Game, Sacramento. 1995. P. 110.

19. H. C. Lunn. "The Conibear Trap—Recommendations for its Improvement," Humane Trap Development Committee of Canada, Canadian Federation of Humane Societies. 1973.

20. G. Proulx, et al. "Assessment and Preliminary Development of the Rotating-Jaw Conibear 120™ Trap to Effectively Kill Marten (Martes americana)" *Canadian Journal of Zoology* 67 (1989): 1074-1079; G. Proulx, et al. "The C120 Magnum with Pan Trigger: A Humane Trap for Mink (Mustela vison)." *Journal of Wildlife Diseases* 26 (1990): 511–517; G. Proulx and M. W. Barrett. "Evaluation of Mechanically Improved Conibear 220™ Traps to Quickly Kill Fisher (Martes pennanti) in Simulated Natural Environments." *Journal of Wildlife Diseases* 29 (1993): 317–323; G. Proulx, et al. "A Humane Killing Trap for Lynx (Felis lynx): the Conibear 330™ with Clamping Bars." *Journal of Wildlife Diseases* 31 (1995): 57–61.

21. T. Krause. "Killing Trap Technology." *American Trapper* 29 (Jan./Feb. 1989): 22.

22. The Federal Provincial Committee on Humane Trapping, "Findings and Recommendations." Federal Provincial Wildlife Conference. Canada. 1981.

23. Garrett. Alternative Traps.

24. D. J. Onderka, et al. "Injuries to Coyotes and Other Species Caused by Four Models of Footholding Devices." *Wildlife Society Bulletin* 16 (1990): 303–307.

# A CRITICAL REVIEW OF TRAP RESEARCH

*Christopher M. Papouchis*

## Introduction

The trapping of wildlife has a long history in North America and has faced intense opposition for nearly a century largely because of the cruel and non-selective nature of traditional traps and questions about the legitimacy of trapping as a management tool (Gentile 1987). To address these criticisms and validate the continued existence of trapping, trap manufacturers and researchers have modified some traditional traps and developed new devices. Some advances have reduced limb injuries and the frequency of non-target captures caused by restraining traps and improved the ability of killing traps to kill target species quickly (see Proulx 1999a). The issue remains sharply polarized, however, as increasing opposition to trapping has been bolstered by the unwillingness of trappers to employ improved devices in the field (Novak 1992, International Association of Fish and Wildlife Agencies [IAFWA] 1993, Proulx et al. 1999a).

This paper reviews the scientific literature as it pertains to the most common traditional traps, the modification of traditional traps, and development of new trapping devices. Specific information on many of the studies cited here can be found in the annotated bibliography of trap studies in Appendix II.

Note: This review should not be read as an endorsement of any particular type or brand of restraining trap. The Animal Protection Institute opposes the use of all body-gripping traps, which inherently cause animals pain and suffering.

## Restraining Traps

### Steel-Jaw Leghold Traps

Steel-jaw leghold traps (hereafter leghold traps) are the most commonly used traps in the U.S. (IAFWA 1993). These devices can cause severe injuries to trapped animals (Linscombe 1976; Waller 1981; Novak 1981; Todd 1987; Linhart et al. 1986; Olsen et al. 1986, 1988; Linscombe and Wright 1988; Kreeger et al. 1988, 1990; Onderka et al. 1990) and can capture large numbers of non-target animals (Novak 1981, Turkowski et al. 1984).

*Injuries*

Animals can incur injury in leghold traps from the clamping of the trap's metal jaws onto the animal's appendage and during the animal's struggle to escape. The range of injuries includes but is not limited to severe swelling, lacerations, joint dislocations, fractures, damage to teeth and gums, self-mutilation, amputation, and death. Atkeson (1956) reported that > 24% of mink (*Mustela vison*), raccoon (*Procyon lotor*), red fox (*Vulpes vulpes*), and gray fox (*Urocyon cinereoargenteus*) were crippled while escaping from leghold traps set on a National Wildlife Refuge in Alabama over a four-year period. During a population dynamics study of arctic fox (*Alopex lagopus*) in Canada, MacPherson (1969) observed that most foxes caught in leghold traps had mutilated themselves and ingested pieces of their own hair, bone, and skin. Van Ballenberghe (1984) found that 44% of 109 gray wolves (*Canis lupus*) captured in leghold traps had severely injured feet and legs. Olsen et al. (1986) reported that 91% of coyotes (*Canis latrans*) caught in leghold traps sustained leg fractures, while 3 of 4 kit foxes (*Vulpes macrotis*) had nearly or completely amputated their trapped leg.

Damage to teeth and gums can occur when a trapped animal attacks the trap trying to free itself (MacPherson 1969, Englund 1982, Van Ballenberghe 1984, Keuhn et al. 1986, Kern et al. 1994, Hubert et al. 1997), though this type of injury is generally ignored by most trapping studies (Onderka et al. 1990). Englund (1982) found severe dental injuries in 58% of adult red foxes captured in leghold traps while Van Ballenberghe (1984) reported injuries to teeth, lips, and gums in 46% of 109 wolves captured. These and other injuries caused by steel-jaw leghold traps have been observed in numerous studies (see Berchielli and Tullar 1980, Novak 1981, Englund 1982, Van Ballenberghe 1984, Tullar 1984, Kuehn et al. 1986, Linhart et al. 1988, Olsen et al. 1988, Onderka et al. 1990, Phillips et al. 1992, Kern et al. 1994, Mowat et al. 1994, Proulx et al. 1994, Phillips et al. 1996, Hubert et al. 1997).

## Non-selectivity

Beasom (1974), Berchielli and Tullar (1980), and Novak (1981) found that non-target animals comprised 56%, 32%, and 76% of leghold captures, respectively. Palmi-sano and Dupuie (1975) and Linscombe (1976) observed large numbers of non-target species caught in leghold traps in coastal Louisiana. In field tests, No. 3

Victor double coil-spring traps set for coyotes captured and severely injured or killed a variety of non-target species, including red fox, porcupine (*Erethizon dorsatum*), lynx (*Lynx canadensis*), snowshoe hare (*Lepus americanus*), birds, and domestic cats and dogs (Onderka et al. 1990, Skinner and Todd 1990). Similarly, Mowat et al. (1994) caught wolverine (*Gulo gulo*) and a number of other species in No. 3 Victor traps set for lynx.

Although the capture and release of non-target animals does not always result in death, any injury or disfigurement invariably affects an animal's ability to survive. Predators face additional problems due to their physiology and methods of obtaining food:

> Reduced fitness and a shortened life span ultimately resulting from capture caused injuries may be as important to consider as proximate mortality. Although difficult to evaluate, the long-term effects of broken canine teeth, missing feet, severed tendons, or poorly healed bones seem obvious for cursorial predators that kill by biting. (Van Ballenberghe 1984:1428)

Besides its impact on individual animals, trapping can impact the long-term viability of wildlife populations, especially of sensitive, threatened, or endangered species. For example, a 1999 U.S. Forest Service report on lynx, a species listed as threatened under the federal Endangered Species Act, concluded: "Trapping for other large furbearers in areas occupied by lynx may pose a risk. Lynx appear to be extremely susceptible to trapping, and where trapping is permitted it can be (and has been) a significant source of mortality" (Ruggiero et al. 1999:11).

Raptors are frequently the unintended victims of leghold traps (Redig 1981, Bortolotti 1984, Stocek and Cartwright 1985), which is a concern because of their low population densities and reproductive rates (Stocek and Cartwright 1985). Gerrard and Bortolotti (1988:132) warned, "one of the more serious, widespread causes of mortality is the accidental trapping of eagles in leg-hold traps set for other animals." Of the bald eagles admitted to the University of Minnesota Raptor Research and Rehabilitation Program over an 8-year period, 21% had been caught in leghold traps (Redig 1981). Of these, 64% had sustained injuries that proved fatal. Bortolotti (1984) examined golden eagle (*Aquila chrysaetos*) and bald eagle (*Haliaeetus leucocephalus*) museum skins and reported that traps set for furbearers and predators were responsible for 42% of golden eagle and 5% of bald eagle mortalities when cause of death could be identified.

The incidence of non-target captures with leghold traps and leg snares (see below) can be reduced by the use of pan tension devices (PTDs), which allow trappers to adjust the trap to close only when sufficient weight is applied to the trigger. When used properly, pan tension devices can exclude up to 98% of non-target animals weighing less than the target species (Turkowski et al. 1984, Phillips and Gruver 1996). They do not, however, exclude species of similar or greater weight; therefore, a leghold trap set to target coyotes will not exclude bobcats (*Lynx rufus*) or large foxes. It is unknown wheather PTDs are used widely by commercial and recreational trappers since they also reduce capture rates of target species, add to the total cost of traps, and are not required by most state wildlife agencies.

## Padded Leghold Traps

The development of the padded-jaw leghold trap, introduced by the Woodstream Corporation as the Soft Catch trap in 1984, has been touted by trapping proponents and some researchers as a "humane" trap. Padded leghold traps can cause fewer and less severe limb injuries than traditional steel-jaw leghold traps to a number of species, including coyotes (Olsen et al. 1986, 1998, Linhart et al. 1988, Phillips et al. 1992, Phillips et al. 1996), bobcats (Olsen et al. 1988), red foxes (Englund 1982, Tullar 1984, Olsen et al. 1988, Kreeger et al. 1990, Kern et al. 1994), gray foxes (Englund 1982, Tullar 1984, Olsen et al. 1988), and kit foxes (Olsen et al. 1986). However, padded traps do not reduce injuries for all species. Like leghold traps, padded traps capture, and injure or kill, non-target species (Onderka et al. 1990, Skinner and Todd 1990, Mowat et al. 1994).

### Injuries

Tullar (1984) tested a prototype padded No. 1 Victor double coil-spring leghold trap with reduced spring tension at the request of the trap's maker, the Woodstream Corporation. He concluded that it caused fewer foot injuries and had a similar capture efficiency as the same trap without pads for foxes and raccoons. However, in addition to a small sample size ($n < 14$ animals/trap), Tullar (1984) failed to distinguish between injuries to red foxes and gray foxes, which are smaller and thus more likely to be injured in a trap (Olsen 1988). Olsen et al. (1986) found that using three different types of padded traps reduced limb injuries to coyotes by 48–71% over an unpadded No. 3 Victor long spring trap. However, the padded traps caused fractures in $\geq$ 15% of captured coyotes and in two of four kit foxes. Linhart et al. (1988) reported reduced limb injuries in coyotes caught with padded traps, but with a significantly lower capture efficiency. Olsen et al. (1988) found fewer limb injuries for red and gray foxes and coyotes captured in padded traps.

Kreeger et al. (1990) examined the physiological responses of trapped red foxes and concluded that padded traps caused less trauma than unpadded

traps, although heart rate responses and the time the foxes spent struggling in traps did not differ. Onderka et al. (1990) found the mean leg injury score of the padded leghold trap for coyotes was a third of that for an unpadded trap. Kern et al. (1994) noted that a padded trap caused less severe leg injuries in captured red foxes than a leghold trap with offset and laminated jaws and an unpadded trap. Similarly, Phillips et al. (1996) reported that the padded No. 3½ EZ Grip double long spring trap produced fewer injuries than both the unpadded Sterling MJ600 with four coil-springs and offset jaws and the unpadded No. 3 Northwoods with laminated and offset jaws. All three traps, however, caused fractures, self-mutilation, and severed tendons and ligaments.

Padded traps do not reduce injuries for all species. Raccoons have a tendency to mutilate themselves by chewing on their trapped toes or foot, regardless of the type of trap used (Berchielli and Tullar 1980, Tullar 1984, Kern et al. 1994). Tullar (1984) and Olsen et al. (1988) reported that padded traps reduced injuries to raccoons but Olsen et al. (1988:306) cautioned that "injury scores [from padded traps] are still high and more work is needed to further improve padded traps for raccoons." Further, bobcats sustained fewer injuries from No. 3 Soft Catch traps but not from the smaller No. 1½ Soft Catch traps (Olsen et al. 1988).

Several problems are associated with the use of padded traps. Because they do not break the skin, padded traps create a tourniquet effect, cutting off the blood flow to a trapped appendage and causing numbness, self-amputation (as the animal chews on the numb foot or toes), and gangrene. In northern latitudes, the tourniquet effect can cause the freezing and eventual loss of the trapped appendage. Onderka et al. (1990) found padded traps caused freezing of the trapped limb in 46% of 21 trapped coyotes. Mowat et al. (1994) did not recommend the No. 3 Soft Catch trap for lynx after observing freezing of the feet or digits in 39% of 23 captured lynx caught in these traps. Most other trapping studies have failed to consider freezing or amputation largely because injury examinations do not consider the potential long-term impacts on survival.

Padded traps are used extensively in research studies and translocation programs. Serfass et al. (1996) recommended the No. 1½ Soft Catch trap for translocating river otters (*Lutra canadensis*) over an unpadded trap, although 38% of otters captured in the padded traps sustained tooth breakage and 40% sustained appendage injuries. Blundell et al. (1999) found the unpadded Sleepy Creek No. 11 had a lower escape rate, lower dental injury rate, and similar appendage injury rate for capturing otters when compared to Serfass et al.'s (1996) findings on the No. 1½ Soft Catch.

The ability to capture and safely release animals is critical in research. Capturing animals in padded leghold traps, however, can negatively impact their long-term survival after the animal is released (Seddon et al. 1999). Seddon et al. (1999) found that only 8% of Ruppell's foxes (*Vulpes rueppellii*, Saudi Arabia) captured in padded leghold traps were alive six months later, compared to 48% of foxes caught in cage traps:

> Even apparently minor injuries assessed at the time of release may result in lameness which, directly through increase risk of predation, or indirectly through reduced ability to find food in combination with possible stress of capture, could significantly reduce the likelihood of survival. (Seddon et al. 1999:76)

Despite the recommendations of some researchers, many trappers have been unwilling to use padded traps. In 1992, fewer than 2% of traps used in the U.S. were padded leghold traps (International Association of Fish and Wildlife Agencies 1993). Avoidance of the padded traps is likely due to their higher cost (Siemer 1994, Phillips et al. 1996) and the perception by trappers that they are less efficient than standard traps (Linscombe and Wright 1988). While early models of the padded jaw trap were not as efficient as standard traps (Linhart et al. 1986, Linscombe and Wright 1988), later versions have demonstrated efficiency equivalent to unpadded traps (Skinner and Todd 1990, Linhart and Dasch 1992, Phillips et al. 1992, Phillips and Mullis 1996). Most trappers, however, remain skeptical (Hubert et al. 1997).

## Non-selectivity

Because padded leghold traps are basically steel-jaw leghold traps with padded jaws, they share the propensity for capturing non-target species. In field studies, No. 3 Victor Soft Catch leghold traps set for lynx captured a number of non-target species, including wolverines and red fox (Mowat et al. 1994), while the same traps set for coyotes captured, and injured or killed, red fox, porcupine, lynx, snowshoe hare, birds, and domestic cats and dogs (Onderka et al. 1990, Skinner and Todd 1990).

## Other Leghold Trap Modifications

Other modifications to standard leghold traps have been developed in attempts to reduce trap-related injuries, including offsetting and/or laminating jaws, the use of additional or heavier "beefer" springs to reduce movement and "pull-outs" by a captured animal, adding a base plate to allow center-mounting of the anchor chain, use of a shock-absorbing springs on the anchor chain, enclosing leghold traps to reduce the incidence of self-mutilation by raccoons, and using tranquilizer tabs to reduce injuries to canids.

Keuhn et al. (1986) suggested that researchers use No. 14 OS (offset) jaw leghold traps for capturing wolves for research as they caused fewer severe injuries then other traps studied, although > 95% of wolves caught in these traps had lacerations. Houben et al. (1993) found that the No. 3 Northwoods (laminated and offset jaws, center mounted anchor chain with shock-absorbing spring) and the padded No. 3 Soft Catch trap with increased spring tension caused similar injuries to coyotes. Kern et al. (1994) found that the No. 1½ Victor laminated jaw trap and the Butera offset jaw trap caused less serious injuries to red foxes than a No. 1½ Victor steel-jaw trap, but more than a No. 1½ Soft Catch trap. Phillips et al. (1996) found that leg injury scores of coyotes captured in Sterling MJ600 traps with offset jaws and modified No. 3 Northwoods coil-spring traps with unpadded, offset, wide laminated jaws and center-mounted chains were significantly higher than those of coyotes caught in padded jaw No. 3½ EZ grip long spring traps.

Hubert et al. (1997) compared an unpadded No. 3 Bridger coil-spring trap with laminated and offset jaws, two additional coil-springs, and center-mounted anchor chains with two swivels to a standard unpadded Bridger leghold trap. They found no statistically significant reductions in injury scores using the modified trap and concluded it was unlikely that the modifications they examined would create the reductions in injury scores previously observed for padded traps.

Increasing clamping force by adding additional coil-springs to No. 3 Soft Catch traps reduced lacerations and serious injuries to coyotes when compared to unmodified Soft Catch traps (Gruver et al. 1996), although lacerations and edema were common in both traps. The authors postulated that the increased clamping force (which likely produces increased pain) reduced movement of the trapped leg and therefore reduced the likelihood of more severe injuries.

The EGG trap, an enclosed leghold trap, was designed in an attempt to reduce the incidence of self-mutilation in raccoons captured in leghold traps. Proulx et al. (1993c) tested the EGG trap in a simulated natural environment and deemed it "humane" for raccoons, despite soft tissue and tendon macerations. In field studies the EGG trap caused fewer injuries than the unpadded No. 1 Victor double coil-spring trap, but still had an unacceptable injury score as several raccoons had fractures, subluxations, and amputated limbs (Hubert et al. 1996). Hubert et al. (1999) concluded that the EGG trap caused significantly fewer severe injuries to Virginia opossums (*Didelphis marsupialis*) than unpadded No. 2 coil-spring leghold traps.

Tranquilizer trap devices (TTDs) can be used with leghold traps to reduce capture-related injuries to canids. TTDs are attached to the jaw of a leghold trap and contain a chemical tranquilizer that depresses the central nervous system. An animal attacking the trap after being captured bites into the TTD and ingests the tranquilizer. The use of TTDs has successfully reduced leg injuries to coyotes (Balser 1965, Linhart et al. 1981) and wolves (Sahr and Knowlton 2000). However, damage to teeth and gums can occur prior to sedation and is not reduced by using TTDs (Sahr and Knowlton 2000). TTDs may allow the safe release of substantially more non-target animals (Sahr and Knowlton 2000). To date, the U.S. government has not approved their use.

## Leg Snares

Several studies compared leghold traps to leg snares (also called foot snares) with regard to injuries (Bercheilli and Tullar 1980, Novak 1981, Englund 1982, Onderka et al. 1990, Mowat et al. 1996) and capture efficiency (Berchielli and Tullar 1980, Skinner and Todd 1990, Mowat et al. 1996). While these studies generally show that leg snares cause significantly less severe leg injuries than steel-jaw leghold traps, comparisons of capture efficiency have been equivocal and incidences of non-target captures are common.

### Injuries

The ability of leg snares to reduce the occurrence of injuries to animals when compared to unpadded leghold traps depends on snare design, diameter of the snare cable (Onderka et al. 1990), and the model of unpadded trap (Berchielli and Tullar 1980, Novak 1981, Onderka et al. 1990). Snare design, material, and the use of plastic casing may also determine whether injuries to teeth and gums are reduced (Englund 1982, Onderka et al. 1990).

Berchielli and Tullar (1980) reported the Ezyonem leg snare yielded similar injury rates as No. 1½ double coil-spring leghold traps for a variety of small- to medium-sized furbearers, but with a significantly lower capture rate. Only six animals were caught in the leg snare. Novak (1981) reported that the Novak leg snare caused significantly fewer leg injuries and non-target captures than the No. 2 coil-spring and No. 4 long spring leghold traps. Englund (1982) captured red foxes in Sweden in freezing conditions using plastic-coated Åberg leg snares and found they caused less severe and fewer dental and leg injuries than unpadded No. 2 and No. 3 double long spring leghold traps. Steel cable leg snares were found to cause fewer injuries to wolves than leghold traps, although the sample size for leg snares was small (*n* = 12) (Van Ballenberghe 1984).

Onderka et al. (1990:181) concluded: "Both the padded trap and the Fremont [leg] snare appear vastly superior to the unpadded trap and the Novak snare for capturing and holding terrestrial furbearers with minimal injury." Padded leghold traps and Fremont snares caused no limb fractures, while roughly 50% of coyotes trapped in unpadded leghold traps and Novak snares had fractures. The authors speculated that the difference in injuries between the Fremont and Novak snares stemmed from the Fremont's larger diameter cable, which may have reduced constriction pressure. In addition, the Fremont's snare loop was designed to remain attached to the spring arm after firing, thereby reducing lunging damage. In a companion study, however, Skinner and Todd (1990) found that the Novak and Fremont leg snares were three times less efficient and had a lower capture rate than a No. 3 unpadded and a Soft Catch leghold trap for capturing coyotes.

Mowat et al. (1994) recommended a modified Fremont leg snare over the Soft Catch leghold trap and two sizes of Tomahawk box traps for live-capture of lynx in winter. Shivik et al. (2000) compared the Belisle, Panda, and Wildlife Services leg snares with the Collarum, a neck snare designed to be non-lethal. They found that the devices with the highest capture rates (Belisle, Wildlife Services) also had the lowest selectivity and caused the most injuries. The Collarum displayed the greatest selectivity and lowest injury rate; however, it also caused hemorrhaging or swelling of the neck/head, chipped teeth, tooth fractures, and one death (brought about by a failure of the stop on the snare cable). None of these devices met the basic thresholds for injury of captured animals as determined by an agreement between the U.S. and European Union, i.e., 80% of captured animals cannot show injury indicators of poor welfare (United States of America/European Community 1997) (also see Chapter Four).

The disparate conclusions of these studies, especially with regard to capture efficiency, likely stem from different methodologies and terminologies and possibly varying familiarity of trappers with leg snares (Skinner and Todd 1990). Most studies encompassed only a single

trapping season or portion thereof, which may have compounded the problem since trappers did not have enough time to familiarize themselves with the devices (Linscombe and Wright 1988).

*Non-selectivity*

Studies have generally failed to consider the degree to which leg snares capture non-target species. An analysis of Novak's (1981) data reveals non-target species comprised 57% of all captures. Onderka et al. (1990) and Skinner and Todd (1990) reported that the Novak and Freemont leg snares were responsible for capturing a variety of species, including furbearers, porcupines, snowshoe hares, and birds, but did not provide an analysis.

## Anchoring Techniques for Restraining Traps

The method of anchoring restraining traps can affect injuries. Most studies generally standardize the method (Onderka et al. 1990), choosing either drag poles (Englund 1982) or stakes (Berchielli and Tullar 1980, Novak 1981, Tullar 1984, Olsen et al. 1988, Houben 1993, Kern et al. 1994, Phillips et al. 1996, Gruver et al. 1996, Hubert et al. 1997). Fur trappers commonly use a drag pole and chain to allow an animal to escape to cover, thereby reducing the occurrence of pelt damage from predation. But drag poles and chains can increase the chance of dislocation or fracture since an animal can entangle the trap and chain in brush (Mowat et al. 1994). Onderka et al. (1990) varied anchoring techniques but found no difference in injury scores for coyotes. Alternately, Mowat et al. (1994) reported numerous dislocations in lynx captured by fur trappers in leghold traps, many of which were anchored to drag poles. The authors noted that lynx had weaker leg bones than coyotes, and suggested a fixed anchor, shock absorber, and a 20 cm chain with at least two swivels could reduce injuries to this species. Some wildlife advocates suggest that the use of drags is preferable to anchor stakes because of the reduced stress and lower possibility of predation (Cathy Liss, Animal Welfare Institute, pers. comm.).

# Kill Traps

## *Rotating Jaw (Conibear, Sauvageau, Bionic, Kania)*

Research into kill traps, of which the Conibear type is the most commonly known and used, has come primarily from Canada, where conventional (unmodified) leghold traps are prohibited in land sets for capturing most furbearers. While modified leghold traps such as the padded or offset jaw leghold traps are still permitted in Canada, as are steel-jaw leghold traps in water sets, Conibear traps have also been promoted for capturing small furbearers (Proulx et al. 1990). Kill traps, however, often fail to cause instant death in captured animals as intended (Gilbert 1981, Waller 1981, Proulx 1999a) and frequently capture non-target species (Barrett et al. 1989, Naylor and Novak 1994).

### *Injuries*

Designing traps that cause rapid death in trapped animals is difficult because of the numerous variables needed to produce a killing blow to the neck or head (i.e., correct sized animal entering the trap at the correct angle and speed). One of the most common killing traps is the Conibear 120 (C120), used throughout North America for trapping mink (*Mustela vison*), marten (*Martes americana*), muskrat (*Ondatra zibethica*), and weasel (*Mustela erminea*) (Gerstall 1985). The C120's original two-prong trigger system did not consistently position animals to promote a killing blow to the head or neck region (Gilbert 1981a) and did not wield sufficient energy to kill marten effectively in accordance with kill threshold standards established by the Canadian General Standards Board (CGSB) (1984), i.e., it did not cause irreversible unconsciousness within three minutes. Proulx and Barrett (1994) later argued that for testing, "state-of the art" killing traps would be defined as those with the potential, at a 95% confidence level, to render $\geq$ 70% of target animals irreversibly unconscious $\leq$ 3 minutes. It is important to note that the determination of the three-minute threshold standard resulted from political negotiations (see Chapter Four).

The C120 Mark IV, a modified C120 with larger springs and rectangular bars welded onto the opposing jaws, performed better than the standard C120 but still required further improvements to meet the kill CGSB threshold standard time frame (Proulx et al. 1989a). Subsequently, the Conibear 120 Magnum was designed to provide more than double the striking and clamping forces of the commercially available C120. The C120 Magnum satisfied experimental requirements to qualify for field tests on marten (Proulx et al. 1989b) and caused rapid death in marten struck in the head-neck region in field testing (Barrett et al. 1989), but not mink struck in the neck (Proulx and Barrett 1989). Proulx et al. (1990) speculated that this result might be due to the larger neck muscles and stronger bones of the mink and argued that since double strikes to the head neck region by both the distal and proximal rotating-jaws had provided consistent unconsciousness in marten, a C120 Magnum modified specifically for mink might yield similar results. Indeed, when the C120 Magnum was equipped with a pan trigger to promote double strikes to the neck and thorax region of mink, tests in a simulated natural environment killed 9 of 9 mink in $\leq$ 3 minutes (Proulx et al. 1990). In field tests, the C120 Magnum struck 87% of captured mink in the neck and posterior thorax to anterior lumbar regions and was recommended as a "humane" killing trap for mink (Proulx and Barrett 1993c).

Proulx and Barrett (1993b) attempted to duplicate their previous results with the C120 Magnum for mink and marten by modifying the Conibear 220 to increase the spring strength and by adding clamping bars to the striking jaws to capture fisher (*Martes pennanti*). However, the mechanically improved Conibear 220 failed to pass preliminary kill tests and was not recommended as a "humane" trap for fisher. A variety of modified Conibear and Sauvageau 2001-8 rotating-jaw traps tested on raccoons also did not meet the standards of the Canadian General Standards Board (Proulx and Drescher 1994). The Sauvageau 2001-8 with an offset baited trigger did render 9 of 9 arctic foxes irreversibly unconscious in $\leq$ 3 minutes when tested in a simulated natural environment (Proulx et al. 1993a). In field studies, Proulx et al. (1994a) confirmed these results, observing that the Sauvageau 2001-8 struck arctic fox in the head or neck 100% of the time. No arctic foxes were found alive in the trap (trap check times averaged one and eight days for the two traplines used) and 86.7% of 60 foxes necropsied had received major traumatic lesions involving mostly the nervous system. Tests of a modified Conibear 330 with increased spring strength and clamping bars were found to render 9 of 9 lynx unconscious in ≤ 3 minutes in a simulated natural environment (Proulx et al. 1995). To date, no field study has been conducted to verify these results.

Two other kill traps used for trapping small and medium furbearers are the mousetrap style Bionic and Kania traps. Gilbert (1980) found the Bionic trap rendered 3 of 3 mink irreversibly unconscious in ≤ 3 minutes. No field tests were conducted, however, (Dwyer 1984) and the sample size of three was judged to be too small for an acceptable analysis (Proulx et al. 1989a). During re-analysis of the device, Proulx and Barrett (1991b) found that the Bionic trap, using a 6 cm aperture plastic cone to position entering mink, killed 9 of 9 mink in a simulated natural environment. Average times to loss of consciousness and heartbeat were < 60 sec and 340 sec, respectively. Based on these results, Proulx and Barrett (1993a) tested the Bionic trap on fisher in a simulated natural environment and found that the device, using a 10 cm aperture cone, killed 9 of 9 fisher with an estimated time to unconsciousness and loss of heartbeat of < 55 sec and 305 sec, respectively. They concluded that the trap could be expected to produce irreversible unconsciousness in < 3 minutes in ≥ 70% of captured minks and fishers. In field tests on marten, Proulx (1999b) concluded that the Bionic trap could be expected, at a 95% confidence level, to render ≥ 70% of martens captured on traplines unconscious in ≤ 3 min. Proulx et al. (1993b) found that the Kania trap killed 9 of 9 red squirrels in enclosures with a mean time to loss of consciousness and heartbeat of ≤ 64 seconds and ≤ 91 seconds, respectively.

While these studies suggest that the ability of kill traps to produce rapid death has been greatly improved, though largely in controlled situations, traditional kill traps that do not correspond to "state-of the art" technology are still wildly used in the field (Proulx and Barrett 1991a, Proulx 1999a).

*Non-selectivity*

Conibear traps are notoriously non species-specific and may catch up to two non-target animals per target animal when used in standard sets (Novak 1987, Barrett et al. 1989, Proulx and Barrett 1993c). Despite this problem, only one study has endeavored to reduce the incidence of incidental captures. Naylor and Novak (1994) compared the efficiency and selectivity of Conibear 120, C120 Magnum, and leghold and cage traps placed in a variety of set types. They noted that for trappers to accept a technique that reduces non-target captures, capture efficiency must be comparable with standard traps and pelt damage must not occur. Their results indicated that increased selectivity came at the expense of capture efficiency or pelt damage and therefore they were unable to recommend a specific trap device or set placement.

## Neck and Body Snares

While lethal neck and body snares are commonly used by commercial fur trappers to capture coyotes, red foxes, gray wolves, bobcats, lynx, and beaver (Baker and Dwyer 1987) and by government trappers for depredation management programs, the literature is surprisingly deficient in studies examining their killing efficiency or selectivity (Phillips 1996).

*Injuries*

Proulx and Barrett (1990) tested the King, Mosher, and Olecko power neck snares and reported that 8 of 16 foxes captured had to be euthanized because of prolonged consciousness and 4 of the remaining 8 remained conscious for 5 to 6 minutes. They concluded, "power snares developed to quickly kill large furbearers appear to have limited application as we search for humane trapping methods" (Proulx and Barrett 1990:30). Proulx et al. (1994) concluded that snares are not humane devices for trapping snowshoe hare after a specially designed neck snare took, on average, 18 minutes to kill snowshoe hares. Philips et al. (1996) reported that the Gregerson, Kelley, and Denver Wildlife Research Center (DWRC) snares killed 71%, 68%, and 94% of coyotes snared by the neck, respectively. They did not, however, record trap check times and it is therefore unknown how long the coyotes struggled in the traps before dying.

*Non-selectivity*

Proulx and Barrett (1990) concluded that power snares should not be used because of their potential for seriously injuring non-target animals. Proulx et al. (1994b) designed a neck snare for snowshoe hares that successfully released accidentally trapped marten but produced prolonged death for hares (see above). Phillips (1996) found that the Gregerson, Kelley, and Denver Wildlife Research Center (DWRC) neck snares killed, respectively, 67%, 33%, and 46% of deer captured incidentally during the study and recommended that these snares not be used in areas frequented by livestock or deer.

### Live-Traps (Cage, Box, and Log Traps)

Cage and box traps offer an attractive alternative to leghold traps and snares because of the significantly reduced incidence of injury sustained by captured animals and the ability of a trapper to release non-target species relatively unharmed. Several types of cage and box traps are available commercially, although there is a paucity of research on these devices.

White et al. (1991:75) compared the responses of red fox captured in the Model 109 Tomahawk cage trap to those trapped by Kreeger et al. (1990) in padded and unpadded leghold traps and concluded that "factors associated with limb restraint directly contribute to the trauma experienced by trapped red foxes and, therefore, foxes caught in box traps undergo less trauma than foxes restrained by a limb in a padded or unpadded-jaw [leg]hold trap."

Perhaps the safest live trap in use is the log trap, a 1 m high x 1 m wide x 2 m long log box with a heavy log lid constructed completely (except for the trigger) of materials gathered on-site. This trap has been used for commercial harvest of furbearers in Canada and for a wolverine study in central Idaho (Copeland et al. 1995). Researchers captured 12 individual wolverines a total of 37 times in 10 log traps without injury, showing that these animals did not develop an aversion to capture in this device (Copeland et al. 1995). Marten, fox, and black bear were also captured in these traps but were released unharmed simply by propping open the lid. Proulx (1999a) noted that the log trap could be used to capture lynx, bobcat, red fox, American marten, fisher, American badger, and striped skunk.

## Limitations of Trap Studies

Many trapping studies suffer from significant flaws that limit their usefulness and undermine their conclusions. For example, when assessing the injuries caused by leghold traps and leg snares, the majority of studies examined only the trapped limb, and did not account for other capture-related traumas that are caused by the trap. Other methodological problems include the failure to consider the time an animal spends in the trap, small sample sizes, and the potential introduction of trapper bias.

### Assessment of Injuries

While studies of restraining traps have documented the broad variety of injuries caused by leghold traps, most underestimated the extent of injuries because they limited their analysis to trapped limbs (Tullar 1984; Olsen et al. 1986, 1988; Houben et al. 1993; Gruver et al. 1996; Phillips et al. 1996) or to the leg plus the head (Van Ballenberghe 1984, Kern et al. 1994). Whole body necropsies have been used in only three studies in an attempt to consider all trap-related trauma (Onderka et al. 1990, Hubert et al. 1996, Hubert et al. 1997). Hubert et al. (1997:862) found that whole body scores were approximately 15% higher than leg injury scores and stressed that previous "studies fail[ed] to tabulate all trap-related injuries that should be assigned to an individual coyote. Whole body necropsies should be conducted to insure no type of trap-related physical trauma is overlooked."

Several studies relied on trappers (Phillips et al. 1992, Mowat et al. 1994) or researchers (Berchielli and Tullar 1980) to evaluate the injuries sustained by captured animals, which may have led to the under-reporting of injuries since these individuals may have missed, or failed to report, some injuries. To avoid any perception of bias, only veterinary pathologists should be used to evaluate injuries.

### Omission of Trap Time

The failure to control the duration of time an animal is left in a trap is nearly universal to all field trapping studies. Animals held for a longer time can receive more severe injuries (see Proulx et al. 1994), especially if the animal struggles or is attacked by another animal. Trapping studies, however, generally consider animals held for different lengths of time as similar with regards to injury determinations.

### Other Methodological Problems

Statistically small sample sizes ($n < 26$ animals/trap) are common in studies of restraining traps (see Berchielli and Tullar 1980, Tullar 1984, Olsen et al. 1986, Linhart et al. 1988, Onderka et al. 1990, Phillips et al. 1992, Proulx et al. 1993c, Houben et al. 1993, Mowat et al. 1994, Hubert et al. 1997, Blundell 1999). Some studies included, but did not account for, the effects of other modifications to traps, including variations in chain length and use of shock springs (Olsen et al. 1986, Linhart et al. 1988, Phillips et al. 1992). Lastly, in a few padded-trap studies, representatives of trap manufacturers were allowed to perform (Tullar 1984) or oversee (Phillips et al. 1992, Linhart and Dasch 1992) trapping. At best, their presence improved the performance of the traps beyond what a trapper without mastery of the device would have experienced. At worst, their interest in putting their traps in the best light might have resulted in skewed data.

## Conclusions

In recent years, changing public attitudes have forced trappers and researchers to consider the effects of trapping on captured animals and on sensitive wildlife populations. Despite some advances in trapping devices, however, the continued use of older traps indicates that trappers are unwilling to consider new devices (see Proulx and Barrett 1991a, Novak 1992, IAFWA 1993, Proulx 1999a). State wildlife agencies have been slow to require use of improved devices, e.g., as of December 1, 2000, only eight states (AZ, CA, CO, FL, CT, MA, TN, WA) require the use of padded traps and then only under specific circumstances (see Chapter Five).

The padded leghold trap, when used properly, can reduce, though not eliminate, the severity and occurrence of limb injuries to some species by 48–85% when compared to conventional steel-jaw leghold traps (Saunders and Roswell 1984, Olsen et al. 1985, Onderka et al. 1990). However, padded traps still cause severe injuries including swelling, freezing, and amputation of limbs, as well as other capture-related trauma. Padded traps can also significantly impact long-term survival of captured and released animals (Seddon et al. 1999). Moreover, trappers have been unwilling to accept these devices because of their greater cost and the perception that they are less efficient than standard traps.

Some research suggests that certain leg snares may be a better alternative to jaw-type leghold traps and could be effective in research, translocation, and relocation programs. At this time, leg snares appear to be less efficient than padded leghold traps, although this may be a result of trapper inexperience with leg snares. While several leg snares do seem promising, including the Fremont, research on these devices has been limited.

Kill traps, like leghold traps, have also been highly modified during the past few decades. By adding clamping bars and increasing spring strength, researchers have made these devices more effective in producing rapid death in some target species. However, "successful" field tests have only been conducted on the Conibear 120 Magnum for mink and marten, the Sauvageau 2001-8 for arctic fox, and the Bionic trap for marten. Since field conditions can vary widely from controlled settings, as can animal behavior, results of controlled tests should not be extrapolated to natural conditions. Further, surprisingly little effort has been expended on reducing the frequency of non-target captures associated with kill traps, which is of special concern since the traps are designed for specific-sized animals and are likely to seriously maim or kill non-target species. Even if these shortcomings are addressed, however, fur trappers may be unwilling to use these improved devices because of their greater cost and increased strength, which make them more dangerous to trappers.

Studies on traps have suffered from a variety of problems that raise questions about their ability to accurately assess the impacts of traps on wildlife. Several problems, including small sample sizes and failure to control the duration of time an animal is held in a trap, are methodological in nature. Other problems highlight the importance of removing potential bias from trapping research, including the documentation of limb injuries rather than whole body injuries, field determination of injuries by trappers rather than through necropsies by veterinary pathologists, the varied experience of trappers with new trap designs, and the presence of trap manufacturer representatives during field testing.

Finally, no device has been shown to restrain animals without injury, except perhaps the log trap. While public opposition to the commercial and recreational exploitation of wildlife continues to grow, there remains a need to develop humane, species-specific capturing devices for programs designed to benefit wildlife, including some research, translocations, and relocation of animals. Future research must continue to build on the foundation of past studies while avoiding the continuous reanalysis of already well-established findings. In some cases it appears that replication, an integral part of research, has become redundancy, especially in tests of the steel-jaw leghold trap. With the overwhelming evidence of the severe injuries caused by these devices, continued testing is unjustified. To remain credible, researchers should acknowledge the inappropriateness of traditional trapping devices and focus their efforts on more humane and socially acceptable methods of capturing wild animals.

## Literature Cited

Atkeson, T. Z. 1956. Incidence of crippling loss in steel trapping. *Journal of Wildlife Management* 20:323–324.

Baker, J. A. and P. M. Dwyer. 1987. Techniques for commercially harvesting furbearers. Pp. 970–995 *in* M. Novak, J. A. Baker, M. E. Obbard, and B. Malloch, eds. *Wild furbearer management and conservation in North America*. North Bay; Ontario Trappers Association.

Balser, D. S. 1965. Tranquilizer tabs for capturing wild carnivores. *Journal of Wildlife Management* 29:438–442.

Barrett, M. W., G. Proulx, and N. Jotham. 1988. Wild fur industry under challenge — The Canadian response. *North American Wildlife and Natural Resources Conferences* 53:180–190.

Barrett, M. W., G. Proulx, D. Hobson, D. Nelson, and J. W. Nolan. 1989. Field evaluation of the C120 Magnum trap for marten. *Wildlife Society Bulletin* 17:299–306.

Beasom, S. L. 1974. Selectivity of predator control techniques in south Texas. *Journal of Wildlife Management* 38:837–844.

Berchielli, L. T. and B. F. Tullar. 1980. Comparison of a leg snare with a standard leg-gripping trap. *NY Fish and Game Journal* 27:63–71.

Bortolotti, G. R. 1984. Trap and poison mortality of golden and bald eagles. *Journal of Wildlife Management* 48:1173–1179.

Buech, R. R. 1983. Modification of the bailey live trap for beaver. *Wildlife Society Bulletin* 11:66–68.

Canadian General Standards Board. 1984. *Animal traps, humane mechanically-powered, trigger activated*. Re. No. CAN2-144.1-M84. Ottawa, Ontario.

Cook, S. R., and G. Proulx. 1989. Mechanical evaluation and performance improvement of the rotating jaw Conibear 120 trap. *Journal of Testing and Evaluation* 17:190–195.

Copeland, J. P., E. Cesar, J. M. Peek, C. E. Harris, C. D. Long, and D. L. Hunter. 1995. A live trap for wolverine and other forest carnivores. *Wildlife Society Bulletin* 23:535–538.

Dwyer, P. M. 1984. *Humane trap field testing during 1981–83*. Alberta Energy and Natural Resources Progress Report, Edmonton, Alberta, Canada, 100 pp.

Englund, J. 1982. A comparison of injuries to leghold trapped and foot-snared red foxes. *Journal of Wildlife Management* 46:1113–1117.

Gerrard, J. M. and G. R. Bortolotti. 1988. *The Bald Eagle: haunts and habits of a wilderness monarch*. Smithsonian Institute Press.

Gerstall, R. 1985. *The steel trap in North America*. Harrisburg. Stackpole Books.

Gilbert, F. F. 1980. Bionic trap-kill tests (mink). University of Guelph report submitted to the Federal Provincial Committee for Humane Trapping, Guelph, Ontario, Canada, 4 pp.

Gilbert, F. F. 1981. Maximizing the humane potential of traps — the Vital and the Conibear 120. Pp. 1630–1646 in J. A. Chapman and D. Pursley, eds. *Proceedings of the Worldwide Furbearer Conference*, University of Maryland, Frostburg.

Gilbert, F. F. and N. Gofton. 1982. Terminal dives in mink, muskrat and beaver. *Physiology & Behavior* 28:835–840.

Gruver, K. S., R. L. Phillips, and E. S. Williams. 1996. Leg injuries to coyotes captured in standard and modified Soft Catch®traps. *Proceedings of the Vertebrate Pest Conference* 17:91–93.

Guthery, F. S. and S. L. Beasom. 1978. Effectiveness and selectivity of neck snares in predator control. *Journal of Wildlife Management* 42:457–459.

Houben, J. M., M. Holland, S. W. Jack, and C. R. Boyle. 1993. An evaluation of laminated offset jawed traps for reducing injuries to coyotes. *Proceedings of the Great Plains Wildlife Damage Control Conference* 11:148–153.

Hubert, G. F., Jr., L. L. Hungerford, G. Proulx, R. D. Bluett, and L. Bowman. 1996. Evaluation of two restraining traps to capture raccoons. *Wildlife Society Bulletin* 24:699–708.

Hubert, G. F., L. L. Hungerford, and R. D. Bluett. 1997. Injuries to coyotes captured in modified foothold traps. *Wildlife Society Bulletin* 25:858–863.

Hubert, G. F., Jr., G. K. Wollenberg, L. L. Hungerford, and R. D. Bluett. 1999. Evaluation of injuries to Virginia opossums captured in the EGG trap. *Wildlife Society Bulletin* 27:301–305.

International Association of Fish and Wildlife Agencies Fur Resources Subcommittee. 1993. *Ownership and use of traps by trappers in the United States in 1992*. Washington; Fur Resources Committee of the International Association of Fish and Wildlife Agencies and The Gallup Organization.

International Organization for Standardization. TC191. 1999. Animal (mammal) traps — Part 5: Methods for testing restraining traps. International Standard ISO/DIS 10990-5.

Geneva; International Organization for Standardization.

Kern, J. W., L. L. McDonald, D. D. Strickland, and E. Williams. 1994. *Field evaluation and comparison of four foothold traps for terrestrial furbearers in Wyoming*. Cheyenne; Western EcoSystems Technology.

Krause, T. 1989. *National Trappers Association trapping handbook*. Sutton; Spearman Publishing and Printing.

Kreeger, T. J., P. J. White, U. S. Seal, and J. R. Tester. 1990. Pathological responses of red foxes to foothold traps. *Journal of Wildlife Management* 54:147–160.

Kuehn. D. W., T. K. Fuller, L. D. Mech, J. P. William, S. H. Fritts, and W. E. Berg. 1986. Trap-related injuries to gray wolves in Minnesota. *Journal of Wildlife Management* 50:90–91.

Linhart, S. B., F. S. Blom, G. J. Dasch, and R. M. Engeman. 1988. Field evaluation of padded jaw coyote traps: effectiveness and foot injury. *Proceedings of the Vertebrate Pest Conference* 13:226–229.

Linhart, S. B. and G. J. Dasch. 1992. Improved performance of padded jaw traps for capturing coyotes. *Wildlife Society Bulletin* 20:63–66.

Linhart, S. B., G. J. Dasch, and F. J. Turkowski. 1981. The steel leghold trap: techniques for reducing foot injury and increasing selectivity. *Proceedings of the Worldwide Furbearer Conference* 3:1560–1578.

Linhart, S. B., G. J. Dasch, C. B. Male, and R. M. Engeman. 1986. Efficiency of unpaddedand padded steel foothold traps for capturing coyotes. *Wildlife Society Bulletin* 14:212–218.

Linscombe, G. 1976. An evaluation of the No. 2 Victor and 220 Conibear traps in coastal Louisiana. *Proceedings of the Annual Conference of the Southeastern Association of Fish & Wildlife Agencies* 30:560–568.

Linscombe, R. G. and V. L. Wright. 1988. Efficiency of padded foothold traps for capturing territorial furbearers. *Wildlife Society Bulletin* 16:307–309.

Macpherson, A. H. 1969. The dynamics of Canadian arctic fox populations. Canadian Wildlife Service Report Series — 8. 8pp.

Mowat, G., B. G. Slough, and R. Rivard. 1994. A comparison of three live capturing devices for lynx: capture efficiency and injuries. *Wildlife Society Bulletin* 22:644–650.

Novak, M. 1981. The foot-snare and the leg-hold traps: a comparison. Proceeding of the Worldwide Furbearer Conference 3:1671–1685.

Novak, M. 1987. Traps and trap research. Pp. 941–969 *in* M. Novak, J. A. Baker, M. E. Obbard, and B. Malloch, eds. *Wild furbearer management and conservation in North America. North Bay*; Ontario Trappers Association.

Naylor, B. J. and M. Novak. 1994. Catch efficiency and selectivity of various traps and sets used for capturing American martens. *Wildlife Society Bulletin* 22:489–496.

Olsen, G. H., S. B. Linhart, R. A. Holmes, G. J. Dasch, and C. B. Male. 1986. Injuries to coyotes caught in padded and unpadded steel foothold traps. *Wildlife Society Bulletin* 14:219–223.

Olsen, G. H., et al. 1988. Reducing injuries to terrestrial furbearers by using padded foothold traps. *Wildlife Society Bulletin* 16:303–307.

Onderka, D. K. 1999. Pathological examinations as an aid for trap selection guidelines: usefulness and limitations. Pp. 47–52 *in* G. Proulx, ed. *Mammal trapping*. Sherwood Park; Alpha Wildlife Research & Management Ltd.

Onderka, D. K., D. L. Skinner, and A. W. Todd. 1990. Injuries to coyotes and other species caused by four models of footholding devices. *Wildlife Society Bulletin* 18:303–307.

Palmisano, A. W. and H. H. Dupuie. 1974. Unpublished manuscript. An evaluation of steel traps for taking fur animals in coastal Louisiana. Louisiana Cooperative Wildlife Unit. Louisiana State University. Baton Rouge, Louisiana. 12 pp.

Pawlina, I. M. and G. Proulx. 1999. Factors affecting trap efficiency: a review. Pp. 95–115

*in* G. Proulx, ed. *Mammal trapping*. Sherwood Park; Alpha Wildlife Research & Management Ltd.

Phillips, R. L, F. S. Blom, G. J. Dasch, and J. W. Guthrie. 1992. Field evaluation of three types of coyote traps. *Proceedings of the Vertebrate Pest Conference* 15:393–395.

Phillips, R. L. 1996. Evaluation of 3 types of snares for capturing coyotes. *Wildlife Society Bulletin* 24:107–110.

Phillips, R. L. and K. S. Gruver. 1996. Performance of the Paws-I-Trip™ pan tension device on 3 types of traps. *Wildlife Society Bulletin* 24:119–122.

Phillips, R. L. and C. Mullis. 1996. Expanded field testing of the No. 3 Victor Soft Catch® trap. *Wildlife Society Bulletin* 24:128–131.

Phillips, R. L., K. S. Gruver, and E. S. Williams. 1996. Leg injuries to coyotes captured in three types of foothold traps. *Wildlife Society Bulletin* 24:260–263.

Proulx G. 1999a. Review of current mammal trap technology in North America. Pp. 1–46 *in* G. Proulx, ed. *Mammal trapping*. Sherwood Park; Alpha Wildlife Research & Management Ltd.

Proulx G. 1999b. The Bionic: An effective marten trap. Pp. 79–87 *in* G. Proulx, editor. *Mammal trapping*. Sherwood Park; Alpha Wildlife Research & Management Ltd.

Proulx, G. and M. W. Barrett 1989. On the development and implications of the Conibear 120 Magnum trap to harvest marten and mink. Pp. 194–209 *in* R. Lafond, ed. Proceedings Northeast Fur Resources Technical Committee. Beauport, Quebec, Canada.

Proulx, G. and M. W. Barrett. 1990. Assessment of power snares to effectively kill red fox. *Wildlife Society Bulletin* 18:27–30.

Proulx, G. and M. W. Barrett. 1991a. Ideological conflict between animal rightists and wildlife professionals over trapping wild furbearers. *Transactions North American Wildlife and Natural Resources Conference* 56:387–399.

Proulx, G. and M. W. Barrett. 1991b. Evaluation of the Bionic trap to quickly kill mink (*Mustela vison*) in simulated natural environments. *Journal of Wildlife Diseases* 27:276–280.

Proulx, G. and M. W. Barrett. 1993a. Evaluation of the Bionic® trap to quickly kill fisher (*Martes pennanti*) in simulated natural environments. *Journal of Wildlife Diseases* 29:310–316.

Proulx, G. and M. W. Barrett. 1993b. Evaluation of mechanically improved Conibear 220™ traps to quickly kill fisher (*Martes pennanti*) in simulated natural environments. *Journal of Wildlife Diseases* 29:317–323.

Proulx, G. and M. W. Barrett. 1993c. Field testing the C120 Magnum for mink. *Wildlife Society Bulletin* 21:421–426.

Proulx, G., M. W. Barrett, and S. R. Cook. 1989a. The C120 Magnum: an effective quick-kill trap for marten. *Wildlife Society Bulletin* 17:294–298.

Proulx, G., M. W. Barrett, and S. R. Cook. 1990. The C120 Magnum with pan trigger: A humane trap for mink (*Mustela vison*). *Journal of Wildlife Diseases* 26:511–517.

Proulx, G., S. R. Cook, and M. W. Barrett. 1989b. Assessment and preliminary development of the rotating-jaw Conibear 120 trap to effectively kill marten (*Martes americana*). *Canadian Journal of Zoology* 67:1074–1079.

Proulx, G. and R. K. Drescher. 1994. Assessment of rotating-jaw traps to humanely kill raccoons (*Procyon lotor*). *Journal of Wildlife Diseases* 30:335-339.

Proulx, G. M., A. Kolenosky, M. J. Badry, P. J. Cole, and R. K. Drescher. 1993a. Assessment of the Sauvageau 2001-8 trap to effectively kill arctic fox. *Wildlife Society Bulletin* 21:132–135.

Proulx, G., A. J. Kolenosky, M. J. Badry, P. J. Cole, and R. K. Drescher. 1994a. Snowshoe hare snare system to minimize capture of marten. *Wildlife Society Bulletin* 22:639–643.

Proulx, G. M., A. J. Kolensosky, and P. J. Cole. 1993b. Assessment of the Kania® trap to humanely kill red squirrels (*Tamiasciurus hudsonicus*) in enclosures. *Journal of Wildlife Diseases* 29:324–329.

Proulx, G., A. J. Kolenosky, P. J. Cole, and R. K. Drescher. 1995. A humane killing trap for lynx (Felis lynx): the Conibear 330™ with clamping bars. *Journal of Wildlife Diseases* 31:57–61.

Proulx, G., D. K. Onderka, A. J. Kolenosky, P. J. Cole, R. K. Drescher, and M. J. Badry. 1993c. Injuries and behavior of raccoons (Procyon lotor) captured in the Soft Catch™ and the Egg™ traps in simulated natural environments. *Journal of Wildlife Diseases* 29:447–452.

Proulx, G., I. M. Pawlina, D. K. Onderka, M. J. Badry, and K. Seidel. 1994b. Field evaluation of the number 1½ steel-jawed leghold and the Sauvageau 2001-8 traps to humanely capture arctic fox. *Wildlife Society Bulletin* 22:179–183.

Redig, P. 1981. Significance of trap-induced injuries to bald eagles. Pp. 45–53 in Eagle Valley Environmental Technical Report BED 81. University of Minnesota. St. Paul.

Ruggiero, L. F., K. B. Aubry, S. W. Buskirk, G. M. Koehler, C. J. Krebs, K. S. McKelvey, and J. R. Squires. 1999. The scientific basis for lynx conservation: qualified insights. *in* Ruggiero, L.F., et al., tech. eds. The scientific basis for lynx conservation in the contiguous United States. Gen. Tech. Rpt. RMRS-GTR-30. Ogden: U.S. Dept. Agriculture, Forest Service, Rocky Mountain Research Station.

Sahr, D. P., and F. F. Knowlton. 2000. Evaluation of tranquilizer trap devices (TTDs) for foothold traps used to capture gray wolves. *Wildlife Society Bulletin* 28:597–605.

Saunders, B. P. and H. C. Roswell. 1984. Padded trap testing in British Columbia. *Proceedings Western Conference of the International Association Fish and Wildlife Agencies* 64:136–142.

Seddon, P. J., Y. V. Heezik, and R. F. Maloney. 1999. Short- and medium- term evaluation of foot hold trap injuries in two species of fox in Saudi Arabia. Pp. 67–77 *in* G. Proulx, ed. *Mammal trapping*. Sherwood Park; Alpha Wildlife Research & Management Ltd.

Serfass, T. L., et al. 1996. Considerations for capturing, handling, and translocating river otters. *Wildlife Society Bulletin* 24:25–31.

Shivik, J. A., K. S. Gruver, and T. J. DeLiberto. 2000. Preliminary evaluation of new cable restrains for capturing coyotes. *Wildlife Society Bulletin* 28:606–613.

Siemer, W. F., G. R. Batcheller, R. J. Glass, and T. L. Brown. 1994. Characteristics of trappers and trapping participation in New York. *Wildlife Society Bulletin* 22:100–111.

Skinner, D. L. and A. W. Todd. 1990. Evaluating efficiency of footholding devices for coyote capture. *Wildlife Society Bulletin* 18:166–175.

Stocek, R. F and D. J. Cartwright. 1985. Birds as non-target catches in the New Brunswick furbearer harvest. *Wildlife Society Bulletin* 13:314–317.

Sweitzer, R. A., B. J. Gonzales, I. A. Gardner, D. Van Vuren, J. D. Waithman, and W. M. Boyce. 1997. A modified panel trap and immobilization technique for capturing multiple wild pig. *Wildlife Society Bulletin* 25:699–705.

Tullar, B. F. 1984. Evaluation of a padded leg-hold trap for capturing foxes and raccoons. *NY Fish and Game Journal* 31:97–103.

Turkowski, F. J., A. R. Armistead, and S. B. Linhart. 1984. Selectivity and effectiveness of pan tension devices for coyote foothold traps. *Journal of Wildlife Management* 48:700–708.

United States of America / European Community. 1997. Agreed minute and annex: Standards for the humane trapping of specified terrestrial and semi-aquatic mammals. Brussels.

Van Ballenberghe, V. 1984. Injuries to wolves sustained during live-capture. *Journal of Wildlife Management* 48:1425–1429.

Waller, D. J. 1981. Effectiveness of kill-type traps versus leg-hold traps utilizing dirt-hole sets. *Proceedings of the Annual Conference of the Southeastern Association Fish & Wildlife Agencies* 35:256–260.

White, P. J., 1991. Pathological responses of red foxes to capture in box traps. *Journal of Wildlife Management* 55:75–80.

# THE USE OF INJURY SCALES IN THE ASSESSMENT OF TRAP-RELATED INJURIES

*Elizabeth Colleran, Christopher M. Papouchis, Jean C. Hofve, and Camilla H. Fox*

The trapping industry has been under pressure for over two decades to develop and use humane methods of trapping wild furbearing animals. In an attempt to standardize the assessment of the humaneness of various body-gripping traps and to compare different traps or trapping techniques, several injury scales have been developed to quantify the degree of injury caused by each of these devices. The scales discussed here were developed by Tullar,[1] Olsen et al.[2], Onderka et al.,[3] Hubert et al.,[4] Phillips et al.,[5] and the International Organization for Standardization (ISO)[6] (see Tables 3.2 and 3.3).

Injury scoring is not an unusual method for standardizing the evaluation of injury. Triage systems in human and veterinary medicine are equivalent tasks designed to identify the most critical cases and prioritize the order of treatment. This approach provides a standardized method for the evaluation and treatment of life-threatening injuries.

The analogy of injury scoring to triage reveals the profound deficiencies of the trapping injury scales currently in use. Because leghold traps and snares are intended to grasp limbs, the vast majority of injuries included in scales are the localized injuries to the limb or foot. Early scales, including Tullar and Olsen, examined only the feet or limbs of trapped animals, respectively. Later, Onderka performed full necropsies on trapped animals and considered injuries to the neck, shoulder, chest, teeth, and mouth, but did not incorporate these in the scoring system. Hubert utilized Onderka's

## TABLE 3.2

*Injury scales used in the assessment of trap-related injuries.*

| | POINTS SCORED | | | | | | |
|---|---|---|---|---|---|---|---|
| INJURY | TULLAR (1984) | OLSEN ET AL. (1986) | OLSEN ET AL. (1988) | ONDERKA ET AL. (1990) | HUBERT ET AL. (1996) | PHILLIPS ET AL. (1996) | DRAFT ISO[a] (1998) |
| Edematous swelling and/or hemorrhage | 5 | 5 | 5 | 1–5 | 1–5 | 5–15 | 5 |
| Avulsed nail | — | — | — | — | 5 | — | 2 |
| Cutaneous laceration less than or equal to 2 cm long | 5 | 5 | 5 | 5 | 5 | 5 | 5 |
| Cutaneous laceration greater than 2 cm long | 10 | 10 | 10 | 10 | 10 | 10 | 10 |
| Permanent tooth fracture exposing pulp cavity | — | — | — | — | 10 | — | 30 |
| Subcutaneous muscle laceration or maceration | — | — | — | 10–20 | 10–20 | 10–30 | 10–30 |
| Tendon or ligament maceration with partial severance | 20 | 20 | 20 | 20–40 | 20–40 | 25 | 100[b] |
| Damage to periosteum | — | — | — | — | 30 | 10–30 | 10–30 |
| Partial fracture of metacarpi or metatarsi | — | — | — | 30 | 30 | — | 100 |
| Fracture of digits | — | — | — | 30–40 | 30–50 | — | — |
| Joint subluxation | 30 | 30 | 30 | — | 100 | — | — |
| Joint luxation | 50 | 50 | 50 | 50 | 50 | 30–100 | 30–100 |
| Luxation at elbow or hock joint | — | — | — | 200–300 | 200 | — | 100 |
| Compression fracture above or below carpus or tarsus | — | 30 | 30 | — | — | 100 | — |
| Simple fracture above carpus or tarsus | 50 | 100 | 100 | 100 | 100 | 100 | 100 |
| Simple fracture below carpus or tarsus | 50 | 50 | 50 | 50 | 50 | 50 | 50 |
| Damage or severance of tendons below carpus or tarsus | — | — | — | 50 | 20–50 | — | — |
| Major laceration on foot pads | — | — | — | — | — | 30 | 30 |
| Amputation of digit(s) | 150 | — | 50–200 | 30–40 | 30–50 | 25–100 | 25–100 |
| Compound fracture below carpus or tarsus | 100 | 75 | — | 75 | 75 | 100 | 100[c] |
| Compound fracture above carpus or tarsus | 200 | 200 | 200 | 200 | 200 | 100 | 100 |
| Amputation of limb | 400 | 400 | 400 | 400 | 400 | 100 | 100 |

[a]Only Draft ISO injury categories shared by other scales included here. See Table 3.3 for complete Draft ISO scale.
[b]Totally severed tendon or ligament          [c]Simple fracture.

system, but added categories for avulsed (torn off) nail, permanent tooth fracture exposing pulp cavity, and damage to the periosteum (fibrous covering of bones which contains nerves and blood vessels). Hubert found that the whole body scores were approximately 15% higher than leg injury scores and stressed that previous "studies fail[ed] to tabulate all trap-related injuries that should be assigned to an individual coyote. Whole body necropsies should be conducted to insure no type of trap-related physical trauma is overlooked."[7]

Of the scales, only the ISO acknowledges the potential for damage apart from the specific trap-induced injuries observed. For example, tongue,

### TABLE 3.3

*Draft International Organization for Standardization (ISO)*
*trauma scale for restraining traps (1998).*

| Pathological Observations | Points Scored | Pathological Observations | Points Scored |
|---|---|---|---|
| Claw Loss | 2 | Simple fracture to the carpsus or tarsus | 50 |
| Edematous swelling or hemorrhage | 5 | Compression fracture | 50 |
| Minor cutaneous laceration | 5 | Comminuted rib fracture | 50 |
| Minor subcutaneous soft tissue maceration or erosion (contusion) | 10 | Amputation of 2 digits | 50 |
| Major cutaneous laceration, except on foot pads or tongue | 10 | Major skeletal muscle degeneration | 55 |
| Minor periosteal abrasion | 10 | Limb ischemia | 55 |
| Severance of minor tendon or ligament | 25 | Amputation of 3 or more digits | 100 |
| Amputation of 1 digit | 25 | Any fracture or joint luxation on limb proximal to carpus or tarsus | 100 |
| Permanent tooth fracture exploring pulp cavity | 30 | Any amputation above digits | 100 |
| Major subcutaneous soft tissue maceration or erosion | 30 | Spinal cord injury | 100 |
| Major laceration on foot pads or tongue | 30 | Severe internal organ damage (internal bleeding) | 100 |
| Severe joint hemorrhage | 30 | Compound or comminuted fracture at or below carpus or tarsus | 100 |
| Joint luxation below carpus or tarsus | 30 | Severance of major tendon or ligament | 100 |
| Major periosteal abrasion | 30 | Compound rib fracture | 100 |
| Simple rib fracture | 30 | Ocular injury resulting in blindness of an eye | 100 |
| Eye lacerations | 30 | Myocardial degeneration | 100 |
| Minor skeletal muscle degeneration | 30 | Death | 100 |

tooth, and eye lacerations are included in the mild and moderate categories. Similarly, severe trauma includes the direct or indirect effects of injuries. The ISO scale also recognizes the potential for internal bleeding, organ damage, and self-mutilation associated with pain. Some of the injuries specified in the ISO scale are an indirect result of being trapped, a consideration not apparent in the other scales. For example, the ISO scale includes degeneration of the skeletal muscle and myocardia (heart muscle), progressive conditions indicating deterioration of a tissue or an organ *over time*.

With the exception of the ISO, the injury scales are similar with regard to the injuries considered and their scoring, largely because each system was based on its predecessor. However, the reasoning behind the values assigned to some of the injuries is difficult to understand from a veterinary point of view. In most of the scales evaluated here, a total injury score of less than 50 points is considered minor, from 50 to 150 points moderate, and over 150 points severe (on the ISO scale, less than 25 is considered mild, 25–50 moderate, 50–99 moderately severe, and 100 or more severe). Low scores have been assigned to injuries known to be very painful, given the current understanding of the neurology of pain. Hemorrhages, regardless of severity, and lacerations are always considered minor. Lacerations have been divided into those less than and greater than 2 cm (slightly over ¾ inch), but there is no maximum over which they would be considered moderate or severe. No consideration is given to the size of the animal, although a 2 cm laceration on a 2 lb. marten or 4 lb. snowshoe hare may be much more critical than on a 40 lb. coyote. Joint luxations (dislocations)

## TABLE 3.4

*Sample scoring system for assessing trap-related injuries.*

| Observation | Normal/Absent | Mild | Moderate | Severe |
|---|---|---|---|---|
| Consciousness | Alert | Depressed | Delirious | Unconscious |
| Vision | Normal | Uneven pupils | | Blind |
| Posture/Spine | Normal | Weak | Unable to rise | Rigid or flaccid paralysis |
| Repiratory rate, pattern, effort | Normal | Rapid | Rapid shallow or slow | Undetectable |
| Pain | Absent | Uncomfortable | Occasional vocalizing | Constant vocalizing, biting |
| Shivering | Absent | Mild, occasional | Continuous | Frostbite present |
| Bleeding from head | Absent | Skin wound | Oral cavity, nose | Ears |
| Position of head | Normal | | | Cervical (neck) fracture |
| Chest movement | Symmetical | Rapid | | Asymmetrical |
| Abdominal wound | Absent | < 1cm, no abdominal contents | > 1 cm or hemorrhage or old | Visible abdominal organs |
| Bleeding | Absent | Little | Moderate | Hemorrhage |
| Oral cavity color | Pink | Pale pink | Pale | White, bluish, or very dark red |
| Fracture - closed | Absent | Digit | Simple, distal limb | Malpositioned limb |
| Fracture - open | Absent | Digit | Distal limb | Proximal limb, joint, ischemic, and amputation |
| Wound size (each), give location | Absent | < 1 cm no hemorrhage | > 2 cm | > 2 cm, contaminated, old, parasitized |

are also given universally low scores (50 or less on all scales). Even the more comprehensive ISO scale errs in this way. Tooth fractures with pulp exposure and eye lacerations, which are recognized as extremely painful in a traditional medical setting, are given low values in scales that identify and score these injuries. In the ISO scale, an elbow or hock joint luxation (dislocation) is given a score of 50 points, whereas Onderka and Hubert score the same injuries from 200 to 300 points. Similarly, ISO gives 100 points to limb amputations, while the other scales typically give 400 points. It is not unreasonable to presume that these injuries cause the same severity of pain to wild animals as they do to humans. One must therefore conclude that pain was simply not considered in the assignment of values.

The injury scales appear to be designed more to legitimize the use of leghold traps and snares than to provide a meaningful measurement of the effects of these traps. The higher scoring injuries may have been given high scores mostly because they are less common, not because they cause higher levels of pain or distress. This premise is faithfully carried through all of the tables, including the ISO scale. Compound fractures and limb amputations (rare injuries) were given very high scores, while edema (occurring in nearly every animal) was given a uniformly low score. To statistically demonstrate that a trap does not cause highly painful, debilitating injuries, one can simply assign the lowest scores to the most common injuries. While this may be too cynical an interpretation, it is consistent with the data and the unique context in which these injuries are interpreted.

In a veterinary examination of an acutely injured animal, specific cutaneous (skin) or bone injuries are not the first concern. A standard evaluation would instead include an overall assessment of the animal, starting with critical systems (breathing and circulation) and life-threatening injuries (e.g., arterial hemorrhage), and once these are stabilized, moving on to an appraisal of potential internal injuries, and lastly dealing with injuries to the limbs. Certainly, shock and cardiovascular injuries must be included in a comprehensive evaluation of injury severity.

An example of a more comprehensive injury scoring system is given in Table 3.4. It assesses the severity of all injuries occurring in the trapping environment. Regardless of the trap design or investigator's intent, this type of evaluation would provide a more complete, and therefore more humane, analysis of the real effects of trapping in animals. The very nature of this scoring system requires the involvement of a trained veterinary pathologist in the field or laboratory, depending on the study's setting. At a minimum, post-mortem necropsies should be performed by a veterinary pathologist with no foreknowledge of the type of trap used to capture a particular specimen. This criterion removes potential bias introduced by the participation of an untrained practitioner, especially one with a vested interest in the outcome.

The need to quantify injuries may indeed help to assess traps, settings, and techniques. Current methods, however, are woefully inadequate and do not represent a realistic portrayal of the experience of trapped animals. These scales have attempted to deliberately minimize the suffering, pain, and terror that a trapped animal must endure. Humaneness in any true sense of the word is not a factor.

If trapping were ever evaluated by the degree to which it causes pain and suffering, justification of the use of any body-gripping traps would be impossible.

## NOTES

1. Tullar.

2. Olsen, et al. "Injuries to coyotes."

3. Onderka, et al. "Injuries to coyotes."

4. Hubert, et al. "Evaluation of two restraining traps."

5. R. L. Phillips, K. S. Gruver, and E. S. William. "Leg injuries to coyotes captured in three types of foothold traps." *Wildlife Society Bulletin* 24 (1996): 260–263.

6. International Organization for Standardization. TC 191, "Animal (mammal) traps — Part 5: Methods for testing restraining traps." International Standard ISO/DIS 10990-5. Geneva: International Organization for Standardization, 1999.

7. Hubert et al. "Injuries to coyotes."

# CHAPTER FOUR

# The Development of International Trapping Standards

*Camilla H. Fox*

*It is my opinion that the end result of the humane trap programs will be to bury the unfavourable leghold trap problem under a depth of misrepresentations and label it acceptably humane.*

— ED CESAR, TRAPPER FOR NEARLY 40 YEARS

---

*"Extensive testing of leghold traps has already been conducted. In fact, of approximately 187 trapping field studies conducted in North America from 1975 through 1996, 153 of them involved leghold traps. The vast array of less cruel traps, including box traps, instant killing traps (sic) and spring-activated, cushioned foot snares, has not received the attention they warrant. Additional leghold trap testing is both inhumane and duplicative."*

(Congressional sign-on letter authored by Congresswoman Elizabeth Furse dated July 22, 1998, to Robert Livingston, Chairman of the House Appropriations Committee, opposing use of federal funds for the National Trap Testing Program and "any further testing of leghold-type traps.")

---

## INTRODUCTION

In the 1950s, in response to renewed and growing opposition to trapping, trap manufacturers and researchers began developing new devices in an effort to reduce the severity and occurrence of injuries in captured animals.[1] Most of this research was conducted in the United States and Canada. In the search for a "humane trap," millions of dollars were spent, and tens of thousands of animals were sacrificed designing and testing hundreds of trap prototypes.

Traps used in the field, however, have changed little in the last 50 years. Steel-jaw leghold traps, strangulation neck snares, and the more recently developed Conibear-type kill traps are the most commonly used traps in North America, despite three decades of research indicating that such traps can cause severe injuries, stress, and pain to trapped animals.

## Early Trap Inventions and Research

From 1920 to 1950, substantial cash prizes were offered in Canada and the U.S. for "humane trap" inventions to replace the leghold trap. Thousands of entries were submitted by trappers, inventors, and humane groups from around the world.

One of the winners was Frank Conibear, a Canadian trapper and trap inventor who, in the early 1950s, designed what became known as the Conibear kill trap. Conibear was never awarded the full cash prize because his instant-kill trap did not meet all of the criteria set forth by the trap review committee (the trap often malfunctioned in cold weather and was not suitable for large furbearing animals). Despite these significant flaws, Canadian trapping interests quickly touted the new invention as the "humane" device that would replace the leghold trap. However, the Conibear's humane label did not last long. The Federal Provincial Committee for Humane Trapping (FPCHT) of Canada conducted tests clearly indicating that the Conibear often failed to kill animals instantly because of trigger and positioning problems.[2]

In the late 1950s and early 1960s, Canada led the way in trap research with support from the Canadian government and the establishment of a national trap testing facility in Vegreville, Alberta. Much of Canada's research focused on kill-type traps, which were considered more humane and more practical for use in cold, wilderness habitats where traplines are not checked frequently and where leghold traps often suffer from trigger problems.

The Fur Institute of Canada (FIC) carries out most trap-related research with joint funding by the federal government and the International Fur Trade Federation. Founded in 1983, the FIC's mission is to "promote the conservation and optimum development of Canada's fur resources." The FIC places ads in international newspapers and magazines promoting fur, and courts well-known fashion designers by flying them to Europe and offering intensive training in fur garment design.

The FIC's trap research division spent over 20 million Canadian tax dollars between 1983 and 1997 and conducted over 2,000 tests on thousands of animals with more than 100 different trap types. The FIC identified seven kill traps and two restraining traps as humane for eight different furbearing animals.* The FIC did little, however, to promote devices it deemed humane. The FIC continues to promote redundant testing of standard Conibear and leghold traps, almost twenty years after Canada's FPCHT proclaimed:

> Research and field studies have demonstrated that the standard steel-jaw leghold trap is non-specific, causes injury in all species studie[d], and results in observable distress and probably pain in many individuals [and] observations of animals dying in Conibear traps [indicated that] the struggle was more violent than that seen in legholds.[3]

Ed Kania, a Canadian trap inventor whose marten-capturing Kania trap was selected by the FIC as one of the seven humane killing systems, believes that the FIC continued to promote the use of standard leghold traps and Conibear traps throughout North America because of its relationship with the Pennsylvania-based Woodstream Corporation, once the largest manufacturer of leghold and Conibear traps in the world.[4] Woodstream was involved in a number of the initial studies of leghold and Conibear traps — research that resulted in glowing reports of both traps.† A Woodstream board member was also on the FIC board.

While Canada has focused its testing on kill-type traps, the U.S. has almost exclusively tested leghold traps. Leghold traps are used more often than kill-type traps or neck snares in the U.S., in part because the close proximity of traps to human habitation and recreation areas makes the use of kill-traps a significant hazard to humans and domestic animals. The United States has refused to research alternative, more humane restraining devices, and has only reinforced the use of the leghold trap in this country.

## The Search for International Trapping Standards

An international debate over trapping at the 1983 Conference of the Parties to the Convention on International Trade in Endangered Species (CITES) led to a resolution calling for a global trade ban on animal products obtained through cruel methods, including the

---

* Kill trap: A trap designed and set with the intention of killing an animal. Restraining trap: A trap designed and set with the intention of live-capturing an animal such as a leghold trap or cage trap.

† In 1999, Woodstream Corporation got out of the leghold and Conibear trap business after 75 years of manufacturing and selling an estimated 145 million traps.

steel-jaw leghold trap. The official sponsor of the resolution was Gambia, which had originally sponsored a resolution to list the heavily-slaughtered harp and hooded seals under CITES. This resolution, however, was rejected by a majority of participating countries as being outside CITES's jurisdiction.* The matter was then turned over to the Geneva-based International Organization for Standardization (ISO),† with the aim of establishing internationally accepted trap standards. Gambia's proposed re-solution sent a strong message that cruel trapping methods would become an increasingly controversial international issue.

By 1984, Canada had established its own national humane trap standard and began pushing for an internationally accepted standard to deflect attempts to restrict trade in furs, as rumors began circulating that some European countries were considering fur-labeling requirements.‡ In 1985, the Canadian government hired Washington public communications analysts Gray & Company to provide recommendations for how to improve the international public image of trapped fur. Gray & Company proposed that Canada label its fur products, "so as to assure the wearer that the animal was caught humanely and by a 'caring' and interested community where environmental balance is always a key consideration. This can be a major public relations coup with a logo approaching the credibility, in the long term, of the Good Housekeeping 'Seal of Approval'."[5] Gray & Company also recommended that Canada ban the steel-jaw leghold trap, stating, "If a fur campaign is going to be effective, the leghold trap is a necessary sacrifice." The Canadian government chose not to follow this advice.

But then came a painfully ironic twist for Canada. In April 1988, Alan Clark, then the United Kingdom (U.K.) Minister of Trade and Industry, proposed his own fur labeling plan for the U.K. that ran directly against Gray & Company's recommendations. Clark stated, "This is a question of public enlightenment, not a statutory thing. It is saying that the public is able to make its own decisions, provided that it knows what is at stake."[6] Identifying eight wild-caught (not fur-farmed) furbearing species, Clark sought to require — under a British Trade Description Act order — that any garment containing their pelts be labeled: "Includes fur from animals caught in leghold traps."

The Canadian government strongly opposed Clark's proposal, as did the U.S. State Department. However, 33 members of the U.S. House of Representatives addressed a letter to the British Prime Minister in support of Clark's plan. Ultimately, the U.K. government rejected the proposal, allegedly because of threats from Canada to withhold a $5 billion order from Britain for Canadian submarines.[7]

Two months later, Clark's campaign was reignited in the European Parliament by British environment ministers Barbara Castle and Madron Seligman, who called for a ban in the European Union (EU) on the manufacture, sale, and use of the leghold trap. Their declaration also proposed labeling of all fur products from animals caught in leghold traps. More than half of the European Parliament members supported the declaration.

Canada once again lobbied against the proposal, claiming that fur labeling would result in "cultural genocide" of Canadian natives — a

---

* Gambia's resolution to ban trade in furs caught in leghold traps was declared ultra vires by the CITES technical committee because it did not address a conservation problem specific to endangered species, which is CITES's mandate.

† The International Organization for Standardization is a federation of national standards bodies from more than 90 countries aimed at developing internationally agreed upon standards to facilitate international trade and communication.

‡ The Canadian General Standards Board (CGSB)'s Committee on Development of Humane Trapping Standards approved a national standard for killing traps in 1984. Canada's definition of a humane kill-trap in 1984 was "… one in which an animal suffers minimal distress …. achieved by rendering the animal unconscious or insensitive to pain as rapidly as possible with inevitable subsidence into death without recovering consciousness." "Minimal distress" and "[as] rapidly as possible" were concepts not defined. Since 1984, the "humane trap" definition has changed within Canada a number of times. In the late 1990s, the CGSB focused its efforts on establishing standards for restraining and submersion trapping systems; in 1996, the CGSB approved standards for "mechanically powered, trigger-activated killing traps for use on land."

strategic public relations tactic recommended by Gray & Company. Subsequently, the European Parliament backed down from the proposal.

At the same time the European Union was debating fur labeling, a Technical Committee (TC 191) was established under the auspices of the ISO to develop an internationally agreed upon humane trapping standard for killing and restraining traps. Participating countries were granted either "participatory" or "observer" status (depending upon their level of involvement). Both the U.S. and Canada were granted "participatory" status and had voting privileges at all plenary sessions of TC 191. Further, most U.S. and Canadian participants were strongly biased in favor of continued use of leghold traps, and both countries were granted more voting positions than any other countries involved.

In a *Vancouver Sun* article (April 18, 1988) titled, "Trapping methods, by any standard, are simply cruel," author Nicholas Read accurately described the activities of the ISO as "legitimizing cruelty." Read wrote:

> The meeting is a government sponsored and supported committee of people — some of them trappers and trapping industry representatives — who are trying to establish a set of standards by which trapping cruelty can be measured ... Among the ways the ISO committees have considered measuring cruelty is with something called the Olsen scale. According to this scale, points are accorded different injuries. For example, a claw pulled off warrants two points. Broken teeth warrant 10. Broken tendons, 20. Fractured ribs, 30. And broken bones, 50 to 75.

On November 4, 1991, the European Union adopted Council Regulation 3254/91, a precedent-setting international regulation aimed at prohibiting imports of fur from countries that had not banned leghold traps. Regulation 3254/91, known as the "leghold trap fur import ban," had two objectives: first, to prohibit the use of leghold traps in all 15 European Union member countries by January 1, 1995*; second, to prohibit, after January 1, 1996, the import of pelts from 13 species of furbearing animals from countries that refused to stop using leghold traps.[†]

Animal welfare advocates hoped Regulation 3254/91 would provide the necessary impetus to force the U.S., Canada, and Russia (the three largest fur-exporting nations in the world) to ban the use of leghold traps. Not surprisingly, the second objective alarmed the North American fur industry, since Europe was one of the largest fur markets and imported more than 70% of wild-caught furs exported by the U.S. and Canada.[8]

The first objective of Regulation 3254/91 was implemented without delay. However, leghold trap proponents induced the EU to add an option to the second provision: instead of banning steel-jaw traps, fur-exporting countries could adopt "internationally agreed humane trapping standards," even though no such international trap standards existed at the time. Inclusion of this provision helped legitimize the trap standards process already underway within the ISO and provided a one-year grace period for fur-producing nations if they could demonstrate that "sufficient progress" was being made toward the development of such standards. The fur industry looked to the ISO TC 191 committee to develop trap standards that would allow the major fur-exporting countries to continue selling furs to Europe under Regulation 3254/91 indefinitely. Fur-exporting countries also saw the provision as a way to avoid a total ban on leghold traps, especially if modified leghold traps, such as the padded version, could meet the ISO standards.

By 1994, progress in developing international trap standards under TC 191 was beginning to break down. Disputes intensified over what defined a humane trap. The very word "humane" became a major issue of contention and was ultimately removed from the title of the proposed standards in 1994. It was apparent no agreement would emerge from ISO that could avert the European

---

* Countries that comprise the European Union: Austria, Belgium, Denmark, Finland, France, Germany, Greece, Ireland, Italy, Luxembourg, Netherlands, Portugal, Spain, Sweden, United Kingdom.

† The species listed in the Annex to the regulation are: beaver (North American), otter (North American), coyote, wolf, lynx (North American), bobcat, sable, raccoon, muskrat, fisher, badger (North American), marten, and ermine. The list of species was later expanded to 19 to include the raccoon dog, pine marten, and the European species of beaver, otter, lynx, and badger.

leghold trap fur ban. In 1997, TC 191 ended its efforts to develop international trap standards and began focusing solely on trap testing methodology.

## The U.S. Thwarts International Efforts to Ban the Leghold Trap

By 1997, the ISO trap standards process had failed and the U.S. had successfully stalled implementation of the fur import ban for two years by threatening the EU with trade reprisals. Fur-producing nations could no longer avert the EU fur import ban by arguing that "sufficient progress" was being made toward the "development of humane trapping standards." Fearing the loss of the European fur market, U.S. trapping and fur interest groups took action. Led by the International Association of Fish and Wildlife Agencies (IAFWA)* and the National Trappers Association (NTA), a national trapping work group was formed in the U.S. with the primary aim of avoiding the EU fur import ban and maintaining public acceptance of trapping in the United States.

This trapping work group achieved its first goal by heavily lobbying then–U.S. Trade Representative Charlene Barshefsky, arguing that a European Union ban of American furs would violate the free trade provisions under GATT (General Agreement on Trade and Tariffs). In addition, the IAFWA and the NTA were successful in convincing the EU that the U.S. was making "sufficient progress toward the development of humane trapping" standards through a new trap-testing program. With the backing of the Clinton Administration and an initial federal aid grant of $350,000, the coalition sold the European Commission and the U.S. Trade Representative on a hollow promise to develop national Best Management Practices (BMP) trapping guidelines under a newly established National Trap Testing Program (NTTP), funded by U.S. tax dollars.

Fearing a U.S. and Canadian challenge of Regulation 3254/91 under the free-trade provisions of the World Trade Organization (WTO), the European Union accepted the United States' proposed BMP trap testing program. On December 18, 1997, the U.S. signed an "understanding"† with the EU, averting the fur ban while maintaining the use of leghold traps nationwide.

Europe's acquiescence was a bitter disappointment to those who had worked for more than six years to ensure compliance with Europe's fur ban regulation and to end the use of leghold traps worldwide. The U.S. government's threat of trade retaliation and its refusal to ban the leghold trap demonstrated the power of the consumptive wildlife use lobby.

## The U.S./EU Understanding

The 1997 understanding between the U.S. and the European Union is composed of two vaguely worded documents: the "Agreed Minute" and the "Side Letter." The understanding also includes "Standards for the Humane Trapping of Specified Terrestrial and Semi-Aquatic Mammals" (also referred to as the "technical standards," which are the same standards annexed to the agreement signed between the EU and Canada and Russia).

The "Agreed Minute" is the key document in this bilateral understanding. It affirms that the technical trapping standards annexed to the "Agreed Minute" provide a "common framework" and "basis for cooperation" on the development and implementation of the trapping standards by the "competent authorities" (i.e., state governments). It expresses the intention of the U.S. and the EU to support trap research conducted by their competent authorities.

---

* The International Association of Fish and Wildlife Agencies (IAFWA) is a quasi-governmental organization whose members include the fish and wildlife agencies of the states, provinces, and federal government of the U.S., Canada, and Mexico. One of IAFWA's stated objectives is "to promote the sustainable use of natural resources."

† The "understanding" the U.S. signed with the EU is much weaker than an international "agreement" and does not require formal ratification. An "agreement" is binding, while an "understanding" is non-binding.

The "Side Letter" affirms that the regulation of trapping in the U.S. is primarily a responsibility of the states and tribal wildlife management authorities (thereby absolving the federal government of any real obligation in implementing the understanding). It also states that "competent authorities" in the U.S. intend to carry out the understanding through the BMP trap testing process.

In essence, the understanding calls for the gradual phasing out of "conventional" leghold traps within the U.S. over a six-year period, after Canada and Russia ratify their agreements with the EU (by December 1999, Canada had ratified and Russia had not). The term "conventional," however, remains undefined. The U.S. and Canada pushed for a narrow interpretation that would exclude modified leghold traps such as padded or offset traps. Animal welfare advocates within Europe, Canada, and the U.S. support a broad interpretation that would include all leghold traps, reflecting the original intent of the EU Regulation.

The understanding also stipulates that the U.S. prohibit all jaw-type restraining traps for capturing ermine (weasel) and muskrat over a four-year period—a progressive sounding provision, but one that is virtually meaningless. Leghold traps used as killing or drowning devices (as opposed to being used as restraining devices) are exempt from all provisions concerning restraining traps within the understanding. Leghold traps used to trap muskrat are almost invariably set as drowning devices, while leghold traps used for capturing ermine are often set as killing traps (and ermine are seldom targeted by trappers as fur demand has been very low for this species).

Other loopholes in the understanding could completely nullify any potential gains in animal welfare, since the provisions are dependent upon the progress of fur-exporting countries in establishing "humane" trap standards. Specifically, one clause allows "competent authorities" in the U.S. to authorize continued use of unapproved traps (i.e., steel-jaw leghold traps) until testing produces traps that meet certain standards included in the understanding. In addition, the use of unapproved traps may be used whenever such traps are deemed necessary to control animals "pos[ing] a threat to the environment, public health, safety or private property."

Perhaps the most disturbing aspect of the U.S./EU understanding is that it is non-binding and defers the federal government's responsibility to regulate trapping to the states. State fish and wildlife agencies, represented by the IAFWA and heavily influenced by consumptive wildlife-use lobby groups such as the National Trappers Association, argued that the regulation of trapping is a state issue and therefore should not involve the federal government. Not wanting to become embroiled in a national states-rights debate, the Clinton Administration bowed to this pressure and ensured that the U.S./EU trapping understanding would be non-binding.

Under the U.S./EU understanding, states are not obligated to prohibit use of leghold traps and replace them with more humane devices, even after close to one million tax dollars have been spent testing leghold traps and other capture devices under the federal BMP National Trap Testing Program (BMP NTTP). In fact, the BMP NTTP, upon which the U.S./EU trapping understanding is based, will most likely be used to legitimize and further entrench the use of leghold traps under the guise of science. This sentiment was summed up by Tom Krause, former president of the National Trappers Association, in a trapping trade magazine article about the BMP NTTP:

> If we are going to continue to have sufficient support from the public to trap furbearers and predators, it will help a great deal to be able to use indisputable science to inform the public we are using appropriate trapping tools and methods.[9]

Backers of the BMP NTTP program have refused to allow public review of trap research projects and have prevented the participation of representatives from the humane community in the national trapping work group or in the BMP development process. Animal advocates were even denied "observer" status, while two representatives from the National Trappers Association were granted voting powers. Public oversight and accountability, if allowed, would have revealed the waste of U.S. tax dollars on redundant and unnecessary trap research that has done little to prevent cruelty to trapped animals.

The BMP NTTP will likely result in a list of guidelines recommending standard and modified leghold traps for the list of species covered under

## TRAPS MEETING REQUIREMENTS OF EU/CANADIAN AND RUSSIAN AGREEMENTS ON INTERNATIONAL HUMANE TRAPPING STANDARDS

(September 9, 1999, Fur Institute of Canada News Release):

### RESTRAINING TRAPS

*(These traps meet the injury and behavioral thresholds as set out in the Agreement)*

**Lynx:**  Victor No. 3 Soft Catch equipped with 4 coil-springs
Victor No. 3 equipped with 3/16 inch laminated jaw and 4 coil-springs

**Bobcat:** Belisle foot snare          **Coyote:**  Belisle foot snare

### KILLING TRAPS

*(These traps meet the time to loss of consciousness and sensibility thresholds as set out in the Agreement)*

**Beaver:**  Woodstream, Conibear 330 underwater & on land
Woodstream, Conibear 330 modified/underwater

**Weasel:**  Victor, Rat Trap          **Fisher:**  Sauvageau, 2001-8

**Marten:**  Sauvageau, 2001-5
Sauvageau, C 120 Magnum
Belisle Super X 120

**Muskrat:** Woodstream, Conibear 120/on land
Jaw-type leghold traps/with submersion system

**Lynx:**  Woodstream, Conibear 330          **Raccoon:** Woodstream, Conibear 160
Woodstream, Conibear 160          Woodstream, Conibear 220

---

the U.S./EU trapping understanding. State and federal wildlife agencies, however, will not be required to implement any of the recommended guidelines. There will be no enforcement, legislation, or regulatory changes to mandate modifications in trapping devices or methods used. The leghold trap will continue to be the trap of choice for capturing the majority of furbearing species in the U.S.* Moreover, wildlife agencies will have pseudo-science and an international bilateral understanding to legitimize their refusal to implement humane alternatives. It is ironic that the international regulation against use of the leghold trap has ultimately led to more testing and manipulation of data designed to further entrench its use.

## The Agreement on International Humane Trapping Standards

In July 1997, six months before the EU member states approved the trapping understanding with the U.S., Canada and Russia signed an "Agreement on International Humane Trapping Standards" with the European Union. This agreement allows Canada and Russia to continue selling furs from trapped animals to the EU if both countries phase out traps that do not meet the annexed technical trapping standards (the same standards later annexed to the U.S./EU "Agreed Minute").

---

* As of September 1999, more than $1 million tax dollars were spent testing 28 different trap types on 9 species in 20 states as part of the NTTP. Four out of five traps tested were leghold traps.

The U.S. refused to sign this agreement, arguing that it was too restrictive and that the federal government could not dictate trapping methodology at the state level. Unlike the U.S. understanding, this trilateral agreement is binding and does not include the large loopholes included in the U.S./EU understanding. This agreement falls short, however, of substantively improving animal welfare by still allowing the use of traps known to cause significant injuries, pain, and suffering to trapped animals.

The trilateral agreement requires Canada and Russia to phase out the use of "conventional" steel-jaw leghold traps for certain species within two to four years of ratification. Other types of leghold traps (padded, modified steel-jaw) can still be used for another eight years or more as trap testing continues.

## Standards for the Humane Trapping of Specified Terrestrial and Semi-Aquatic Mammals

Contained in the trilateral agreement between the EU, Russia, and Canada and annexed to the "Agreed Minute" of the U.S./EU understanding are "Standards for the Humane Trapping of Specified Terrestrial and Semi-Aquatic Mammals." Ostensibly developed to improve animal welfare, the actual aim of these technical standards is reflected in the preamble, which states, "The primary purpose of any international technological standard is to improve communications and facilitate trade." Clearly, with the threat of a World Trade Organization challenge by the U.S. and Canada,* free trade and avoidance of a trade dispute became the overriding goal of the international trapping agreements — a far cry from the EU Regulation's original intent to prevent excessive cruelty by encouraging countries to ban leghold traps.

The "Standards for the Humane Trapping of Specified Terrestrial and Semi-Aquatic Mammals" (SHTM) describe the technical criteria for the performance of traps. For restraining traps (leghold traps), injuries to captured animals are measured according to a trauma scale that applies points for different trap-related injuries. For kill-type traps, thresholds are measured by time to irreversible unconsciousness. The U.S. agreed to use the standard only as a reference for further testing on leghold traps.

### Restraining Traps

The SHTM set no limit on the amount of time animals can be left in restraining traps. Therefore, in parts of Canada, the U.S., and Russia, animals could be left for days or weeks in leghold traps and other restraining devices. As long as the traps have met the standards set forth in the agreement, they would be considered humane.

The SHTM fails to specify a humane method for killing animals captured in restraining traps. Clubbing and suffocation — the standard methods for killing trapped animals — will continue unabated.

Under these weak standards, leghold traps would still be labeled humane even if as many as 20% of animals tested in them suffer from fractured limbs, severe internal trauma, and spinal cord injuries. The SHTM fails to include an assessment of pain and physiological parameters related to trap injuries, confining assessment almost exclusively to injuries of the trapped limb. Injuries are awarded points according to severity rated on a "trauma scale" included in the annexed technical trap standards (which reflects the draft ISO trap injury scale [see Chapter Three]). Animal advocates objected to the labeling of the injury scale as a "trauma scale," as complete assessment of trauma would necessarily include pain and physiological factors, which the standards fail to incorporate.

---

* The Russian federation was unable to make trade reprisal threats to the European Union because it was not a member of the WTO.

## *Kill Traps*

Kill traps are considered acceptable if they render species covered under the agreement unconscious and insensible within a specific time frame. Ermine must be rendered unconscious and insensible by the trap within 45 seconds; marten, sable, and pine marten within 120 seconds; and all other species covered within 300 seconds. The agreement requires a committee to "evaluate the time limit at the three-year review ... where data warrants such action, to adapt the time limit requirement on a species-by-species basis, with a view to lowering the 300 second time limit to 180 seconds, and to define a reasonable time-frame for implementation."

## Conclusion

Despite the European Union's good intentions, Regulation 3254/91 has done little to improve the plight of trapped animals. While there is hope that Canada and possibly Russia may prohibit the most heinous traps that fail to meet the agreement, the same cannot be said for the United States. Political forces in the U.S. succeeded in forcing the EU to accept an "understanding" that, according to the U.S. Trade Representative's office, "allows the trade of wild furs [to European markets] to continue uninterrupted." *

NOTES

1. M. W. Barrett, et al. "Wild fur industry under challenge: the Canadian response." *Transactions of the North American Wildlife and Natural Resources Conference* 53 (1988): 180–190.

2. The Federal Provincial Committee on Humane Trapping. "Findings and Recommendations." Federal Provincial Wildlife Conference. Canada. 1981.

3. Executive Summary Report of the Federal Provincial Committee for Humane Trapping. 1981.

4. "Fur Institute of Canada Fails to Recognize Humane Traps." *The Animal Welfare Institute Quarterly* 44 (Summer 1995).

5. Gray & Company Public Communications International, "Defense of the Fur Trade." 1985.

6. "Labeling of Furs Caught in Steel Jaw Leghold Traps." *The Animal Welfare Institute Quarterly* 37 (Spring/Summer 1988).

7. Ibid.

8. "National Trappers Association Fights Regulation Against Steel Jaw Leghold Traps." *The Animal Welfare Institute Quarterly* 43 (Spring 1994).

9. Tom Krause. "Trap Standards." *American Trapper* 37 (January/February 1997): 26–31.

---

* Canada ratified the trilateral agreement on June 1, 1999. By December 1999, Russia had not yet ratified. Because the "Agreed Minute" signed between the U.S. and the EU is only an "understanding" and is not binding, no ratification is necessary for the U.S.

# CHAPTER FIVE

# State Trapping Regulations

*Camilla H. Fox*

*A disturbing lack of concern for the furbearers is standard operating procedure throughout the United States. Most state wildlife agencies have little or no relevant data available regarding the short- and long-term impacts that trapping has on their respective furbearer species. But what's even worse than not having the data to support these large-scale killing campaigns is the fact that some states are trying to create technical smoke screens to hide their ignorance.*

— THOMAS EVELAND, *WILDLIFE BIOLOGIST*

In the United States, trapping is regulated at the state level. Regulations vary tremendously from state to state: Some, such as Louisiana and Nevada, have very loose restrictions; others have more restrictive and complex regulations, including Connecticut and Colorado.

Animal advocates have had some success in banning or limiting certain traps and trapping practices through the administrative, legislative, and ballot-initiative processes (see Chapter Seven). However, most state wildlife agency commissions (or boards or councils) are controlled and dominated by "consumptive wildlife users," those who hunt, trap, and kill wildlife for recreation or "sport," making change through the administrative process slow. Wildlife is seen as a resource to be stocked, managed, culled, thinned, harvested, hunted, and trapped for the benefit of consumptive users, as reflected in the fact that many state wildlife agencies are still called fish and game departments. State wildlife agencies

depend heavily upon revenues obtained from hunting, trapping, and fishing license sales, and excise taxes levied on hunting and fishing gear. As a result, agencies have effectively ignored the opinions of the vast majority of their constituents. Agency funds are disproportionately spent on "game" animals while "nongame" animals receive little or no consideration. Funding for sensitive species is often so low that in many states, threatened and endangered species lack recovery plans.

Most states review trapping regulations annually or biennially, primarily to establish future seasons and bag limits. Some states, including California and Alaska, allow citizens to propose regulation changes pertaining to trapping, hunting, and fishing, although most only allow public comment on proposals promulgated by the state wildlife agency. Generally, oversight commissions rubber-stamp department proposals, giving little consideration to the views of the non-consumptive majority, who may prefer that wildlife be managed less intrusively. Unfortunately, the views and voices of wildlife advocates have been sorely missing (or suppressed by those in power) in this process, which has only helped to maintain the status quo. Fortunately, this trend is beginning to shift as more and more wildlife advocates learn how to participate in this process.

## Problems with State Trapping Regulations

### Lack of Enforcement

Many states, by their own admission, lack the enforcement personnel necessary to ensure compliance with state trapping (and hunting) regulations in the field. Surveys of game wardens indicate that violations of trapping regulations are commonplace. Common violations include failure to check traps as frequently as state regulations require, using traps without personal iden-

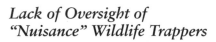

tification (most states require that a tag with the trapper's identity be affixed to traps used in the field), trapping for species out of season, and using traps that do not comply with state regulations.

### Species with No Protections

Some state trapping regulations only cover certain trapped species, for example those classified as "furbearer" or "small game." Species classified as "nongame" or "predatory" are exempt from any protections or regulatory oversight, meaning they can be killed at will. In some states species designated as "predatory" or "nongame" can be trapped and/or hunted at any time of the year, in any number, without a license. In most states, gophers, moles, voles, rats, and mice may be trapped without any restrictions. Following are some examples of such regulations:

**Arkansas:** "Beavers causing damage may be trapped the entire year with water sets and snares."

**Mississippi:** "Beavers are classed as predators and may be trapped throughout the year."

**Nebraska:** Coyotes, prairie dogs, and woodchucks are designated as "unprotected nongame species" and may be killed year-round without a license or permit.

**New Mexico:** Residents do not need a trapping license to trap coyotes or skunks (designated as "unprotected furbearers").

**Ohio:** No trapping license is required to trap coyotes, although a hunting license is required.

**Oregon:** "The general furbearer regulations do not apply to the trapping of gophers, moles, ground squirrels and mountain beaver." In addition, badgers, coyotes, nutria, opossums, porcupines, striped and spotted skunks, and weasels can be trapped year-round by licensed trappers.

**Tennessee:** Beaver can be trapped in parts of the state year-round with no bag limit.

**Texas:** Bobcats and coyotes can be killed year-round with no bag limit.

### Lack of Oversight of "Nuisance" Wildlife Trappers

A growing concern among animal advocates in the U.S. is the exponential growth and privatization of the nuisance wildlife control field, an industry based upon the removal and, most often, killing of animals deemed "pests" or a "nuisance." This industry has almost no regulatory oversight at either the state or federal level. Although many wildlife control operators (WCOs) use the same traps as do fur trappers (and many sell the pelts of the animals they trap), few states require that persons employed in this business obtain a state trapping license or report the species or number of animals killed. In most states, wildlife agencies have almost no oversight over private WCOs even though nuisance trappers kill wild animals over which the state wildlife agency has management authority. In those states where trapping has been banned or restricted through the ballot initiative process, it is likely that many trappers have turned from commercial and/or recreational fur trapping to "pest control" trapping. According to a 1992 national Gallup survey of trappers, "nuisance" trapping for private landowners was performed by nearly 70% of fur trappers in the Midwest and West, 60% of trappers in the Northeast, and 55% of trappers in the South.[1]

A 1997 national study found that few WCOs have any knowledge about wild animals, "most have a high school diploma, but little specific training in wildlife damage management in general," and "more than half of WCOs surveyed in one study had not attended a trapper-education course."[2] WCOs commonly use "illegal methods," including "toxicants to control bats or to euthanize animals." According to the study, common methods used to kill "pest" animals include the use of strangulation snares, drowning, injections of paint thinner or other toxicants, clubbing, and suffocation by standing on the animal's chest.

In 1997, Connecticut passed a precedent-setting bill banning WCOs from killing wildlife using inhumane methods. The bill requires that wildlife control trappers follow the humane euthanasia guidelines of the American Veterinary Medical Association and that they receive mandatory training in non-lethal, humane capture methods.

## Unregulated Killing Methods

Most state regulations do not address how animals found alive in traps are to be killed. The most common killing methods used by trappers are clubbing, suffocation (standing on the chest), and strangulation (with a "choke stick" or "catch pole"). Fur trappers do not like to shoot trapped animals because bullet holes and blood damage pelts and reduce the value of furs. *Get Set to Trap*, a trapper education manual published by the California Department of Fish and Game (DFG), recommends clubbing trapped animals and standing on their chests as the preferred method. Specifically, the DFG suggests using a heavy object such as a "heavy iron pipe about 18-24 inches long, or an axe handle," and striking the animal two times, "once to render it unconscious and again to render it either dead or comatose." In addition, it suggests that trappers "pin the head with one foot and stand on the chest (area near the heart) of the animal with the other foot for several minutes." At least eight other states produce similar trapper educational manuals recommending the same methods. New York's

trapping regulations allow for "use [of] any legal method to kill a trapped animal. You do not need a hunting license to use a firearm to kill a legally trapped animal." Georgia is the only state to mandate that trappers "… carry a weapon of .22 cal. rimfire while tending traps and to use that weapon to dispatch any furbearing animal to be taken." Alabama requires that "any person trapping fur-bearing animals in the state of Alabama must carry with him a choke stick while running traps … When legally trapped fur-bearing animals are dispatched with a firearm, only standard .22 caliber rimfire firearms may be used."

## Inaccuracy of State Wildlife Agency Trap-Kill Figures

The majority of state wildlife agencies do not require trappers to report the number or species of animals they trap each season. Instead they rely on "fur dealer or buyer reports," which have little correlation to the actual number of animals trapped. Fur buyer or dealer reports only record those pelts purchased by licensed fur buyers within the state. Unsold and/or damaged pelts or pelts sold out of state are not recorded in these figures. These reports, therefore, underestimate the total number of animals trapped statewide. States that require seasonal trapping reports from trappers often obtain their information through random telephone or mail surveys. Response rates to such surveys vary from 10% to 60%. State wildlife agencies then extrapolate the total number of animals trapped each year from these partial reports.

In a letter from the Kansas Department of Wildlife & Parks to the Animal Protection Institute, dated April 30, 1997, the head Furbearer Biologist makes this point: "Harvest reports are only what they say, harvest reports. Not population trends. Numbers presented in these reports do not reflect the total take of each species either. We get a 20% response rate to our survey. Therefore, we infer our numbers based on who sent their surveys back … You must realize that population trends in furbearers can not be interpreted from trends in the harvest reports."

States that allow commercial trapping of river otters, bobcats, lynx, and gray wolves are required to issue tags for trappers to affix to the pelt and to closely monitor annual take. This requirement is a federal mandate under the Convention on International Trade in Endangered Species (CITES) of Wild Fauna and Flora, which lists the above species on Appendix II, the category designating species that are threatened or likely to become so if heavily traded.

**States that require trappers to report annual trap kill numbers (of target animals only):** Alabama, Arizona, California, Georgia, Idaho, Mississippi, New Hampshire, Oregon, Rhode Island, South Carolina, Vermont, Washington, Wisconsin.

**States that require fur dealers to report annual in-state fur-buying records:** Alabama, Alaska, Arizona, Arkansas, California, Florida, Georgia, Illinois, Indiana, Iowa, Kentucky, Maine, Maryland, Massachusetts, Minnesota, Mississippi, Missouri, Nebraska, New Hampshire, New Mexico, North Carolina, North Dakota, Ohio, Oklahoma, Pennsylvania, South Carolina, South Dakota, Tennessee, Texas, Vermont, Virginia, West Virginia, Wisconsin, Wyoming.

**States that do not require any reporting by trappers or fur dealers:** Colorado, Connecticut, Delaware, Kansas, Louisiana, Michigan, Montana, Nevada, New Jersey, New York, Utah.

### Poor (or Nonexistent) Reporting of Non-Target Animals Trapped

Very few states require that trappers report non-target animals trapped. Although some states require that incidentally trapped threatened and endangered species, domestic animals, and farm animals be reported and/or turned in to the state wildlife agency, most states do not. Some states, including Idaho, New Mexico, Washington, and Wyoming, require that non-target trapped animals be released either "immediately" and/or "unharmed." (How one determines or ensures that an animal is "unharmed" after struggling for hours or days in a trap is never mentioned.) Such regulations, however, do little to ensure an accurate tally of the numbers of non-target animals trapped.

### Private Landowners Exempted from Trapping Regulations

In a number of states, private landowners do not need a license to trap and kill certain species on their property. The following are provisions that usually, but not always, exempt landowners from the state trapping regulations:

**Indiana:** "Landowners may take coyotes at any time on the land they own or provide written permission for others to take coyotes on their land at any time."

**Kansas:** Owners and legal occupants of land may kill (includes trapping) furbearers found in or near buildings or doing damage if non-lethal efforts have failed to solve the problem.

**Maryland:** Private landowners do not need a license or permit to trap certain species on their property.

**Massachusetts:** "No license is required by any legal resident of the Commonwealth or member of his immediate family for trapping on land owned or leased by him which is used principally for agriculture, if he is actually domiciled on that land." A public ballot initiative passed in 1996, however, limits the traps allowed under this provision.

**Rhode Island:** "Landowners are permitted to take nuisance furbearers provided that any carcass, except rabbits, is presented to the Department of Environmental Management within 24 hours." A permit is required for use of leghold traps.

**Texas:** "Landowners or their agents may take nuisance fur-bearing animals by any means at any time on that person's land without the need for a hunting or trapping license."

**Wisconsin:** "The owner or occupant of any land, and family members do not need a license to trap beaver, foxes, raccoon, woodchucks, rabbits and squirrels on the land year-round."

### Trappers Rights vs. Landowners Rights

Trespassing by trappers has been a problem for private landowners for years. Statutes and regulations vary from state to state, with some favoring landowners and others favoring trappers. Every state recognizes a landowner's right to exclude trappers from his or her land by erecting "No Trespassing" or "No Hunting/Trapping" signs. Many states require that trappers obtain either written or verbal permission from landowners even if they landowner has not posted his or her land. Conversely, some states favor trappers by requiring that landowners who wish to exclude trappers post No Trespassing signs, or by enacting burdensome posting requirements.

Below are some examples of state landowner posting and permission requirements. (contact your state wildlife agency for information pertaining to your state.)

**Examples of states requiring trappers to obtain permission (either written or oral) to trap on private land:**

**Nebraska:** "It shall be unlawful for anyone to take any wildlife upon private land *without permission of the owner*. It shall be unlawful for anyone to trap or otherwise harvest fur-bearing animals upon the lands of another without his or her consent. Animals and the pelts thereof taken contrary to this section may be retrieved by the owner of the lands. For purposes of this section, owner means the actual owner of the land and any tenant or agent in possession or charge thereof for him or her." (Emphasis added).

**Oklahoma:** "No person may trap on the inhabited land of another without first procuring from the owner or occupant thereof a *written permit* to do so. Such permit must be kept on the person of such trapper whenever he tends his traps and must be presented for inspection upon demand of any officer authorized to enforce the wildlife conservation laws of this state." (Emphasis added).

**Examples of states that require private landowners to post their land to exclude trappers:**

**Arizona:** "Landowners or lessees of private land who desire to prohibit hunting, fishing or trapping on their lands without their written permission *shall post such lands closed to hunting, fishing or trapping using notices or signboards*." (Emphasis added).

**Utah:** "While taking wildlife or engaging in wildlife related activities, a person may not: (a) without permission of the owner or person in charge, enter upon privately owned land that is cultivated or *properly posted*; (b) refuse to immediately leave the private land if requested to do so

by the owner or person in charge; or (c) obstruct any entrance or exit to private property." (Emphasis added).

**Examples of states which have specific posting requirements:**

**Idaho:** "No person shall enter the real property of another and shoot any weapon or enter such property for the purposes of hunting, fishing or trapping, without the permission of the owner or person in charge of the property, which property is either cultivated or posted with legible 'No trespassing' signs, is posted with a minimum of one hundred (100) square inches of fluorescent orange paint except that when metal fence posts are used, the entire post must be painted fluorescent orange, or other notices of like meaning, placed in a conspicuous manner on or near all boundaries at intervals of not less that one (1) sign, paint area or notice per six hundred sixty (660) feet provided that where the geographical configuration of the real property is such that entry can reasonably be made only at certain points of access, such property is posted sufficiently for all purposes of this subsection if said signs, paint areas or notices are posted at such points of access."

**Vermont:** "Notices prohibiting the taking of wild animals shall be erected upon or near the boundaries of lands to be affected with notices at each corner and not over 400 feet apart along the boundaries thereof ... Legible signs must be maintained at all times and shall be dated each year. These signs shall be of a standard size and design as the commissioner shall specify ... The owner or person posting the lands shall record this posting annually in the town clerk's office of the town in which the land is located ... The town clerk shall retain a fee of $5.00 for this recording." The signs prohibiting trapping on land must be "(1) of a size not less than 11 ½" wide by 8" high; (2) lettering and background must be of contrasting colors; (3) contain the wording that hunting, fishing or trapping or any combination of the three are prohibited or forbidden ..."

## Weak or Nonexistent Trap Check Time Requirements

*(Note: States listed with an asterisk (\*) next to them indicate more information is provided in the section, "Notes on State Trapping Regulations" on p. 88.)*

Even though numerous scientific studies indicate that frequent trap checks greatly reduce injuries to trapped animals, a number of states still allow animals to languish in traps for days. *Four states have no trap check time requirement at all.* The trap check time requirements for traps set on land and traps set in water in each state are detailed below.

**"Daily" trap check time for land sets:** Arizona, Arkansas, California, Colorado\*, Illinois, Kansas, Louisiana, Maine, Maryland, Massachusetts, Minnesota\*, Missouri, Nebraska, New Hampshire, North Carolina, South Carolina, Virginia, West Virginia, Wisconsin. (A "daily" requirement can extend the amount of time an animal suffers in a trap beyond 24 hours. For example, under a "daily" trap check requirement in Minnesota, a trapper may legally first tend his trap at 5 a.m. Monday and then not again until as late as 10 p.m. Tuesday. As a result an animal caught just after 5 a.m. on Monday would remain in the trap for almost 41 hours.)

**"Daily" trap check time for water sets:** Arizona, California, Colorado\*, Illinois, Kansas, Louisiana, Massachusetts, Missouri, New Hampshire, North Carolina, South Carolina, Virginia, West Virginia.

**24-hour trap check time for land sets:** Alabama, Connecticut, Delaware, Florida, Georgia, Indiana, Iowa, Kentucky, New Jersey, New Mexico\*, New York, Ohio, Oklahoma, Rhode Island, Vermont, Washington\*.

**24-hour trap check time for water sets:** Connecticut, Delaware, Florida, Georgia, Indiana, Kentucky, New Jersey, New Mexico\*, New York\*, Ohio, Oklahoma, Rhode Island.

**36-hour trap check time for land sets:** Mississippi, Pennsylvania, Tennessee, Texas.

**36-hour trap check time for water sets:** Maryland, Mississippi, Pennsylvania, Tennessee, Texas.

**48-hour trap check time for land sets:** Michigan (Zone 2 and 3)\*, Oregon\*, South Dakota, Utah.

**48-hour trap check time for water sets:** Michigan (Zone 2 and 3)\*, Nebraska, Oregon, South Dakota.

**72-hour trap check time for land sets:** Idaho\*, Michigan (Zone 1)\*, Wyoming.

**72-hour trap check time for water sets:** Alabama, Arkansas, Idaho, Maine\*, Michigan (Zone 1)\*, Minnesota\*, Vermont.

**96-hour trap check time for land sets:** Nevada (if traps are not set to kill).

**96-hour trap check time for water sets:** Utah, Wisconsin.

**NO trap check time for land sets:** Alaska, Montana\*, North Dakota\*.

**NO trap check time for water sets:** Alaska, Iowa, Montana\*, Nevada (if traps are set to kill), North Dakota\*, Wyoming.

## Lack of Trapper Safety Educational Courses

While Canada requires that all trappers take an educational trapping course before obtaining a license, in the U.S., only 21 states mandate trapper education. In many of these states, the requirement is limited to young or first-time trappers, thereby exempting long-time trappers.

**States that require a trapper education course:** Alabama, Arizona, California, Connecticut, Illinois, Iowa, Kansas, Maine, Maryland, Massachusetts, New Hampshire, New Jersey\*, New York, Ohio, Oregon, Pennsylvania, Utah, Vermont, Washington, West Virginia, Wisconsin.

**States that offer a trapper education course, but do not mandate taking a course to obtain a trapping license:** Delaware, Indiana, Montana, Rhode Island, South Carolina, Virginia.

**States that neither offer nor require a trapper education course:** Alaska, Arkansas, Colorado, Delaware, Florida, Georgia, Idaho, Indiana, Kentucky, Louisiana, Michigan, Minnesota, Mississippi, Missouri, Montana, Nebraska, Nevada, New Mexico, North Carolina, North Dakota, Oklahoma, Rhode Island, South Carolina, South Dakota, Tennessee, Texas, Virginia, Wyoming.

## Bidding Programs on State Lands

Four states currently operate programs that allow the highest bidder exclusive rights to trap on particular areas of state lands. Typically, interested persons can bid on particular parcels a few months before the trapping season begins. For example, since 1986, animal advocates in Connecticut have attempted to limit trapping in their state by submitting bids on states land allotments. In 1998, the animal advocates succeeded in securing 35 of 122 available tracts, a total of 47,000 acres, which they then posted off-limits to trapping. In response, the Connecticut Department of Environ-mental Protection (DEP) initiated a regulation change requiring that prospective bidders prove they had trapped furbearing animals during a minimum of four previous trapping seasons. On September 17, 1999, the animal advocates filed a lawsuit claiming that the regulation blocked their participation in the bidding process and was, therefore, discriminatory. As part of a settlement agreement reached in that case, the DEP Commissioner withdrew the 1999 invitation to bid and stipulated that the DEP would not require bidders to provide proof of actual harvesting until regulations or law permitted such a condition. The following season the DEP sought to require proof of trapping activity on the land after the bids had been awarded and the animal advocates sued to enjoin the trapping program. The plaintiffs argued that the permit conditions violated the 1999 settlement agreement. The court, however, refused to enjoin the program, finding that the balance of equities weighed heavily against shutting down the 2000 fur-bearing trapping season.

### States that currently have bidding programs:

**Connecticut:** "Trapping privileges shall, on some lands, be assigned on the basis of monetary bids for described units. All bids shall be on forms furnished by the state."

**Delaware:** "No trapping on state areas without a valid lease. Leases will be bid in September of each year."

**Indiana:** Trapping in the past has been available on state lands through a bidding program. Individuals must contact the particular trapping area for information on the rules and regulations (bidding programs are not being used for all areas because there are not enough interested trappers).

**Maryland:** Trapping on state lands (including wildlife management areas) is done through a bidding program. An application to enter the bid program is available in September at the Maryland Forest, Park and Wildlife Service Office.

## Drawing or Lottery Programs on State Lands

Many states allow interested individuals to enter a drawing or lottery for exclusive trapping rights on state lands. Typically, a current trapping license is all that is required.

Activists might consider obtaining a trapping license and entering drawings/lotteries to secure land away from trappers.

### The following states currently have a drawing or lottery program:

**California:** The department may limit the number of hunters, trappers, or other users on state lands and will issue entry permits on a first-come, first-served basis, or by a drawing to be held at a designated department office. Check with the Department of Fish and Game to determine whether they hold drawings to parcel out state lands. Since the passage of Proposition 4 in 1998, however, trapping with body-gripping traps is not allowed for recreational or commercial purposes.

**Idaho:** There is a drawing system in place for which applicants can submit their name for particular units of land on any of eight wildlife management areas. Applicants not drawn for

CULL OF THE WILD

their first choice unit will automatically be entered into a second choice drawing, provided their second choice has not been filled. Applications must be submitted in July.

**Illinois:** There are 32 parcels of state management areas that require a special permit to trap. These permits are allocated by a drawing held prior to the opening of the season. To enter, applicants must be present. Applicants must have either a current or previous year trapping license and a habitat stamp.

**Kentucky:** There is a drawing program for furbearer trapping from December 1 through 10 for water sets only for the Peal Wildlife Management Area.

**Montana:** A predetermined number of trapping licenses are selected through a random drawing for the Mt. Haggin Management Area, Freezeout Lake Wildlife Management Area, Canyon Ferry Wildlife Management Area, Upper Madison Beaver Management Area, Blackfoot-Clearwater Wildlife Management Area, and the Lake Helena Wildlife Management Area.

**Nevada:** Permits are issued through a drawing process and may designate specific trapping areas, dates or other restrictions for the following state wildlife management areas only: Overton, Key Pittman, W.E. Kirch, Scripps, Humboldt, Fernley, Mason Valley, and Alkali Lake wildlife management areas.

**New Hampshire:** There is a lottery program held in every even year. The permit to trap on a particular parcel of land is held for two continuous years.

**New York:** There is a quota system in place for Wetlands, Restricted Areas, and the State Wildlife Refuges. Trappers must provide their current trapper stamp number when applying for a permit. If, by one week prior to the starting date of trapping, the number of applicants exceeds a quota, a random drawing will be held to fill that quota.

**Ohio:** The division may accept bids for trapping rights on properties owned, controlled, or maintained by the division where limited access is maintained, or where animal removal is needed for management or research purposes.

**Utah:** There is a drawing program for trapping muskrats on Wildlife Management Areas.

**Wisconsin:** There is a drawing program for some of the Wildlife Management Areas and state lands. To determine the participating areas contact the Department of Natural Resources.

**Wyoming:** There are limited quota trapping permits for specific state lands. Permit holders are chosen by a random computer selection for a specific area.

## No Bidding/Drawing Program in Place

The majority of states currently have no bidding/drawing or lottery programs for trapping on state lands.

**States with no bidding/drawing/lottery programs:** Alabama, Alaska, Arkansas, Colorado (only live trapping is permitted on state lands), Iowa, Kansas, Louisiana, Maine, Massachusetts, Michigan, Minnesota, Mississippi, Missouri, Nebraska, New Jersey, New Mexico, New York, North Carolina, North Dakota, Ohio (presently, there is no bidding program in place for state lands and wildlife management areas in Ohio; however, the regulations allow for the division to accept bids for trapping rights on properties owned, controlled, or maintained by the division with limited access or where animal removal is needed for management or research purposes), Oklahoma, Oregon, Pennsylvania, Rhode Island, South Dakota, Tennessee, Texas, Vermont, Virginia, Washington.

## No Trapping Allowed on State Lands

Arizona, Florida, Georgia, Hawaii, South Carolina, West Virginia.

## State Regulations Pertaining to Trap Types

*(For more information about specific trap types, see Chapter Three. For states that have an asterisk (\*) next to them see "Notes on State Trapping Regulations" on p. 88 for more details).*

## Leghold Traps

Only eight states have banned or severely restricted the use of leghold traps, despite decades of legislative, legal, and administrative attempts to prohibit their use at the national, state, and local levels. Five states have banned leghold traps for commercial or recreational trapping through the initiative process (Arizona in 1994 on public lands, Colorado and Massachusetts in 1996, California in 1998, and Washington in 2000). Two states have banned or severely restricted the use of leghold traps through legislation: Rhode Island passed a law in 1977 banning the use of leghold traps except under permit for "animal damage control"; New Jersey followed suit in 1984, with stronger legislation banning the use, manufacture, sale, import, transport, and possession of steel-jaw leghold traps. Florida (1972) is the only state to have severely restricted the use of leghold traps through the administrative regulatory process (leghold traps are only allowed under permit for "animal damage control"). In addition, a number of states have implemented regulations restricting the maximum size of leghold traps allowed for use in land and/or water sets.

**States that have banned leghold traps for commercial or recreational trapping:** Arizona (on public lands only), California, Colorado, Florida, Massachusetts, New Jersey, Rhode Island, Washington.

**States that have restricted the size of leghold traps used in land sets:** Alabama, Alaska, Arizona, Arkansas, Connecticut, Delaware, Georgia, Illinois, Indiana, Iowa, Kentucky, Maryland, Minnesota, New Mexico, New York, North Carolina*, Ohio, Oklahoma, Oregon, Pennsylvania, South Carolina, Tennessee*, Virginia, Washington, West Virginia, Wisconsin.

**States that have restricted the size of leghold traps used in water sets:** Alaska, Arkansas, Connecticut, Illinois, Maryland, Minnesota, New Mexico, New York, North Carolina, Oklahoma, Oregon, Pennsylvania, South Carolina.

For more information about leghold traps and countries that have banned these devices see Chapter One. For additional information pertaining to state ballot initiatives and legislation banning or restricting the use of leghold traps and other body-gripping devices, see Chapter Seven.

## Leghold Traps with Teeth

Despite claims made by trapping and fur proponents that traps with teeth are no longer legal, nineteen states allow their use in land sets and twenty-six states do not prohibit their use for water sets.

**States that have not banned the use of teeth or serrations on leghold traps used in land sets:** Alaska, Delaware, Florida, Georgia, Idaho, Kansas, Maine, Michigan, Minnesota, Mississippi, Montana, Nevada, New Hampshire, North Dakota, South Carolina, South Dakota, Texas, Utah, Wyoming.

**States that have not banned the use of teeth or serrations on leghold traps used in water sets:** Same states listed above plus Alabama, Iowa, Kentucky, New Mexico, Tennessee, Virginia, Wisconsin.

## Padded Leghold Traps

Few states mandate the use of padded leghold traps instead of traditional leghold traps, even though wildlife managers are quick to claim that the padded leghold trap is more humane than the standard steel-jaw variety. (See Chapter Three for research findings regarding injuries caused by padded leghold traps.) In addition, a national survey indicated that less than 2% of traps owned by U.S. trappers are padded leghold traps.[3]

### States requiring that only padded leghold traps be used in land sets:

**Arizona:** Padded or offset jaws required on private lands (trapping on public lands with body-gripping traps is banned).

**California:** Although California banned leghold traps in 1998, padded leghold traps can still be used by "federal, state, county, or municipal government employees or their duly authorized agents in the extraordinary case where the otherwise prohibited padded-jaw leghold trap is the only method available to protect human health or safety." (See Proposition 4 update in Chapter 7.)

**Colorado:** Banned leghold traps in 1996; however, padded leghold traps may be used under a limited exemption for "animal damage control purposes."

**Connecticut:** Restrictions on use of padded leghold traps: "1) Opening greater than 51 5/16" is prohibited, except that traps with an opening of up to 7½" may be set for beaver in waters frequented by beaver; 2) May only be used in the burrow of a wild animal or below the surface of the water in a pond, lake, stream, spring hole, or tidal water."

**Florida:** Permits may be issued to trap nuisance animals with padded leghold traps.

**Tennessee:** "Cushion-hold traps ... are the only steel traps legal for trapping in the open and on top of the ground." Steel-jaw leghold traps can be used only in water and inside burrows and holes.

**Washington:** Although Washington banned leghold traps in 2000, padded leghold traps can still be used by permit for human health/safety, endangered species protection, wildlife research, and animal damage control.

**States requiring that only padded leghold traps be used in water sets (the same restrictions that apply to padded leghold traps used on land may aply to water sets; see "padded leghold traps on land"):** Arizona (or offset jaws), California, Colorado, Florida, Washington.

## Offset Leghold Traps

A number of states mandate the use of offset jaws

when standard steel-jaw leghold traps are used in water or land sets. The small gap between the jaws (usually 3/16") ostensibly allows small non-target animals to escape and reduces trap injuries in larger animals. This claim has not been substantiated by research (see Chapter Three for details).

### *States that require offset leghold traps used in land sets:*

**Arizona:** Offset or padded jaws required on private lands (trapping on public lands with body-gripping traps is banned).

**Arkansas:** "To be used on land ... all leghold traps with a jaw spread greater than 5 inches must have offset jaws."

**Indiana:** "It is illegal to take any furbearing animal with leg hold traps size No. 3 or larger without offset jaws unless the trap is completely covered in water."

**Nevada:** "All steel leg hold traps size No. 2 or larger or with an outside jaw spread of 5 ½ inches or larger used in the taking of any wildlife must have lugs, spaces or similar devices permanently attached so as to maintain a minimum trap opening of three-sixteenths of one inch."

**New Mexico:** "All foot-hold traps must be off-set."

**North Carolina:** Leghold traps must be "horizontally offset with closed jaw of at least 3/16 inch for a trap with a jaw spread of more than 5 ½ inches ... This provision does not apply if the trap is set in the water with a quick-drown type set."

**Oregon:** It is illegal to use "a No. 3 or larger leghold trap not having a jaw spacing of at least 3/16 of one inch when the trap is sprung ... and when the set is not capable of drowning the trapped animal."

**Utah:** "All long spring, jump, or coil-spring traps, except rubber-padded jaw traps, that are not completely submerged under water when set must have spacers on the jaws which leave an opening of at least 3/16 of an inch when the jaw is closed."

### States that require offset leghold traps used in water sets:

Arizona (padded or offset jaws required on private lands), Nevada (only 5 ½" jaw spread or larger), New Mexico.

## Conibear Traps

Also known as kill traps, Conibear traps are restricted in a number of states because of the dangers posed to non-target animals, particularly domestic dogs and cats.

In its 1998 Trapping Regulations publication, Wisconsin's Department of Natural Resources advises trappers: "Consider all placement to avoid contact with humans and domestic animals. We strongly encourage the use of cubbys [a trap enclosure which permits only smaller animals to enter] and elevated sets when using Conibear type traps on dry land. Future use of Conibear type traps depends on it!" Yet, these are only recommendations.

**States that prohibit the use of Conibear traps on land:** Connecticut, Florida (also prohibited in water), Maryland, New Jersey, Oklahoma, Pennsylvania, South Carolina, South Dakota, West Virginia.

**States that restrict the size of Conibear traps used in land sets:** Alabama, Alaska, Arizona, Arkansas, California, Delaware, Georgia, Illinois, Iowa, Kansas, Kentucky, Maine, Minnesota, Missouri, Nebraska, New Hampshire, New York, North Carolina, North Dakota, Ohio, Oregon, Rhode Island, Tennessee, Texas, Vermont, Virginia, Washington, Wisconsin.

**States that restrict the size of Conibear traps used in water sets:** Alaska, Arkansas, Connecticut, Delaware, Illinois, New Jersey, North Carolina, Pennsylvania, Rhode Island, Tennessee.

### States with specific restrictions on the use of Conibear traps:

**Arizona:** Only permits the use of Conibear 110 traps (5" jaw spread) on private lands (trapping on public lands with body-gripping traps is banned).

**California:** Banned Conibear traps and other body-gripping devices for commercial and recreational trapping; however, Conibear traps can still be used in California for animal damage control purposes.

**Colorado:** Voters banned the use of body-gripping traps, including Conibears in 1996; however, Conibear traps may still be used under specified limited exemptions.

**Massachusetts:** Conibears may only be used with a special permit for animal damage control after voters banned the use of body-gripping traps in 1996.

**Oklahoma:** Only allows the use of Conibear traps by trappers who obtain a 30-day permit specifically for beaver trapping.

**Washington:** Banned Conibear traps and other body-gripping devices for commercial and recreational trapping; however, Conibear traps can still be used in Washington for human health/safety, endangered species protection, wildlife research, and animal damage control.

## Snares

Because of the indiscriminate and lethal nature of strangulation neck and body snares, a number of states have banned or restricted their use. Some states have specific regulations pertaining to snare use, such as the requirement of "locks" or "stops" that prevent the snare from closing smaller than a set diameter, "breakaway" devices that ostensibly allow animals over a certain weight to escape, limits on the snare loop size, and the distance snares can be set off the ground or from public roads or residences (see chart and notes on State Trapping Regulations at the end of this chapter for details). Some states have very specific regulations pertaining to snares. Maryland, for example, requires that snares be "designed or set with the intent of capturing an animal by the neck" (to strangle the animal). Few states differentiate between neck, body, and foot (or "leg") snares.

**States that have banned snares:** Arizona, Connecticut, Massachusetts, New York, Oklahoma, Rhode Island, Vermont.

**States in which snares are explicitly banned for use on land (but allowed in water sets):** Illinois, Michigan, Missouri, New Hampshire, North Carolina, Pennsylvania, South Carolina, Wisconsin.

### Some specific state restrictions on the use of snares:

**Alabama:** No neck/body snares allowed on land, except powered foot snares with a maximum loop of 5 ½ inches.

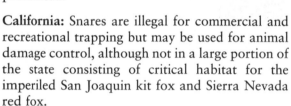

**Arkansas:** "Only non-locking snares may be used on land. No land snare may be placed in a public road right-of-way nor touch a fence when fully extended. Spring-loaded snares are prohibited."

**California:** Snares are illegal for commercial and recreational trapping but may be used for animal damage control, although not in a large portion of the state consisting of critical habitat for the imperiled San Joaquin kit fox and Sierra Nevada red fox.

**Colorado:** Snares can only be used for animal damage control under a one-time-per-year-per-landowner 30-day requested exemption, and/or for the "protection of human health and safety (by state, federal, and county officials and/or authorized contractors)."

**Georgia:** "Snares may be used for trapping beaver provided that snares are set in water or on land within 10 feet of water. All snares must be marked with the trapper's name or identification number."

**Iowa:** "No person shall set or maintain any snare in any public road or right of way ... Snares cannot be attached to a drag. All snares must have a functional deer lock ..."

**Kansas:** "Snares are prohibited for use in dryland sets within 50 feet of the outside edge of a public road or within five feet of a fence bordering a public road." (Landowners are exempt.) "Snares must be tagged with the user's name and address."

**Maine:** Allows snares for beaver trapping in water sets, neck-snaring of coyotes for damage control, and leg-snaring of black bears.

**Maryland:** Snares must be "designed to set with the intent of capturing an animal by the neck."

**Michigan:** Only allows snares for beaver and river otter trapping.

**Minnesota:** "Bobcats and bears cannot be taken with snares ... Snare cable or wire may not have a diameter exceeding ⅛"... Snares may not be used with spring poles ..."

**Nebraska:** "During upland game bird seasons, it is unlawful to use snares on any land owned or controlled by the Game and Parks Commission, on U.S. Fish and Wildlife Service waterfowl production areas, or on U.S. Army Corps of Engineers lands at Harland County Reservoir."

**New Hampshire:** Only allows snares for beaver and river otter trapping.

**North Carolina:** Only allows snares for beaver trapping in water sets.

**Ohio:** Snares must have a relaxing lock and stop, may not by used in public hunting areas, and may not be spring-loaded or mechanical.

**Pennsylvania:** A trapper may set up to 10 snares submerged underwater for beaver. "A metal ferrule shall be crimped on the cable to prevent the snare loop from closing to a circumference less than 20 inches." The snare may not be spring-activated.

**South Carolina:** Allows the use of snares for beaver trapping in water sets with a depredation permit.

**South Dakota:** "Snares must have a mechanical lock, swivel device on the anchor end and stop device ... attaching snares to a drag is prohibited."

**Tennessee:** "Spring activated snares are prohibited."

**Washington:** Snares are illegal for commercial and recreational trapping but may be used by permit for human health/safety, endangered species protection, wildlife research, and animal damage control.

**West Virginia:** Neck and body-gripping snares are illegal in land sets, while foot snares of 6 ½" in diameter are legal on land.

**Wisconsin:** Cable length of snare may not exceed five feet; must be constructed of galvanized aircraft cable; cable or wire diameter may not exceed ⅛ inch; must have a mechanical lock and swivel; must be non-spring activated.

## Pole Traps

Pole traps generally consist of leghold traps (sometimes snares or Conibear traps are used) set above the ground and attached to a pole, log, or tree branch. When an animal becomes trapped, it will dangle in the air, unable to gnaw or twist its caught appendage free of the trap, thereby preventing the loss of a pelt for the trapper. Pole traps are legal in most states.

The use of pole traps has been the subject of controversy for a number of years, primarily because of the threat such traps pose to eagles, other raptors, and non-target animals. As a result, several states have outlawed pole traps if they are set in a way that may capture birds. Some states, such as New York, ban the use of all pole traps by prohibiting the setting of traps "in such a manner that causes a captured animal to be suspended in the air." Other states ban pole traps explicitly or exclude them from their lists of legal traps. Most states are silent on the use of these traps, which generally indicates that they can legally be used.

**States that have banned pole traps only if set for birds:** Maine, South Dakota (raptors only), Wisconsin.

**States that have banned pole traps (either explicitly or by exclusion from an enumerated list of legal trap types):** Alabama, California, Florida, Massachusetts, Minnesota*, New Jersey, New York, North Carolina, Pennsylvania, Rhode Island, Tennessee, Washington, West Virginia.

## Deadfall Traps

A deadfall trap is a kill trap consisting of a baited trigger attached to a heavy object, such as a rock or tree limb, that falls and kills the animal pulling on the trigger. Though not commonly used today, the deadfall trap is still explicitly allowed in some states. Most states are silent on the use of deadfalls, which generally indicates that they can legally be used.

**States that have banned deadfall traps (either explicitly or by exclusion from enumerated list of legal trap types):** Arkansas, Delaware, Illinois, Maine, Maryland, Massachusetts, Michigan, Missouri, Ohio, Oklahoma, Pennsylvania, South Carolina, Tennessee, Texas, Virginia, West Virginia.

**States that explicitly allow deadfall traps:** Alabama, California, Connecticut, Idaho, Kansas, Kentucky, New York.

## Pitfall Traps

A pitfall trap is a restraining trap consisting of a concealed pit or dugout hole large enough to hold an animal. The animal is attracted to the baited trap and falls into the hole where it is unable to escape. Not commonly used today, pitfall traps are still legal in a number of states. A few states explicitly ban their use, while other states have made them illegal by excluding pitfalls from the list of permitted traps. Most states are silent on the use of pitfalls, which generally indicates that they can legally be used.

**States that have banned pitfall traps (either explicitly or by exclusion from enumerated list of legal trap types):** Alaska, Arkansas, Delaware, Illinois, Kentucky, Maine, Maryland, Massachusetts, Michigan, Missouri, Oklahoma, Texas.

**States that explicitly allow pitfall traps:** Arizona (five-gallon size or smaller), Idaho (dirt hole must be covered if baited).

## Colony Traps
## (Also Known as Submarine Traps)

A colony trap is a cage or box trap set in water to capture and drown multiple animals. Colony traps are explicitly banned in a number of states. Most states are silent on their use, which generally indicates that they can legally be used.

**States that have banned the use of colony traps:** Illinois, Delaware, Massachusetts, Missouri, New York, Pennsylvania, Wisconsin.

**States that explicitly allow the use of colony traps:** Colorado, Iowa (muskrats only), Michigan (muskrats only), South Dakota.

NOTES

1. International Association of Fish and Wildlife Agencies (IAFWA) Fur Resources Technical Committee. "Ownership and Use of Traps by Trappers in the United States in 1992." Fur Resources Technical Committee of the International Fish and Wildlife Agencies and the Gallup Organization, Washington, D.C. 1993.

2. T. G. Barnes. "State Agency Oversight of the Nuisance Wildlife Control Industry." *Wildlife Society Bulletin* 25 (1997): 185–188.

3 IAFWA. "Ownership and Use of Traps."

## TABLE 5.1

### U.S. State Trapping Regulations (See p. 87 for key to codes)

| State | Source of Trapping Data | Trapper Report Required | Fur Dealer Report Required | Leghold Permitted (Land) | Teeth Allowed (Land) | Leghold Permitted (Water) | Teeth Allowed (Water) | Max Size Leghold (Land) | Max Size Leghold (Water) | Conibear Permitted (Land) | Conibear Permitted (Water) | Max Size Conibear (Land) | Max Size Conibear (Water) | Snares Permitted (Land) | Snares Permitted (Water) | Max Size Snare (Land) | Max Size Snare (Water) | Trap Check Time (Land) | Trap Check Time (Water) | Trap ID Required | Educational Course Required | Bait Distance From Trap | Bobcat Trapping | Otter Trapping |
|---|---|---|---|---|---|---|---|---|---|---|---|---|---|---|---|---|---|---|---|---|---|---|---|---|
| Alabama | FR | Y | Y | Y | N | N/S | N/S | 6" | N/S | Y | N/S | 5" | N/S | Y* | N/S | 5 ½" | N/S | 24 | 72 | Y | Y | 25' | Y(N/L) | Y(N/L) |
| Alaska | PS/FR | N | Y | Y | Y | Y | Y | 9" | 9" | Y | Y | 11" | 11" | Y | Y | N/S | N/S | None | None | N | N | N/S | Y(N/L) | Y |
| Arizona | TR/FR | Y | Y | Y* | N | Y* | N | 6 ½" | N/S | Y* | N/S | 5" | N/S | N | N | N/A | N/A | Daily | Daily | Y | Y | 30' | Y | N |
| Arkansas | FR | N | Y | Y* | N | Y* | N | 5 ⅝" | 8 ½" | Y | Y* | 6" | 10" | Y* | Y* | 12" | N/S | Daily | 72 | Y | N | 20' | Y(N/L) | Y(N/L) |
| California | TR/FR | Y | Y | N* | N | N* | N | N/A | N/A | Y* | Y* | 8"* | N/S | Y* | Y* | N/S | N/S | Daily | Daily | Y | Y | 30' | Y(N/L) | N |
| Colorado | TS | N | N | Y3* | N | Y3* | N | N/S* | N/S* | Y3* | Y3* | N/S* | N/S* | Y3* | Y3 | 8-10"* | N/S* | Daily* | Daily* | N/S | N | 30' | Y | Y(8) |
| Connecticut | TS/PS | N | N | Y2* | N | Y* | N | 5 15/16" | 7 ½"* | N | Y* | N/A | 10"* | N | N | N/A | N/A | 24 | 24 | Y | N2 | N/S | N | Y(N/L) |
| Delaware | TS/FS | N | N | Y3* | N/S | Y3* | N/S | No.1 ½ | N/S | Y | Y | 5" | 5" | Y | N/S | N/S | N/S | 24 | 24 | Y | N2 | N/S | N | Y(N/L) |
| Florida | FR | N | N | Y | N/S | Y3* | N/S | N/S | N/S | N | N | N/A | N/A | Y | Y | N/S | N/S | 24 | 24 | N/S | N | N/S | Y | Y |
| Georgia | TR/FR | Y | Y | Y | N/S | Y* | N/S | 5 ¾" | N/S | Y* | Y* | 9 ½" | N/S | Y* | Y | N/S | N/S | 24 | 24 | Y | N | N/S | Y | Y |
| Hawaii | NO COMMERCIAL OR RECREATIONAL TRAPPING ALLOWED | | | | | | | | | | | | | | | | | | | | | | | |
| Idaho | TR | Y | N | Y | Y | Y | Y | N/S | N/S | Y | Y | N/S | N/S | Y | Y | N/S | N/S | 72* | 72 | Y | N | 30' | Y | N |
| Illinois | TS/FR | N | Y | Y | N | Y | N | 6 ½" | 7 ½" | Y | Y | 7" | 10" | N | Y | N/A | 15" | Daily | Daily | Y | Y | 30' | N | N |
| Indiana | TS/FR | N | Y | Y* | N | Y | N | No.3* | N/S | Y | Y | 7 ½" | N/S | Y* | Y | 15"* | N/S | 24 | 24 | N/S | Y | N/S | N | N |
| Iowa | FR | N | Y | Y | N | Y | Y | 7" | N/S | Y* | Y | 8" | N/S | Y* | Y | 11" | N/S | 24 | N/S | Y | Y | 20' | Y(N/L) | N |
| Kansas | TS | N | N | Y | N/S | Y | N/S | N/S | N/S | Y | Y | 8" | N/S | Y* | Y | N/S | N/S | Daily | Daily | Y | Y | N/S | Y(N/L) | N |
| Kentucky | TS/FR | N | Y | Y* | N | Y | N/S | 6"* | N/S | Y | Y | 220 | N/S | Y | Y | N/S | N/S | 24 | 24 | Y | Y | N/S | Y(2) | N |
| Louisiana | FS | N | Y | Y | N | Y | N | N/S | N/S | Y | Y | N/S | N/S | Y* | Y | N/S | N/S | Daily | Daily | N/S | N | N/S | Y(N/L) | Y |
| Maine | PS/FR | N | Y | Y | Y | Y* | Y | N/S | N/S | Y | Y | 8"* | N/S | Y* | Y* | N/S | N/S | Daily* | 72* | Y | Y | N/S | Y(N/L) | Y(N/L) |
| Maryland | FR | N | Y | Y* | N | Y | N | 5 ¾" | 7 ¼" | N | Y* | N/A | N/S | Y* | Y* | N/S | N/S | Daily | 36 | N/S | Y | N/S | N | Y(5) |

| State | Source of Trapping Data | Trapper Report Required | Fur Dealer Report Required | Leghold Permitted (Land) | Teeth Allowed (Land) | Leghold Permitted (Water) | Teeth Allowed (Water) | Max Size Leghold (Land) | Max Size Leghold (Water) | Conibear Permitted (Land) | Conibear Permitted (Water) | Max Size Conibear (Land) | Max Size Conibear (Water) | Snares Permitted (Land) | Snares Permitted (Water) | Max Size Snare (Land) | Max Size Snare (Water) | Trap Check Time (Land) | Trap Check Time (Water) | Trap ID Required | Educational Course Required | Visible Bait Distance from Trap | Bobcat Trapping | Otter Trapping |
|---|---|---|---|---|---|---|---|---|---|---|---|---|---|---|---|---|---|---|---|---|---|---|---|---|
| Massachusetts | FR/PS | N | Y | Y* | N | Y* | N | N/A | N/A | Y3* | Y3* | N/S | N/S | Y* | Y* | N/A | N/A | Daily | Daily | Y | Y | N/S | Y(N/L) | Y(N/L) |
| Michigan | TS | N | Y | Y* | N/S | Y | N/S | N/S | N/S | Y* | Y | N/S* | N/S | N | Y* | N/A | N/S | 72/48* | 72/48* | Y | N | N/S* | Y(3) | Y(3) |
| Minnesota | TS/FR/PS | N | Y | Y | N/S | Y | N/S | 8¾" | 8¾" | Y | Y | 7½" | N/S* | Y* | Y | 10" | 10" | Daily* | 72 | Y | N | 20' | Y(5) | Y(4-8) |
| Mississippi | TR/FR | Y | Y | N/S | N/S | N/S | N/S | N/S | N/S | N/S | N/S | N/S | N/S | N/S | N/S | N/S | N/S | 36 | 36 | Y | N | N/S* | Y(N/L) | Y(N/L) |
| Missouri | FR/PS | N | Y | Y | N | Y | N | N/S | N/S | Y* | Y | 5" | N/S | N | Y | N/S | 15" | Daily | Daily | Y | N | N/S | Y(N/L) | Y(N/L) |
| Montana | TS/PS | N | N | Y | N/S | Y | N/S | N/S | N/S | Y | Y* | N/S | N/S | Y* | Y | N/S | N/S | None* | None* | Y | N2 | 30' | Y(7-N/L) | Y(1) |
| Nebraska | TS | N | N | Y* | N | Y | N | N/S* | N/S | Y* | Y* | 8"* | N/S | Y | Y | N/S | N/S | Daily | 48 | Y | N | 30' | Y | N |
| Nevada | TS/PS | N | N | Y* | N/S | Y | N/S | N/S* | N/S | Y | Y | N/S | N/S | Y* | Y | N/S | N/S | 96 | None | N | N | 30' | Y | Y |
| New Hampshire | TR/FR | Y | Y | Y* | N/S | Y | N/S | N/S | N/S | Y* | Y | 220* | N/S | N | Y* | N/S | N/S | Daily | Daily* | Y | Y | N/S | N | Y(10) |
| New Jersey | TS/PS | N | Y | N | N/A | N | N/A | N/A | N/A | N | Y* | N/A | 10"* | Y* | Y* | 8" | N/S | 24 | 24 | Y | Y* | 30'* | N | Y(1) |
| New Mexico | FR | N | Y | Y* | N | Y* | N/S | 6½" | 12" | Y* | Y | N/S | N/S | Y* | Y | N/S | N/S | 24 | 24 | Y | N | 25'* | Y(N/L) | N |
| New York | TS/PS | N | Y | Y* | N | Y | N | 5¾" | 7¼" | Y* | Y | 7½" | N/S* | Y* | Y* | N/A | N/A | 24* | 24* | Y | Y | N/S | Y(N/L) | Y(N/L) |
| North Carolina | FR | N | Y | Y | N | Y | N | 7½"* | 7½" | Y | Y | 7½" | 330 | N* | N | N/S | N/S | Daily | Daily | Y | Y | N/S | Y | Y |
| North Dakota | TS/FR | N | Y | Y | N/S | Y | N/S | N/S | N/S | Y | Y | 8"* | N/S | Y | Y* | 12" | N/S | None* | None* | Y* | N | 25' | Y | N |
| Ohio | FR | N | Y | Y* | N | Y* | N | 5⅝" | N/S | Y | Y* | 5" | N/S | Y* | Y* | 15" | 15" | 24 | 24 | Y | Y | * | Y | Y |
| Oklahoma | FR | N | Y | Y | N | Y | N | 8" | 8" | N | Y | N/A | N/S* | N | N | N/A | N/A | 24 | 24 | Y | N | N/S | Y(20) | N |
| Oregon | TR/PS | Y | N | Y | N | Y | N | 9" | 9"* | Y* | Y | 9" | N/S | Y | N | N/S | N/S | 48* | 48 | Y | Y | 15'* | Y | Y(5-N/L) |
| Pennsylvania | TS/FR | N | Y | Y | N | Y | N | 6½" | 6½" | N | Y | N/A | 10"* | N | Y | N/A | N/A | 36 | 36 | Y | N | N/S* | N | N |
| Rhode Island | TR | Y | N | Y3* | N/A | Y3* | N/A | N/A | N/A | Y* | Y* | 6½" | 8" | N | Y3* | N/A | N/A | 24 | 24 | Y | N2 | N/S | N | N |
| South Carolina | TR/FR/PS | Y | Y | Y* | N/S | Y* | N/S | No. 2 | No. 3 | N | Y | N/A | N/S | Y* | Y* | N/S* | N/S* | Daily | Daily | Y | N2 | N/S | Y(N/L) | Y(N/L) |
| South Dakota | FR | N | N | Y* | N/S | Y | N/S | No. 4* | N/S | N | Y | N | N/A | Y* | Y | N/S* | N/S* | 48 | 48 | N/S | N | 30' | Y | Y |
| Tennessee | FR | N | Y | Y* | N | Y | N/S | N/S | N/S | Y | Y | 10" | 10" | Y* | Y | N/S | N/S | 36 | 36 | Y | N | N/S | Y(N/L) | Y(N/L) |
| Texas | FR | N | Y | Y* | N/S | Y | N/S | N/S | N/S | Y | Y | 10" | N/S | Y | Y | N/S | N/S | 36 | 36 | N/S | N | N/S | Y | Y(N/L) |

# TABLE 5.1 (CONTINUED)
## U.S. State Trapping Regulations

| State | Source of Trapping Data | Trapper Report Required | Fur Dealer Report Required | Leghold Permitted (Land) | Teeth Allowed (Land) | Leghold Permitted (Water) | Teeth Allowed (Water) | Max Size Leghold (Land) | Max Size Leghold (Water) | Conibear Permitted (Land) | Conibear Permitted (Water) | Max Size Conibear (Land) | Max Size Conibear (Water) | Snares Permitted (Land) | Snares Permitted (Water) | Max Size Snare (Land) | Max Size Snare (Water) | Trap Check Time (Land) | Trap Check Time (Water) | Trap ID Required | Educational Course Required | Visible Bait Distance From Trap | Bobcat Trapping | Otter Trapping |
|---|---|---|---|---|---|---|---|---|---|---|---|---|---|---|---|---|---|---|---|---|---|---|---|---|
| Utah | TS/PS | N | N | Y* | N/S | Y | N/S | N/S* | N/S | Y* | Y | N/S | N/S | Y | Y | N/S | N/S | 48 | 96 | Y | Y | 30' | Y(7) | N |
| Vermont | TR/FR/PS | Y | Y | Y | N | Y | N | N/S | N/S | Y | Y | 8" | N/S | N | N | N/A | N/A | 24 | 72 | Y | Y | N/S | Y(N/L) | Y(N/L) |
| Virginia | FR/PS | N | Y | Y | N | Y | N/S | 6½" | N/A | Y* | Y | 7½"* | N/S | Y* | N/S | <12"* | N/S | Daily | Daily | Y | N2 | N/S | Y(12)* | Y(N/L) |
| Washington | TR/PS | Y | N | Y* | N | Y* | N | 7½" | * | N | Y | 7½"* | N/S | Y* | Y* | 6½" | N/S | 24 | 24 | Y | Y | 30' | Y(N/L) | Y(6-N/L) |
| West Virginia | FR | N | Y | Y | N | Y | N | 6½" | N/S* | N | Y | N/A | N/S | Y* | Y | 6½" | N/S | Daily | Daily | Y | Y | N/S | Y(2) | N |
| Wisconsin | TS/PS | Y | Y | Y | N | Y | Y | 8" | N/S | Y* | Y* | 7"* | N/S | Y* | Y* | N/S | N/S | Daily | 96 | Y | Y | 25' | Y(1) | Y(1) |
| Wyoming | TS/FR | N | Y | Y | N/S | Y | N/S | N/S | N/S | Y | Y | N/S | N/S | Y | Y | N/S | N/S | 72 | None | Y* | N | N/S | Y(N/L) | N |

**Codes:**

N/A = Not Applicable
N/L = No Limit
N/S = Not Specified (Unless otherwise stated, if a state does not indicate that a particular trap is illegal, then one can assume it is legal to use in that state.)
Y1 = Written permission required to trap on private land
N2 = Educational course is not required, but is available
* = See state notes beginning on page 88 for specific regulations
Y2* = Only padded leghold traps allowed for use on land; see state notes for specific regulations
Y3* = Allowed under permit only; see state notes for specific regulations
TR = Mandatory Trapping Report
FR = Mandatory Fur Dealer Report
TS = Random Trapper Mail Survey (voluntary)
FS = Random Fur Dealer Report (voluntary)
PS = Pelt Sealing (tag attached to the pelt or unskinned animal)

Numbers in parentheses under Bobcat and Otter Trapping () indicate seasonal bag limits (max. number of animals that can be trapped in a season.)

**Note:** Trap sizes provided reflect state regulations. Some states give trap size in inches between trap jaws; other states give trap size as indicated. Please use following conversions:

Size 110 Conibear = 5 inches
Size 160 Conibear = 6 inches
Size 220 Conibear = 7 inches
Size 280 Conibear = 8 inches
Size 330 Conibear = 9 to 12 inches

# NOTES ON STATE TRAPPING REGULATIONS

These notes work in conjunction with the previous chart on state trapping regulations and provide more detailed information about specific regulations. State trapping regulations may vary from one year to another. The information provided here is based upon regulations available at the time of publication from state fish and wildlife agencies. Only selected regulations have been included in the chart and notes; contact your state wildlife agency for complete and updated information.

## ALABAMA

### Three Primary Trapped Species (96/97)

Muskrat, raccoon, beaver

### Traps

No neck/body snares allowed on land, except powered foot snares with a maximum loop of 5 ½ inches.

### Trap Placement

"It shall be illegal to set a trap on top of a post or stake elevated above ground level."

"No person using traps for the purpose of taking or catching fur-bearing animals shall be permitted to set or have set in any one day more than 150 traps."

### Misc.

■ "Any person trapping fur-bearing animals in the State of Alabama must carry with him a choke stick while running traps. When legally trapped fur-bearing animals are dispatched with a firearm, only standard .22 caliber rimfire firearms may be used."

## ALASKA

### Three Primary Trapped Species (96/97)

Beaver, marten, otter (Note: These three species are the top three trapped species that are "sealed" (tagged and registered with the state wildlife agency). Most trapped species in Alaska are not sealed or tracked. Species including coyote, fox, and muskrat may be caught in greater numbers than sealed species, but, since no records are kept, one cannot accurately report the primary trapped species in Alaska.

### Traps

**Conibear** "YOU MAY NOT take furbearers with … a conventional steel trap with an inside jaw spread over 9 inches, except that the 'Conibear' style trap with a jaw spread of less than 11 inches may be used."

### Misc.

■ "YOU MAY NOT use poisons, except with written permission from the Board of Game."

■ "YOU MAY NOT disturb or destroy beaver houses or any furbearer den (except that muskrat pushups or feeding houses may be disturbed in the course of trapping)."

■ An Alaska resident under the age of 16 does not need a trapping license to trap furbearers.

■ "Before you may buy, sell, or barter beaver, land otter, lynx, wolf, or wolverine taken anywhere in the state, as well as marten trapped in Units 1-7, 13E, 14, 15 and 16, the hide must be sealed … You may sell any part of an animal taken under a trapping license."

■ "You may obtain a permit from the department to capture and possess, but not export from Alaska, furbearers for fur farming purposes …The purpose of this permit is to allow existing resident fur farmers to improve their genetic stock; it is not intended to allow individuals to start new fur farms from wild stock."

# ARIZONA

A state ballot initiative banning body-gripping traps on public lands passed in 1994 by a margin of 59% to 41% (the regulations provided below reflect the ballot initiative).

## Three Primary Trapped Species (97/98)

Coyote, fox, bobcat

## Traps

A 1994 ballot initiative banned trapping with body-gripping traps on public lands (82% of state). On private lands, traps allowed are padded or rubber-jawed, or unpadded jaws permanently offset to minimum of ³⁄₁₆ inch.

**Land sets** (on private lands only): "Any trap with a jaw spread exceeding six and one-half inches" is illegal. In addition, it is unlawful to "use a body-gripping or other instant kill trap with an open jaw spread exceeding five inches for any land set."

**Leghold** (allowed on private lands only) "The only traps lawful for use are commercially manufactured padded or rubber-jawed traps and traps with unpadded jaws permanently offset to a minimum of ³⁄₁₆ inch ... An anchor chain shall be attached to the trap frame within one-half inch of the center of the trap ... An anchor chain longer than twelve inches shall be equipped with swivels at each end and at least one swivel positioned near the middle of the anchor chain; an anchor chain twelve inches or shorter shall contain at least two swivels, one at each end ... The anchor chain shall be equipped with a shock-absorbing spring requiring less than forty pounds of force to extend or open the spring ... the trap shall be used with a device to allow for pan tension adjustment."

**Other** Pitfall traps are legal: 5-gallon size max.

## Trap Placement

*IT IS UNLAWFUL TO:*

- "Set a trap within one-half mile of any of the following areas developed for public use: a boat launching area, picnic area, camping area, or roadside rest area."

- "Set a trap within 100 yards of any interstate highway or any other highway maintained by the Arizona Department of Transportation, within 25 yards of any other road ... or within 50 feet of any trail maintained for public use by a government agency."

## Landowner Permission

The trapper must obtain permission from the owner or resident to "set a trap within one-half mile of any occupied residence or building."

## Misc.

- "A trapper shall release without additional injury all animals that cannot lawfully be taken by trap. Every trapper shall possess while in the field a device designed or manufactured to restrain trapped animals so that they can be removed from the traps when their release is required by this rule."

# ARKANSAS

## Three Primary Trapped Species (97/98)

Raccoon, beaver, opossum

## Traps

**Leghold** "To be used on land, leghold traps must have a jaw spread no greater than 5 ⅝ inches, and all leghold traps with a jaw spread greater than 5 inches must have offset jaws ... For a legal water set with a leghold trap, the trap must be entirely submerged."

**Conibear** "For land sets, the maximum jaw spread for Conibear-type traps is six inches. For water sets, the maximum jaw spread is 10 inches and the trap's jaw opening, when the trap is set, must be at least half-submerged."

**Snare** "Snares must be constructed of braided cable with a 12-inch (or smaller) loop with the bottom of the loop no more than 10 inches off the ground. Snares set farther than 20 feet from water must a have a "deer stop" that prevents the snare loop from closing smaller than 2½ inches. Only non-locking snares may be used on land. No land snare may be placed in a public road right-of-way nor touch a fence when fully extended. Spring-loaded leg snares are prohibited."

**Other** "Box traps may be used for trapping rabbits with interior dimensions no larger than eight inches in width and 10 inches in height. Licensed fur takers may use box traps of any size during furbearer season."

## Misc.

- "Beavers causing damage may be trapped the entire year with water sets and snares."

- "To import, sell, barter or trade live coyotes or foxes, a "Live Fox and Coyote Permit" must be purchased ... Any fox or coyote, whether imported or originating from Arkansas, requires a health certificate issued not more than 10 days before shipment."

- "Nuisance animals may also be removed by landowners (or their designees) at any time. Trapping in towns must be in compliance with municipal ordinances. Live trapped wildlife must be released unharmed outside the municipality's boundaries within 24 hours except nuisance furbearers are not required to be released alive. Live traps must have the trapper's name and address or his vehicle operator's license number or the current vehicle license number registered to the trap-user."

## CALIFORNIA

A state ballot initiative banning body-gripping traps for commercial and recre-

ational trapping passed in 1998 by a margin of 58% to 42% (the regulations provided below reflect the ballot initiative). Statute reads: "It is unlawful for any person to trap for the purposes of recreation or commerce in fur any fur-bearing mammal or nongame mammal with any body-gripping trap. A body-gripping trap is one that grips the mammal's body or body part, including but not limited to, steel-jawed leghold traps, padded-jaw leghold traps, Conibear traps, and snares. Cage and box traps, nets, suitcase-type live beaver traps, and common rat and mouse traps shall not be considered body-gripping traps." In addition, the statute makes it "unlawful for any person to buy, sell, barter ... the raw fur ... of any fur-bearing mammal or nongame mammal that was trapped in this state, with a body-gripping trap ..." Persons may still purchase a trapping license in California and trap animals for their fur with non body-gripping traps.

### Three Primary Trapped Species (97/98)

Muskrat, gray fox, coyote

### Traps

**Leghold** "It is unlawful for any person, including an employee of the federal, state, county, or municipal government, to use or authorize the use of any steel-jawed leghold trap, padded or otherwise, to capture any game mammal, fur-bearing mammal, nongame mammal, protected mammal, or any dog or cat ... The prohibition in this sub-division does not apply to federal, state, county, or municipal government employees or their duly authorized agents in the extraordinary case where the otherwise prohibited padded-jaw leghold trap is the only method available to protect human health or safety."

**Conibear** This was banned for commercial or recreational trapping, but is still legal for animal damage control purposes. "Traps of the Conibear-type with a jaw opening larger than 8" x 8" may be used only in sets where the trap is wholly or partially submerged in water or is: (A) Within 100 feet of permanent water. (B) Within 100 feet of seasonally flooded marshes, pastures, agricultural lands or floodways when standing or running water is present. (C) Within the riparian vegetation zone … where the take of beaver is permitted."

**Snare** This was banned for commercial or recreational trapping, but is still legal for animal damage control purposes.

### Trap Placement/Landowner Permission

"Conibear-type traps and snares, except those totally submerged, and deadfall traps are prohibited" in large portions of the state designated as Sierra Nevada Red Fox and San Joaquin Kit Fox Protection Zones … Traps may not be set within 150 yards of any structure used as a permanent or temporary residence, unless such traps are set by a person controlling such property by a person who has and is carrying with him written consent of the landowner to so place the trap or traps … It is unlawful to set traps on land without the owner's written permission where such land are fenced, posted or under cultivation."

### Misc.

- Fisher, marten, river otter, wolverine, kit fox, red fox, island fox, and ringtail may not be taken at any time.

# COLORADO

In 1996, by a 52% to 48% margin, Colorado voters approved a constitutional amendment creating a "method of take" prohibition for wildlife with respect to the use of leghold and Conibear-type traps, snares, and poisons (the regulations below reflect the ballot initiative).

### Three Primary Trapped Species (96/97)

Coyote, beaver, muskrat

### Traps

Live traps (cage and box) are legal for all types of trapping in Colorado, including

recreational, commercial, or animal damage control.

There are four limited exemptions to the ban on body-gripping traps that allow certain types of traps to be used for the following reasons:

- To control wildlife damage to commercial crops and livestock on private land (one 30-day period per land parcel per calendar year allows for use of padded jaw leghold traps on land, any leghold trap in water sets, Conibear-type kill traps, and snares for certain species. If live traps are used to control damage, no 30-day permit is necessary);

- To protect human health and safety by Health Departments and "authorized contractors";

- For bona fide scientific research, falconry, relocation, or medical treatment of the animal;

- For management of fish and non-mammalian aquatic wildlife by the Division of Wildlife.

(See regulations for details.)

### Trap Check Time

When used for recreational or commercial trapping, live traps (cage, box, and colony traps) must be checked daily. Trap check time requirements with body-gripping traps used under the limited exemption provisions vary from once daily to once every seven days. (See regulations for details.)

# CONNECTICUT

### Three Primary Trapped Species (96/97)

Muskrat, beaver, raccoon

### Traps

"Furbearing animals for which there is an open trapping season may be taken by Box Traps, Live Traps, Deadfalls, Padded and Unpadded Metal Traps, Smooth Wire Traps, and Species Specific Traps subject to the following restrictions."

### Leghold

*Unpadded Metal Trap Restrictions:*

- Opening greater than 5¾" is prohibited, except that traps with an opening of up to 7½" may be set for beaver in waters frequented by beaver.

- May only be used below the surface of the water in a pond, lake, stream, spring hole, or tidal water.

*Padded Metal Trap Restrictions:*

- Opening greater than 5 ¹⁵⁄₁₆" is prohibited, except that traps with an opening of up to 7½" may be set for beaver in waters frequented by beaver.

- May only be used in the burrow of a wild animal or below the surface of the water in a pond, lake, stream, spring hole, or tidal water.

*Smooth Wire Trap Restrictions:*

- Opening greater than 6½" is prohibited, except that Conibears and similar smooth wire traps with an opening of up to 10" may be set for beaver in waters frequented by beaver.

- May only be used below the surface of the water in a pond, lake, stream, spring hole, or tidal water. Except, smooth wire traps having an opening of 4¾" or less may extend above the surface of the water provided a portion of the trap frame remains in contact with the water.

*The Following Are Prohibited:*

- The use of any type of snare.

- Traps placed, set, or tended within 10 feet of the waterline of a muskrat or beaver house, including bank beaver.

## Misc.

- "A special permit, based upon competitive bids every 4 years, is required to trap on state forests, lands leased to or owned by the state and lands managed under agreement by DEP."

# DELAWARE

## Three Primary Trapped Species (96/97)

Muskrat, raccoon, opossum

## Traps

**Leghold** "Leghold traps may only be used with permission of the landowner and only during the muskrat season, except in certain areas where they may be used throughout the year (except on Sundays) to trap raccoons in eastern New Castle and Kent Counties ... Leghold traps larger than No. 1½ or No. 1 coil-spring may only be used in tidal areas ... River otters may be trapped in mill ponds and streams with a special free permit from the Division."

## Misc.

*IT IS UNLAWFUL TO:*

- Use traps to take game animals except muskrats, mink, and otter ....

- Set any type of trap except in marshes, streams or ditches (rabbit, raccoon and opossum box traps may be set elsewhere).

- Use diving or box traps for muskrats."

# FLORIDA

## Three Primary Trapped Species (96/97)

Raccoon, otter, opossum

## Traps

**Leghold** "The use or possession of any steel or leg-hold trap where wildlife might be found is prohibited unless authorized by a permit from the Executive Director of the Commission." Permits may be issued to trap nuisance animals with padded leg traps.

## Trap Check Time

Live traps and snares must be visited at least every 24 hours.

### Misc.

- "Furbearers may be taken with guns, live traps, or snares."

- "Trapping or shooting any fox is prohibited. Fox may not be killed, but may be chased by the use of dogs year round."

- "Raccoon, opossum, skunk, nutria, beaver and coyote may be live-trapped, hunted with dogs, or taken with snares and guns year-round."

## GEORGIA

### Three Primary Trapped Species (96/97)

Raccoon, beaver, opossum

### Traps

**Conibear** "Body gripping traps in excess of 9½ inches square may be used only in water or within 10 feet of water."

**Snare** "Snares may be used for trapping beaver provided that snares are set in water or on land within 10 (ten) feet of water, including swamps, marshes, and tidal areas. All snares must be marked with the trapper's name or identification number."

### Trap Placement

"It is unlawful to trap any wildlife upon the right-of-way of any public road or highway of this state."

### Misc.

- "It is unlawful to fail to carry a weapon of .22 cal. rimfire while tending traps and to use that weapon to dispatch any furbearing animal to be taken."

- "It is unlawful to fail to carry a choke stick or similar device while tending traps and to use that device to release domestic animals."

- "It is unlawful to sell the fur, hide or pelt of any domestic dog or cat caught by a trap."

## IDAHO

### Three Primary Trapped Species (96/97)

Muskrat, beaver, red fox

### Traps

All commonly used traps, snares, deadfalls, or other devices commonly used to capture wildlife are legal.

### Trap Check Time

"No person shall place snares or traps for furbearing animals, predatory or unprotected wildlife, EXCEPT pocket gophers, most species of ground squirrels and other unprotected rodents, without visiting every trap or snare once every 72 hours and removing any catch therein. Trappers acting under authority of the U.S. Department of Agriculture, Animal Plant Health Inspection Service, Wildlife Services are exempt from this rule."

### Landowner Permission

"No person may enter private land to hunt, fish or trap without permission from the landowner if the land is cultivated or posted with legible 'No Trespassing' signs."

### Misc.

- "There is NO open season for fisher, kit fox, lynx, otter, wolverine or wolf."

- "The Department will reimburse trappers $5.00 for each lynx, otter, or fisher caught accidentally and turned in."

### "It Is Unlawful:

- To destroy or damage a muskrat or beaver house.

- To trap in or on a muskrat house.

- To possess alive furbearers taken from the wild."

## ILLINOIS

### Three Primary Trapped Species (97/98)

Raccoon, muskrat, opossum

### Landowner Permission

"Hunters and trappers must obtain permission from the landowner or tenant before entering his land regardless of whether or not the land is fenced or posted ... Railroad rights-of-way are private property and you need permission from the owner before hunting or trapping."

### Misc.

- "It is unlawful to destroy any feed bed, nest, den, house or other animal cavity. A feed bed is defined as a mound, pile or mat of branches, cattails or other vegetation gathered and piled by muskrats or beaver."

- "It is unlawful to take or possess bobcat or river otter at any time."

## INDIANA

### Three Primary Trapped Species (96/97)

Raccoon, muskrat, opossum

### Traps

**Leghold** "It is illegal to take any furbearing animal with leg hold traps size No. 3 or larger without offset jaws unless the trap is completely covered by water."

**Snare** "The maximum circumference for snares is 15 inches. Trappers are permitted to use snares greater than 15 inches in circumference on their own land or with written permission of a landowner as long as at least half of the snare loop is covered by water or if the snare employs a relaxing snare lock."

### Misc.

- "There is no distance limitation in setting traps at openings to tile drains or entrances to beaver lodges."

- "Landowners may take coyotes at any time on the land they own or provide written permission for others to take coyotes on their land at any time."

## IOWA

### Three Primary Trapped Species (97/98)

Raccoon, muskrat, mink

### Traps

**Leghold** "You cannot set or maintain on land any foothold or leghold trap with metal serrated jaws, metal toothed jaws or a spread inside the set jaws of greater than seven inches."

**Conibear** "You cannot set or maintain any body-gripping or Conibear-type trap on any public road right of way within five feet of any fence ... Conibear-type traps and snares must not be set on the right of way of a public road within 200 yards of the entry to a private drive serving a residence without the permission of the occupant. You cannot set or maintain any snare or Conibear-type trap within any public road right of way within 200 yards of buildings inhabited by humans unless a resident of the dwelling adjacent to the public road right of way has given permission or unless the body-gripping or Conibear-type trap is completely under water or at least one-half of the loop of a snare is underwater. This does not limit the use of foothold traps or box-type live traps in public road rights-of-way."

**Snare** "No person shall set or maintain any snare in any public road right of way so the snare when fully extended can touch any fence. A snare set on private land other than roadsides within 30 yards of a pond, lake, creek, drainage ditch, stream or river must have a loop size of 11 inches or less in horizontal measurement. All other snares must have a loop size of eight inches or less in horizontal measurement, except for snares with at least one-half of the loop under water. Snares cannot be attached to a drag. All snares must have a functional deer lock which will not allow the snare loop to close smaller than two and one-half inches in diameter."

"It is illegal to set any mechanically-powered snare designed to capture an animal by the neck or body unless the snare is placed completely underwater."

## Other

"A person shall not use colony traps in taking, capturing, trapping or killing any game or fur-bearing animals except muskrats as determined by rule of the commission. Box traps capable of capturing more than one game or fur-bearing animal at each setting are prohibited."

## Trap Placement

"To protect river otters, no trapping is allowed within 10 yards of active or inactive beaver lodges or dens in Linn County on the Cedar River and Indian Creek floodplains between Hwy. 30, Hwy. 151, Business 151 and Interstate 380."

## Misc.

■ "You cannot molest or disturb, in any manner, any den, lodge or house of a fur-bearing animal or beaver dam except by written permission of an officer appointed by the director of the DNR. You cannot use any chemical, explosive, smoking device, mechanical ferret, wire, tool, instrument or water to remove fur-bearing animals from their dens. This section does not prohibit a property owner from destroying a den to protect their property."

# KANSAS

## Three Primary Trapped Species (97/98)

Raccoon, opossum, coyote

## Traps

Snare "Snares are prohibited for use in dryland sets within 50 feet of the outside edge of a public road or within five feet of a fence bordering a public road. However, landowners and tenants or their immediate families or agents may use snares in the right-of-way adjacent to their lands. Snares must be tagged with the user's name and address."

Other Deadfall traps are legal.

## Landowner Permission

"Without the owner's permission, it is illegal to hunt, shoot, pursue, or trap any animal on private land, or any traveled public road or railroad right-of-way adjoining private land … Written permission is required to enter land posted with hunting and/or trapping 'by Written Permission Only' signs."

# KENTUCKY

## Three Primary Trapped Species (96/97)

Raccoon, muskrat, opossum

## Traps

Leghold "Dry-land sets are limited to Number 2 or smaller smooth-jawed foothold traps, padded foothold traps having a jaw spread of six inches or less."

Snare "The following dry-land sets are permitted … (6) Non-locking snares."

## Other

"Deadfalls, wire cages and boxtraps are also permitted. Any traps may be used for water sets, except during the extended beaver season."

## Trap Placement

"Traps set on land must be at least 10 feet apart and not be set in trails or paths commonly used by humans or domestic animals."

## Misc.

■ "A trapping license is required of all trappers, regardless of age, residency or physical condition. Resident landowners, tenants, and members of their immediate families trapping on their own property must possess a valid trapping license."

■ When trapping beaver "Trappers must use water sets. The following traps are permitted:

  ■ No. 3 or larger smooth-jawed foothold traps,

- Padded foothold traps having a jaw spread 5½ inches or larger, or

- Conibear-type traps having a jaw spread of eight inches or larger, or snares."

# LOUISIANA

### Three Primary Trapped Species (93/94)

Nutria, raccoon, muskrat

### Landowner Permission

Trappers must have landowner consent "to trap upon marsh, or low prairie, or swamplands."

### Misc.

- "Licensed trappers may hold in captivity live furbearers during the open trapping season. Such animals must have been obtained by legal trapping methods. Such animals must be released or pelted by the last day of the open season."

- "Furbearers can be taken only with traps. Firearms are illegal except as provided to take nutria, coyote, raccoon and opossum …."

# MAINE

### Three Primary Trapped Species (97/98)

Beaver, marten, fisher (Note: Maine stopped tracking raccoon take after the 1988/89 trapping season when 6,439 raccoon pelts were reported. Maine does not keep records of muskrats whose "harvest" is probably higher that raccoons and beavers.)

### Traps

**Leghold** "Ordinary foothold traps may be used to trap for all legal species of furbearing animal, except that:

(1) foothold traps with auxiliary teeth added to the jaws may not be used anywhere in the State unless they are covered by water at all times (auxiliary teeth are teeth which were not built into the trap at the

time it was manufactured), and

(2) foothold traps manufactured with teeth may not be used in Wildlife Management Districts 12, 15, 16, 17, 20, 21, 22, 23, 24, 25, and 26 prior to the start of the firearm season on deer unless they are covered by water at all times."

### Conibear

- "Killer-type traps with a jaw spread of 5 inches or less are the **only** killer-type traps which you are allowed to set at ground or snow level (They may also be set above ground or under water.)

- Killer-type traps with a jaw spread from 5 to 8 inches may be used **only** if they are set completely underwater **or** at least 4 feet above the ground or snow.

- Killer-type traps with a jaw spread greater than 8 inches may be used **only** during the beaver trapping season **and** must be set completely underwater."

**Snare** Snares may be used only in the following situations:

- Snares may be used to trap for beaver, but they must be set completely underwater.

- Snares may sometimes be used to trap coyotes for purposes of animal damage control; and

- Foot snares (cable traps) may be used **only** to trap for bear as explained below. Ordinary foothold traps also may be used for bears; (see regulations for details).

### Trap Placement

"If you use an ordinary foothold trap, you must enclose the trap, as follows: It is unlawful to set a bear trap unless it is enclosed by 2 strands of wire, one 2 and 4 feet from the ground. The wire must be held securely in position not less than 5 yards nor more than 10 yards from the enclosed trap. The enclosure must be marked with signs bearing the words 'BEAR TRAP' in letters at least 3 inches in height, and the signs must be spaced around the enclosure, securely attached to the top of wire, at intervals of not more than 20 feet."

"It is unlawful to place, set or tend any trap within a) 10 feet of a beaver house, muskrat den or house; b) 5 feet of a beaver dam, or c) 4 feet of a beaver trap which has been set by another trapper ... It is unlawful for any person to trap outside his/her own land, within ½ mile of the compact, built-up portion of a city or village, except by the use of cage-type live traps and water sets."

## Landowner Permission

"It is unlawful for any person to trap, except for beaver, on land in any organized or incorporated place, without first obtaining written permission from the owner or occupant. It is also unlawful for any person to trap, except for beaver, without written permission from the owner or occupant, on the following lands in unorganized places: a) Cultivated or pasture land which is used for agricultural purposes and on which is located an occupied dwelling; and, b) Land within 200 yards of any occupied dwelling (organized towns also)."

## Trap Check Time

"A person who traps in any organized or incorporated place is required to visit each trap, except killer-type traps and under-ice water sets for beaver and muskrat, at least once in every calendar day. Each killer-type trap, except under ice water sets for beaver and muskrat, must be visited at least once in every 3 calendar days ... A person who traps in any unorganized township is required to visit each trap, except killer-type traps and water sets, so-called, at least once in every calendar day. Each killer-type trap or water set, so called, except under-ice water sets for beaver or muskrat, must be visited at least once in every 5 calendar days."

## Misc.

- "The harvest of marten will be limited to 25 marten per trapper statewide ... Licensed trappers may lawfully possess any otter taken by accident [after the otter trapping season has closed] in a legal beaver or muskrat set."

- "The raw skin of any beaver, bobcat, coyote, fisher, fox, marten, mink, or otter must be presented to a warden or other agent of the Commissioner for tagging."

- "No person may have more than 2 traps set for bear at any one time ... All bear traps must be visited by the trapper at least once in each calendar day ... Cable traps with a closing diameter of not less than 2½ inches may be used in trapping for bear."

- Only one bear may be taken a year, either by trapping or hunting.

# MARYLAND

## Three Primary Trapped Species (93/94)

Muskrat, raccoon, red fox

## Traps

**Leghold** Leghold traps may not be used on land in Anne Arundel, Baltimore, Montgomery, and Prince George's counties.

**Conibear** Conibear traps are allowed only if: "(1) equal to or less than 8 inches in diameter and set in tidal wetlands, flooded non-tidal wetlands, freshwater marshes, shrub swamps, wooded swamps, bogs, or where water covers the surface of the soil or the soil is water-logged to the surface; or, (2) larger than 8 inches in diameter and set completely submerged in water."

**Snare** Snares may not be used in Anne Arundel, Baltimore, Carroll, Cecil, Harford, Montgomery, and Prince George's counties.

## Trap Check Time

"Traps must be checked once per calendar day except in tidal marshes and waters, where they must be tended every 36 hours."

### Misc.

- A landowner does not need a trapping license to trap on his/her own property.

- "Dens or houses of furbearers may not be disturbed at any time."

- "Beaver, otter and fisher pelts must be tagged."

- "In tidal areas, landowners and their agents or lessees have exclusive rights to muskrats and other furbearers above the mean low water line."

## MASSACHUSETTS

A state ballot initiative banning body-gripping traps passed in 1996 by a margin of 64% to 36% (the regulations below reflect the ballot initiative).

### Three Primary Trapped Species (96/97)

Muskrat, raccoon, beaver

### Traps

"The only traps which may be used for the taking of furbearing mammals are cage or box traps and common rat traps. Hancock and Bailey type traps may be used only when the trapper has been trained in their use, and may be used only for the taking of beaver. Common rat traps may be used only for the taking of weasels … **Steel-jaw leghold traps,** padded jaw traps, body-gripping (**Conibear**) traps (see below), **snares,** deadfalls, and any traps other than those specified above are **PROHIBITED**. Such traps may not be set, tended, used, or possessed in the field … There is a detailed procedure for obtaining a special permit to use a body gripping (Conibear) trap for certain types of wildlife damage." (Emphasis added.)

### Trap Placement

"It is illegal to … Trap in a public way, cart road or path commonly used by humans or domestic animals [or to] trap within 10 feet of the waterline of a muskrat house."

### Landowner Permission

Trappers must obtain landowner permission only if land is posted against trapping.

### Misc.

- "No license is required by any legal resident of the Commonwealth or member of his [or her] immediate family for trapping on land owned or leased by him [or her] which is used principally for agriculture, if he is actually domiciled on that land."

  - "It is illegal to … Tear open or disturb a muskrat or beaver house or beaver dam … Pick up any road-killed furbearers during the closed season, or to pick up road-killed furbearers during the open season without a valid trapping license."

  - "It is illegal to … Use poison or use a trap that takes more than one animal at a time."

## MICHIGAN

### Three Primary Trapped Species (96/97)

Muskrat, raccoon, beaver

### Traps

"*It is unlawful to:*

- Use any kind of trap other than a steel trap. [Both leghold traps and Conibear-type steel traps are legal.]

- Use a steel trap with a jaw spread exceeding a number 2-foothold trap when taking mink or muskrat.

- Use **snares** (exceptions for beaver and otter trapping). (Emphasis added.)

- Set a body-gripping or **Conibear** type trap in Zone 1 Upper Peninsula larger than six inches in diameter on dry land, unless it is four feet or more above the ground or placed in a box or similar container inaccessible to dogs." [Conibear-type traps used throughout the rest of the state have no size limit, whether used on land or water.] (Emphasis added.)

- "As a substitute for leghold traps, trappers may use live traps capable of taking only one animal at a time within 150 yards of an occupied dwelling and associated buildings during a legal time for trapping the target animal. Live traps must be checked daily." "Multiple catch or colony traps" submerged below the water are legal for taking muskrats.

## Trap Check Time

"It is illegal to set any catching device designed to hold an animal alive unless it is checked at least once within each 48-hour period in Zones 2 and 3, and at least once within each 72-hour period in Zone 1." See regulations for zone descriptions and maps.

## Trap Bait

"We recommend that bait be placed where it is not visible to nontarget species such as owls, hawks, and eagles." This is not a legal requirement.

## Misc.

- "It is unlawful to molest or disturb the house, hole, nest, burrow, or den of a badger, beaver, mink, muskrat, or raccoon, whether occupied or not, or molest or destroy a beaver dam, except under a DNR Wildlife Damage Investigation and Control Permit."

- Fisher (limit 3), otter (limit 1 or 3 depending on the zone) and badger (limit 1 in 1998–99) may all be trapped and they must be tagged.

# MINNESOTA

## Three Primary Trapped Species (96/97)

Muskrat, beaver, raccoon

## Traps

**Snare** See regulations for snare restrictions in certain zones of the state.

"Bobcats and bears cannot be taken with snares."

"Snare cable or wire may not have a diameter exceeding ⅛ inch."

"Snares may not be used with spring poles or other devices that wholly or partly lift from the ground an animal caught in the snare."

## Trap Placement

"No person may place a foot or leghold trap on a pole, post, tree stump, or other perch more than 3 feet above the ground, except by federal permit ... No person may set, place, or operate a snare in a culvert, except as a completely submerged waterset ... Snares may not be set in deer trails ... No snare may be set in such a way that the top of the loop is more than 16 inches above the ground or, when the ground is snow-covered, more than 16 inches above the bottom of a person's footprint made in the snow beneath the snare with the full body weight on the foot ... A person may not set a trap within 50 feet of any water other than temporary surface water within 30 days before the open season for mink and muskrat in that area, except by permit."

## Landowner Permission

Trapping and hunting are allowed on private lands unless landowner posts against it. Trappers do not need permission to trap on unposted private land (unless it is agricultural land).

## Trap Check Time

"Any trap capable of capturing a protected* animal and not capable of drowning the animal must be tended at least once each calendar day, except for body gripping or Conibear-type traps. Any trap capable of drowning the captured animal and any body-gripping or Conibear-type trap must be tended at least once each third calendar day, except for traps set under the ice. When the trap is tended, any animal captured must be removed." "All snares not capable of drowning the captured animal must be tended at least once each calendar day."

* In wildlife management terminology, a "protected" animal usually means a species for which a hunting or trapping season and perhaps a bag limit have been set thereby "protecting" the animal from unregulated killing.

### *Misc.*

- "No person may possess, transport, or pelt a fisher, otter, pine marten, fox, bobcat, lynx, or timber wolf that was accidentally killed, except when authorized beforehand."

- "Nonresidents may not trap in Minnesota."

- "No person may disturb, injure, or destroy any muskrat house or den, except that traps may be set at natural entrances to muskrat burrows and opening may be made in muskrat houses for trapping if all material removed is wetted and used to plug the opening."

- "No person may disturb, injure, or destroy any beaver house, dam, burrow, or den."

- "Mink may not be taken by digging or with the aid of dogs."

## MISSISSIPPI

### *Three Primary Trapped Species (96/97)*

Raccoon, beaver, opossum

### *Trap Placement*

"No traps may be placed on or set within 100 feet of any street or public highway."

### *Trap Bait*

"State law prohibits the use of baits with traps; however, liquid scents may be used."

### *Misc.*

- "Beavers are classed as predators and may be trapped throughout the year."

## MISSOURI

### *Three Primary Trapped Species (97/98)*

Raccoon, muskrat, opossum

### *Traps*

"Traps must be metal traps with smooth

or rubber jaws only, EGG-type traps, live traps, cage-type traps, or snares set underwater only. You may not use pitfalls, deadfalls, snares in a dry-land set, nets or colony traps."

**Conibear** "Conibear-type traps with a jaw spread not greater than 8 inches may be set 6 feet or more above ground level in buildings."

**Snare** "Snares must be set underwater and have a loop 15 inches or less in diameter when set. They also must have a stop device that prevents the snare from closing to less than 2½ inches in diameter. The cable used to make the snare must be between $5/64$ inch and ⅛ inch in diameter and must have a mechanical lock and anchor swivel."

### *Trap Placement*

"Traps may not be set in paths made or used by people or domestic animals, and Conibear-type traps may not be set along public roadways, except underwater in permanent waters. Within communities having 10,000 or more inhabitants, traps may not be set within 150 feet of any residence or occupied building."

### *Misc.*

- "The homes, nests or dens of furbearers must not be molested or destroyed."

- "No person shall accept payment for furbearers taken by another."

## MONTANA

### *Three Primary Trapped Species (95/96)*

Muskrat, beaver, coyote

### *Landowner Permission*

As of 1998, resident trappers must obtain permission of the landowner, lessee, or their agent before trapping on private land. Non-resident trappers must obtain written permission from the landowner before trapping on private property. But "a trapper who injures livestock in a snare is liable for damage and this constitutes a misdemeanor."

### Trap Check Time

A 48-hour trap check time is recommended, but not required.

### Misc.

- Lynx, wolverine, marten, fisher, bobcat, and river otter may be trapped in Montana and must be tagged.

## NEBRASKA

### Three Primary Trapped Species (96/97)

Raccoon, muskrat, coyote

### Traps

"Furbearers may be trapped only with snares, metal spring traps with smooth jaws or box traps."

Conibear "It is unlawful to use a Conibear-type trap with a jawspread larger than 5 inches except when placed under water or at least 6 feet above the ground on any lands owned or controlled by the Game and Parks Commission, U.S. Fish and Wildlife Service waterfowl production areas, U.S. Army Corps of Engineers lands at Harlan County Reservoir, or on any road rights-of-way. It is unlawful in Nebraska to use any Conibear-type trap with a jawspread over 8 inches unless it is totally under water or at least 6 feet above the ground."

Snare "During upland game bird seasons, it is unlawful to use snares on any lands owned or controlled by the Game and Parks Commission, on U.S. Fish and Wildlife Service waterfowl production areas, or on U.S. Army Corps of Engineers lands at Harlan County Reservoir."

### Misc.

- Coyote, prairie dog and woodchuck are designated as "unprotected nongame species" and may be killed year-round without a license or permit.

## NEVADA

### Three Primary Trapped Species (96/97)

Muskrat, coyote, bobcat

### Traps

Leghold "All steel leg hold traps size No. 2 or larger or with an outside jaw spread of 5½ inches or larger used in the taking of any wildlife must have lugs, spacers or similar devices permanently attached so as to maintain a minimum trap opening of three-sixteenths of an inch."

### Trap Placement

It is "unlawful to set any steel trap used for the purpose of trapping mammals, larger than a No. 1 Newhouse trap, within 200 feet of any public road or highway within this state." (See regulations for exemptions.)

### Trap Check Time

"Traps or snares not designed to cause immediate death to be visited once every 96 hours."

## NEW HAMPSHIRE

### Three Primary Trapped Species (97/98)

Beaver, muskrat, fisher

### Traps

Conibear "It is unlawful to set any 'Conibear' traps or similar trap of a size larger than number 220, except when the trap is: five feet or more above the ground or surface of the snow; in water for trapping beaver or otter; set for bear [under certain provisions]."

**Snare** It is illegal to use snares for taking or killing furbearing animals, with the exception that a permit may be obtained to trap beaver and otter with snares set under water or ice.

## Trap Placement

"No person may set or arrange any trap in a public way, cart road, or path commonly used as a passageway by human beings or domestic animals ... No person may set or arrange any trap in or under any bridge, ditch or drainage system, whether artificial or natural, within the limits of the right-of-way of any public highway except by special permission of the executive director."

## Trap Check Time

"A trapper must visit traps set at least once each calendar day. A person trapping beaver through the ice must visit his traps at least once each 72 hours."

## Misc.

- "It is unlawful to disturb or interfere with the dams or houses of beaver without obtaining a special permit ... or to at any time destroy or injure a muskrat house, den or burrow or place a trap within 15 feet thereof."

- Ten fisher may be taken by hunting and/or trapping (1999 season).

# NEW JERSEY

## Three Primary Trapped Species (97/98)

Muskrat, raccoon, red fox

## Traps

**Leghold** "It is illegal to possess or use steel-jawed leghold traps anywhere in New Jersey."

**Conibear** "No Conibear or killer-type trap shall be used unless submerged underwater. In tidal water, such traps must be completely covered at normal high tide. In non-tidal waters, such traps must be completely submerged when the water is at the normal level. It is illegal to use, set or possess a Conibear or killer-type trap having a jaw spread greater than 6 inches without a permit for beaver or otter. A Conibear or kill-type trap with a jaw spread of no more than 10 inches may be used for beaver or otter ... Beaver and otter trap tags must be placed above the water line and exposed to view."

**Snare** See regulations for specific requirements regarding the use of snares.

## Landowner Permission

"Hunters and trappers are required to secure permission prior to entering private agricultural lands to hunt. The enacted law provides that these lands need not be posted to enforce the trespass law."

## Trapper Educational Course

"New Jersey requires that anyone applying for a trapping license must show a previous resident trapping license from NJ or any other state, or proof of completion of a trapper education course. In addition, persons wanting to use body-gripping restraining snares must carry proof of training in the proper use of the snare."

## Trap Bait

"All natural or artificial baits used in trapping with body gripping restraining snares must be covered or concealed from view except when placed or located a distance of 30 feet or greater from any set snare."

## Misc.

- "Beaver and otter may be trapped by special permit only."

- "Any person (including a farmer) who traps a coyote must notify a division law enforcement office within 24 hours."

## NEW MEXICO

### Three Primary Trapped Species (97/98))

Coyote, gray fox, muskrat

### Traps

"No steel trap with an outside jaw spread larger than 6½ inches and no tooth-jawed trap may be used in making a land set, except Conibear-type traps set on land for beaver. All foot-hold traps must be off-set ... No steel trap with an outside jaw spread larger than 12 inches may be used in making a water set."

### Trap Placement

"No land set may be placed within one-quarter (¼) mile of an occupied dwelling without prior, written permission of the dwelling's occupant, except for a land set placed by a landowner on his own land ... No land set may be placed within 25 yards of any Forest Service or Bureau of Land Management system trail designated by the agency on a map provided for the general public, or within 25 yards of the shoulder of any public road that is graded and annually maintained with public funds ... No land set may be placed within 50 yards of any man-made livestock or wildlife watering, except on private land with written permission of the landowner."

### Trap Check Time

"A licensed trapper or his representative (agent) must make a visual inspection of each trap every 24 hours. If wildlife is held captive in the trap, the trapper or representative must remove the wildlife. All traps must be personally checked by the trapper every 48 hours and all wildlife removed. Each trapper will be allowed one representative who must possess written permission from the trapper."

### Misc.

- New Mexico residents do not need a trapping license to trap coyotes or skunks (designated as "unprotected furbearers").

## NEW YORK

### Three Primary Trapped Species (96/97)

Muskrat, raccoon, beaver

### Traps

**Leghold** "Foothold traps larger than 4" set on land must have a pan tension device and be covered when set ... On land, foothold traps must be 5¾" or smaller. During beaver or otter season, foothold traps up to 7¼" are allowed if set underwater. When the beaver or otter season is closed, foothold traps set in water for mink or muskrat may not be larger than 5¾"."

**Conibear** "Body-gripping traps more than 7½" may only be used in water during an open beaver or otter season."

**Other** Box and cage traps are legal. Traps designed to take more than one muskrat at a setting are illegal.

### Trap Placement

- "You may not set a trap in such a manner that it causes a captured animal to be suspended in the air ... You may not set a trap on a public road ... Foothold traps larger than 4" must be covered when set on land."

- "You may set a trap in a permanent body of water only when the mink, muskrat, otter, or beaver season is open."

- "You are not allowed to set a trap within 100 feet of a house, school, playground or church unless you have permission from the owner of the land where the trap is set."

- "Traps may not be set on or within 15 feet of a beaver lodge at any time ... You may not disturb a beaver lodge, beaver dam, or muskrat house or den."

- "Traps may not be set on or within 15 feet of a beaver dam except during an open otter season ... You may not set a trap on or within 5 feet of a muskrat house."

### Trap Check Time

In certain wildlife management units, traps only have to be checked once every 48 hours (see regulations for details).

### Landowner Permission

Recommended, but not required to trap on private lands.

### Misc.

- "You may use any legal method to kill a trapped animal. You do not need a hunting license to use a firearm to kill a legally trapped animal."

- Beaver, coyote, otter, bobcat, fisher and marten pelts must be sealed.

## NORTH CAROLINA

### Three Primary Trapped Species (96/97)

Raccoon, muskrat, beaver

### Traps

**Leghold and Conibear-type traps** must be "horizontally offset with closed jaw offset of at least ³⁄₁₆ inch for a trap with a jaw spread of more than 5½ inches. This provision does not apply if the trap is set in the water with a quick-drown type set." It is illegal to "set a steel-jaw or leghold trap on dry land with solid anchor with a trap chain longer than 8 inches from trap to anchor unless fitted with a shock-absorbing device approved by the Commission."

**Conibear** Conibear traps size 330 or larger are illegal unless "at least one-half of the trap is covered by water."

**Snare** Snares are illegal except for trapping beaver.

### Trap Placement

It is illegal to "set or use a trap so that animals or birds will be suspended when caught."

### Misc.

- See state regulations for specific local laws that restrict trapping in certain counties and designated "game lands."

- Groundhogs may be legally trapped.

## NORTH DAKOTA

### Three Primary Trapped Species (95/96)

Muskrat, red fox, raccoon

### Traps

**Conibear** There are restrictions on size and placement of Conibears during certain times of year, but from January through the end of August, there are no restrictions. See regulations for specific details.

**Snare** See regulations for details.

"Use of relaxing snares is permitted ... Galvanized or stainless steel cable snares only of ¹⁄₁₆ inch diameter or larger ... are legal."

### Trap ID

Only snares must be tagged with the trapper's ID.

### Trap Check Time

It is recommended, but not required, that trappers check their traps once every 48 hours.

### Misc.

- "Furbearers may be taken with firearms, archery equipment (including cross bows), dogs, traps, and snares except mink and muskrat may be taken with traps and snares only."

- "Beaver dams may be dismantled when their presence causes property damage."

## OHIO

### Three Primary Trapped Species (96/97)

Muskrat, raccoon, opossum

### Traps

**Leghold** "It is unlawful to use leghold traps except those of 5 ⅝" spread or smaller when raccoon and mink season is closed" (mid-March to mid-November in most counties).

"Leghold traps set on land must be covered."

**Conibear** "Body gripping traps set on land, or in a tile, den, or burrow on land shall not have a jaw spread greater than 5 inches in diameter."

**Snare** "All snares must have a relaxing lock and a stop to prevent the opening of the snare from closing to a diameter of less than 2½ inches in diameter, or a relaxing lock system with a breaking point of not greater than 350 pounds."

The following practices are unlawful: "[to] use snares on public hunting areas; [to] use any snare constructed of any material other than multi-strand steel cable ... [to] ... set a snare with a loop diameter of more than 15 inches ... [or to] ... have attached to the snare any spring loaded or mechanical device to assist the snare in closing."

**Other** Deadfall traps are illegal.

### Trap Placement

"Except for live traps, no traps may be set within 150 feet of another person's occupied residence without advising the resident ... No traps, including snares, shall be set in a path commonly used by humans or domestic animals." It is unlawful to "set, maintain, or use a trap or snare in or upon any cart or wagon road, or in or upon any path ordinarily used by domestic animals or human beings."

### Landowner Permission

Written permission is required only if using snares on private property.

### Trap Bait

"All flesh baits must be totally covered."

#### Misc.

■ No trapping license is required to trap coyotes although a hunting license is required.

## OKLAHOMA

### Three Primary Trapped Species (96/97)

Raccoon, opossum, beaver

### Traps

**Legal Traps** "Box traps; smooth-jawed, single-spring, leg-hold steel traps with a jaw spread no greater than eight inches; smooth-jawed, double-spring offset jawed, leg-hold traps with a jaw spread no greater than eight inches."

**Illegal Traps** Conibear type traps and snares are illegal in Oklahoma; however, trappers can obtain a 30-day permit to trap beaver with Conibears. Conibear-type traps used for this purpose can only be used in water sets.

### Trap Placement

"No trap may be set 'in the open' or in paths, roads or runways commonly used by persons, dogs or other domestic animals."

### Trap Posting

"When double-spring offset jawed steel traps are used, signs must be posted conspicuously to the right and left of all entrances from public roads and highways and from adjacent lands at corners of perimeter fences." Signs must have minimum dimensions of 5 inches by 8 inches and the wording "Traps" must be included and be conspicuous on the signs and printed in letters at least 2 inches tall.

### Misc.

- "Persons trapping under the general trapping license may use no more than 20 traps. There is no limit for persons holding the professional license."

## OREGON

### Three Primary Trapped Species (97/98)

Muskrat, nutria, beaver

### Traps

It is illegal to use "a No. 3 or larger leghold trap not having a jaw spacing of at least $3/16$ of one inch when the trap is sprung (measurement excludes pads on padded jaw traps) and when the set is not capable of drowning the trapped animal."

### Trap Check Time

Oregon's 48-hour trap-check time requirement does not apply to traps set for predatory animals.

### Trap Bait

It is illegal to use "the flesh of any game bird, game fish or game mammal for trap bait," or "sight bait within 15 feet of any leghold trap set for carnivores."

### Misc.

- "The general furbearer regulations do not apply to the trapping of gophers, moles, ground squirrels and mountain beaver."

- Marten may be legally trapped in Oregon. River otter trapping season runs from November 15 to March 15 and there is no bag limit.

- "It is unlawful for any person to damage or destroy any muskrat house at any time except where such muskrat house is an obstruction to a private or public ditch or watercourse."

## PENNSYLVANIA

### Three Primary Trapped Species (97/98)

Muskrat, raccoon, opossum

### Traps

It is unlawful to "... (3) use pole traps, jaw-toothed traps, deadfalls, poison, explosives, chemicals, snares, or traps with a jaw-spread exceeding six and half inches; (4) set body-gripping traps outside a watercourse, waterway, marsh, pond, or dam."

"It is unlawful to (1) use a cage or box trap in water; and (2) use a cage or box trap capable of capturing more than one animal at a time."

**Snare** A trapper may set up to 10 traps or snares submerged under water for beaver. "A metal ferrule shall be crimped on the cable to prevent the snare loop from closing to a circumference less than 20 inches" and may not be spring-activated.

### Trap Placement

It is unlawful to "set traps within five feet of a hole or den, except for underwater sets."

### Trap Bait

It is unlawful to "set a trap with bait visible from the air."

### Misc.

- "It is unlawful to (1) destroy, disturb or interfere with a beaver dam or house; ... (3) place or tend a trap within 15 feet of a dam or beaver house, measured from directly above the trap across the water, ice or land to the nearest point of the structure; (4) set or tend more than a total of 10 traps, of which two may be body-gripping types no larger than 10x10 inches, except up to 10 body-gripping traps or snares may be used in Bradford, McKean, Potter, Susquehanna, Tioga, and Wayne counties."

## RHODE ISLAND

### Three Primary Trapped Species (96/97)

Muskrat, raccoon, mink

### Traps

**Leghold** "No person shall use, set, place, maintain or tend any steel jawed leghold trap to capture any furbearing mammal or other animal except by special permit from the Director of the DEM."

**Conibear** "Size 220 (or their equivalent, not to exceed 8 inch jaw spread) shall be permitted only if such trap is completely submerged in water, or placed at least six (6) feet above the surface of water or ground (i.e. trees)."

**Snare** "Use of wire snares or poison prohibited."

### Trap Placement

"Traps must be so placed as to be inaccessible to domestic animals."

### Landowner Permission

"Written landowner permission is required to trap private land."

### Misc.

- "Landowners permitted to take nuisance furbearers provided that any carcass, except rabbits, is presented to the DEM within 24 hours."

- "Permits to trap state management areas are required (to be) presented to the DEM within 24 hours."

- "Permits to trap state management areas are required."

## SOUTH CAROLINA

### Three Primary Trapped Species (96/97)

Raccoon, gray fox, beaver

### Traps

**Leghold** Leghold traps are restricted in certain zones in South Carolina. In Clarendon, Georgetown, and Williamsburg counties, "rubber padded foot-hold traps of a size No.2 or smaller" may be used "for land sets for live foxes. Any other furbearer so captured must be immediately released. Foothold traps may not be used in Chesterfield, Kershaw and Marlboro Counties."

**Conibear** "Conibear-type or body gripping traps may be used statewide without bait or scents in water sets or slide sets only. These traps may be set in a vertical position only."

**Snare** "The Department may issue special depredation permits to allow the use of snares for beavers in water sets."

**Other** "Live traps may be used statewide."

### Trap Placement

"No trap may be set in the open, in paths commonly used by persons or domestic animals."

### Misc.

- "There is no trapping on Wildlife Management Area lands."

## SOUTH DAKOTA

### Three Primary Trapped Species (96/97)

Muskrat, raccoon, coyote

### Traps

**Snare** "Snares must have a mechanical lock, swivel device on the anchor end, and stop device to prohibit the restraint loop from closing to a diameter less than ½–2½ inches … Attaching snares to a drag is prohibited."

**Other** Colony traps for muskrats are legal (with some size restrictions).

Pole traps are illegal if set "in a manner that a raptor may be captured, injured or killed."

### Trapping License

A Furbearer Stamp is not required for trappers under 16 years of age, or for landowners trapping on their own lands.

### Trap Placement/Landowner Permission

"No person may attach a trap, including snares, to any part of a fence along a public road right-of-way adjacent to private land without permission from the adjoining landowner ... No person, except the adjoining landowner or a person receiving written permission from the adjoining land-owner, may trap on public road rights-of-way within 660 feet of a home, church or schoolhouse ... Snares may not be set within fenced pastures, cropland, feedlots or fenced areas containing domestic livestock without permission of the landowner or the operator ... Traps, except live traps and snares, cannot be placed or set in water or within 30 feet of water from Oct. 1–30."

### Misc.

- "No person may take pine marten, swift fox, fisher river otter, wolf, mountain lion or black bear."

- "A person must have a [free] permit issued by the park manager to trap in a state park or recreation area."

- It is illegal, except in Haakon, Jackson, Jones, Lyman, and Stanley counties, to "destroy a muskrat house, except that in open season a house may be opened in a manner that will not destroy or damage it as a place of habitation."

## TENNESSEE

### Three Primary Trapped Species (96/97)

Raccoon, muskrat, beaver

### Traps

Leghold "Number 4 steel leg-hold traps and smaller steel traps must be placed at least 12 inches inside the entrance to a burrow or hole except in the case of a water set. Water sets are defined as traps set in water adjacent to and part of streams, ponds, lakes, wetlands or other water courses, and include floating sets."

Padded Leghold "Woodstream Soft-Catch and Butera Cushion Catch traps meet the definition of a cushion-hold trap. These traps are the only steel traps legal for trapping in the open and on top of the ground, provided that the trapper has specific written permission from the landowner to use the trap."

Snare "Steel cable snares having a minimum cable diameter of 5/64 inch and maximum cable diameter of 3/32 inch" are legal. "Spring activated snares prohibited." Snares are restricted in certain parts of state; see regulations for details.

### Misc.

- Beaver may be trapped and hunted in parts of the state year-round with no bag limit.

## TEXAS

### Three Primary Trapped Species (97/98)

Raccoon, opossum, nutria

### Trap Placement

"It is illegal to take fur-bearing animals with a leghold or Conibear style trap within 400 yards of any school."

### Misc.

- "Landowners or their agents may take in any number nuisance fur-bearing animals by any means at any time on that person's land without the need for a hunting or trapping license."

## UTAH

### Three Primary Trapped Species (96/97)

Muskrat, coyote, red fox

### Traps

**Leghold** "All long spring, jump, or coil-spring traps, except rubber-padded jaw traps, that are not completely submerged underwater when set must have spacers on the jaws which leave an opening of at least 3/16 of an inch when the jaws are closed."

### Trap Placement

See regulations for details about beaver trapping and trapping restrictions near rivers and tributaries.

### Landowner Permission

"A person may not set any trap or trapping device on posted private property without the landowner's permission ... Any trap or trapping device set on posted property without the owner's permission may be sprung by the landowner."

### Misc.

- Marten may be legally trapped in Daggett, Duchesne, Summit, and Uintah counties with a free marten trapping permit in addition to a furbearer license.

## VERMONT

### Three Primary Trapped Species (97/98)

Muskrat, beaver, raccoon

### Traps

**Conibear** "It is unlawful to set a body gripping trap with a jaw-spread over eight inches, unless the trap is set five feet or more above the ground or in water."

### Misc.

- Fisher may be legally trapped with no bag limit. The season in 1998 was Dec. 5–20.

- "No person shall set a trap within 10 feet of the nearest point, above the water, of a beaver house or dam. No person may interfere with dams or dens of beaver except in protection of property."

- "It is unlawful to disturb a muskrat house or place a trap therein, thereon, or at the entrance thereof, or in the entrance or inside a muskrat burrow."

## VIRGINIA

### Three Primary Trapped Species (97/98)

Muskrat, raccoon, beaver

### Traps

**Conibear** "It shall be unlawful to set above the ground any body gripping trap with a jaw spread in excess of 5 inches, baited with any lure or scent likely to attract a dog."

**Snare** "No deadfall or snares, except that on land snares with loops less than 12 inches in diameter with the top of the snare loop not more than 12 inches above the ground may be used with written permission of the landowner."

### Trap Placement

"No trapping within 50 feet of a highway in Clarke, Fauquier, and Loudoun counties."

## WASHINGTON

A state ballot initiative banning body-gripping traps for commercial and recreational trapping passed in 2000 by a margin of 55% to 46% (the regulations provided below reflect the ballot initiative). Statute reads: "It is unlawful to use or authorize the use of any steel-jawed leghold trap, neck snare, or other body-gripping trap to capture any mammal for recreation or commerce in fur." In addition, the statute makes it "unlawful to knowingly buy, sell, barter, or otherwise exchange, or offer to buy, sell, barter, or otherwise exchange the raw fur of a mammal or a mammal that has been trapped in this state with a steel-jaw leghold trap or any other body-gripping trap, whether or not pursuant to permit ... Nothing in this section prohibits the use of a Conibear trap in water, padded leghold trap, or a nonstrangling type foot snare with a special permit granted by the director" for protecting human health and safety, wildlife conflicts (permit not to exceed 30 days for this purpose and non-lethal control tools

109

must be attempted first), protection of threatened and endangered species, and for use in "legitimate wildlife research" (excluding Conibear traps). "Every person granted a special permit to use a trap or device ... shall check the trap or device at least every twenty-four hours." In addition, the U.S. Fish and Wildlife Service or its employees or agents may use Conibear traps in water, padded leghold traps, or nonstrangling type foot snares for protection of threatened and endangered species.

## Three Primary Trapped Species (97/98)

Muskrat, beaver, coyote

### Misc.

■ Marten may be legally trapped.

## WEST VIRGINIA

### Three Primary Trapped Species (96/97)

Raccoon, muskrat, beaver

### Traps

**Leghold** Leghold traps with an open jaw spread of more than 6½ inches may only be used under water to trap beaver.

**Snare** It is illegal to "set or maintain neck or body gripping snares or spring pole snares" in land sets (water sets are legal). Foot snares are legal on land.

**Other** Deadfall traps are illegal.

### Trap Placement

"It is illegal to set or maintain any trap or trapping device in human foot trails and/or livestock paths ... It is illegal to set or maintain any trap, trapset or snare upon any tree, post or other natural or man-made object at any points more than 3 linear feet from the surface of the earth ... It is illegal to trap within 15 feet of the waterline on the structure of any beaver house or burrow."

### Misc.

■ Fisher may be legally trapped. The 1998 season bag limit was one fisher.

■ "It is illegal to destroy, disturb, or in any manner interfere with dams, houses, or burrows of beavers while trapping for or attempting to trap for beavers."

## WISCONSIN

### Three Primary Trapped Species (97/98)

Muskrat, raccoon, beaver

### Traps

**Conibear** See regulations for details regarding the use of Conibear traps sized 220 (7"x7").

**Snare** It is illegal to "set, place, or operate any snare regardless of the noose size, unless one-half of the snare noose is located underwater at all times." Snares must conform to the follow specifications:

■ Cable length may not exceed 5 feet.

■ It must be galvanized aircraft cable.

■ The cable or wire diameter may not exceed ⅛ inch.

■ It must have a mechanical lock and anchor swivel.

■ It must be non-spring activated.

### Other

Colony traps (traps capable of taking more than one animal) are illegal.

The WI DNR distinguishes between snares (only allowed in water sets) and "cable restraint devices" which are allowed on land for trapping coyotes and foxes. Please see regulations for specific details.

## Trap Placement

- "Elevated traps are legal for furbearers as long as the sight exposed bait law is followed."

- "It is illegal to operate trap sets which permit the trapped animal to reach water, except when the muskrat, beaver or otter trapping season is open in the zone you are trapping."

- "It is illegal to set any trap or snare closer than 15 feet from any beaver dam," unless done by a landowner for beaver damage control.

- Conibear traps greater than 6" or any snare cannot be set "within 3 feet of any federal, state, or county road right-of-way culvert unless completely submerged in water; within 3 feet of any woven or welded wire fence; within 100 yards of any building devoted to human occupancy without the owner's consent."

## Trap Check Time

"There is no mandated trap checking period for sets made under the ice."

## Misc.

- "The owners or occupants of any land, and family members, do not need a license to trap beaver, foxes, raccoon, woodchucks, rabbits and squirrels on the land year-round."

- "Landowners, occupants, and family members may hunt or trap beaver on their land at anytime without a license. Landowners may also trap on beaver dams. Beaver dams may be removed without a permit."

- Fisher and river otter may be legally trapped (season limit = one per permit of each species).

# WYOMING

## Three Primary Trapped Species (96/97)

Coyote, red fox, beaver

## Trap I.D

According to the regulations, only "steel leg hold traps" must bear the trapper's identity.

## Misc.

- Marten may be legally trapped in Wyoming.

- "Persons possessing a valid trapping license may use dogs to pursue and take bobcats during the bobcat trapping season."

## CHAPTER SIX

# Trapping on Public Lands: National Wildlife Refuges

*Camilla H. Fox*

### MISSION OF THE NATIONAL WILDLIFE REFUGE SYSTEM:

*To administer a national network of lands and waters for the conservation, management, and where appropriate, restoration of the fish, wildlife, and plant resources and their habitats within the United States for the benefit of present and future generations of Americans.*

— 1997 MISSION STATEMENT, U.S. FISH AND WILDLIFE SERVICE

Commercial and recreational trapping is allowed on the vast majority of public lands in the U.S. The only public lands where trapping is expressly prohibited, except where specifically sanctioned by Congress, is the National Park System. Perhaps most disturbing is that trapping is allowed on the majority of the nation's National Wildlife Refuges, which were specifically created to protect wildlife.

The National Wildlife Refuge system is the most comprehensive and diverse collection of fish and wildlife habitats in the world, encompassing 93 million acres in all 50 states. The 552 refuge units and 40 affiliated wetland management districts, administered by the U.S. Fish and Wildlife Service, harbor more than 240 listed threatened and endangered species (24% of all listed species), over 700 kinds of birds, 220 mammals, 250 reptiles and amphibians, and 200 kinds of fish.

In 1903, when Theodore Roosevelt established the first wildlife refuge on Pelican Island, Florida, hunting and trapping were prohibited. In the 1950s and 1960s, as hunters and trappers gained greater political power, consumptive wildlife uses were expanded on refuges through new legislation and amendments to existing laws. Today, more than half of all wildlife refuges allow commercial or recreational killing of wildlife. Yet, most people think of National Wildlife Refuges (NWRs) as sanctuaries for wildlife: 78% of Americans believe that hunting and trapping are prohibited on NWRs, according to a 1999 Decision Research poll (see page 114).

A 1997 U.S. Fish and Wildlife Service (FWS) survey reported that from 1992 to 1996, 280 of the 517 National Wildlife Refuge units had trapping programs.* As a result, bobcats, river otters, badgers, beavers, foxes, raccoons, coyotes, and other

---

* When the U.S. Fish and Wildlife Service conducted its national survey of refuges regarding trapping in 1997, there were 517 refuges. This figure constantly changes as additional refuges are added to the system. At press time, there were 552 refuge units within the National Wildlife Refuge System.

## PUBLIC ATTITUDES TOWARD TRAPPING ON NATIONAL WILDLIFE REFUGES

A national public opinion survey conducted by Decision Research for the Animal Protection Institute found that 79% of Americans oppose the trapping of wildlife on National Wildlife Refuges. This opposition crosses all demographic lines, including hunting households where 71% disapprove of trapping. The survey reported that 78% of Americans mistakenly assume that hunting and trapping are illegal on refuges. Further, 78% of Americans oppose the spending of tax dollars to administer commercial fur trapping programs on refuges. A majority (59%) of Americans supports ending all recreational killing of wildlife at refuges.

The public's desire to protect animals on refuges extends beyond opposition to killing for recreation and profit. The survey found that 78% of respondents oppose allowing U.S. Fish and Wildlife officials to kill wildlife with any means necessary, such as trapping and poisons. Moreover, 71% feel that "as long as wildlife refuge officials can remove dangerous animals, there is no reason to allow any other killing of animals on wildlife refuge property."

Findings from this survey are consistent with those of previous polls, which found that Americans object to trapping because it causes pain and suffering to captured animals. The survey found that 76% of Americans believe an animal's right to live free of suffering should be as important as a person's right.

When survey respondents were asked which activity should be the priority for National Wildlife Refuges, 88% identified, "Preserving the natural, undeveloped landscape and preserving the habitat and wildlife. Only 9% thought "Providing opportunities for commercial and recreational hunters and trappers" should be the priority.

### About the Survey

Telephone interviews for the API survey were conducted throughout the United States with 800 Americans 18 years of age or older. Interviews were conducted April 8–11, 1999. The overall margin of error for the sample is ±4% at the 95% confidence level, signifying that in 95% of all samples drawn from the same population, the findings would not differ from those reported by more than 4%.

wild animals are trapped, crippled, and maimed on refuges each year for their fur and for "wildlife management" purposes. Countless non-target animals are also trapped and killed in the process, including bald and golden eagles, owls, migratory birds, and threatened and endangered species.

Although trapping threatens the very species refuges are intended to safeguard, the FWS and Congress continue to sanction and promote the expansion of trapping and hunting on the National Wildlife Refuge System (NWRS) each year.* The public has almost no say as to whether trapping is

allowed on refuges, unless the FWS determines that the proposed trapping program may have a significant impact on the human environment. Such a determination requires the FWS to comply with the National Environmental Policy Act (NEPA)[†] and invite public comment. Refuge managers must also prepare environmental documentation when developing a new trapping plan or making major modifications to an existing plan.[‡] FWS policy relieves managers of this responsibility if an existing "generic" environmental assessment or environmental impact statement addresses trapping.[§]

---

* In July 1999, the House of Representatives voted 259–166 to restrict trapping (and ban leghold traps and neck snares) on the refuge system for commercial and recreational purposes. But pro-trapping and fur-interest lobby groups pressured the Senate to table the amendment by a 64–32 vote. The amendment was then killed in Conference Committee in October 1999.

† 42 U.S.C. § 4321, et seq.

‡ U.S. Fish and Wildlife Service Manual, March 12, 1982, 7 RM § 15.9.

§ Ibid.

Unfortunately, wildlife-killing "sports" in the refuge system are destined to increase due to the National Wildlife Refuge System Improvement Act of 1997,* which designates hunting and fishing as "priority uses" and stipulates that they "receive enhanced consideration" by refuge managers.

## Laws and Regulations Governing Consumptive Wildlife Uses on National Wildlife Refuges

Various laws, regulations, and policies regulate trapping on National Wildlife Refuges (see Figure 6.1). Where trapping is permitted on refuges, trappers must follow the applicable state laws. Trapping programs conducted for "resource management" are carried out by refuge staff, by trappers under contract, and by the public through issuance of refuge special use permits. Trapping for recreational or commercial purposes requires that the trapper obtain a refuge special use permit, except on most Alaska refuges (which encompass 54 million acres or 83% of the total NWRS land area) and most Waterfowl Production Areas, the majority of which are in the Midwest.

## History of NWRS Trapping Survey

Public outcry against trapping on refuges prompted Congress to include language in the 1997 Appropriations Bill directing the FWS to convene a task force to "study the use of animal traps in the National Wildlife Refuge system [and to] consider the humaneness of various trapping methods ... and other relevant issues." It also stipulated that the task force include "interested outside parties."

The FWS argued, however, that a task force could not be convened in the allotted time, and convinced Congress to replace it with a nationwide survey that was distributed to every refuge unit manager in January 1997. The

ultimate intent of the survey, which requested specific information pertaining to trapping programs on those refuges that allow this activity, was never fully clear.

Unable to ignore growing public concern about trapping on National Wildlife Refuges, the FWS posted a notice in the *Federal Register* allowing the public less than 60 days to submit comments on the issue of "the use of animal traps within the National Wildlife Refuge System." Despite the short comment period, 969 public comments were submitted, according to the FWS. In May 1997, the FWS forwarded four volumes of unedited public comments to the Chairmen of the Appropriations Subcommittee on Interior & Related Agencies, in addition to a summarized version of the questionnaires returned by the 517 National Wildlife Refuge managers.

## U.S. Fish and Wildlife Service Summarizes NWRS Trapping Survey

In its final 87-page report to Congress, the FWS offered a glowing, self-serving account of the benefits of trapping, concluding it is "a professional wildlife management tool" providing "important benefits for public health and safety and recreational, commercial, and subsistence opportunities for the public." However, a copy of the raw survey data obtained by the Animal Protection Institute (API) through the Freedom of Information Act revealed that the FWS's official conclusions did not accurately reflect the information submitted by the refuge managers.

## Animal Protection Institute Summarizes NWRS Trapping Survey

In the survey, refuge managers were asked how many active trapping programs were in place between 1992 and 1996 on their refuge, the primary "purposes" of these trapping programs, the types of traps allowed, who carried out the

* 16 U.S.C. § 668dd, *et seq.*

115

---

### Figure 6.1

*Primary legal authorities under which trapping occurs on National Wildlife Refuges*

STATUTES:

---

- The National Wildlife System Improvement Act of 1997, Pub. L. No. 105-57, 111 Stat. 1252 (1997) (codified at 16 U.S.C. § 668dd, *et seq.*).

- The National Wildlife Refuge System Administration Act of 1966, Pub. L. No. 89-669, 80 Stat. 927 (1966) (codified as amended at 16 U.S.C. § 668dd, *et seq.*).

- The Refuge Recreation Act of 1962, Pub. L. No. 87-714, 76 Stat. 653 (1962) (codified at 16 U.S.C. § 460k, *et seq.*).

- Migratory Bird Conservation Act of 1929, Ch. 257, § 1, 45 Stat. 1222 (1929) (codified as amended at 16 U.S.C. § 715, *et seq.*).

- Migratory Bird Hunting Stamp Act of 1934, Act of Mar. 16, 1934, Pub. L. No. 73-124, ch. 71, 48 Stat. 451 (1934) (codified as amended at 16 U.S.C. § 718, *et seq.*).

- Alaska National Interest Lands Conservation Act of 1980, Pub. L. No. 96-487, 94 Stat. 2371 (1980) (codified at 16 U.S.C. § 3101, *et seq.*).

REGULATIONS:

---

- Title 43 C.F.R. § 24.4(e) discusses management of public activities on Federal lands (refuges). It affirms the Secretary of Interior's authority to determine whether units of the NWRS shall be open to public uses, and on what terms such access shall be granted. It also affirms that such public uses shall, to the maximum extent practicable, be consistent with state laws and regulations.

- Title 50 C.F.R. § 29.1 provides for public or private economic use of the natural resources of any wildlife refuge area where the use may contribute to, or is related to, the administration of the area. It provides for use by refuge special use permit only when the authorized activity will not be incompatible with the purposes for which the refuge was established.

- Title 50 C.F.R. § 31.2 authorizes trapping as a method of "surplus wildlife" population control.

- Title 50 C.F.R. § 31.16 requires persons trapping on refuges (other than in Alaska and within WPAs) where trapping has been authorized to obtain federal and state permits. This section specifies that lands acquired as WPAs are to be open to trapping without a federal permit.

- Title 50 C.F.R. § 36.14 and § 36.32(c)(1) authorizes trapping on Alaska refuges for subsistence and other reasons without a Federal permit.

POLICIES:

---

The U.S. Fish and Wildlife Service Refuge Manual, 7 RM 15, Ch. 15, Mar. 12, 1982, contains current policy on trapping within units of the NWRS. Where trapping is permitted on refuges, trappers are required to follow applicable state law. According to the FWS, trapping programs conducted for "resource management" reasons are carried out by refuge staff, by trappers under contract, and by the public through issuance of refuge special use permits. Trapping programs conducted primarily for recreational or commercial purposes require that the trapper obtain a refuge special use permit, except on most Alaska refuges (which encompass 54 million acres or 83% of the total NWRS land area) and most Waterfowl Production Areas (WPAs), the majority of which are in the Midwest.

trapping programs, the cost of implementing the trapping programs, which target and non-target species were trapped, whether or not there were trap-related refuge-specific regulations in place, and whether alternative methods of control were considered if trapping was conducted for wildlife damage or management purposes.

Though included in the survey, vital information such as the traps used and incidents of non-target species being trapped on refuges was not mentioned in the FWS report to Congress.

### The Number of Trapping Programs

Between 1992 and 1996 there were 489 trapping programs in the NWRS. Of the 517 refuge units surveyed, 280 (54.2%) had at least one trapping program.

### Primary Purposes for Trapping on Refuges

The FWS told Congress and the public that trapping on refuges is conducted primarily for "facilities protection" and for the protection of migratory birds and threatened and endangered species; trapping for "recreation/commerce/subsistence" is listed as the last of 11 reasons for trapping on refuges. API found, however, that the single most common purpose cited by refuge managers for trapping was for "recreation/commerce/subsistence" (see Figure 6.2). Clearly, the FWS has attempted to obscure the fact that many animals trapped on refuges are killed primarily for their fur.

### Types of Traps Used on the NWRS

Most managers indicated that more than one type of trap was used on their refuge. Of the 280 refuges that allowed trapping, 171 (61.1%) utilized Conibear-type devices, 157 (56.1%) utilized live enclosure traps, 140 (50%) utilized steel-jaw leghold traps, 74 (26.4%) utilized kill snares, and 66 (23.6%) utilized "other body-hold devices."

### Who Traps on the NWRS?

A variety of government personnel carried out the 489 trapping programs. There were also private trappers who trapped primarily for fur. To implement these trapping activities, 56.6% of the programs involved refuge staff or volunteers (some of whom may trap primarily for fur), 24.7% involved private individuals who obtained Special Use Permits (SUP) (this category also includes fur trappers), 12.1% involved other Federal or State agency personnel, 6.5% involved individuals hired under contracts for which the refuge must pay, 5.1% involved federal Animal Damage Control (now called Wildlife Services) trappers, and 15.3% involved other persons, which may include trappers trapping in Waterfowl Production Areas and Easements and in Wetland Management Districts (these trappers are required to hold a state trapping license, but not an SUP).

### Cost of Implementing Trapping Programs on the NWRS

According to the survey, the estimated cost of trapping on all refuge units, including labor, materials, salaries, and construction costs, was $2,840,000. The total cost is undoubtedly higher, since the FWS indicated that many refuge managers did not accurately report the cost of their trapping programs and three managers failed to specify any cost for their trapping programs.

### Target Species Trapped on the NWRS

Choosing from a list of 40 target species, managers noted that raccoons were the most frequently targeted: 176 (36%) of the 489 trapping programs targeted this species. Beavers were second, targeted by 156 (31.9%) programs. A total of 130 (26.6%) programs targeted red foxes, 127 (26%) targeted mink, and 126 (25.8%) targeted striped skunks. Other target species included feral dogs, feral cats, gray/timber wolves, bobcats, lynx, and coyotes.

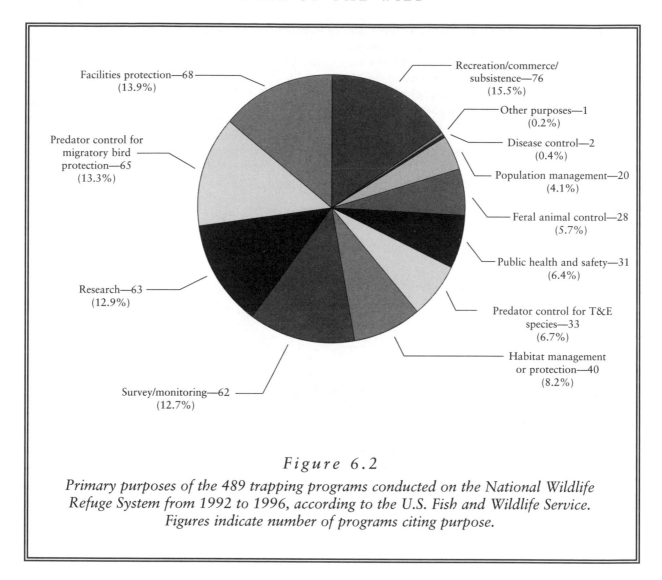

Facilities protection—68
(13.9%)

Predator control for
migratory bird
protection—65
(13.3%)

Research—63
(12.9%)

Survey/monitoring—62
(12.7%)

Recreation/commerce/
subsistence—76
(15.5%)

Other purposes—1
(0.2%)

Disease control—2
(0.4%)

Population management—20
(4.1%)

Feral animal control—28
(5.7%)

Public health and safety—31
(6.4%)

Predator control for T&E
species—33
(6.7%)

Habitat management
or protection—40
(8.2%)

### Figure 6.2

*Primary purposes of the 489 trapping programs conducted on the National Wildlife Refuge System from 1992 to 1996, according to the U.S. Fish and Wildlife Service. Figures indicate number of programs citing purpose.*

## Non-Target Species Trapped on the NWRS

As with any activity involving indiscriminate body-gripping traps, refuge trapping programs include the capture of non-target species as well as target species. The most commonly trapped non-target species were river otters, reportedly captured in 52 (10.6%) of the 489 trapping programs. Forty-four (9%) programs involved the accidental capture of feral and domestic cats, 39 (8%) of rabbits and hares, and 37 (7.6%) of feral and domestic dogs. Other non-target species trapped included Canada geese, alligators, ducks, hawks, owls, eagles, and bears. This list may be incomplete because a significant number of refuge managers failed to specify non-target species.

## Refuge-Specific Trapping Regulations

Of the 280 refuges with trapping programs, only 30.4% had refuge-specific regulations, while 61% lacked such regulations. The other 8.6% failed to specify whether refuge-specific regulations exist.

Only 53.9% of the 280 refuge managers had established refuge-specific trap-check time requirements, which ranged anywhere from three times per day to once every four days. According to the survey data, 37.2% of the 280 refuges do not have any refuge-specific trap-check time requirements (however, these refuges are supposed to follow state trap-check time requirements) and 8.9% failed to specify.

## Conclusion

Most refuge visitors do not trap. They visit refuges to hike, bird-watch, take photographs, and enjoy nature. Visitors expect to be safe and to have the opportunity to view wildlife without the fear of stepping into a trap or witnessing the pain and suffering of a trapped animal.

Commercial and recreational trapping and the use of body-gripping traps should be prohibited on all refuges. The vast majority of Americans agree with this sentiment as evidenced by a 1999 national Decision Research public opinion poll commissioned by the Animal Protection Institute that showed 79% of Americans oppose trapping on National Wildlife Refuges. Humane concerns aside, leghold traps, neck snares, and other body-gripping devices pose a serious hazard to non-target wildlife, including threatened and endangered species. Trappers can already access millions of acres of public lands outside the refuge system. As lands specifically set aside to provide animals a safe home, refuges should be inviolate sanctuaries for wildlife, not playgrounds for trappers and other consumptive wildlife users.

*For more detailed information about trapping on individual refuges, see Appendix III.*

# CHAPTER SEVEN

# Targeting Trapping through Public Policy

*Dena Jones*

*Riding along on a wave of sentiment that was fostered largely by the women voters, the antisteel trap law was voted into effect in Tuesday's election by a plurality estimated at more than 250,000 votes.*

— *Boston Globe,* 6 NOVEMBER 1930

## Introduction

No issue received more attention from American animal protection advocates during the twentieth century than the use of body-gripping traps. To affect the use of these traps, animal activists have tried three main public policy approaches: 1) banning traps; 2) restricting the use of traps; and 3) prohibiting commerce in products from animals caught in traps. Restricting the use of traps has been the most frequently used approach and the most successful, as illustrated by the specific and complex rules that govern trapping in individual states described in Chapter Five. Outright bans on the devices or on commerce in the products taken from animals caught in them have been more difficult to achieve.

Laws banning or restricting the use of traps have been enacted through legislation, including ballot referenda, and administrative agency regulation at the state level and through ordinance and referenda at the municipal and county levels. Although it is possible to limit the use of traps through federal legislation and administrative agency regulation, to date, all attempts through

this avenue have failed. This chapter summarizes federal, state, and local public policy initiatives to limit trapping in the United States. Litigation related to trapping and trapping prohibitions is also noted.

## State Legislation and Regulation

Statewide attempts to restrict trapping have persisted continuously since 1901, when a bill was introduced in the New Hampshire Legislature. Geography professor John Gentile, in a 1984 dissertation titled "The Evolution and Geographic Aspects of the Anti-trapping Movement: A Classic Resource Conflict," documented no less than 450 anti-trapping bills introduced in state legislatures between 1901 and 1982.[1] According to Gentile, state legislation has been the most popular avenue for anti-trapping activity, with 50% of all public policy efforts at the state level, 30% at the local level, and 20% at the federal level.

Gentile noted three distinct phases in anti-trapping activity in the U.S.: 1925 to 1939, which he designated "The Idealistic Phase," characterized by legislative efforts to ban trapping; 1940 to

1968, "The Institutional Phase," characterized by regulatory reform and compromise; and 1969 on, "The Insight Phase," characterized by renewed interest and refined strategies. Attempts to ban trapping at the state level have occurred during each of these phases.

The formation of the Anti-Steel-Trap League in 1925 signified the beginning of an organized approach to reform trapping in the United States. Unlike previous efforts that were motivated by concerns for dwindling furbearer numbers, the Anti-Steel-Trap League crusaded to save wild animals from unnecessary "pain and suffering." According to Gentile, fox and raccoon hunters concerned about the risks trapping posed to their dogs lent support to the effort. However, the primary opposition to trapping during this time came from those pushing for an end to the cruelty of the leghold trap. The Anti-Steel-Trap League succeeded in forming a broad base of support ranging from the Massachusetts Rod and Gun Club to the Ohio Academy of Sciences and, as a result, legislation to limit trapping was passed in several states, including South Carolina, Georgia, Arkansas, New Jersey, Pennsylvania, and Kentucky.

After 1940, many of the bans were overturned and anti-trapping activity in the U.S. dropped significantly. In fact, 30 years passed before another state legislated trapping restrictions. In 1969, Massachusetts passed a law requiring that all traps be designed to kill animals instantly or take them alive, unhurt. In 1972, by administrative rule, the Florida Game and Fresh Water Fish Commission outlawed the leghold trap, except by permit. This prohibition remains the only major restriction of leghold traps initiated by a state wildlife agency.

In 1974, Massachusetts extended its ban to all leghold traps except water sets and those placed in and under buildings, and Tennessee banned the use of leghold traps except in burrows. The following year, South Carolina banned the sale, manufacture, and use of leghold traps except size 3 or smaller, near buildings or on personal land. In 1977, Connecticut banned use of leghold traps except in burrows, and Rhode Island banned leghold traps except by permit for 90 days or less. A complete leghold trap ban, offering no exemptions, was enacted by the New Jersey Legislature in 1984, following ten years of lobbying by animal advocates (text on p. 125). Since that time, no significant restrictions have been passed by state legislatures or by state wildlife agencies on the use of the leghold trap, although a few state agencies have mandated use of the padded version of the trap. Table 7.1 shows how and when the current state leghold trapping bans were enacted.

A notable legal challenge to the legislature-enacted trapping ban in Massachusetts came in the late 1980s. As mentioned above, in 1974 the Massachusetts Legislature prohibited the use of any steel-jaw leghold trap on land as well as the setting of any other device "in such a manner that it will knowingly cause continued suffering to such a mammal caught therein, or which is not designed to kill such a mammal at once or take it alive unhurt." In January 1989, a District Court decision on a criminal complaint found that the padded leghold trap was not a "steel-jaw leghold trap" within the meaning of the law. As a result, the state Division of Fisheries and Wildlife promulgated regulations allowing the use of padded traps to take furbearers, once again permitting trapping on open land in Massachusetts. Arguing that the regulation was inconsistent with the statute, animal advocacy groups sued the Division in late 1989. On hearing the case, a Superior Court judge sided with the plaintiffs, noting that the animal advocates had presented "uncontradicted evidence, including scientific studies, that the padded jaw traps authorized by the Regulation hurt animals ...." However, in June 1995 the ruling was overturned by the state Supreme Judicial Court on the grounds that the statute did not prohibit the use of traps that do not take an animal "alive unhurt," but only those

# TABLE 7.1

## State leghold trapping bans

| STATE | EXCEPTION(S) | LAW | HOW ENACTED |
|---|---|---|---|
| **Leghold:** | | | |
| Arizona | public lands; human health/ safety, rodent control, wildlife research/relocation (jaws must be padded or offset) | ARIZ, REV. STAT. ANN. § 17-301 D ARIZ. ADMIN. CODE 12-4-307 | Initiative/ Regulation |
| California | human health/safety (jaws must be padded) | CAL. FISH & GAME CODE § 3003.1 | Initiative |
| Colorado | human health/safety, rodent control, wildlife research/ relocation, by permit for animal damage control for up to 30 days (jaws must be padded) | COLO. REV. STAT. §§ 33-6-203, 33-6-207, 33-6-208; 8 COLO. CODE REGS. § 1201-12 | Initiative/ Regulation |
| Florida | by permit for animal damage control (jaws must be padded) | FLA. ADMIN. CODE ANN. R. 68A-12.009(4), 68A-24.002(3); FL HUNTING HANDBOOK & REGULATIONS | Regulation/ Policy |
| Massachusetts | human health/safety | MASS. GEN. LAWS CH. 131, § 80A | Initiative |
| New Jersey | none | N.J. REV. STAT. §§ 23:4-22.1 TO 23:4-22.7 | Legislation |
| Rhode Island | by permit for animal damage control for up to 90 days | R.I. GEN. LAWS § 20-16-8 | Legislation |
| Washington | by permit for human health/ safety, endangered species protection, wildlife research, animal damage control for up to 30 days (jaws must be padded) | WASH. REV. CODE § 77.15 | Initiative |
| **Conibear (Kill):** | | | |
| Arizona | public lands; human health/ safety, rodent control, wildlife research/relocation | ARIZ. REV. STAT. ANN. § 17-301 D | Initiative |
| California | all purposes except recreation or commerce in fur | CAL. FISH & GAME CODE § 3003.1 | Initiative |
| Colorado | human health/safety, rodent control, by permit for animal damage control for up to 30 days | COLO. REV. STAT. §§ 33-6-203, 33-6-207, 33-6-208 | Initiative |
| Connecticut | water sets | CONN. AGENCIES REGS. § 26-66-5 | Regulation |
| Florida | none | FLA. ADMIN. CODE ANN. R. 68A-24-002(3) | Regulation |
| Maryland | water sets | MD. REGS. CODE TIT. 08, § 03.06.03 | Regulation |
| Massachusetts | human health/safety, by permit for beaver/muskrat damage control | MASS. GEN. LAWS CH. 131, § 80A | Initiative |
| New Jersey | water sets | N.J. REV. STAT. § 23:4-38.2 | Legislation |
| Oklahoma | water sets | OK DEPT. OF WILDLIFE CONSERVATION HUNTING REGULATIONS | Policy |
| Pennsylvania | water sets | PA GAME COMMISSION HUNTING & TRAPPING REGULATIONS | Policy |
| South Carolina | water sets | S.C. CODE ANN. § 50-11-2410 | Legislation |
| South Dakota | water sets | S.D. ADMIN. R. 41:08:02:06 | Regulation |

# TABLE 7.1

*State leghold trapping bans*

| State | Exception(s) | Law | How Enacted |
|-------|--------------|-----|-------------|
| Washington | water sets by permit for human health/safety, endangered species protection, animal damage control for up to 30 days | Wash. Rev. Code § 77.15 | Initiative |
| West Virginia | water sets | W. Va. Code St. R. § 58-53-3 | Regulation |
| **Snare:** | | | |
| Alabama | water sets; powered foot snares with max loop of 5 $1/2$ in. (neck/body snares illegal on land) | Ala. Admin. Code r. 220-2-.30 | Regulation |
| Arizona | None | Ariz. Admin. Code 12-4-307 | Regulation |
| California | all purposes except recreation or commerce in fur | Cal. Fish & Game Code § 3003.1 | Initiative |
| Colorado | human health/safety, rodent control, wildlife research/ relocation (nonlethal), by permit for animal damage control for up to 30 days | Colo. Rev. Stat. §§ 33-6-203, 33-6-207, 33-6-208 | Initiative |
| Connecticut | none | Conn. Gen. Stat. § 26-72 | Legislation |
| Illinois | water sets | 520 Ill. Comp. Stat. 5/2.33 | Legislation |
| Maine | foot snares for bear; water sets for beaver | Me. Rev. Stat. Ann. tit. 12, §§ 7432, 7452, 7453-B | Legislation |
| Massachusetts | human health/safety | Mass. Gen. Laws ch. 131, § 80A | Initiative |
| Michigan | water sets | Michigan Dept. of Natural Resources Hunting & Trapping Guide | Policy |
| Missouri | water sets | Mo. Code Regs. Ann. tit. 3, § 10-8.510 | Regulation |
| New Hampshire | water sets for beaver and otter | N.H. Rev. Stat. Ann. § 207:10 | Legislation |
| New York | none | N.Y. Envtl. Conserv. Law § 11-1101 | Legislation |
| North Carolina | water sets for beaver | N.C. Gen. Stat. §§ 113-291.1, 113-291.9 | Legislation |
| Oklahoma | none | Okla. Stat. tit. 29, § 29-5-502 | Legislation |
| Pennsylvania | water sets for beaver | 58 Pa. Code § 141.6 | Regulation |
| Rhode Island | none | R.I. Gen. Laws § 20-16-6 | Legislation |
| South Carolina | water sets for beaver | S.C. Code Ann. § 50-11-2410 | Legislation |
| Vermont | none | Vt. Stat. Ann. tit. 10, § 4706 | Legislation |
| Washington | foot snare by permit for human health/safety, endangered species protection, wildlife research, animal damage control for up to 30 days | Wash. Rev. Code § 77.15 | Initiative |
| West Virginia | water sets; foot snares with max loop of 6 $1/2$ in. (neck/body snares illegal on land) | W. Va. Code St. R. § 58-53-3 | Regulation |
| Wisconsin | water sets | Wis. Admin. Code § NR 10.13 | Regulation |

---

### State of New Jersey, Introduced December 12, 1983, An Act Concerning Steel-Jaw Leghold Type Animal Traps

*Be it enacted by the State and General Assembly of the State of New Jersey:*

(1) 1. No person shall manufacture, sell, offer for sale, possess, import or transport an animal trap of the steel-jaw leghold type.

2. No person shall take or attempt to take any animal by means of a trap of the steel-jaw leghold type.

3. The possession of a trap of the steel-jaw leghold type shall be prima facie evidence of a violation of section 2 of this act except under the circumstances indicated by section 5 of this act.

4. Mouse and rat traps designed for use in or under buildings shall not be classified as steel-jaw leghold traps for the purpose of this act.

5. This act shall not be construed to prevent the use of steel-jaw leghold traps for the purpose of exhibition by humane or educational institutions and organizations, or the possession of such traps by a person in the act of turning over the traps to a law enforcement agency.

6. A person violating this act shall for each illegal trap involved be fined not less than $50.00 nor more than $250.00 for a first offense; not less than $250.00 nor more than $500.00 for a second offense; not less than $500.00 nor more than $2,500.00, or imprisonment for six months, or both fine and imprisonment, for a third and each subsequent offense.

7. All equipment used in, or animals and pelts obtained by a violation of section 2 of this act shall be confiscated by any law enforcement agency enforcing the act. This bill shall not be construed to authorize the confiscation of animals and pelts other than those which have been obtained in violation of section 2 of this act and which are either held by a trap or in the possession of a violator.

---

not designed and intended to take animals alive and unhurt. In the judge's opinion, the padded jaw trap was designed to accomplish that objective and, therefore, could be used to take furbearers in the state.* Animal advocates responded to the court loss by sponsoring a successful ballot initiative in 1996 that not only banned all versions of the leghold trap, but also ended most uses of Conibear traps.

While Florida's ban on the leghold trap ban is currently the only prohibition on leghold traps approved by a state wildlife agency, several state agencies have eliminated Conibears and snares and mandated padding of leghold traps in response to animal protection concerns (see Table 7.1). As mentioned previously, the Massachusetts Division of Fisheries and Wildlife required padded traps in 1989, as did the California Fish and Game Commission in 1990, the Arizona Game and Fish Commission in 1993, and the Colorado Division of Wildlife in 1995. All were under pressure to ban the leghold trap entirely by animal advocates who eventually succeeded in reaching their goal through the initiative process. In addition, several state wildlife agencies have closed trapping seasons on individual animal species at the behest of animal activists. California canceled plans for trapping of red fox in 1996; Colorado eliminated trapping of kit fox in 1994 and trapping of swift fox, gray fox, mink, marten, and weasel in 1995; Idaho rejected a proposal by trappers to sell pelts of river otters trapped incidentally in 1998, and Montana ended trapping of lynx in 1999.

Since 1986, animal advocates in Connecticut have pursued a creative approach to limiting trapping by bidding on state land allotments. In 1998, the animal protectionists succeeded in securing 35 of 122 available tracts, a total of 47,000 acres, which they then posted off-limits to trapping. In response, the Connecticut Department of Environmental Protection (DEP) initiated a regulation change requiring that prospective bidders prove they had trapped furbearing animals during a minimum of four previous trapping seasons. On September 17, 1999, the animal advocates filed a lawsuit claiming that the regulation blocked their participation in the bidding process and was, therefore, discriminatory. Review of DEP records demonstrated inadequate biological justification for the conduct of the state

---

* "Massachusetts Society for the Prevention of Cruelty to Animals v. Division of Fisheries and Wildlife." 420 Mass. 639, 651 N.E.2d 388 (Mass. 1995.)

trapping program. Faced with the disclosure, DEP agreed to rescind all bids for the 1999–2000 season and reconsider the bidding process and other aspects of the state trapping program.

Each state must review its trapping regulations every one to three years, with the wildlife department proposing changes that are then submitted to an oversight commission or board for approval. During this process, most states publish proposed regulation changes and hold hearings where members of the public may testify or submit comments. In addition, some states such as California and Alaska give citizens the opportunity to actually propose changes to the trapping regulations. Because wildlife management agencies depend heavily upon the revenues obtained from hunting, trapping, and fishing license sales, they have traditionally catered to consumptive users. As a result, the regulatory process has been used far less frequently than legislation for initiating trapping restrictions. However, the regulatory process tends to be less costly in terms of time and money than either legislation or ballot initiative and offers animal advocates an alternative when these other options are prohibitive or unavailable.

While a complete ban on the use of a particular trapping device may be difficult to achieve, animal advocates can accomplish incremental change through campaigns to do one or more of the following:

- Ban traps with teeth or limit maximum size of traps.

- Shorten trap check periods.

- Restrict the use of body-gripping traps in high-use recreation areas.

- Mandate that trappers obtain written permission to trap on private lands.

- Prohibit trapping on state lands.

- Require trappers to post lands where traps have been placed.

- Restrict trapping to protect sensitive species.

## State Ballot Initiatives

Citizen-initiated ballot measures are one method, along with legislation and administrative agency regulation, by which trapping-related laws may be enacted or amended. Twenty-seven states currently allow citizens to initiate or refer proposed changes in the law to voters for approval. The initiative process allows citizens to gather petition signatures to place a proposed statutory or constitutional amendment before the voters. Those states where the initiative process is available are: Alaska, Arizona, Arkansas, California, Colorado, Florida, Idaho, Illinois, Maine, Massachusetts, Michigan, Mississippi, Missouri, Montana, Nebraska, Nevada, North Dakota, Ohio, Oklahoma, Oregon, South Dakota, Utah, Washington, and Wyoming. Citizens in all but two of these states (Florida and Misssissippi), as well as three additional states — Kentucky, Maryland, and New Mexico — also have available the popular referendum, which allows them to gather petition signatures to refer a law recently passed by the legislature to the voters; the law in question does not go into effect until approved by the voters.

Initiative processes differ by state. Some states have the direct version, where the measure is submitted to voters without legislative action. In states with the indirect version, the legislature is required to act upon the measure within a reasonable period of time before it is voted on by the electorate. The time period to collect signatures and the percentage of voters required to sign petitions to place a measure on the ballot varies widely. Among the states where the process is available, some have held very few ballot measure contests, while others offer dozens at each general election. Ballot propositions are most popular in western states, where the process originated at the end of the last century.

The first anti-trapping success at the ballot box came in 1930 when Massachusetts voters approved by two-to-one a measure to outlaw the use of trapping devices that cause suffering. (The ban was later repealed.) In 1977 and 1980, animal advocates in Ohio and Oregon, respectively, tried unsuccessfully to advance trapping bans through the initiative process. The Ohio loss was especially devastating, costing animal protection groups more than $1 million. Another negative impact of that campaign was the formation of the Wildlife Legislative Fund of America, a hunting lobby that originally came into being to fight the Ohio trapping ban and then stayed around after the

## TABLE 7.2

### *State trapping initiatives, 1930–2000.*

| Year | State | Description | Outcome | Vote in Favor |
|------|-------|-------------|---------|---------------|
| 1930 | Massachusetts | To ban use of trapping devices not designed to kill animals outright or take alive unhurt except for damage control | Approved (later repealed) | 69% |
| 1977 | Ohio | To ban use of leghold traps and any trapping devices causing prolonged suffering | Rejected | 37% |
| 1980 | Oregon | To ban use, sale of snares and leghold traps except for human health and safety and for predator control until 1985 | Rejected | 37% |
| 1992 | Arizona | To ban use of leghold, instant kill, and snare traps on public lands except for rodent control, human health and safety, wildlife research and relocation | Rejected | 38% |
| 1994 | Arizona | To ban use of leghold, instant kill, and snare traps on public lands except for rodent control, human health and safety, wildlife research and relocation | Approved | 58% |
| 1996 | Colorado | To ban use of leghold, instant kill, and snare traps except for damage control, rodent control, human health and safety, wildlife research and relocation | Approved | 52% |
| 1996 | Massachusetts | To ban use of steel-jaw leghold traps, padded leghold traps, Conibear traps, and snares except for human health and safety | Approved | 64% |
| 1998 | Alaska | To ban use of snares to take wolves; ban sale and possession of wolf skins taken with a snare | Rejected | 37% |
| 1998 | California | To ban use of all body-gripping traps for recreation or commerce; ban use of steel-jaw leghold traps for all purposes except use of padded leghold trap for human health and safety | Approved | 57% |
| 2000 | Oregon | To ban use of all body-gripping traps for recreation or commerce; ban use of body-gripping traps for other purposes except Conibear trap in water, padded leghold trap, and foot snare by permit for human health and safety, endangered species protection, wildlife research, or damage control for period not to exceed 30 days | Rejected | 39% |
| 2000 | Washington | To ban use of all body-gripping traps for recreation or commerce; ban use of body-gripping traps for other purposes except Conibear trap in water, padded leghold trap, and foot snare by permit for human health and safety, endangered species protection, wildlife research, or damage control for period not to exceed 30 days | Approved | 54% |

election to assist hunters and trappers in opposing subsequent measures in other states.

As a result of these losses, animal advocates became frustrated and disillusioned with the initiative process. This changed in 1990 when a broad coalition of environmental and animal protection groups came together in California to stop the planned trophy hunting of mountain lions and to set aside funds for the purchase of wildlife habitat. Unlike previous efforts, the mountain lion campaign was managed and coordinated by individuals with political, public relations, and grassroots organizing expertise. The win in California was a turning point for animal protection initiatives. It demonstrated to the animal protection movement that well-run campaigns, taking advantage of the unique strengths of profes- sional organizations and grassroots activism, could be successful.

Encouraged by the win in California, anti-trapping activists opted to pursue the initiative recourse to address their concerns. The results have been dramatic. Since 1994, the initiative process has been used to ban or restrict trapping in five states — Arizona, California, Colorado, Massachusetts, and Washington. Table 7.2 presents the results of all ballot initiatives held to date related to trapping. As noted in the table, the specific provisions of the measures have differed, and although the initiatives have included more exemptions than the laws passed by the New Jersey and Rhode Island legislatures, they also covered trapping devices in addition to the leghold trap. The Massachusetts initiative also banned the use of hounds to hunt bears and bobcats and changed the requirements of membership on the state wildlife board. And the Arizona, California, Colorado, and Washington measures all restricted the use of poisons to kill wildlife.

One likely reason for the recent success of anti-trapping initiatives is the public's increased awareness of, and support for, ending inhumane animal practices. This coincides with a shift from rural to urban residence in this country. Research for the author's master's thesis showed that population density is the demographic factor most frequently associated with the outcome of animal related ballot measures. Voting on these measures appears to be related in a positive direction with population of residence and in a negative direction with reliance on natural resource income. Both of these factors have shifted drastically in the U.S. since the beginning of the century. The percent of Americans living in urban areas has increased 50%, while the percent employed in agriculture has declined more than 90%. The trends in these areas are projected to continue.

Changing demographics is not the only explanation for the turnaround in animal initiatives. The animal protection movement has also learned how to get its message out to the public. After being outspent in several animal-related initiatives, leaders of animal protection campaigns now acknowledge that it takes money to deliver an effective message. Activities such as trapping are far removed from the experiences of the average American; free and paid media are necessary to educate voters about what these practices are and how they affect animals.

The American public has indicated through its votes on initiatives that it wants a say in how this country's wildlife is treated. Until state and federal governments accept that message and begin to act as responsible trustees of the nation's wildlife, citizen-initiated ballot measures offer one option for gaining reforms. Environmental scholar Roderick Nash noted: "It's a situation where the public has to get out in front and drag some of these bureaucracies along."

Ballot initiatives are not, however, a panacea for ending the cruelties of trapping or any other form of animal exploitation. They take a commitment of considerable time and money. The process is complex, and the outcome of ballot measures is dependent upon a number of factors, many of which are not under the control of those sponsoring the measures. Moreover, legal decisions, even when made by the voters themselves, are rarely final;

initiative results can be challenged in the state legislature, in court, or brought before the voters again at a subsequent election.

Following passage of the trapping ban in Arizona in 1994, four fur trappers appealed criminal convictions for violating the new law. Their appeal was based on the argument that the trapping ban, which applies only to public lands in Arizona (more than 80% of the state), violates the equal protection clauses of the Arizona and U.S. Constitutions by conferring special privileges and benefits to private landowners. On October 8, 1998, an Arizona Superior Court judge ruled upholding the constitutionality of the statute. The decision was appealed and subsequently upheld by the Court of Appeals, State of Arizona.[2]

Soon after Proposition 4, the California anti-trapping measure, passed, the National Audubon Society and four other organizations sued California to allow the use of leghold traps to protect federally-endangered bird species from predation.[3] Intervening in the case, Prop. 4 proponents argued that the initiative could be interpreted so as not to conflict with the federal conservation efforts. The court held, however, that the Endangered Species Act, the Migratory Bird Treat Act, and the Property Clause of the U.S. Constitution allowed the federal government to trap on its property for any purpose. Prop. 4 proponents and the State appealed the decision.

In September 2002, the 9th Circuit Court of Appeals found that Prop. 4 cannot be enforced against the federal trapping programs pursuant to the Endangered Species Act and the National Wildlife Refuge Systems Improvement Act. As a result, the federal government may trap on all National Wildlife Refuges and to protect endangered or threatened species. The 9th Circuit Court of Appeals found, however, that the federal government could not trap pursuant to the Migratory Bird Treaty Act. At press time, the case was being heard in district court to determine whether trapping may occur in California pursuant to the Animal Damage Control Act.

## State Anti-Cruelty Laws

Although every state has enacted anti-cruelty legislation, these laws have not provided animals with protection from inhumane trapping devices. Hunting, fishing, and trapping activities are specifically exempt from the cruelty statute of 34 states.* Generally, an activity is not regarded as falling under the cruelty law if it is regulated by a state agency. For example, in a recent case in New Mexico a rancher was charged and found guilty of animal cruelty for killing two deer by catching them in snares. The decision was upheld by the New Mexico Court of Appeals, but later reversed by the New Mexico Supreme Court on the grounds that the state Game and Fish Commission has exclusive authority to regulate the manner in which "game" animals are killed.[4]

## Local Legislation and Ballot Initiatives

Local bans on trapping have been the easiest to accomplish. As evidence of this, John Gentile, in his dissertation on the anti-trapping movement, documented trapping bans enacted in 84 U.S. cities and counties between 1925 and 1939. According to Gentile, by 1925 protectionists had realized that efforts to get women to give up furs were futile and better enforcement of existing trapping laws was unlikely, so enacting legislation at the local and state level became the strategy of choice. In many cases the primary purpose of the local ban was to prevent cruelty to animals, but a number of counties in states such as Arkansas, Texas, and Pennsylvania passed trapping prohibitions during this time to conserve dwindling numbers of furbearers. Some local bans were passed by the municipality itself and others by the state legislature.

By the time the U.S. became involved in World War II, anti-trapping activity had nearly ceased, and by 1948, trapping bans remained in effect in only a few scattered counties. Gentile documented no anti-trapping attempts at the local level between 1940 and 1967. However, public policy initiatives to end trapping resumed in the late 1960s. Between 1968 and 1982, local trapping

---

* P. D. Frasch, *et al.* "State Animal Anti-Cruelty Statutes: An Overview." *Animal Law* 5 (1999): 69–80. The states that exempt wildlife from their animal cruelty statute are: Alaska, Arizona, Arkansas, California, Colorado, Connecticut, Delaware, Georgia, Idaho, Illinois, Indiana, Iowa, Kansas, Kentucky, Louisiana, Maine, Maryland, Michigan, Missouri, Nebraska, New Jersey, New Mexico, North Carolina, Oregon, Pennsylvania, Rhode Island, South Carolina, South Dakota, Tennessee, Utah, Vermont, Washington, West Virginia, and Wisconsin.

---

### An Ordinance Adding Section 6.49 to the Sacramento City Code
### Prohibiting the Use of Steel-Jawed Leg-Hold Traps

*Be it enacted by the Council of the City of Sacramento:*

SECTION 1.

Section 6.49 is hereby added to the Sacramento City Code, to read as follows:

Section 6.49 Steel-Jawed Leg-Hold Traps Prohibited.

(a) Purpose. The purpose of this section is to protect the public health and safety by prohibiting the use of steel-jawed leg-hold traps which pose great potential for injury to domestic pets and children.

(b) Findings. The City Council finds as follows:

   (1) In an urbanized area, steel-jawed leg-hold traps present a risk of injury or death to domestic pets and persons, especially small children.

(2) Steel-jawed leg-hold traps are inhumane. Studies cited by the Humane Society of the United States show that up to 59.8% of animals caught in steel-jawed leg-hold traps sustain visible injuries caused by the type of trap employed.

(3) Steel-jawed leg-hold traps do not discriminate between the target animal and non-target animals. According to the Humane Society of the United States, by design of the trap, a trapper can never be sure of finding the desired animal caught in the steel-jaws of the trap.

(4) Alternatives to steel-jawed leg-hold traps are available for those circumstances in which the need to trap an intruding animal is great.

(5) A prohibition on the use of steel-jawed leg-hold traps within the City of Sacramento is necessary to protect the public health and safety of the City's human and pet population.

(c) Definition. For purposes of this section, "steel-jawed leg-hold trap" shall mean any spring-powered device or trap which captures or holds an animal by exerting a lateral force with fix-mounted jaws on the leg, toe, paw, or any other part of the animal's body.

(d) Use prohibited. It shall be unlawful and a misdemeanor for any person to use, set, place, maintain or tend, or cause to be used, set, placed, maintained or tended, any steel-jawed leg-hold trap.

---

bans were enacted in numerous areas, including 10 counties in Alabama, 3 counties in Maryland, 10 counties in New Jersey, at least 3 counties in North Carolina, and 24 towns and cities in Minnesota.

Anti-trapping initiatives at the local level continued into the 1990s. Protection of people and companion animals has been most often cited as the primary goal of local bans as illustrated by the "Purpose" and "Findings" section of the anti-trapping ordinance passed by the city of Sacramento, California in 1991 (text above). While city-wide bans such as Sacramento's do not threaten commercial trapping, prohibitions enacted at the county level are another story. In the mid-1980s, states — often with the urging of trapping and agricultural groups — began challenging county-wide bans in court.

In 1986, the Suffolk County [New York] Legislature voted to ban the use of steel-jaw leghold traps on the basis that the traps presented a hazard to children and companion animals. In vetoing the measure, the County Executive claimed that although he supported the ban, it could only be enacted through the State Legislature. The Suffolk County Legislature overrode the veto, but in 1988 the state Department of Environmental Conservation (DEC) sued to repeal the ban. The court found in the state's favor, agreeing that the DEC had authority over management of wildlife in the state. In 1997, the County of Rockland passed a similar ban that was also struck down by the courts on the basis that the county's authority in this area is circumscribed by the New York Constitution.[5]

California's San Francisco, Santa Cruz, and Nevada counties all passed leghold trap bans in the mid-1980s. In 1987, the state Department of Fish and Game requested an Attorney General opinion of whether a county may prohibit the use of leghold traps in its jurisdiction. The conclusion was that "a county may, by ordinance, ban the use of steel-jawed leg-hold traps within its jurisdiction where such action is necessary to protect the public health and safety and where the ordinance only incidentally affects the field of hunting preempted by the Fish and Game Code." The Attorney General cited the section of the State Constitution

# TABLE 7.3

*Federal anti-trapping legislation, 1973–2000.* *

| Session | # of Bills | Purpose | Number of Sponsors | Hearings Held |
|---|---|---|---|---|
| 1973–74 | 12 | To limit inhumane trapping devices on federal lands | 63 | No |
| 1973–74 | 3 | To ban commerce in steel-jaw leghold traps and in furs from animals trapped with leghold or steel-jaw traps | 4 | No |
| 1975–76 | 18 | To limit inhumane trapping devices on federal lands | 105 | Yes |
| 1975–76 | 5 | To ban commerce in steel-jaw leghold traps and in furs from animals trapped with leghold or steel-jaw traps | 5 | No |
| 1977–78 | 12 | To limit inhumane trapping devices on federal lands | 98 | No |
| 1977–78 | 7 | To ban commerce in steel-jaw leghold traps and in furs from animals trapped with leghold or steel-jaw traps | 21 | No |
| 1979–80 | 3 | To limit inhumane trapping devices on federal lands | 71 | No |
| 1979–80 | 2 | To ban commerce in steel-jaw leghold traps and in furs from animals trapped with leghold or steel-jaw traps | 114 | No |
| 1981–82 | 1 | To limit inhumane trapping devices on federal lands | 2 | No |
| 1981–82 | 2 | To ban commerce in steel-jaw leghold traps and in furs from animals trapped with leghold or steel-jaw traps | 87 | No |
| 1983–84 | 2 | To ban commerce in steel-jaw leghold traps and in furs from animals trapped with leghold or steel-jaw traps | 128 | Yes |
| 1985–86 | 2 | To ban commerce in steel-jaw leghold traps and in furs from animals trapped with leghold or steel-jaw traps | 121 | No |
| 1985–86 | 1 | To control trapping within the National Park Service and on other public lands | 8 | No |
| 1989–90 | 1 | To ban commerce in steel-jaw leghold traps and in furs from animals trapped with leghold or steel-jaw traps | 70 | No |
| 1991–92 | 2 | To ban commerce in steel-jaw leghold traps and in furs from animals trapped with leghold or steel-jaw traps | 120 | No |
| 1993–94 | 2 | To ban commerce in steel-jaw leghold traps and in furs from animals trapped with leghold or steel-jaw traps | 116 | No |
| 1995–96 | 2 | To ban commerce in steel-jaw leghold traps and in furs from animals trapped with leghold or steel-jaw traps | 98 | No |
| 1997–98 | 2 | To ban commerce in steel-jaw leghold traps and in furs from animals trapped with leghold or steel-jaw traps | 98 | No |
| 1999–00 | 2 | To ban commerce in steel-jaw leghold traps and in furs from animals trapped with leghold or steel-jaw traps | 103 | No |

* Data from Library of Congress (http://thomas.loc.gov).

granting the Legislature authority to enact laws for the protection of fish and wildlife, but also noted that the purpose of the ordinance would be significant: "An ordinance banning steel-jawed leg-hold traps in the City and County of San Francisco, an almost entirely urbanized area, would likely be held to have public safety as its principal purpose with hunting only incidentally affected. On the

## H.R. 1581, 106th Congress, Introduced by Representative Lowey, April 27, 1999, to End the Use of Steel-Jawed Leghold Traps on Animals in the United States [abridged]

*Be it enacted by the Senate and House of Representatives of the United States of America in Congress assembled,*

SECTION 1. DECLARATION OF POLICY.

It is the policy of the United States to end the needless maiming and suffering inflicted upon animals through the use of steel-jawed leghold traps by prohibiting the import or export of, and the shipment in interstate commerce of, such traps and of articles of fur from animals that were trapped in such traps.

SECTION 2. DEFINITIONS

As used in this Act:

(1) The term "article of fur" means—

(A) any furskin, whether raw or tanned or dressed; or

(B) any article, however produced, that consists in whole or part of any furskin.

For purposes of subparagraph (A), the terms "furskin", "raw", and "tanned or dressed" have the same respective meanings as those terms under headnote 1 of chapter 43 of the Harmonized Tariff Schedule of the United States.

(2) The term "interstate commerce" shall have the same meaning as that given to such term in section 10 of title 18, United States Code.

(3) The term "import" means to land on, bring into, or introduce into, any place subject to the jurisdiction of the United States, whether or not such landing, bringing, or introduction constitutes an entry into the customs territory of the United States.

(4) The term "person" includes any individual, partnership, association, corporation, trust, or any officer, employee, agent, department, or instrumentality of the Federal Government or of any State or political subdivision thereof, or any other entity subject to the jurisdiction of the United States.

(5) The term "Secretary" means the Secretary of the Interior.

(6) The term "conventional steel-jawed leghold trap" means any spring-powered pan- or sear-activated device with two opposing steel jaws, whether the jaws are smooth, toothed, padded, or offset, which is designed to capture an animal by snapping closed upon the animal's limb or part thereof.

SECTION 3. PROHIBITED ACTS AND PENALTIES

(a) Prohibition.—No article of fur shall be imported, exported, or shipped in interstate commerce if any part or portion of such article is derived from an animal that was trapped in a conventional steel-jawed leghold trap.

(b) Offenses.—It is unlawful for any person knowingly—

(1) to import, export, ship, or receive any article of fur in contravention of subsection (a);

(2) to import, export, deliver, carry, transport, or ship by any means whatever, in interstate commerce, any conventional steel-jawed leghold trap;

(3) to sell, receive, acquire, or purchase any conventional steel-jawed leghold trap that was delivered, carried, transported, or shipped in contravention of paragraph (2); or

(4) to violate any regulation prescribed by the Secretary under this section.

(c) Penalties.—any person who knowingly commits an act which violates subsection (a) or (b), or any regulation issued under this section, shall, in addition to any other penalty that may be imposed—

(1) for the first such violation, be guilty of an infraction under title 18, United States Code; and

(2) for each subsequent violation, be imprisoned for not more than two years, or fined in the amount set forth in title 18, United States Code, or both.

other hand, contrary findings might be expected with respect to the same ban in a rural county with a significant fur trapping tradition."[6]

Following issuance of the opinion, the State of California, joined by the California Farm Bureau, sued to overturn the leghold trap ban in primarily rural Nevada County. The state Fish and Game Department explained that it hadn't challenged other county and city prohibitions because those areas did not have large coyote populations that it felt could be controlled only with use of the trap. The case was heard in Nevada County Superior Court where the judge sided with the State, striking down the trapping prohibition.

## Federal Legislation and Regulation

The first national anti-trapping bill was introduced in the U.S. Congress in 1957. If enacted, it would have discouraged the use of steel-jaw leghold traps by directing the Secretary of the Interior to issue regulations prescribing acceptable methods for trapping mammals and birds on Federal lands. Similar bills were introduced in the next three sessions of Congress.

Anti-trapping efforts at the national level increased sharply in the early 1970s, coinciding with the birth of the modern environmental movement and the passage of landmark animal protective legislation such as the Endangered Species Act and the Marine Mammal Protection Act. In 1973, in addition to the public lands trapping bill, legislation was introduced to ban commerce in steel-jaw leghold traps and in furs from animals taken in leghold traps (partial text of the 1999–2000 version is given on p. 132). Similar legislation has been introduced in all but one subsequent session of Congress. Table 7.3 presents a summary of these federal bills. A total of 23 anti-trapping bills with 110 co-sponsors were introduced during 1975–76 session alone. Despite the persistence of the effort and considerable legislative and public support, only two hearings have been held and as yet no anti-trapping legislation has been reported out of committee.

The first congressional vote on trapping came in 1999 when an amendment was offered to the Department of the Interior appropriations bill to eliminate funding of commercial or recreational trapping programs using steel-jaw leghold traps or neck snares on National Wildlife Refuges. The House of Representatives approved the measure by a vote of 259 to 166. Following strong lobbying by hunters, trappers, and state wildlife agencies, however, the Senate killed a similar amendment by voting 64 to 32 to table it.

Failure of federal anti-trapping legislation has been credited to opposition from powerful lobbying groups representing hunting, trapping, agricultural, and commercial fur interests, and to opposition by federal and state agencies that vigorously defend the activity and, in some cases, participate in it themselves. In fact, the Wildlife Services program of

the U.S. Department of Agriculture, operating under the authority of the Animal Damage Control Act of 1931, is the single largest user of traps in the United States. Each year, tens of thousands of wild animals are caught in leghold traps set in a dozen western states by agents of Wildlife Services. In recent years, animal protectionists have attempted unsuccessfully to indirectly limit the use of traps by this agency by promoting congressional cuts in its funding for lethal animal control.

To date, few efforts have been made to limit trapping through changing federal agency regulation or policy. Trapping is permitted on federal lands administered by the Department of the Interior's Bureau of Land Management and the Department of Agriculture's Forest Service, subject to state laws and regulations. Trapping on the National Wildlife Refuge System, administered by the Department of Interior's Fish and Wildlife Service (FWS), is generally allowed under the authority of FWS regulations described in Chapter Six. Trapping on national park lands, however, also administered by the Department of Interior, is prohibited except where specifically sanctioned by Congress.

The National Park Service rule limiting hunting and trapping to parks where specifically mandated by federal statutory law was challenged by the National Rifle Association of America and the Wildlife Legislative Fund of America in 1984, shortly after the regulation was promulgated. The plaintiffs argued that the regulation arbitrarily reversed a Park Service policy of permitting hunting and trapping in recreational areas of the park system. The government and intervening advocacy defendants responded that the philosophy of the Park Service has always been exclusively protectionist; that hunting and trapping had never been permitted in traditional parks and monuments; and that, while the Park Service erred in allowing the activities in certain recreational areas in the 1960s and 1970s, it was conforming to the constant congressional intent of legislation governing national park lands. The U.S. District Court hearing the case found in favor of the Park Service.[7] Trapping currently occurs only in a very few park units where the activity was specifically granted by federal enabling acts.

## Restricting the Sale of Fur

Animal advocates have also approached trapping by attempting to restrict the sale of products from animals taken with certain traps. Anti-trapping legislation introduced in the U.S. Congress has focused on interstate commerce in products from animals caught with the leghold trap to bring the issue under federal jurisdiction. And California's and Washington's successful anti-trapping initiatives included a prohibition on the sale of raw fur of animals trapped with body-gripping traps to eliminate the economic incentive to trap animals for damage control with traps other than the leghold, which was banned outright in the measure.

In addition, two municipalities have held contentious and highly publicized debates on selling finished fur products. In 1986, the City Council of Aspen, Colorado, voted 3 to 2 to prohibit the sale of furs from animals caught in areas allowing use of the steel-jaw leghold trap. However, an outcry from local businesses put the issue before the voters in February 1990, when it was soundly defeated. In 1999, animal activists in Beverly Hills, California, placed a measure on the city ballot that would have required fur sellers to attach labels to their products explaining how the animals were killed. Any item costing more than $50 would have carried warnings that the animals may have been electrocuted, gassed, poisoned, clubbed, stomped, drowned, or caught by steel-jaw leghold traps. On voting day, May 11, 1999, the measure lost 38% to 62% after winning intense international publicity.

## Conclusion

The political power of hunters and the fur industry makes a federal ban on trapping unlikely in the near future, although additional bans at the state level would probably help prospects significantly. While trapping bans at the local level have been relatively easy to attain, their impact is affected by the limited amount of commercial and damage control trapping that occurs in these areas. Statewide bans, accomplished through legislation or citizen initiative, appear to offer the best hope of eliminating the use of specific trapping devices. To date, partial or complete statewide bans have been enacted on the use of

leghold traps in 8 states, Conibear traps in 14 states, and snares in 21 states (see Table 7.1).

Efforts of animal advocates to restrict the use of trapping devices have been countered by those with an interest in keeping use of the devices legal. Some municipal and county-wide bans have been overturned on constitutional grounds. Attempts have been made to repeal statewide trapping restrictions through litigation and legislative action, although none has been successful to date. Six states (Alabama, Michigan, Minnesota, North Dakota, Utah, and Virginia) have taken preemptive steps by passing laws that guarantee the right to hunt or restrict the availability of the citizen initiative process for wildlife management issues.

Despite minimal success with winning an outright ban of the activity, the legal status of trapping in the U.S. has been altered significantly since the first anti-trapping bill was introduced in 1901. Restrictions are in place in most states on who can trap, what animals can be trapped and when, the type and size of devices that can be used, where traps can be used, and how often they must be checked. In many instances, these limits were won by animal advocates through their participation in the legislative and regulatory process.

The public remains firmly opposed to the commercialization of wildlife and to the use of indiscriminate and inhumane trapping devices. This disapproval, combined with a declining interest in trapping as a recreational activity, puts the long-term future of trapping in serious doubt. There is cause for optimism that policy initiatives to restrict trapping, accompanied by efforts to decrease the demand for fur products and promotion of alternatives for damage control, will eventually lead to the elimination of body-gripping traps in the U.S.

### NOTES

1. J. R. Gentile. "The Evolution and Geographic Aspects of the Anti-trapping Movement: A Classic Resource Conflict." Doctoral dissertation, Oregon State University, 1984.

2. "State of Arizona v. Kurt Bonnewell, et al." No. CR 98-0093; State of Arizona v. Kurt Bonnewell, et al., ___Ariz.___

3. "National Audubon Society, et al. v. Pete Wilson, et al." No. 98-4610 (D. Ca. Filed Dec. 3, 1998.)

4. "New Mexico v. Cleve." No. 24, 734 (N.M. Mar. 11, 1999).

5. "State of New York, et al. v. County of Rockland, et al." No. 0973/98 (N.Y. Sup. Ct. May 27, 1998).

6. 70 Cal. Atty. Gen. Ops. 210, 214.

7. "Natl. Rifle Assn. of Am. v. Potter." 628 F. Supp. 903 (D.D.C. 1986).

# AFTERWORD

Around 1964, I decided to do something about a trapping situation in the California county where I lived. I met others who shared my feelings of outrage and disgust at the cruelty and suffering inherent in trapping and the fur trade. A new friendship was born, beginning a partnership in humane work that soon led to the founding of the Animal Protection Institute.

From its earliest days, API's core mission has been the protection of animals. To accomplish our mission, we work continually to change state and federal policies and regulations. We inform the public of the abuses of animals everywhere. We teach fledgling activists how to work for change in their own communities.

*Cull of the Wild* is the culmination of API's extensive research and advocacy on trapping issues. Here, in one concise publication, is the history and current status of trapping in the United States. That history is a shameful record of cruelty and indifference to the pain and suffering of the trapper's "harvest."

Today's trappers believe they are a part of history, continuing what they see as a great tradition dating back to the days before the Old West turned to gunslingers and cowboys. They don't understand that those gory days of "glory" are gone, a shameful relic of an unenlightened time.

API hopes that *Cull of the Wild* will open the eyes of anyone who cares about animals. Government officials, whatever their level in the decision-making process, need this book to show them that trapping is archaic, inhumane, and ecologically damaging. Grassroots activists will find the tools they need to help convince these same government officials that the cruelty of trapping must end.

Are there humane alternatives to trapping? You bet. Can the would-be grassroots activist find step-by-step instructions on how to get involved and what to do? Absolutely. *Cull of the Wild* works hand in hand with API's website, www.api4animals.org, which offers a wealth of resources. And help is always available by contacting API's headquarters.

The animal rights movement has come a long way since API came into being. Attitudes and practices that were taken for granted only a generation or so ago have been reformed. We're proud to have helped shape that journey, in the process saving untold numbers of animals and empowering thousands of caring, compassionate people to do something about the injustices they see around them.

Your participation can help eliminate trapping and ensure that the present generation of trappers is the last. With education and understanding, with compassion and advocacy, we can put an end to the shame and cruelty of trapping in the United States.

*Kenneth E. Guerrero*
*Chairman Emeritus*
*Animal Protection Institute*

# Additional References and Resources

## Websites

For those who want to find additional information regarding trapping and the fur industry online, the following websites will get you started. Many of these sites have additional links to other useful sites. State and federal government websites are also provided for information pertaining to trapping laws and regulations.

### Pro-Wildlife/Anti-Trapping/Fur Websites

*www.BanCruelTraps.com*

*www.api4animals.org*

The Animal Protection Institute (API) websites provide information about API's major campaigns, wildlife-related state and federal legislation, timely action alerts, and links to other useful sites. Visit API's websites for current information about anti-trapping/fur campaigns and legislation.

*www.infurmation.com*

Fur Free Alliance website. Provides information about trapping and fur farming worldwide.

*www.worldanimal.net*

World Animal Net is a worldwide network of societies campaigning to improve the status and welfare of animals.

*www.furfreeaction.com* — Humane Society of the United States

*www.respectforanimals.org* — Respect for Animals

*www.caft.org.uk* — The Coalition to Abolish the Fur Trade–UK

*www.banlegholdtraps.com* — The Fur-Bearer Defenders

### Pro-Fur/Trapping Websites

*www.nationaltrappers.com*

The official site of the National Trappers Association, providing information on state trapping regulations, recent fur auction results, and links to other useful sites.

These sites provide information about the North American fur industry and provide many links to other sites:

*www.furcouncil.com* — The Fur Council of Canada

*www.fur.org* — Fur Information Council of America

*www.furcommission.com* — Fur Commission USA

*www.iftf.com* — International Fur Trade Federation

*www.naiaonline.org*

The National Animal Interest Alliance is a coalition of trappers, hunters, fur industry representatives, vivisectors, and agribusiness representatives whose goal is "to provide balancing information and services where animal rights activities or other forms of animal exploitation have diverted attention from facts and foundation issues."

*www.furbearermgmt.org*

The official site of the International Association of Fish and Wildlife Agencies Furbearer Resources Technical Work Group. Information on BMP trap testing carried out with federal funding and other trapping related information.

*www.wlfa.org*

In their own words, "The US Sportsmen's Alliance (Formerly the Wildlife Legislative Fund of America 'WLFA') provides direct lobbying and grassroots coalition support to protect and advance the rights of hunters, fishermen, trappers and scientific wildlife management professionals." Site provides information on current trapping/hunting legislation.

## Government Sites

### Federal Government

*www.lawchek.net*

Wealth of information on federal and state laws, federal agencies, and U.S. Congress.

*www.fedworld.gov*

Federal government source of statistics, including those on the fur industry.

*www.senate.gov*

Wealth of information on the U.S. Senate.

*www.house.gov*

Wealth of information on the U.S. House of Representatives.

*www.access.gpo.gov*

*GPO Access* is a service of the U.S. Government Printing Office that provides free electronic access to a wealth of important information products produced by the Federal Government.

*http://thomas.loc.gov*

Provides information on current and previous federal legislation.

*http://laws.fws.gov*

Provides access to state and federal wildlife related laws, the Federal Code of Regulations, federal wildlife-related acts and treaties, and links to other useful sites.

*https://foia.aphis.usda.gov*

The U.S. Department of Agriculture's Animal and Plant Health Inspection Service Freedom of Information Act (FOIA) Home Page. Provides a "Guide for Freedom of Information Act (FOIA) Requesters" with instructions on how to use the site to obtain frequently requested information and records.

*www.washlaw.edu*

Washburn Law Library, which provides links to the federal court system.

### State Government

*www.msue.msu.edu/wildlife/links/statenragencies.html*

Access to all 50 state fish and wildlife agency websites.

*www.lawsonline.net/directories_info/stleg.htm*

Access to state legislative websites.

*www.washlaw.edu*

Washburn Law Library, which provides links to all 50 states' legislative and court systems.

*http://ipl.unm.edu/cwl*

Website of the Center for Wildlife Law, the Institute for Public Law, University of New Mexico School of Law. Provides information on state and federal wildlife laws.

## Printed Materials

### Books/Publications

Animal Welfare Institute. *Animals and Their Legal Rights: A Survey of American Laws from 1641 to 1990.* Washington: Animal Welfare Institute, 1990.

Eveland, Thomas. *Jaws of Steel.* Silver Spring: The Fund For Animals, Inc. 1991.

Garrett, Tom. *Alternative Traps: The Role of Spring Powered Killing Traps in Modern Trapping, the Role of Cage and Box Traps in Modern Trapping, and the Role of Legsnares in Modern Trapping.* Washington: Animal Welfare Institute, 1999.

Gerstell, Richard. *The Steel Trap in North America: The Illustrated Story of Its Design, Production, and Use with Furbearing and Predatory Animals, from Its Colorful Past to the Present Controversy.* Harrisburg: Stackpole Books, 1985.

Humane Society of the United States. *What Is That They're Wearing? A Humane Society of the U.S. report regarding the international trade in dog and cat fur.* Washington: Humane Society of the United States, 1999.

McKenna, Carol. *Fashion Victims: An Inquiry into the Welfare of Animals on Fur Farms*. World Society for the Protection of Animals, August 1998.

Musgrave, Ruth S., *et al. State Wildlife Laws Handbook*. Center for Wildlife Law, Univ. of New Mexico. Rockville, Maryland: Government Institutes Inc., 1993. (*Federal Wildlife Laws Handbook* also available. Published in 1998).

Nilsson, Greta, *et al. Facts About Furs*. Washington: Animal Welfare Institute, 1980.

**Trapping/Fur Trade Publications**

*American Trapper*. Published six times a year by the National Trappers Association. Provides a plethora of information pertaining to trapping. Telephone: 309-829-2422. *www.nationaltrappers.com.*

*The Trapper & Predator Caller*. Published ten times a year. Provides fur market reports, news reports on trapping-related legislation, fur auction information, and reports from all state trapping associations. Telephone: 1-800-258-0929.

# APPENDIX II

# State Wildlife Agencies

(Before sending correspondence, please double-check agency contact information since it may have changed since the publication of this book)

**Alabama**
Alabama Department of Conservation and
Natural Resources
Division of Wildlife & Freshwater Fisheries
64 N. Union Street
Montgomery, AL 36130-1456
205-242-3565
*www.dcnr.state.al.us/agfd*

**Alaska**
Alaska Department of Fish and Game
Division of Wildlife Conservation
P.O. Box 25526
Juneau, AK 99802-5526
907-465-4190
*www.state.ak.us/local/akpages/FISH.GAME/wild
life/wildmain.htm*

**Arizona**
Arizona Department of Game and Fish
2221 West Greenway Road
Phoenix, AZ 85023-4399
602-942-3000
*www.gf.state.az.us*

**Arkansas**
Arkansas Game and Fish Commission
2 Natural Resources Drive
Little Rock, AR 72205
800-364-GAME
*www.agfc.state.ar.us*

**California**
California Department of Fish and Game
1416 Ninth Street
Sacramento, CA 95814
916-445-0411
*www.dfg.ca.gov*

**Colorado**
Colorado Division of Wildlife
6060 Broadway
Denver, CO 80216
303-297-1192
*wildlife.state.co.us*

**Connecticut**
Connecticut Department of Environmental
Protection
Bureau of Natural Resources—Wildlife Division
79 Elm Street
Hartford, CT 06106-5127
860-424-3011
*dep.state.ct.us*

**Delaware**
Delaware Department of Natural Resources and
Environmental Control
Division of Fish & Wildlife
89 Kings Highway
Dover, DE 19901
302-739-5295
*www.dnrec.state.de.us/dnrec2000*

**Florida**
Florida Fish and Wildlife Conservation
Commission
Division of Wildlife
620 South Meridian Street
Tallahassee, FL 32399
850-488-3831
*www.floridaconservation.org*

**Georgia**
Georgia Deptpartment of Natural Resources
Wildlife Resources Division
2070 U.S. Highway 278 SE
Social Circle, GA 30025
404-656-3500
*georgiawildlife.dnr.state.ga.us*

**Idaho**
Idaho Fish and Game Department
600 S. Walnut, P.O. Box 25
Boise, ID 83707
208-334-3700
*www2.state.id.us/fishgame/fishgame.html*

**Illinois**
Illinois Department of Natural Resources
One Natural Resources Way
Springfield, IL 62701-1271
217-782-6384
*dnr.state.il.us*

**Indiana**
Indiana Department of Natural Resources
Division of Fish and Wildlife
402 W. Washington Street, Room W273
Indianapolis, IN 46204
317-232-4080
*www.in.gov/fishwild/index.html*

**Iowa**
Iowa Deptartment of Natural Resources
Fish and Wildlife Division, Wildlife Bureau
502 East 9th Street
Des Moines, IA 50319-0034
515-281-5918
*www.state.ia.us/wildlife*

**Kansas**
Kansas Department of Wildlife and Parks
Office of the Secretary
1020 S. Kansas
Topeka, KS 66612-1327
785-296-2281
*www.kdwp.state.ks.us*

**Kentucky**
Kentucky Department of Fish and Wildlife
1 Game Farm Road
Frankfort, KY 40601
800-858-1549
*www.kdfwr.state.ky.us*

**Louisiana**
Louisiana Department Of Wildlife and Fisheries
200 Quail Drive
Baton Rouge, LA 70808
225-765-2800
*www.wlf.state.la.us/apps/netgear/page1.asp*

**Maine**
Main Department of Inland Fisheries and Wildlife
284 State Street
41 State House Station
Augusta, ME 04333-0041
207-287-8000
*www.state.me.us/ifw/homepage.htm*

**Maryland**
Maryland Department of Natural Resources
Wildlife and Heritage Division
Tawes State Office Building, E-1
580 Taylor Avenue
Annapolis, MD 21401
*www.dnr.state.md.us*

**Massachusetts**
Massachusetts Division of Fisheries and Wildlife
251 Causeway Street, Suite 400
Boston, MA 02114-2152
617-626-1590
*www.state.ma.us/dfwele/dpt_toc.htm*

**Michigan**
Michigan Department of Natural Resources
Wildlife Division
Mason Building, 4th Floor
P.O. Box 30444
Lansing, MI 48909-7944
517-373-1263
*www.michigan.gov/dnr*

**Minnesota**
Minnesota Department of Natural Resources
500 Lafayette Road
St. Paul, MN 55155-4040
651-296-6157
*www.dnr.state.mn.us/index.html*

**Mississippi**
Mississippi Department of Wildlife, Fisheries & Parks
1505 Eastover Drive
Jackson, MS 39211-6374
601-432-2400
*www.mdwfp.com*

**Missouri**
Missouri Department of Conservation
P.O. Box 180
Jefferson City, MO 65102-0180
573-751-4115
*www.conservation.state.mo.us*

**Montana**
Montana Department of Fish, Wildlife, and Parks
1420 East Sixth Avenue
P.O. Box 200701
Helena, MT 59620-0701
406-444-2535
*www.fwp.state.mt.us*

**Nebraska**
Nebraska Game and Parks Commission
2200 North 33rd Street
Lincoln, NE 68503
402-471-0641
*ngpc.state.ne.us*

**Nevada**
Nevada Department of Wildlife
1100 Valley Road
Reno, NV 89512
775-688-1500
*http://ndow.org*

**New Hampshire**
New Hampshire Fish & Game Department
2 Hazen Drive
Concord, NH 03301
603-271-3211
*www.wildlife.state.nh.us*

**New Jersey**
New Jersey Department of Environmental
Protection
Division of Fish and Wildlife
P.O. Box 400
501 East State Street, 3rd Floor
Trenton, NJ 08625-0400
609-292-2965
*www.state.nj.us/dep/fgw*

**New Mexico**
New Mexico Department of Game and Fish
Division of Wildlife
1 Wildlife Way
Santa Fe, NM 87507
505-476-8000
*www.gmfsh.state.nm.us*

**New York**
New York State Department of Environmental
Conservation
Division of Fish, Wildlife, and Marine Resources
625 Broadway
Albany, NY 12233-4750
518-402-8924
*www.dec.state.ny.us*

**North Carolina**
North Carolina Wildlife Resources Commission
Division of Wildlife Management
512 North Salisbury Street, Room 325
Raleigh, NC 27604
919-733-7291
*www.ncwildlife.org*

**North Dakota**
North Dakota Game & Fish Department
100 North Bismarck Expressway
Bismarck, ND 58501-5095
701-328-6300
*www.state.nd.us/gnf*

**Ohio**
Ohio Department of Natural Resources
Division of Wildlife
1840 Belcher Drive
Columbus, OH 43224-1329
614-265-6300
*www.dnr.state.oh.us/wildlife*

**Oklahoma**
Oklahoma Department of Wildlife Conservation
1801 North Lincoln
Oklahoma City, OK 73105
405-521-3851
*www.wildlifedepartment.com*

**Oregon**
Oregon Department of Fish and Wildlife
2501 SW First Avenue
P.O. Box 59
Portland, OR 97207
503-872-5268
*www.dfw.state.or.us*

**Pennsylvania**
Pennsylvania Game Commission
2001 Elmerton Ave.
Harrisburg, PA 17110-9797
717-787-4250
*www.pgc.state.pa.us*

**Rhode Island**
Rhode Island Department of Environmental
Management
Stedman Government Center
Dvision of Fish and Wildlife
4808 Tower Hill Road
Wakefield, RI 02879
401-789-3094
*www.state.ri.us/dem*

**South Carolina**
South Carolina Department of Natural
Resources
Rembert C. Dennis Building
1000 Assembly Street
Columbia, SC 29201
803-734-3888
*water.dnr.state.sc.us*

**South Dakota**
South Dakota Department of Game, Fish & Parks
Division of Wildlife
523 East Capitol Avenue
Pierre, SD 57501-3182
605-773-3381
*www.state.sd.us/gfp*

**Tennessee**
Tennessee Wildlife Resources Agency
Ellington Agricultural Center
P.O. Box 40747
Nashville, TN 37204
615-781-6610
*www.state.tn.us/twra*

**Texas**
Texas Parks and Wildlife Department
4200 Smith School Road
Austin, TX 78744
512-389-4800 or
800-792-1112
*www.tpwd.state.tx.us*

**Utah**
Utah Department of Natural Resources
Division of Wildlife Resources
1594 W. North Temple
Suite 2110 / Box 146301
Salt Lake City, UT 84114-6301
801-538-4700
*www.wildlife.utah.gov*

**Vermont**
Vermont Fish and Wildlife Department
10 South Main Street
Waterbury, VT 05671-0501
802-241-3701
*www.anr.state.vt.us/fw/fwhome*

**Virginia**
Department of Game and Inland Fisheries
4010 West Broad Street
Richmond, VA 23230
804-367-1000
*www.dgif.state.va.us*

**Washington**
Washington Department of Fish and Wildlife
600 Capitol Way North
Olympia, WA 98501-1091
360-902-2200
*www.wa.gov/wdfw*

**West Virginia**
West Virginia Division of Natural Resources
Wildlife Resources Section
State Capitol Complex, Building 3, Room 669
1900 Kanawha Boulevard
Charleston, WV 25305-0060
304-558-2771
*www.dnr.state.wv.us*

**Wisconsin**
Wisconsin Department of Natural Resources
101 South Webster Street
Madison, WI 53703
608-266-2621
*www.dnr.state.wi.us*

**Wyoming**
Wyoming Game and Fish Department
5400 Bishop Blvd.
Cheyenne, WY 82006
307-777-4600
*gf.state.wy.us*

# Number of Animals Trapped in the United States 1986–1999

☐ Indicates trapped data.

▨ Indicates trapped, hunted or other data.

N/D No data provided/ available

| State | 1986–87 | 1987–88 | 1988–89 | 1989–90 | 1990–91 | 1991–92 | 1992–93 | 1993–94 | 1994–95 | 1995–96 | 1996–97 | 1997–98 | 1998–99 | Total by state 1986–99 |
|---|---|---|---|---|---|---|---|---|---|---|---|---|---|---|
| **Badger** | | | | | | | | | | | | | | |
| AZ[8] | 780 | 748 | 281 | 89 | 33 | 151 | 69 | 44 | 24 | 8 | 11 | 21 | 27 | ...6 |
| AR[9] | 5 | 1 | 2 | 0 | 0 | 1 | 0 | 0 | 3 | 2 | 3 | 0 | N/D | 17 |
| CA[58] | 194 | 235 | 92 | 72 | 13 | 22 | 25 | 42 | 22 | 23 | 49 | 47 | 5 | 841 |
| CO[59, 19] | 847 | 1,003 | 424 | 259 | 242 | 60 | 527 | 426 | 656 | 186 | 155 | N/D | N/D | 4,78_ |
| ID[16] | 512 | 490 | 246 | 106 | 91 | 212 | 103 | 175 | 137 | 150 | 280 | 145 | 169 | 2_ _ |
| IL | 0 | 0 | 0 | 0 | 0 | 0 | 0 | 0 | 0 | 0 | 50 | 31 | 18 | _99 |
| IA[20] | 2,520 | 1,642 | 1,043 | 468 | 503 | 572 | 621 | 571 | 502 | 614 | 832 | 796 | 642 | _1,_26 |
| KS[7] | 3,009 | 2,402 | 1,417 | 476 | 442 | 571 | 687 | 649 | 781 | 522 | 874 | 876 | 958 | 13,664 |
| MI[26] | 0 | 0 | 0 | 28 | 52 | 35 | 63 | 90 | 124 | 75 | 109 | 117 | 91 | _84 |
| MN[27] | 2,000 | 3,000 | 2,000 | 1,000 | 1,000 | 1,000 | 1,000 | 1,000 | 1,000 | 500 | 1,000 | 1,000 | 500 | _,000 |
| MO[31] | 133 | 84 | 44 | 19 | 8 | 25 | 30 | 44 | 31 | 26 | 44 | 36 | 20 | 544 |
| MT[33] | 2,108 | 2,538 | 1,612 | 727 | 498 | 920 | 482 | 839 | 931 | 491 | 1,819 | 1,071 | 261 | 14_ _7 |
| NE[35] | 3,517 | 3,064 | 1,505 | 715 | 582 | 1,223 | 973 | 1,023 | 1,874 | 1,629 | 2,224 | 3,093 | 2,284 | 23,_ 6 |
| NV[37] | 397 | 366 | 141 | 97 | 55 | 151 | 112 | 233 | 182 | 53 | 96 | 58 | 94 | 2,_35 |
| NM[39] | 942 | 460 | N/D | 173 | 216 | 225 | 325 | 322 | 412 | 68 | 86 | 19 | 16 | 3,264 |
| ND[42] | 3,082 | 5,467 | 2,016 | 446 | 762 | 1,723 | 655 | 634 | 821 | 953 | 1,838 | 2,991 | 106 | 21,494 |
| OH[43] | 29 | 5 | 5 | 1 | 5 | 2 | 0 | 0 | 0 | 0 | 1 | 0 | 0 | _ |
| OK[44] | 176 | 75 | 28 | 4 | 3 | 12 | 5 | 19 | 32 | 14 | 21 | 10 | 10 | 409 |
| OR[45] | 583 | 612 | 149 | 104 | 140 | 136 | 180 | 95 | 166 | 102 | 181 | 1 | 3 | 2,452 |
| SD[49] | 2,356 | 3,411 | 1,493 | 402 | 457 | 809 | 860 | 594 | 1,077 | 825 | 826 | 836 | 441 | 14,387 |
| TX[50] | 1,591 | 1,633 | 1,309 | 811 | 287 | 360 | 578 | 406 | 451 | 299 | 1,015 | 766 | 506 | 10,012 |
| UT[51] | 424 | 459 | 417 | 366 | 172 | 237 | 232 | 238 | 327 | 276 | 222 | 271 | 318 | 3,959 |
| WA[54] | 135 | 85 | 28 | 19 | 21 | 30 | 20 | 17 | 40 | 6 | 11 | 14 | 2 | 428 |
| WY[57] | 1,482 | 2,811 | 1,850 | 773 | 714 | 1,798 | 878 | 404 | 383 | 156 | 333 | 3,900 | 279 | 15,761 |
| **Total** | 26,822 | 30,591 | 16,102 | 7,155 | 6,296 | 10,275 | 8,425 | 7,865 | 9,976 | 6,978 | 12,080 | 16,099 | 6,750 | |

Totals from 1986 through 1999 = 165,414

# APPENDIX III

*Number of Animals Trapped in the United States.*

Indicates trapped data.

Indicates trapped, hunted or other data.

N/D  No data provided/ available

| State | 1986–87 | 1987–88 | 1988–89 | 1989–90 | 1990–91 | 1991–92 | 1992–93 | 1993–94 | 1994–95 | 1995–96 | 1996–97 | 1997–98 | 1998–99 | Total by State 1986–99 |
|---|---|---|---|---|---|---|---|---|---|---|---|---|---|---|
| | | | | | | | **Beaver** | | | | | | | |
| AL[1] | 4,049 | 3,343 | 824 | 216 | 111 | 95 | 43 | 72 | 287 | 663 | 1,110 | 540 | 242 | 11,595 |
| AK[4] | 17,112 | 16,556 | 9,219 | 8,240 | 5,577 | 7,151 | 3,185 | 4,860 | 4,493 | 3,614 | 6,930 | 5,299 | 3,216 | 93,482 |
| AZ[8] | 87 | 127 | 80 | 202 | 28 | 52 | 9 | 0 | 0 | 0 | 19 | 52 | 16 | 672 |
| AR[9] | 10,527 | 8,609 | 4,963 | 4,396 | 1,803 | 2,167 | 3,187 | 4,460 | 9,202 | 15,219 | 19,207 | 14,076 | 12,190 | 110,006 |
| CA[58] | 1,451 | 1,231 | 622 | 586 | 250 | 551 | 345 | 509 | 257 | 299 | 526 | 792 | 313 | 7,732 |
| CO[59, 19] | 5,913 | 7,458 | 4,033 | 6,064 | 3,657 | 3,151 | 3,488 | 3,833 | 5,751 | 2,771 | 2,396 | N/D | N/D | 48,515 |
| CT[32] | 642 | 655 | 702 | 565 | 553 | 594 | 582 | 521 | 1,032 | 553 | 1,180 | 1,163 | 708 | 9,450 |
| DE[12] | N/D | N/D | 3 | 20 | 0 | 15 | 34 | 99 | 11 | 10 | 71 | 309 | 443 | 1,015 |
| FL[60] | 97 | 210 | 9 | 0 | 0 | 0 | 0 | 0 | 4 | 4 | 11 | 53 | 0 | 388 |
| GA[14] | 5,990 | 6,233 | 4,159 | 5,240 | 2,535 | 4,116 | 4,710 | 4,256 | 3,941 | 6,074 | 5,836 | 5,398 | 4,874 | 63,362 |
| ID[16] | 7,388 | 7,148 | 4,477 | 5,459 | 3,206 | 4,268 | 2,043 | 2,581 | 2,307 | 2,403 | 3,626 | 4,076 | 3,528 | 52,510 |
| IL[17] | 8,960 | 8,314 | 5,241 | 3,887 | 2,315 | 2,533 | 1,917 | 2,847 | 5,297 | 3,902 | 6,310 | 9,406 | 3,474 | 64,403 |
| IN[18] | 3,357 | 2,739 | 1,488 | 1,341 | 588 | 1,183 | 1,643 | 1,026 | 1,534 | 1,675 | 1,871 | 3,361 | 2,469 | 24,275 |
| IA[20] | 17,778 | 13,509 | 18,459 | 8,706 | 9,246 | 8,943 | 15,839 | 11,788 | 11,643 | 10,678 | 10,481 | 11,122 | 10,336 | 158,528 |
| KS[7] | 14,732 | 12,474 | 13,989 | 9,607 | 5,214 | 5,429 | 3,044 | 5,288 | 12,123 | 8,089 | 10,653 | 13,337 | 8,606 | 122,585 |
| KY[11] | 2,527 | 1,633 | 1,211 | 1,174 | 801 | 1,021 | 1,035 | 613 | 1,035 | 967 | 2,257 | 2,968 | 2,687 | 19,929 |
| LA[2] | 1,810 | 1,274 | 830 | 864 | 1,303 | 993 | 3,650 | 1,824 | 4,897 | 4,473 | 11,630 | 10,229 | 4,914 | 48,691 |
| ME[23] | 12,152 | 12,611 | 10,311 | 7,839 | 7,522 | 10,636 | 9,619 | 8,177 | 15,251 | 7,336 | 16,640 | 10,547 | 10,432 | 139,073 |
| MD[25] | 693 | 648 | 434 | 550 | 334 | 280 | 537 | N/D | N/D | N/D | N/D | N/D | N/D | 3,476 |
| MA[19] | 1,371 | 1,695 | 1,042 | 1,364 | 1,103 | 1,223 | 1,086 | 1,025 | 2,083 | 1,136 | 623 | 98 | 114 | 13,963 |
| MI[3] | 42,920 | 17,640 | 38,680 | N/D | N/D | N/D | N/D | 25,684 | 56,753 | N/D | 41,671 | 90,699 | 39,987 | 354,034 |
| MN[27] | 172,000 | 158,000 | 47,000 | 79,000 | 44,000 | 51,000 | 56,000 | 61,000 | 113,000 | 66,000 | 86,000 | 83,000 | 94,000 | 1,110,000 |
| MS | 15,214 | 12,952 | 9,753 | 8,591 | 4,475 | 5,110 | 6,203 | 6,563 | 5,929 | 5,654 | 11,404 | 8,894 | 9,620 | 110,362 |
| MO[31] | 10,284 | 8,125 | 7,266 | 5,158 | 2,759 | 3,192 | 2,153 | 3,561 | 5,475 | 5,327 | 9,899 | 9,534 | 4,849 | 77,582 |
| MT[33] | 18,142 | 12,356 | 8,987 | 8,710 | 5,497 | 5,133 | 5,707 | 6,478 | 11,699 | 8,620 | 16,531 | 13,497 | 11,634 | 132,991 |
| NE[35] | 25,439 | 18,302 | 13,273 | 13,436 | 6,339 | 8,764 | 5,157 | 11,368 | 19,357 | 14,039 | 27,823 | 25,267 | 20,359 | 208,923 |
| NV[37] | 1,722 | 675 | 367 | 1,020 | 421 | 1,089 | 254 | 403 | 625 | 398 | 564 | 780 | 421 | 8,739 |
| NH[36] | 4,258 | 4,099 | 3,637 | 3,098 | 2,589 | 3,372 | 2,059 | 3,612 | 5,901 | 4,048 | 4,752 | 3,975 | 3,784 | 49,184 |
| NJ[38] | 134 | 160 | 168 | 132 | 169 | 152 | 168 | 113 | 172 | 266 | 304 | 288 | 329 | 2,555 |
| NM[39] | 584 | 372 | N/D | 428 | 231 | 656 | 234 | 322 | 672 | 74 | 144 | 112 | 9 | 3,838 |
| NY[40] | 23,754 | 21,892 | 16,645 | 19,645 | 13,223 | 15,982 | 13,544 | 21,107 | 31,611 | 26,556 | 31,075 | 23,382 | 14,901 | 273,317 |
| NC[41] | 1,340 | 1,379 | 892 | 1,105 | 401 | 536 | 427 | 913 | 1,915 | 1,396 | 1,935 | 1,975 | 1,653 | 15,867 |
| ND[42] | 5,443 | 5,490 | 1,903 | 1,998 | 1,371 | 833 | 1,171 | 2,487 | 2,051 | 2,185 | 8,213 | 13,319 | 6,658 | 53,122 |
| OH[43] | 4,517 | 3,408 | 3,086 | 2,183 | 1,574 | 3,602 | 1,589 | 1,898 | 3,303 | 3,472 | 3,020 | 4,551 | 1,594 | 37,797 |

| State | 1986–87 | 1987–88 | 1988–89 | 1989–90 | 1990–91 | 1991–92 | 1992–93 | 1993–94 | 1994–95 | 1995–96 | 1996–97 | 1997–98 | 1998–99 | Total by State 1986–99 |
|---|---|---|---|---|---|---|---|---|---|---|---|---|---|---|
| Beaver (continued) | | | | | | | | | | | | | | |
| OK[44] | 4,184 | 2,950 | 1,793 | 1,303 | 540 | 923 | 677 | 342 | 1,006 | 833 | 2,574 | 3,331 | 980 | 21,436 |
| OR[45] | 8,632 | 8,284 | 4,193 | 5,639 | 4,299 | 4,532 | 3,002 | 4,643 | 4,483 | 3,461 | 5,218 | 5,573 | 3,037 | 64,996 |
| PA[46] | 5,272 | 6,490 | 4,721 | 4,678 | 3,439 | 4,107 | 4,506 | 3,606 | 9,360 | 6,454 | 9,789 | 12,628 | 8,727 | 83,777 |
| RI[47] | 0 | 0 | 0 | 0 | 12 | 7 | 0 | 0 | 6 | 19 | 20 | 56 | 72 | 192 |
| SC[48] | 852 | 892 | 1,174 | 689 | 556 | 716 | 1,345 | 1,084 | 917 | 1,594 | 1,974 | 1,751 | 1,866 | 15,410 |
| SD[49] | 3,238 | 2,417 | 2,033 | 900 | 736 | 915 | 538 | 1,864 | 1,764 | 1,506 | 1,871 | 2,677 | 1,188 | 21,647 |
| TN | 2,142 | 1,218 | 408 | 309 | 66 | 225 | 204 | 515 | 706 | 505 | 1,168 | 1,351 | 653 | 9,470 |
| TX[50] | 4,939 | 5,494 | 2,847 | 2,296 | 3,126 | 3,562 | 2,692 | 3,076 | 5,297 | 3,735 | 11,089 | 6,450 | 4,246 | 58,849 |
| UT[51] | 4,138 | 4,716 | 2,721 | 3,436 | 1,551 | 1,492 | 956 | 1,761 | 2,551 | 1,530 | 1,299 | 2,896 | 2,950 | 31,997 |
| VT[52] | 2,670 | 2,452 | 1,345 | 1,640 | 1,137 | 1,070 | 1,060 | 484 | 1,521 | 517 | 3,237 | 2,958 | 2,341 | 22,432 |
| VA[53] | 6,192 | 4,728 | N/D | 1,798 | 2,222 | 3,887 | 1,677 | 1,522 | 5,340 | 2,700 | 9,418 | 6,142 | 1,719 | 47,345 |
| WA[54] | 11,449 | 8,921 | 5,718 | 6,665 | 3,641 | 5,036 | 3,785 | 5,968 | 7,347 | 5,163 | 7,456 | 8,116 | 4,558 | 83,823 |
| WV[55] | 1,748 | 1,905 | 1,131 | 1,170 | 683 | 999 | 759 | 357 | 1,313 | 649 | 2,126 | 2,322 | 1,621 | 16,783 |
| WI[56] | 48,730 | 41,726 | 40,749 | 24,370 | 21,252 | 20,253 | 21,648 | 49,099 | 86,574 | 35,821 | 24,835 | 36,320 | 19,160 | 470,537 |
| WY[57] | 9,477 | 10,484 | 6,995 | 4,920 | 4,131 | 3,528 | 4,136 | 1,876 | 1,774 | 685 | 1,843 | 1,649 | 1,654 | 53,152 |
| Total | 556,050 | 473,994 | 309,581 | 270,637 | 176,586 | 205,074 | 197,647 | 275,485 | 469,570 | 273,073 | 428,629 | 466,319 | 333,132 | |

Totals from 1986 through 1999 = 4,435,777

### Black Bear

| State | 1986–87 | 1987–88 | 1988–89 | 1989–90 | 1990–91 | 1991–92 | 1992–93 | 1993–94 | 1994–95 | 1995–96 | 1996–97 | 1997–98 | 1998–99 | Total by State 1986–99 |
|---|---|---|---|---|---|---|---|---|---|---|---|---|---|---|
| ME[23] | N/D | 77 | 75 | 55 | 50 | 40 | 32 | 35 | 45 | 25 | 41 | 56 | 59 | 590 |
| Total | 0 | 77 | 75 | 55 | 50 | 40 | 32 | 35 | 45 | 25 | 41 | 56 | 59 | |

Totals from 1986 through 1999 = 590

### Bobcat

| State | 1986–87 | 1987–88 | 1988–89 | 1989–90 | 1990–91 | 1991–92 | 1992–93 | 1993–94 | 1994–95 | 1995–96 | 1996–97 | 1997–98 | 1998–99 | Total by State 1986–99 |
|---|---|---|---|---|---|---|---|---|---|---|---|---|---|---|
| AL[1] | 2,566 | 2,968 | 837 | 280 | 22 | 97 | 3 | 3 | 26 | 28 | 70 | 34 | 21 | 6,955 |
| AZ[8] | 6,421 | 6,609 | 3,174 | 1,253 | 322 | 878 | 723 | 1,362 | 181 | 55 | 251 | 286 | 312 | 21,827 |
| AR[9] | 2,067 | 2,399 | 938 | 627 | 199 | 501 | 445 | 595 | 778 | 794 | 2,067 | 994 | 584 | 12,988 |
| CA[58] | 8,587 | 8,275 | 5,208 | 2,534 | 989 | 1,080 | 1,101 | 1,105 | 1,018 | 719 | 984 | 1,059 | 190 | 32,849 |
| CO[59, 19] | 1,238 | 905 | 936 | 690 | 294 | 72 | 735 | 1,068 | 879 | 344 | 345 | N/D | 57 | 7,563 |
| FL[60] | 926 | 1,069 | 375 | 93 | 8 | 13 | 45 | 41 | 50 | 51 | 27 | 34 | 11 | 2,743 |
| GA[14] | 2,555 | 4,045 | 1,743 | 1,115 | 494 | 704 | 622 | 904 | 1,338 | 1,292 | 1,264 | 1,084 | 1,050 | 18,210 |
| ID[16] | 1,064 | 1,023 | 872 | 665 | 343 | 543 | 312 | 312 | 324 | 246 | 569 | 484 | 351 | 7,108 |
| KS[7] | 4,522 | 4,805 | 4,492 | 2,482 | 1,694 | 2,453 | 2,307 | 2,900 | 5,352 | 3,932 | 7,041 | 6,233 | 3,938 | 52,151 |
| KY[13] | 0 | 39 | 34 | 18 | 49 | 47 | 40 | 32 | 49 | 35 | 78 | 92 | 105 | 618 |
| LA[2] | 2,395 | 1,971 | 874 | 419 | 138 | 434 | 214 | 554 | 685 | 678 | 857 | 610 | 283 | 10,112 |
| ME[23] | 179 | 91 | 89 | 152 | 113 | 56 | 64 | 40 | 88 | 70 | 128 | 205 | 150 | 1,425 |
| MA[19] | 11 | 21 | 8 | 6 | 22 | 29 | 8 | 16 | 12 | 14 | 11 | 8 | 8 | 174 |
| MI[3] | 669 | 597 | 497 | 269 | 351 | 371 | 380 | 448 | 795 | 450 | 883 | 1,118 | 704 | 7,532 |

# APPENDIX III

*Number of Animals Trapped in the United States.*

| | Indicates trapped data. |
|---|---|
| | Indicates trapped, hunted or other data. |
| N/D | No data provided/available |

| State | 1986–87 | 1987–88 | 1988–89 | 1989–90 | 1990–91 | 1991–92 | 1992–93 | 1993–94 | 1994–95 | 1995–96 | 1996–97 | 1997–98 | 1998–99 | Total by State 1986–99 |
|---|---|---|---|---|---|---|---|---|---|---|---|---|---|---|
| **Bobcat (continued)** | | | | | | | | | | | | | | |
| MN[30] | 160 | 214 | 140 | 129 | 84 | 106 | 168 | 201 | 238 | 134 | 223 | 359 | 103 | 2,259 |
| MS | 1,945 | 2,521 | 1,686 | 568 | 362 | 360 | 483 | 474 | 419 | 293 | 885 | 631 | 519 | 11,146 |
| MO[31] | 1,049 | 1,189 | 1,014 | 728 | 556 | 681 | 723 | 822 | 1,198 | 990 | 1,198 | 1,391 | 889 | 12,428 |
| MT[33] | 1,438 | 1,277 | 832 | 622 | 370 | 1,062 | 947 | 965 | 1,052 | 762 | 1,041 | 1,206 | 1,093 | 12,667 |
| NE[35] | 173 | 97 | 78 | 68 | 99 | 149 | 156 | 194 | 242 | 278 | 318 | 410 | 396 | 2,658 |
| NV[37] | 1,305 | 1,458 | 2,189 | 2,489 | 939 | 2,476 | 1,175 | 1,820 | 1,270 | 806 | 1,509 | 1,705 | 899 | 20,040 |
| NH[36] | 34 | 30 | 31 | 5 | 6 | 4 | 7 | 5 | 0 | 0 | 0 | 0 | 0 | 122 |
| NM[39] | 2,724 | 1,172 | N/D | 362 | 351 | 656 | 872 | 1,415 | 921 | 246 | 214 | 112 | 59 | 9,104 |
| NY[40] | 199 | 224 | 199 | 139 | 167 | 205 | 209 | 193 | 256 | 225 | 292 | 274 | 285 | 2,867 |
| NC[41] | 673 | 460 | 174 | 155 | 10 | 97 | 19 | 68 | 90 | 42 | 111 | 82 | 47 | 2,028 |
| ND[42] | 263 | 97 | 44 | 41 | 3 | 37 | 26 | 13 | 10 | 33 | 0 | 215 | 42 | 824 |
| OK[44] | 4,515 | 3,452 | 2,372 | 822 | 291 | 654 | 648 | 908 | 1,368 | 738 | 2,007 | 1,887 | 829 | 20,491 |
| OR[45] | 3,524 | 3,366 | 1,873 | 1,086 | 570 | 884 | 803 | 850 | 1,109 | 548 | 1,096 | 2,146 | 1,475 | 19,330 |
| SC[48] | 1,279 | 1,505 | 496 | 190 | 155 | 224 | 200 | 154 | 248 | 260 | 270 | 221 | 263 | 5,465 |
| SD[49] | 105 | 140 | 100 | 42 | 35 | 107 | 86 | 52 | 76 | 49 | 39 | 83 | 52 | 966 |
| TN | 949 | 813 | 278 | 108 | 28 | 109 | 41 | 68 | 90 | 82 | 235 | 120 | 65 | 2,986 |
| TX[50] | 21,154 | 27,031 | 13,807 | 7,817 | 3,226 | 4,415 | 4,657 | 5,009 | 6,275 | 3,392 | 9,201 | 7,315 | 5,838 | 119,137 |
| UT[51] | 1,530 | 1,024 | 1,023 | 1,042 | 843 | 527 | 968 | 1,171 | 1,256 | 896 | 866 | 1,234 | 2,092 | 14,472 |
| VT[52] | 40 | 38 | 35 | 27 | 20 | 9 | 28 | 21 | 15 | 24 | 20 | 31 | 17 | 325 |
| VA[53] | 277 | 263 | N/D | 44 | 16 | 46 | 41 | 20 | 94 | 38 | 198 | 140 | 37 | 1,214 |
| WA[54] | 844 | 690 | 405 | 313 | 267 | 218 | 257 | 245 | 262 | 485 | 207 | 365 | 180 | 4,738 |
| WV[55] | 508 | 579 | 378 | 259 | 290 | 269 | 258 | 287 | 402 | 448 | 596 | 577 | 552 | 5,403 |
| WI[56] | 183 | 247 | 165 | 136 | 98 | 71 | 217 | 160 | 169 | 111 | 166 | 216 | 194 | 2,133 |
| WY[57] | 1,707 | 1,522 | 1,323 | 866 | 634 | 1,877 | 968 | 681 | 471 | 126 | 445 | 2,994 | 380 | 13,994 |
| **Total** | 79,778 | 84,226 | 48,719 | 28,661 | 14,458 | 22,521 | 20,956 | 25,176 | 29,106 | 19,714 | 35,712 | 35,955 | 24,070 | |
| | | | | | | | | | | | Totals from 1986 through 1999 = 469,052 | | | |
| **Coyote** | | | | | | | | | | | | | | |
| AL[1] | 302 | 393 | 30 | 15 | 2 | 2 | 3 | 4 | 2 | 10 | 19 | 18 | 79 | 879 |
| AK[4] | 215 | 143 | 157 | 83 | 80 | 131 | 52 | 68 | 36 | 196 | 150 | 151 | 211 | 1,673 |
| AZ[8] | 14,198 | 13,335 | 6,397 | 3,140 | 1,135 | 2,214 | 2,372 | 2,683 | 654 | 178 | 1,307 | 1,437 | 1,213 | 50,263 |
| AR[9] | 1,129 | 1,229 | 493 | 90 | 39 | 161 | 171 | 222 | 257 | 213 | 673 | 210 | 96 | 4,983 |
| CA[58] | 6,901 | 6,847 | 5,228 | 2,965 | 1,451 | 1,536 | 1,340 | 1,264 | 1,054 | 1,209 | 1,367 | 1,127 | 301 | 32,590 |
| CO[59, 19] | 11,492 | 11,619 | 5,728 | 4,107 | 4,099 | 577 | 7,757 | 5,799 | 8,877 | 3,615 | 4,246 | N/D | N/D | 67,916 |
| CT[10] | 40 | 70 | 56 | 54 | 61 | 23 | 31 | 21 | 43 | 30 | 136 | 166 | 136 | 867 |

| State | 1986–87 | 1987–88 | 1988–89 | 1989–90 | 1990–91 | 1991–92 | 1992–93 | 1993–94 | 1994–95 | 1995–96 | 1996–97 | 1997–98 | 1998–99 | Total by State 1986–99 |
|---|---|---|---|---|---|---|---|---|---|---|---|---|---|---|
| Coyote (continued) | | | | | | | | | | | | | | |
| FL[60] | 10 | 0 | 1 | 0 | 0 | 0 | 0 | 0 | 0 | 0 | 1 | 1 | 0 | 13 |
| GA[14] | 2,353 | 4,680 | 2,111 | 1,961 | 1,198 | 1,656 | 1,715 | 2,420 | 2,827 | 2,667 | 2,651 | 1,971 | 2,510 | 30,720 |
| ID[16] | 5,656 | 7,093 | 2,513 | 1,589 | 1,691 | 2,583 | 1,897 | 1,825 | 1,924 | 1,587 | 2,293 | 1,922 | 1,166 | 33,739 |
| IL[17] | 9,167 | 9,652 | 3,513 | 1,489 | 3,010 | 7,220 | 8,812 | 7,899 | 6,194 | 8,001 | 5,289 | 3,886 | 1,505 | 75,637 |
| IN[18] | 1,143 | 1,549 | 454 | 161 | 249 | 515 | 653 | 1,118 | 1,075 | 1,176 | 1,041 | 1,763 | 940 | 11,835 |
| IA[20] | 3,598 | 3,311 | 1,395 | 978 | 1,419 | 1,303 | 3,703 | 2,486 | 6,986 | 8,462 | 7,159 | 6,992 | 5,786 | 53,578 |
| KS[7] | 40,999 | 41,460 | 25,387 | 15,314 | 11,968 | 15,941 | 16,076 | 16,595 | 17,022 | 14,009 | 19,794 | 14,398 | 12,125 | 261,088 |
| KY[11] | 783 | 1,469 | 1,722 | 1,147 | 695 | 860 | 818 | 1,020 | 831 | 1,261 | 2,219 | 1,989 | 1,975 | 16,789 |
| LA[2] | 937 | 1,212 | 76 | 12 | 21 | 66 | 33 | 83 | 81 | 96 | 253 | 60 | 26 | 2,956 |
| ME[23] | 1,151 | 1,631 | 1,251 | 1,215 | 944 | 1,222 | 1,356 | 1,410 | 1,647 | 1,440 | 1,587 | 1,987 | 2,420 | 19,261 |
| MD[25] | N/D | N/D | N/D | N/D | 1 | 3 | 0 | N/D | N/D | N/D | N/D | N/D | N/D | 4 |
| MA[19] | 0 | 1 | 2 | 45 | 58 | 102 | 95 | 92 | 107 | 153 | 166 | 86 | 97 | 1,004 |
| MI[3] | 1,540 | 2,490 | 2,690 | N/D | N/D | N/D | N/D | 1,221 | 1,878 | N/D | 3,747 | 5,011 | 6,457 | 25,034 |
| MN[27] | 7,000 | 7,000 | 3,000 | 4,000 | 3,000 | 3,000 | 4,000 | 4,000 | 5,000 | 3,000 | 3,000 | 3,000 | 2,000 | 51,000 |
| MS | 1,804 | 2,707 | 2,941 | 1,535 | 1,146 | 1,584 | 1,224 | 909 | 1,283 | 844 | 1,870 | 1,508 | 1,643 | 20,998 |
| MO[31] | 12,279 | 10,812 | 3,123 | 1,544 | 2,236 | 3,919 | 5,962 | 5,485 | 4,508 | 2,903 | 3,543 | 1,944 | 410 | 58,668 |
| MT[33] | 13,550 | 15,958 | 7,838 | 4,750 | 4,559 | 7,432 | 10,862 | 9,766 | 10,079 | 5,495 | 9,354 | 10,510 | 6,059 | 116,212 |
| NE[35] | 32,880 | 36,082 | 18,424 | 11,515 | 13,878 | 16,316 | 23,952 | 29,338 | 28,679 | 26,765 | 36,443 | 36,213 | 28,794 | 339,279 |
| NV[37] | 7,745 | 6,373 | 2,352 | 1,717 | 1,252 | 3,718 | 3,746 | 4,477 | 3,298 | 1,791 | 3,209 | 2,227 | 1,003 | 42,908 |
| NH[36] | 291 | 264 | 253 | 169 | 155 | 227 | 260 | 298 | 342 | 380 | 345 | 398 | 318 | 3,700 |
| NJ[38] | 3 | 3 | 4 | 7 | 4 | 12 | 5 | 3 | 7 | 4 | 12 | 7 | 1 | 72 |
| NM[39] | 20,549 | 8,092 | N/D | 3,660 | 3,521 | 4,927 | 6,966 | 9,580 | 9,236 | 1,714 | 1,678 | 2,041 | 106 | 72,070 |
| NY[40] | 1,503 | 1,678 | 1,248 | 856 | 753 | 1,403 | 1,133 | 1,315 | 1,899 | 2,114 | 2,500 | 2,571 | 2,203 | 21,176 |
| ND[42] | 12,073 | 8,366 | 7,840 | 3,712 | 4,608 | 8,318 | 12,133 | 9,147 | 8,393 | 5,521 | 9,113 | 21,817 | 1,183 | 112,224 |
| OH[43] | 118 | 293 | 256 | 68 | 102 | 219 | 320 | 479 | 642 | 1,755 | 539 | 426 | 464 | 5,681 |
| OK[44] | 7,599 | 5,890 | 2,171 | 603 | 253 | 1,617 | 1,067 | 1,552 | 838 | 1,234 | 687 | 389 | 70 | 23,970 |
| OR[45] | 8,920 | 8,882 | 3,196 | 1,905 | 2,051 | 2,379 | 3,064 | 2,689 | 3,172 | 1,601 | 3,005 | 4,764 | 3,048 | 48,676 |
| PA[46] | N/D | 400 | 500 | 750 | 1,810 | 3,719 | 4,402 | 6,161 | 6,240 | 5,662 | 7,957 | 6,685 | 11,652 | 55,938 |
| RI[47] | 0 | 0 | 0 | 0 | 2 | 0 | 0 | 0 | 0 | 0 | 1 | 2 | 0 | 5 |
| SC[48] | 5 | 8 | 6 | 16 | 25 | 30 | 34 | 30 | 198 | 113 | 142 | 130 | 185 | 922 |
| SD[49] | 8,149 | 8,705 | 5,846 | 1,951 | 2,913 | 6,159 | 9,570 | 8,081 | 8,721 | 5,711 | 6,098 | 5,285 | 2,285 | 79,474 |
| TN | 535 | 437 | 71 | 32 | 45 | 111 | 22 | 115 | 128 | 137 | 87 | 93 | 19 | 1,832 |
| TX[50] | 62,476 | 68,083 | 27,385 | 19,975 | 15,972 | 23,334 | 20,785 | 18,851 | 20,725 | 8,696 | 14,080 | 19,053 | 18,447 | 337,862 |
| UT[51] | 4,947 | 6,919 | 3,200 | 3,331 | 1,831 | 3,255 | 3,666 | 5,247 | 5,267 | 4,372 | 4,017 | 3,228 | 4,337 | 53,617 |
| VT[52] | 359 | 337 | 170 | 76 | 141 | 113 | 197 | 121 | 241 | 109 | 106 | 107 | 59 | 2,136 |
| VA[53] | 0 | 0 | 0 | 0 | 0 | 0 | 0 | 7 | 12 | 0 | 40 | 25 | 10 | 94 |
| WA[54] | 6,330 | 4,573 | 1,827 | 1,360 | 1,359 | 1,875 | 1,610 | 2,341 | 2,288 | 1,770 | 1,364 | 1,606 | 922 | 29,225 |

## APPENDIX III

### Number of Animals Trapped in the United States.

Indicates trapped data.

Indicates trapped, hunted or other data.

N/D  No data provided/ available

| State | 1986–87 | 1987–88 | 1988–89 | 1989–90 | 1990–91 | 1991–92 | 1992–93 | 1993–94 | 1994–95 | 1995–96 | 1996–97 | 1997–98 | 1998–99 | Total by State 1986–99 |
|---|---|---|---|---|---|---|---|---|---|---|---|---|---|---|
| **Coyote (continued)** | | | | | | | | | | | | | | |
| WV[55] | 0 | 0 | 0 | 5 | 1 | 6 | 9 | 3 | 38 | 13 | 28 | 29 | 29 | 161 |
| WI[56] | 9,946 | 13,704 | 14,735 | 19,881 | 9,789 | 18,320 | 18,719 | 32,300 | 19,354 | 19,031 | 12,280 | 23,511 | 29,037 | 240,617 |
| WY[57] | 7,049 | 9,379 | 5,776 | 4,240 | 3,313 | 6,164 | 5,528 | 2,954 | 3,518 | 1,427 | 3,937 | 2,885 | 3,331 | 59,501 |
| Total | 327,724 | 333,129 | 171,366 | 122,023 | 102,840 | 154,282 | 186,120 | 201,479 | 195,601 | 147,465 | 179,533 | 193,627 | 154,660 | |

Totals from 1986 through 1999 = 2,469,847

| State | 1986–87 | 1987–88 | 1988–89 | 1989–90 | 1990–91 | 1991–92 | 1992–93 | 1993–94 | 1994–95 | 1995–96 | 1996–97 | 1997–98 | 1998–99 | Total by State 1986–99 |
|---|---|---|---|---|---|---|---|---|---|---|---|---|---|---|
| **Fisher** | | | | | | | | | | | | | | |
| ME[23] | 1,851 | 2,090 | 1,211 | 1,059 | 1,181 | 1,603 | 1,345 | 1,623 | 1,546 | 1,756 | 1,886 | 3,827 | 1,807 | 21,785 |
| MD[25] | 5 | 6 | 7 | 2 | 1 | 0 | 0 | 0 | 0 | N/D | N/D | N/D | N/D | 21 |
| MA[19] | 201 | 248 | 248 | 165 | 93 | 85 | 111 | 120 | 158 | 226 | 278 | 340 | 395 | 2,668 |
| MI[26] | 0 | 0 | 0 | 99 | 125 | 68 | 140 | 425 | 417 | 208 | 471 | 609 | 455 | 3,017 |
| MN[30] | 1,068 | 1,642 | 1,025 | 1,243 | 746 | 528 | 778 | 1,159 | 1,771 | 942 | 1,773 | 2,761 | 2,695 | 18,131 |
| MT[33] | 14 | 10 | 13 | 9 | 1 | 4 | 5 | 7 | 8 | 2 | 6 | 7 | 8 | 94 |
| NH[36] | 801 | 718 | 881 | 406 | 440 | 442 | 426 | 525 | 722 | 426 | 642 | 1,187 | 923 | 8,539 |
| NY[40] | 1,003 | 1,217 | 807 | 666 | 452 | 498 | 639 | 673 | 758 | 1,228 | 1,368 | 2,899 | 1,230 | 13,438 |
| VT[52] | 431 | 496 | 406 | 93 | 225 | 151 | 247 | 218 | 288 | 103 | 250 | 630 | 387 | 3,925 |
| WV[55] | 8 | 16 | 13 | 9 | 4 | 5 | 2 | 2 | 18 | 15 | 40 | 53 | 45 | 230 |
| WI[56] | 98 | 308 | 260 | 334 | 339 | 204 | 1,647 | 1,564 | 2,085 | 1,360 | 1,388 | 3,644 | 496 | 13,727 |
| Total | 5,480 | 6,751 | 4,871 | 4,085 | 3,607 | 3,588 | 5,340 | 6,316 | 7,771 | 6,266 | 8,102 | 14,957 | 8,441 | |

Totals from 1986 through 1999 = 85,575

| State | 1986–87 | 1987–88 | 1988–89 | 1989–90 | 1990–91 | 1991–92 | 1992–93 | 1993–94 | 1994–95 | 1995–96 | 1996–97 | 1997–98 | 1998–99 | Total by State 1986–99 |
|---|---|---|---|---|---|---|---|---|---|---|---|---|---|---|
| **Arctic Fox** | | | | | | | | | | | | | | |
| AK[4] | 165 | 612 | 361 | 73 | 0 | 42 | 252 | 144 | 149 | 43 | 135 | 51 | 208 | 2,235 |
| Total | 165 | 612 | 361 | 73 | 0 | 42 | 252 | 144 | 149 | 43 | 135 | 51 | 208 | |

Totals from 1986 through 1999 = 2,235

| State | 1986–87 | 1987–88 | 1988–89 | 1989–90 | 1990–91 | 1991–92 | 1992–93 | 1993–94 | 1994–95 | 1995–96 | 1996–97 | 1997–98 | 1998–99 | Total by State 1986–99 |
|---|---|---|---|---|---|---|---|---|---|---|---|---|---|---|
| **Gray Fox** | | | | | | | | | | | | | | |
| AL[1] | 9,824 | 11,223 | 2,441 | 628 | 142 | 212 | 68 | 114 | 124 | 70 | 112 | 46 | 23 | 25,027 |
| AZ[8] | 18,900 | 19,808 | 13,064 | 4,689 | 1,626 | 2,578 | 3,101 | 4,781 | 1,482 | 130 | 583 | 616 | 718 | 72,076 |
| AR[9] | 5,911 | 7,865 | 3,566 | 1,096 | 502 | 790 | 1,119 | 849 | 1,526 | 1,881 | 2,130 | 1,131 | 541 | 28,907 |
| CA[58] | 10,187 | 11,270 | 6,952 | 3,091 | 1,153 | 1,330 | 1,469 | 1,406 | 1,182 | 851 | 822 | 1,267 | 232 | 41,212 |
| CO[59, 19] | 940 | 783 | 879 | 339 | 120 | 11 | 477 | 392 | 576 | 9 | 16 | N/D | N/D | 4,542 |
| CT[10] | 162 | 70 | 71 | 33 | 34 | 20 | 20 | 13 | 14 | 6 | 27 | 40 | 34 | 544 |
| DE[12] | N/D | N/D | 88 | 26 | N/D | 46 | 34 | 4 | 11 | 32 | 28 | 14 | 66 | 349 |
| GA[14] | 12,337 | 17,962 | 6,586 | 3,013 | 2,007 | 2,764 | 1,771 | 2,334 | 3,558 | 3,646 | 3,647 | 3,449 | 3,934 | 67,008 |
| IL[17] | 2,915 | 2,944 | 1,585 | 556 | 308 | 778 | 347 | 333 | 389 | 340 | 257 | 164 | 72 | 10,988 |
| IN[18] | 6,886 | 7,169 | 2,085 | 973 | 672 | 884 | 660 | 642 | 758 | 673 | 602 | 616 | 363 | 22,983 |

| State | 1986–87 | 1987–88 | 1988–89 | 1989–90 | 1990–91 | 1991–92 | 1992–93 | 1993–94 | 1994–95 | 1995–96 | 1996–97 | 1997–98 | 1998–99 | Total by State 1986–99 |
|---|---|---|---|---|---|---|---|---|---|---|---|---|---|---|
| | | | | | | Gray Fox (continued) | | | | | | | | |
| IA[20] | 940 | 578 | 446 | 180 | 169 | 189 | 414 | 359 | 789 | 948 | 721 | 768 | 681 | 7,182 |
| KS[7] | 107 | 123 | 235 | 30 | 34 | 77 | 59 | 55 | 204 | 99 | 179 | 71 | 152 | 1,425 |
| KY[11] | 5,332 | 8,039 | 4,348 | 2,029 | 1,143 | 2,292 | 1,076 | 1,182 | 1,070 | 951 | 1,744 | 1,593 | 775 | 31,574 |
| LA[2] | 2,405 | 3,164 | 579 | 169 | 90 | 279 | 197 | 642 | 642 | 477 | 1,282 | 318 | 207 | 10,451 |
| ME[23] | 67 | 116 | 45 | 60 | 73 | 74 | 58 | 46 | 50 | 104 | 25 | 92 | 75 | 885 |
| MD[25] | 1,747 | 1,323 | 830 | 60 | 508 | 366 | 284 | N/D | N/D | N/D | N/D | N/D | N/D | 5,118 |
| MA[19] | 110 | 83 | 37 | 24 | 31 | 38 | 19 | 10 | 19 | 36 | 20 | 43 | 45 | 515 |
| MI[3] | 2,720 | 3,020 | 2,140 | N/D | N/D | N/D | N/D | 1,152 | 2,320 | N/D | 2,134 | 2,962 | 2,474 | 18,922 |
| MN[27] | 6,000 | 5,000 | 5,000 | 2,000 | 1,000 | 1,000 | 1,000 | 1,000 | 1,000 | 1,000 | 1,000 | 1,000 | 1,000 | 27,000 |
| MS | 4,192 | 5,670 | 3,980 | 1,511 | 839 | 1,092 | 1,050 | 643 | 531 | 400 | 1,323 | 579 | 519 | 22,329 |
| MO[31] | 5,880 | 5,085 | 3,090 | 1,290 | 798 | 1,506 | 1,451 | 1,184 | 1,803 | 1,139 | 2,031 | 1,370 | 658 | 27,285 |
| NE[35] | 5 | 8 | 10 | 10 | 5 | 10 | 6 | 6 | 1 | N/D | N/D | N/D | N/D | 61 |
| NV[37] | 767 | 630 | 439 | 811 | 212 | 443 | 223 | 612 | 354 | 376 | 498 | 565 | 318 | 6,248 |
| NH[36] | 172 | 174 | 106 | 58 | 63 | 76 | 86 | 76 | 97 | 75 | 129 | 104 | 120 | 1,336 |
| NJ[38] | 1,658 | 3,208 | 2,040 | 779 | 520 | 513 | 995 | 480 | 1,027 | 931 | 647 | 383 | 217 | 13,398 |
| NM[39] | 5,987 | 3,292 | N/D | 1,471 | 1,026 | 1,540 | 2,887 | 3,992 | 3,268 | 652 | 342 | 681 | 41 | 25,179 |
| NY[40] | 9,452 | 10,784 | 6,117 | 3,653 | 2,549 | 2,999 | 2,744 | 1,636 | 3,187 | 3,202 | 4,794 | 6,061 | 3,804 | 60,937 |
| NC[41] | 2,772 | 2,246 | 889 | 412 | 48 | 161 | 121 | 40 | 44 | 67 | 279 | 203 | 73 | 7,355 |
| OH[43] | 10,292 | 12,154 | 5,332 | 3,382 | 3,168 | 5,226 | 2,580 | 2,846 | 2,911 | 1,755 | 1,715 | 1,144 | 770 | 53,275 |
| OK[44] | 1,718 | 1,547 | 1,091 | 329 | 84 | 192 | 198 | 142 | 175 | 114 | 399 | 384 | 124 | 6,497 |
| OR[45] | 270 | 284 | 187 | 62 | 57 | 116 | 86 | 69 | 96 | 47 | 157 | 156 | 136 | 1,723 |
| PA[46] | 46,387 | 56,944 | 23,072 | 28,818 | 21,653 | 30,409 | 25,395 | 23,839 | 34,691 | 23,518 | 23,307 | 26,043 | 32,922 | 396,998 |
| RI[47] | 10 | 17 | 9 | 11 | 6 | 4 | 3 | 3 | 0 | 3 | 0 | 6 | 2 | 74 |
| SC[48] | 7,860 | 11,290 | 4,285 | 2,741 | 2,724 | 3,392 | 2,178 | 1,977 | 2,060 | 2,461 | 2,600 | 2,172 | 2,162 | 47,902 |
| SD[49] | 11 | 10 | 7 | 0 | 0 | 31 | 0 | 43 | 0 | 28 | N/D | N/D | N/D | 130 |
| TN | 10,401 | 8,529 | 2,199 | 799 | 245 | 1,113 | 238 | 181 | 392 | 135 | 486 | 83 | 91 | 24,892 |
| TX[50] | 50,458 | 52,766 | 26,167 | 12,293 | 5,373 | 7,402 | 8,284 | 9,106 | 8,066 | 6,088 | 14,406 | 10,537 | 8,709 | 219,655 |
| UT[51] | 1,465 | 1,633 | 1,099 | 941 | 250 | 402 | 422 | 687 | 771 | 828 | 367 | 389 | 870 | 10,116 |
| VT[52] | 224 | 178 | 82 | 52 | 47 | 30 | 116 | 32 | 56 | 17 | 6 | 22 | 12 | 874 |
| VA[53] | 10,850 | 13,081 | N/D | 1,783 | 871 | 2,090 | 1,517 | 1,024 | 2,591 | 1,423 | 2,796 | 2,348 | 866 | 41,240 |
| WV[55] | 10,102 | 10,625 | 3,463 | 1,859 | 1,332 | 2,316 | 1,004 | 611 | 1,766 | 955 | 1,831 | 1,180 | 1,111 | 38,155 |
| WI[56] | 9,632 | 10,537 | 11,471 | 29,557 | 18,022 | 14,064 | 9,108 | 12,276 | 12,869 | 13,839 | 15,458 | 8,156 | 12,427 | 177,416 |
| Total | 278,047 | 311,232 | 146,112 | 111,618 | 69,504 | 88,855 | 72,865 | 76,819 | 92,470 | 69,306 | 88,900 | 76,711 | 77,344 | |

Totals from 1986 through 1999 = 1,559,783

Indicates trapped data.

Indicates trapped, hunted or other data.

N/D  No data provided/available

# APPENDIX III

*Number of Animals Trapped in the United States.*

| State | 1986–87 | 1987–88 | 1988–89 | 1989–90 | 1990–91 | 1991–92 | 1992–93 | 1993–94 | 1994–95 | 1995–96 | 1996–97 | 1997–98 | 1998–99 | Total by State 1986–99 |
|---|---|---|---|---|---|---|---|---|---|---|---|---|---|---|
| **Kit/Swift Fox** | | | | | | | | | | | | | | |
| AZ[8] | 2,100 | 2,201 | 1,452 | 521 | 181 | 286 | 345 | 531 | 165 | 14 | 65 | 69 | 80 | 8,009 |
| CO[59,19] | 1,062 | 624 | 265 | 166 | 166 | 356 | 302 | 395 | 279 | 2 | N/D | N/D | N/D | 3,617 |
| KS[7] | 1,161 | 650 | 442 | 264 | 76 | 93 | 64 | 73 | 34 | 45 | 144 | 25 | 15 | 3,086 |
| NV[37] | 1,345 | 1,004 | 845 | 397 | 87 | 514 | 488 | 537 | 247 | 172 | 195 | 298 | 154 | 6,283 |
| NM[39] | 2,345 | 814 | N/D | 194 | 188 | 139 | 234 | 112 | 273 | 21 | 86 | 68 | 1 | 4,475 |
| TX[50] | N/D | N/D | N/D | N/D | N/D | N/D | 120 | N/D | 363 | 134 | 2,117 | 171 | 26 | 2,931 |
| UT[51] | 547 | 538 | 643 | 365 | 186 | 187 | 191 | 301 | 531 | 218 | 162 | 96 | 168 | 4,133 |
| WY[57] | 73 | 167 | 55 | 11 | 23 | 41 | 38 | 20 | 11 | 3 | 7 | N/D | N/D | 449 |
| **Total** | 8,633 | 5,998 | 3,702 | 1,918 | 907 | 1,616 | 1,782 | 1,969 | 1,903 | 609 | 2,776 | 727 | 444 | |

Totals from 1986 through 1999 = 32,983

| State | 1986–87 | 1987–88 | 1988–89 | 1989–90 | 1990–91 | 1991–92 | 1992–93 | 1993–94 | 1994–95 | 1995–96 | 1996–97 | 1997–98 | 1998–99 | Total by State 1986–99 |
|---|---|---|---|---|---|---|---|---|---|---|---|---|---|---|
| **Red Fox** | | | | | | | | | | | | | | |
| AL[1] | 1,233 | 1,570 | 404 | 82 | 16 | 46 | 6 | 29 | 29 | 17 | 40 | 6 | 5 | 3,483 |
| AR[9] | 0 | 0 | 0 | 0 | 0 | 0 | 0 | 0 | 0 | 3 | 239 | 172 | 46 | 460 |
| CO | 1,366 | 1,895 | 1,496 | 946 | 1,006 | 399 | 1,788 | 1,543 | 3,423 | 523 | 704 | N/D | N/D | 15,089 |
| CT[10] | 412 | 236 | 185 | 80 | 47 | 40 | 26 | 18 | 22 | 15 | 103 | 65 | 49 | 1,298 |
| GA[14] | 3,376 | 3,687 | 1,969 | 917 | 581 | 679 | 472 | 686 | 921 | 699 | 710 | 599 | 569 | 15,865 |
| ID[16] | 3,276 | 3,257 | 1,943 | 1,611 | 1,740 | 3,008 | 1,911 | 2,742 | 2,513 | 2,529 | 2,715 | 2,853 | 1,739 | 31,837 |
| IL[17] | 8,531 | 7,939 | 4,671 | 2,716 | 2,386 | 2,848 | 1,876 | 1,689 | 1,825 | 1,525 | 2,103 | 1,492 | 670 | 40,271 |
| IN[18] | 9,150 | 7,638 | 2,960 | 1,555 | 1,045 | 1,128 | 966 | 829 | 1,393 | 1,064 | 1,063 | 1,799 | 1,125 | 31,715 |
| IA[20] | 11,647 | 10,423 | 8,958 | 6,412 | 6,135 | 6,804 | 5,864 | 5,584 | 12,243 | 14,136 | 12,402 | 12,896 | 11,646 | 125,150 |
| KS[7] | 961 | 1,113 | 672 | 462 | 243 | 509 | 328 | 731 | 1,003 | 753 | 1,232 | 823 | 490 | 9,320 |
| KY[11] | 6,292 | 7,628 | 4,365 | 2,202 | 1,713 | 2,755 | 1,205 | 987 | 1,191 | 1,111 | 1,813 | 1,628 | 892 | 33,782 |
| LA[2] | 396 | 456 | 76 | 18 | 18 | 36 | 7 | 26 | 71 | 73 | 113 | 92 | 14 | 1,396 |
| ME[23] | 4,148 | 4,424 | 2,409 | 2,336 | 1,949 | 1,965 | 1,916 | 1,745 | 2,186 | 1,993 | 1,599 | 1,894 | 1,533 | 30,097 |
| MD[25] | 4,762 | 4,380 | 3,015 | 1,337 | 2,192 | 2,103 | 1,554 | N/D | N/D | N/D | N/D | N/D | N/D | 19,343 |
| MA[19] | 279 | 281 | 124 | 91 | 85 | 131 | 118 | 92 | 78 | 83 | 65 | 31 | 27 | 1,485 |
| MI[3] | 25,620 | 26,260 | 19,460 | N/D | N/D | N/D | N/D | 5,414 | 10,210 | N/D | 6,540 | 10,785 | 7,188 | 111,477 |
| MN[27] | 40,000 | 57,000 | 53,000 | 25,000 | 33,000 | 25,000 | 23,000 | 22,000 | 25,000 | 15,000 | 14,000 | 13,000 | 6,500 | 351,500 |
| MS | 921 | 1,115 | 853 | 269 | 236 | 199 | 167 | 117 | 113 | 76 | 219 | 182 | 250 | 4,717 |
| MO[31] | 3,934 | 3,092 | 2,196 | 1,176 | 634 | 1,198 | 1,109 | 1,289 | 1,590 | 1,550 | 1,672 | 1,239 | 534 | 21,213 |
| MT[33,34] | 8,468 | 11,276 | 9,329 | 3,927 | 3,529 | 6,935 | 5,453 | 6,047 | 6,872 | 3,573 | 5,764 | 4,810 | 2,156 | 78,139 |
| NE[35] | 2,830 | 3,075 | 1,530 | 1,240 | 1,103 | 1,423 | 1,773 | 2,573 | 3,647 | 3,036 | 4,941 | 5,053 | 3,760 | 35,984 |
| NH[36] | 1,249 | 1,301 | 743 | 504 | 415 | 426 | 381 | 378 | 444 | 343 | 264 | 324 | 195 | 6,967 |

| State | 1986–87 | 1987–88 | 1988–89 | 1989–90 | 1990–91 | 1991–92 | 1992–93 | 1993–94 | 1994–95 | 1995–96 | 1996–97 | 1997–98 | 1998–99 | Total by State 1986–99 |
|---|---|---|---|---|---|---|---|---|---|---|---|---|---|---|
| | | | | | | Red Fox (continued) | | | | | | | | |
| NJ[38] | 2,940 | 3,635 | 3,907 | 2,382 | 1,547 | 1,831 | 1,800 | 1,495 | 2,209 | 1,545 | 3,219 | 2,199 | 1,066 | 29,775 |
| NM[39] | 819 | 89 | N/D | 69 | 70 | 7 | 34 | 62 | 65 | 3 | 16 | 6 | 5 | 1,245 |
| NY[40] | 17,933 | 18,597 | 14,170 | 8,076 | 5,776 | 6,534 | 5,636 | 5,079 | 9,411 | 8,918 | 9,543 | 7,861 | 8,613 | 126,147 |
| NC[41] | 971 | 627 | 216 | 87 | 16 | 26 | 7 | 2 | 42 | 12 | 38 | 36 | 9 | 2,089 |
| ND[42] | 32,919 | 28,355 | 18,858 | 10,977 | 9,999 | 12,725 | 12,835 | 10,778 | 11,628 | 21,187 | 21,519 | 23,797 | 1,141 | 216,718 |
| OH[43] | 15,719 | 12,596 | 7,438 | 5,468 | 4,160 | 4,860 | 2,952 | 2,709 | 3,117 | 2,766 | 2,192 | 2,418 | 1,547 | 67,942 |
| OR[45] | 536 | 739 | 444 | 209 | 199 | 220 | 169 | 210 | 202 | 128 | 194 | 167 | 67 | 3,484 |
| PA[46] | 95,330 | 74,590 | 52,737 | 43,525 | 32,699 | 28,495 | 27,611 | 25,862 | 30,649 | 31,110 | 29,623 | 36,923 | 47,202 | 556,356 |
| RI[47] | 55 | 34 | 23 | 12 | 9 | 3 | 0 | 2 | 5 | 2 | 2 | 1 | 8 | 156 |
| SC[48] | 1,781 | 1,917 | 1,227 | 914 | 1,039 | 1,363 | 720 | 810 | 698 | 823 | 783 | 682 | 185 | 12,942 |
| SD[49] | 17,512 | 15,240 | 8,917 | 3,098 | 4,388 | 5,791 | 5,229 | 5,227 | 8,485 | 6,299 | 6,889 | 5,700 | 1,731 | 94,506 |
| TN | 2,341 | 1,614 | 465 | 188 | 52 | 172 | 71 | 74 | 91 | 75 | 112 | 60 | 64 | 5,379 |
| TX[50] | 7,298 | 10,263 | 4,217 | 2,549 | 1,340 | 1,400 | 1,813 | 2,101 | 1,857 | 1,609 | 3,917 | 2,826 | 1,600 | 42,790 |
| UT[51] | 2,446 | 2,545 | 2,446 | 2,250 | 1,993 | 3,662 | 3,126 | 5,055 | 4,378 | 4,116 | 4,274 | 3,744 | 5,600 | 45,635 |
| VT[52] | 827 | 686 | 457 | 213 | 400 | 224 | 330 | 235 | 154 | 106 | 39 | 53 | 44 | 3,768 |
| VA[53] | 6,459 | 5,319 | N/D | 913 | 971 | 1,376 | 812 | 567 | 1,266 | 1,008 | 2,847 | 2,463 | 1,111 | 25,112 |
| WA[34] | 64 | 31 | 13 | 19 | 1 | 9 | N/D | N/D | N/D | N/D | N/D | N/D | N/D | 137 |
| WV[55] | 4,797 | 5,468 | 2,221 | 1,261 | 838 | 813 | 363 | 162 | 558 | 479 | 1,181 | 1,019 | 671 | 19,831 |
| WI[56] | 43,517 | 407,85 | 33,547 | 30,777 | 29,381 | 32,591 | 26,607 | 29,495 | 8,432 | 16,440 | 20,670 | 19,826 | 18,528 | 350,596 |
| WY[57] | 6,754 | 9,621 | 5,978 | 4,673 | 5,260 | 8,585 | 6,581 | 3,865 | 2,252 | 1,298 | 2,228 | 1,971 | 1,502 | 60,568 |
| Total | 399,869 | 390,797 | 277,639 | 170,541 | 158,211 | 168,319 | 146,616 | 148,309 | 160,273 | 146,026 | 167,587 | 171,495 | 130,082 | |

Totals from 1986 through 1999 = 2,635,764

| State | 1986–87 | 1987–88 | 1988–89 | 1989–90 | 1990–91 | 1991–92 | 1992–93 | 1993–94 | 1994–95 | 1995–96 | 1996–97 | 1997–98 | 1998–99 | Total by State 1986–99 |
|---|---|---|---|---|---|---|---|---|---|---|---|---|---|---|
| | | | | | | | Lynx | | | | | | | |
| AK[4] | 1,234 | 1,038 | 1,200 | 1,321 | 1,273 | 2,074 | 1,323 | 1,225 | 788 | 574 | 1,768 | 2,910 | 2,782 | 19,510 |
| MT[33] | 23 | 15 | 22 | 15 | 2 | 3 | 2 | 3 | 5 | 2 | 3 | 6 | 3 | 104 |
| Total | 1,257 | 1,053 | 1,222 | 1,336 | 1,275 | 2,077 | 1,325 | 1,228 | 793 | 576 | 1,771 | 2,916 | 2,785 | |

Totals from 1986 through 1999 = 19,614

| State | 1986–87 | 1987–88 | 1988–89 | 1989–90 | 1990–91 | 1991–92 | 1992–93 | 1993–94 | 1994–95 | 1995–96 | 1996–97 | 1997–98 | 1998–99 | Total by State 1986–99 |
|---|---|---|---|---|---|---|---|---|---|---|---|---|---|---|
| | | | | | | | Marten | | | | | | | |
| AK[4,5] | 27,407 | 27,153 | 30,061 | 20,534 | 2,216 | 4,402 | 1,487 | 3,953 | 4,906 | 5,424 | 4,617 | 3,735 | 3,200 | 139,095 |
| CO[59,19] | 1,160 | 2,383 | 3,006 | 2,664 | 999 | 1,191 | 1,016 | 811 | 2,324 | 23 | N/D | N/D | N/D | 15,577 |
| ID[16] | 2,707 | 2,877 | 3,555 | 1,935 | 1,112 | 736 | 414 | 364 | 330 | 508 | 452 | 537 | 316 | 15,843 |
| ME[23] | 3,951 | 6,424 | 2,698 | 4,554 | 3,266 | 3,292 | 2,090 | 3,119 | 2,199 | 4,478 | 2,208 | 5,736 | 2,160 | 46,175 |
| MN[30] | 798 | 1,363 | 2,072 | 2,119 | 1,349 | 656 | 1,602 | 1,438 | 1,527 | 1,500 | 1,625 | 2,261 | 2,299 | 20,609 |
| MT[33] | 2,366 | 2,393 | 2,426 | 1,283 | 736 | 996 | 603 | 822 | 1,323 | 802 | 830 | 900 | 716 | 16,196 |
| NH[36] | 0 | 2 | 0 | 0 | 1 | 0 | 2 | 0 | 10 | 1 | 0 | 0 | 0 | 16 |
| NY[40] | 57 | 93 | 16 | 44 | 50 | 33 | 44 | 71 | 11 | 82 | 31 | 183 | 14 | 729 |

☐ Indicates trapped data.

▨ Indicates trapped, hunted or other data.

N/D No data provided/available

# APPENDIX III

*Number of Animals Trapped in the United States.*

Total by State 1986–99

| State | 1986–87 | 1987–88 | 1988–89 | 1989–90 | 1990–91 | 1991–92 | 1992–93 | 1993–94 | 1994–95 | 1995–96 | 1996–97 | 1997–98 | 1998–99 | Total by State 1986–99 |
|---|---|---|---|---|---|---|---|---|---|---|---|---|---|---|
| **Marten (continued)** | | | | | | | | | | | | | | |
| OR[45] | 94 | 146 | 159 | 207 | 122 | 52 | 41 | 44 | 16 | 15 | 19 | 92 | 17 | 1,024 |
| UT | 22 | 50 | 10 | 0 | 0 | 0 | 0 | 0 | 0 | 0 | 2 | N/D | N/D | 84 |
| WA[54] | 364 | 178 | 298 | 464 | 241 | 246 | 140 | 67 | 176 | 52 | 74 | 80 | 14 | 2,394 |
| WY[57] | 881 | 1,418 | 1,640 | 559 | 493 | 595 | 414 | 442 | 180 | 92 | 128 | 1,022 | 277 | 8,141 |
| Total | 39,807 | 44,480 | 45,941 | 34,363 | 10,585 | 12,199 | 7,853 | 11,131 | 13,002 | 12,977 | 9,986 | 14,546 | 9,013 | |

Totals from 1986 through 1999 = 265,883

| State | 1986–87 | 1987–88 | 1988–89 | 1989–90 | 1990–91 | 1991–92 | 1992–93 | 1993–94 | 1994–95 | 1995–96 | 1996–97 | 1997–98 | 1998–99 | Total by State 1986–99 |
|---|---|---|---|---|---|---|---|---|---|---|---|---|---|---|
| **Mink** | | | | | | | | | | | | | | |
| AL[1] | 2,795 | 2,318 | 918 | 408 | 425 | 509 | 132 | 94 | 63 | 65 | 112 | 49 | 32 | 7,920 |
| AR[9] | 18,220 | 11,748 | 9,766 | 3,534 | 4,659 | 4,435 | 4,176 | 5,131 | 2,915 | 3,562 | 5,554 | 2,268 | 1,319 | 77,287 |
| CA[58] | 356 | 300 | 171 | 148 | 66 | 220 | 228 | 73 | 26 | 42 | 119 | 76 | 13 | 1,838 |
| CO[59, 19] | 235 | 307 | 246 | 247 | 244 | 134 | 282 | 166 | 774 | 9 | 0 | N/D | N/D | 2,644 |
| CT[32] | 201 | 206 | 111 | 72 | 128 | 139 | 136 | 140 | 215 | 209 | 224 | 262 | 174 | 2,217 |
| DE[12] | N/D | N/D | 5 | 9 | N/D | N/D | N/D | 15 | 3 | 16 | 17 | 3 | N/D | 68 |
| FL[60] | 29 | 39 | 6 | 0 | 0 | 0 | 3 | 0 | 1 | 1 | 1 | 0 | 0 | 80 |
| GA[14] | 1,337 | 1,016 | 517 | 221 | 212 | 254 | 69 | 100 | 154 | 87 | 194 | 31 | 268 | 4,460 |
| ID[16] | 2,836 | 2,487 | 1,910 | 1,444 | 945 | 1,729 | 649 | 588 | 461 | 346 | 744 | 758 | 512 | 15,409 |
| IL[17] | 18,391 | 14,009 | 6,155 | 3,189 | 3,358 | 5,201 | 2,309 | 3,004 | 4,164 | 3,185 | 3,948 | 3,849 | 2,622 | 73,384 |
| IN[18] | 11,746 | 11,853 | 4,198 | 2,696 | 1,976 | 3,890 | 2,348 | 3,125 | 4,594 | 3,253 | 2,765 | 3,337 | 2,230 | 58,012 |
| IA[20] | 31,139 | 27,712 | 13,996 | 8,293 | 7,363 | 8,469 | 12,839 | 13,946 | 11,819 | 20,392 | 18,946 | 16,832 | 16,461 | 208,207 |
| KS[7] | 2,571 | 2,619 | 1,545 | 630 | 423 | 713 | 252 | 368 | 746 | 291 | 473 | 718 | 419 | 11,768 |
| KY[11] | 5,964 | 5,792 | 2,984 | 2,539 | 783 | 2,554 | 1,439 | 836 | 1,186 | 630 | 2,007 | 2,172 | 845 | 29,731 |
| LA[2] | 35,045 | 33,365 | 25,782 | 10,267 | 4,358 | 7,736 | 4,543 | 8,779 | 17,982 | 10,303 | 8,361 | 9,294 | 1,743 | 177,558 |
| ME[23] | 2,072 | 3,466 | 2,550 | 2,366 | 1,513 | 2,068 | 1,803 | 1,881 | 1,549 | 1,341 | 1,365 | 1,177 | 1,519 | 24,670 |
| MD[25] | 335 | 311 | 229 | 123 | 107 | 206 | 144 | N/D | N/D | N/D | N/D | N/D | N/D | 1,455 |
| MA[19] | 1,170 | 1,140 | 751 | 489 | 503 | 631 | 591 | 593 | 559 | 502 | 441 | 49 | 49 | 7,468 |
| MI[3] | 25,520 | 28,000 | 23,280 | N/D | N/D | N/D | N/D | 18,755 | 18,630 | N/D | 20,141 | 32,306 | 21,537 | 188,169 |
| MN[27] | 77,000 | 110,000 | 59,000 | 40,000 | 25,000 | 21,000 | 32,000 | 33,000 | 40,000 | 26,000 | 35,000 | 34,000 | 36,000 | 568,000 |
| MS | 8,881 | 6,201 | 5,291 | 2,106 | 917 | 1,424 | 1,503 | 685 | 326 | 315 | 600 | 674 | 528 | 29,451 |
| MO[31] | 8,578 | 6,299 | 4,406 | 3,166 | 2,280 | 3,402 | 2,131 | 2,399 | 3,570 | 2,479 | 3,937 | 3,235 | 1,561 | 47,443 |
| MT[33] | 3,148 | 3,964 | 3,148 | 2,144 | 1,175 | 1,192 | 841 | 844 | 1,145 | 919 | 1,638 | 1,493 | 1,078 | 22,729 |
| NE[35] | 7,778 | 10,626 | 5,701 | 3,504 | 2,008 | 2,788 | 2,040 | 2,809 | 4,442 | 2,218 | 5,188 | 4,236 | 3,057 | 56,395 |
| NV[37] | 380 | 126 | 113 | 47 | 24 | 80 | 20 | 72 | 116 | 41 | 75 | 80 | 17 | 1,191 |
| NH[36] | 488 | 701 | 618 | 465 | 358 | 537 | 381 | 441 | 513 | 386 | 587 | 429 | 453 | 6,357 |
| NJ[38] | 567 | 449 | 579 | 525 | 541 | 323 | 658 | 114 | 572 | 704 | 828 | 556 | 1,565 | 7,981 |

| State | 1986–87 | 1987–88 | 1988–89 | 1989–90 | 1990–91 | 1991–92 | 1992–93 | 1993–94 | 1994–95 | 1995–96 | 1996–97 | 1997–98 | 1998–99 | Total by State 1986–99 |
|---|---|---|---|---|---|---|---|---|---|---|---|---|---|---|
| **Mink (continued)** | | | | | | | | | | | | | | |
| NY[40] | 15,307 | 17,024 | 13,279 | 9,232 | 9,433 | 10,526 | 10,551 | 8,153 | 10,726 | 8,031 | 14,834 | 17,333 | 10,406 | 154,834 |
| NC[41] | 1,021 | 861 | 312 | 250 | 118 | 227 | 121 | 256 | 136 | 93 | 183 | 101 | 51 | 3,730 |
| ND[42] | 2,704 | 6,035 | 3,965 | 1,980 | 863 | 964 | 682 | 427 | 659 | 438 | 766 | 13,213 | 1,670 | 34,366 |
| OH[43] | 11,296 | 11,937 | 6,100 | 4,479 | 3,233 | 9,886 | 4,155 | 3,635 | 4,544 | 4,371 | 3,763 | 4,664 | 2,548 | 74,611 |
| OK[44] | 1,021 | 932 | 478 | 258 | 54 | 180 | 193 | 58 | 47 | 48 | 112 | 55 | 10 | 3,446 |
| OR[45] | 1,744 | 1,723 | 1,077 | 1,045 | 631 | 742 | 459 | 486 | 367 | 322 | 673 | 607 | 310 | 10,186 |
| PA[46] | 16,008 | 18,513 | 12,914 | 9,669 | 7,053 | 10,355 | 9,157 | 7,808 | 10,208 | 8,602 | 9,315 | 14,063 | 12,238 | 145,903 |
| RI[47] | 76 | 67 | 58 | 63 | 65 | 109 | 65 | 69 | 56 | 71 | 85 | 79 | 54 | 917 |
| SC[48] | 258 | 258 | 116 | 40 | 23 | 63 | 17 | 27 | 21 | 11 | 16 | 15 | 21 | 886 |
| SD[49] | 8,557 | 12,753 | 5,033 | 1,785 | 877 | 625 | 756 | 3,322 | 2,727 | 1,868 | 1,825 | 3,385 | 1,697 | 45,210 |
| TN | 6,464 | 4,566 | 1,889 | 919 | 442 | 2,164 | 667 | 712 | 893 | 444 | 621 | 570 | 253 | 20,604 |
| TX[50] | 4,719 | 1,607 | 1,142 | N/D | 367 | 812 | 430 | 464 | 308 | 303 | 988 | 350 | 160 | 11,650 |
| UT[51] | 828 | 1,037 | 854 | 1,114 | 543 | 723 | 380 | 472 | 350 | 529 | 269 | 337 | 345 | 7,781 |
| VT[52] | 737 | 989 | 1,005 | 645 | 1,042 | 691 | 535 | 566 | 572 | 391 | 412 | 441 | 242 | 8,268 |
| VA[53] | 2,238 | 1,646 | N/D | 400 | 391 | 647 | 382 | 331 | 531 | 274 | 868 | 536 | 187 | 8,431 |
| WA[54] | 1,502 | 1,172 | 809 | 845 | 620 | 732 | 624 | 640 | 720 | 375 | 596 | 607 | 424 | 9,666 |
| WV[55] | 1,393 | 1,746 | 547 | 380 | 268 | 597 | 368 | 260 | 322 | 237 | 521 | 393 | 211 | 7,243 |
| WI[56] | 30,912 | 37,229 | 25,985 | 10,910 | 9,687 | 18,713 | 25,924 | 21,089 | 27,616 | 19,206 | 19,346 | 28,767 | 22,619 | 298,003 |
| WY[57] | 807 | 1,692 | 1,010 | 576 | 891 | 305 | 228 | 301 | 144 | 28 | 177 | 121 | 151 | 6,431 |
| Total | 374,374 | 406,841 | 250,549 | 133,222 | 95,967 | 128,695 | 127,211 | 147,034 | 177,472 | 122,938 | 168,635 | 203,521 | 147,598 | |

Totals from 1986 through 1999 = 2,484,058

| State | 1986–87 | 1987–88 | 1988–89 | 1989–90 | 1990–91 | 1991–92 | 1992–93 | 1993–94 | 1994–95 | 1995–96 | 1996–97 | 1997–98 | 1998–99 | Total by State 1986–99 |
|---|---|---|---|---|---|---|---|---|---|---|---|---|---|---|
| **Muskrat** | | | | | | | | | | | | | | |
| AL[1] | 14,434 | 14,701 | 4,946 | 681 | 358 | 2,117 | 385 | 890 | 2,903 | 853 | 6,685 | 4,873 | 175 | 54,001 |
| AZ[8] | 18 | 23 | 25 | 0 | 0 | 0 | 0 | 12 | 0 | 0 | 41 | 3 | 0 | 122 |
| AR[9] | 25,502 | 23,075 | 17,010 | 4,991 | 3,479 | 3,773 | 3,196 | 2,631 | 3,619 | 4,355 | 3,948 | 2,037 | 1,120 | 98,736 |
| CA[58] | 35,446 | 34,104 | 20,066 | 8,883 | 9,127 | 9,938 | 6,529 | 10,129 | 10,096 | 8,690 | 17,557 | 13,370 | 6,633 | 190,568 |
| CO[59, 19] | 22,930 | 25,078 | 11,715 | 6,994 | 4,102 | 1,280 | 3,420 | 4,706 | 5,963 | 2,126 | 2,373 | N/D | N/D | 90,687 |
| CT[10] | 10,893 | 11,108 | 5,024 | 3,387 | 3,686 | 3,754 | 2,918 | 2,710 | 4,689 | 3,159 | 3,104 | 3,222 | 2,216 | 59,870 |
| DE[12] | 29,200 | 12,000 | 37,519 | 35,515 | 16,576 | 37,417 | 33,892 | 28,807 | 39,590 | 22,560 | 49,271 | 40,476 | 16,800 | 399,623 |
| GA[14] | 4,438 | 4,655 | 2,608 | 1,421 | 1,397 | 2,235 | 629 | 658 | 761 | 496 | 991 | 973 | 705 | 21,967 |
| ID[16] | 78,221 | 68,305 | 34,883 | 24,325 | 18,558 | 33,114 | 13,085 | 14,987 | 12,217 | 12,140 | 23,678 | 21,273 | 13,882 | 368,668 |
| IL[17] | 360,499 | 297,737 | 115,125 | 67,103 | 44,624 | 59,510 | 45,593 | 75,128 | 108,579 | 50,631 | 41,167 | 62,824 | 36,003 | 1,364,523 |
| IN[18] | 276,785 | 247,100 | 83,509 | 64,662 | 48,276 | 80,270 | 53,665 | 84,408 | 84,673 | 48,313 | 37,742 | 72,720 | 53,821 | 1,235,944 |
| IA[20] | 482,811 | 515,611 | 192,214 | 73,415 | 70,133 | 91,206 | 124,638 | 163,842 | 178,683 | 158,241 | 123,460 | 113,621 | 90,126 | 2,378,001 |
| KS[7] | 25,561 | 33,814 | 22,822 | 7,114 | 4,083 | 3,043 | 2,115 | 2,571 | 6,215 | 3,598 | 5,451 | 9,679 | 7,445 | 133,511 |

# APPENDIX III

*Number of Animals Trapped in the United States.*

| | | | | Indicates trapped data. |
| --- | --- | --- |
| | Indicates trapped, hunted or other data. |
| N/D | No data provided/ available |

## Muskrat (continued)

| State | 1986–87 | 1987–88 | 1988–89 | 1989–90 | 1990–91 | 1991–92 | 1992–93 | 1993–94 | 1994–95 | 1995–96 | 1996–97 | 1997–98 | 1998–99 | Total by State 1986–99 |
| --- | --- | --- | --- | --- | --- | --- | --- | --- | --- | --- | --- | --- | --- | --- |
| KY[11] | 84,402 | 79,481 | 36,146 | 24,488 | 8,319 | 17,123 | 11,433 | 5,329 | 10,479 | 5,851 | 14,402 | 17,059 | 5,281 | 319,793 |
| LA[2] | 143,538 | 163,670 | 22,193 | 12,672 | 2,987 | 13,071 | 8,697 | 11,953 | 4,792 | 5,013 | 6,078 | 13,375 | 607 | 408,646 |
| ME[23] | 40,000 | 40,000 | 37,500 | N/D | N/D | N/D | N/D | N/D | N/D | N/D | N/D | N/D | N/D | 117,500 |
| MD[25] | 105,115 | 95,611 | 36,683 | 25,639 | 35,320 | 55,186 | 41,683 | N/D | N/D | N/D | N/D | N/D | N/D | 395,237 |
| MA[19] | 28,404 | 28,656 | 13,780 | 19,958 | 13,519 | 12,519 | 9,474 | 9,595 | 11,341 | 7,873 | 7,062 | 712 | 1,017 | 163,910 |
| MI[3] | 565,080 | 548,630 | 214,340 | N/D | N/D | N/D | N/D | 193,400 | 261,178 | N/D | 222,649 | 275,368 | 178,537 | 2,459,182 |
| MN[27] | 826,000 | 1,007,000 | 185,000 | 118,000 | 55,000 | 45,000 | 92,000 | 202,000 | 355,000 | 195,000 | 202,000 | 194,000 | 131,000 | 3,607,000 |
| MS | 12,142 | 9,097 | 6,853 | 2,506 | 681 | 1,256 | 1,439 | 725 | 238 | 267 | 1,432 | 760 | 443 | 37,839 |
| MO[31] | 68,828 | 60,936 | 40,436 | 21,817 | 9,772 | 14,964 | 11,969 | 13,145 | 18,508 | 13,448 | 19,803 | 21,210 | 7,621 | 322,457 |
| MT[33] | 32,706 | 41,578 | 23,766 | 12,538 | 10,778 | 12,260 | 6,912 | 15,772 | 14,256 | 11,727 | 16,121 | 18,816 | 12,243 | 229,473 |
| NE[35] | 111,041 | 119,545 | 53,819 | 23,847 | 12,400 | 13,072 | 8,601 | 26,949 | 32,718 | 24,110 | 71,472 | 57,010 | 40,351 | 594,935 |
| NV[37] | 14,864 | 12,641 | 2,135 | 149 | 410 | 680 | 100 | 273 | 876 | 1,372 | 6,717 | 9,604 | 3,415 | 53,236 |
| NH[36] | 6,115 | 6,871 | 5,809 | 3,746 | 2,381 | 3,886 | 2,525 | 2,273 | 4,389 | 2,731 | 2,976 | 3,980 | 3,517 | 51,199 |
| NJ[38] | 199,056 | 184,805 | 177,402 | 126,807 | 66,349 | 72,909 | 78,228 | 42,274 | 56,737 | 82,506 | 74,837 | 81,351 | 66,732 | 1,309,993 |
| NM[39] | 8,131 | 2,599 | N/D | 142 | 417 | 311 | 573 | 87 | 346 | 594 | 698 | 481 | 8 | 14,387 |
| NY[40] | 304,313 | 359,700 | 193,720 | 105,388 | 106,362 | 122,751 | 110,133 | 120,883 | 186,358 | 95,701 | 178,475 | 192,382 | 124,560 | 2,200,726 |
| NC[41] | 25,228 | 25,073 | 10,187 | 5,810 | 4,099 | 10,287 | 4,691 | 7,130 | 4,616 | 2,167 | 6,002 | 4,485 | 1,600 | 111,375 |
| ND[42] | 63,219 | 141,882 | 22,158 | 1,020 | 541 | 305 | 621 | 1,266 | 6,105 | 32,032 | 39,312 | 425,452 | 18,897 | 762,810 |
| OH[43] | 392,370 | 331,677 | 144,999 | 155,831 | 111,461 | 215,836 | 142,420 | 163,293 | 172,272 | 127,869 | 84,484 | 154,467 | 70,439 | 2,267,418 |
| OK[44] | 2,809 | 2,159 | 1,214 | 505 | 219 | 353 | 141 | 143 | 137 | 141 | 236 | 176 | 57 | 8,290 |
| OR[45] | 40,826 | 37,914 | 18,571 | 14,641 | 9,349 | 12,154 | 6,412 | 13,190 | 14,053 | 9,042 | 21,222 | 18,156 | 5,615 | 221,145 |
| PA[46] | 440,880 | 346,558 | 229,958 | 141,577 | 112,358 | 156,014 | 135,533 | 121,657 | 178,145 | 130,442 | 146,013 | 216,066 | 148,202 | 2,503,403 |
| RI[47] | 1,337 | 1,211 | 728 | 284 | 473 | 442 | 461 | 367 | 472 | 356 | 417 | 454 | 512 | 7,514 |
| SC[48] | 1,139 | 911 | 465 | 386 | 103 | 435 | 155 | 135 | 94 | 197 | 199 | 284 | 367 | 4,870 |
| SD[49] | 248,126 | 254,185 | 35,623 | 2,949 | 1,085 | 1,392 | 1,175 | 3,130 | 28,123 | 36,770 | 27,327 | 42,874 | 12,024 | 6594,783 |
| TN | 31,767 | 31,028 | 12,286 | 4,924 | 1,655 | 7,357 | 2,563 | 1,545 | 4,041 | 2,161 | 3,488 | 2,261 | 2,094 | 107,170 |
| TX[50] | 192 | 1,063 | N/D | N/D | N/D | N/D | N/D | N/D | 1,022 | 205 | 917 | 733 | 17 | 4,149 |
| UT[51] | 59,382 | 58,560 | 33,400 | 16,898 | 7,102 | 19,547 | 11,623 | 22,488 | 28,369 | 26,260 | 23,371 | 26,907 | 21,895 | 355,788 |
| VT[52] | 21,084 | 14,253 | 7,069 | 3,048 | 6,284 | 4,201 | 4,143 | 3,984 | 4,135 | 1,828 | 3,801 | 6,740 | 3197 | 83,767 |
| VA[53] | 64,579 | 63,464 | N/D | 13,080 | 15,734 | 21,961 | 10,380 | 14,832 | 21,353 | 7,010 | 23,925 | 20,045 | 3,888 | 280,251 |
| WA[54] | 26,132 | 21,843 | 11,181 | 6,662 | 5,138 | 9,275 | 4,420 | 6,005 | 6,056 | 5,335 | 11,028 | 10,924 | 4,117 | 128,116 |
| WV[55] | 34,397 | 34,643 | 13,234 | 6,669 | 4,692 | 11,148 | 7,074 | 5,661 | 8,419 | 4,233 | 9,440 | 7,474 | 2,833 | 149,917 |
| WI[56] | 662,237 | 753,808 | 340,802 | 115,220 | 114,361 | 224,728 | 370,669 | 499,388 | 503,319 | 248,077 | 297,096 | 456,839 | 324,881 | 4,911,425 |
| WY[57] | 8,605 | 16,742 | 9,087 | 4,427 | 2,503 | 2,980 | 2,637 | 1,039 | 989 | 238 | 1,799 | 1,639 | 1,964 | 54,649 |
| Total | 6,040,782 | 6,185,106 | 2,488,010 | 1,290,119 | 946,251 | 1,411,060 | 1,378,950 | 1,901,390 | 2,396,924 | 1,395,718 | 1,840,267 | 2,627,155 | 1,426,857 | |

Totals from 1986 through 1999 = 31,328,574

| State | 1986–87 | 1987–88 | 1988–89 | 1989–90 | 1990–91 | 1991–92 | 1992–93 | 1993–94 | 1994–95 | 1995–96 | 1996–97 | 1997–98 | 1998–99 | Total by State 1986–99 |
|---|---|---|---|---|---|---|---|---|---|---|---|---|---|---|
| **Nutria** | | | | | | | | | | | | | | |
| AL[1] | 228 | 105 | 4 | 0 | 0 | 0 | 0 | 0 | 0 | 0 | 150 | 25 | 15 | 527 |
| AR[9] | 950 | 1,448 | 32 | 22 | 102 | 88 | 197 | 490 | 745 | 931 | 2,169 | 947 | 938 | 9,059 |
| GA[14] | 65 | 64 | 41 | 6 | 1 | 0 | 0 | 4 | 12 | 13 | 21 | 28 | N/D | 255 |
| LA[2] | 986,014 | 617,646 | 223,222 | 292,760 | 134,196 | 240,229 | 129,545 | 215,968 | 171,470 | 188,719 | 327,286 | 359,232 | 114,646 | 4,000,933 |
| MD[25] | 441 | 207 | 1 | N/D | 22 | 18 | 84 | N/D | N/D | N/D | N/D | N/D | N/D | 773 |
| MS | 4,199 | 1,602 | 1,515 | 1,017 | 378 | 254 | 694 | 6,153 | 541 | 620 | 890 | 1,004 | 1,411 | 20,278 |
| NC[41] | 1,067 | 2,047 | 1,131 | 906 | 294 | 493 | 271 | 445 | 153 | 13 | 126 | 202 | 14 | 7,162 |
| OK | 12 | 36 | 0 | 0 | 0 | 0 | 0 | 0 | 0 | 0 | 0 | 0 | 0 | 48 |
| OR[45] | 12,079 | 14,950 | 8,149 | 6,484 | 5,267 | 6,333 | 6,182 | 6,213 | 7,467 | 8,523 | 11,336 | 12,181 | 10,345 | 115,509 |
| TX[50] | 20,908 | 21,899 | N/D | 4,449 | 3,106 | 4,191 | 5,060 | 7,574 | 9,549 | 5,103 | 10,524 | 23,860 | 3,416 | 119,639 |
| VA[53] | 19 | 1,706 | N/D | 0 | 0 | 0 | 55 | 0 | 17 | 24 | 22 | 28 | N/D | 1,871 |
| WA[54] | 575 | 717 | 433 | 517 | 0 | 0 | 0 | 289 | 365 | 320 | 923 | 1,116 | 486 | 5,741 |
| Total | 1,026,557 | 662,427 | 234,528 | 306,161 | 143,366 | 251,606 | 142,088 | 237,136 | 190,319 | 204,266 | 353,447 | 398,623 | 131,271 | |

Totals from 1986 through 1999 = 4,281,795

| State | 1986–87 | 1987–88 | 1988–89 | 1989–90 | 1990–91 | 1991–92 | 1992–93 | 1993–94 | 1994–95 | 1995–96 | 1996–97 | 1997–98 | 1998–99 | Total by State 1986–99 |
|---|---|---|---|---|---|---|---|---|---|---|---|---|---|---|
| **Opossum** | | | | | | | | | | | | | | |
| AL[1] | 8,834 | 5,619 | 741 | 192 | 101 | 191 | 61 | 53 | 122 | 154 | 176 | 78 | 199 | 16,521 |
| AR[9] | 50,183 | 30,635 | 9,461 | 2,160 | 1,720 | 2,792 | 2,630 | 2,100 | 4,286 | 5,575 | 9,335 | 5,068 | 1,043 | 126,988 |
| CA[58] | 913 | 1,138 | 889 | 612 | 267 | 436 | 201 | 609 | 127 | 243 | 526 | 329 | 292 | 6,582 |
| CO[59, 19] | 52 | 132 | 48 | 11 | 14 | 20 | 73 | 57 | 36 | 0 | 7 | N/D | N/D | 450 |
| CT[10] | 973 | 903 | 414 | 455 | 364 | 293 | 210 | 126 | 210 | 189 | 166 | 454 | 104 | 4,861 |
| DE[12] | N/D | N/D | 862 | 819 | 214 | 153 | 323 | 251 | 339 | 372 | 412 | 350 | 235 | 4,330 |
| FL[60] | 1,575 | 952 | 62 | 17 | 0 | 6 | 0 | 3 | 40 | 40 | 66 | 4 | 14 | 2,779 |
| GA[14] | 21,637 | 32,417 | 11,019 | 5,441 | 3,364 | 4,271 | 2,780 | 3,444 | 3,355 | 3,447 | 3,713 | 4,574 | 3,215 | 102,677 |
| IL[17] | 38,502 | 35,749 | 8,137 | 2,441 | 3,097 | 6,758 | 6,006 | 7,022 | 9,813 | 9,509 | 16,693 | 17,847 | 7,502 | 169,076 |
| IN[18] | 11,684 | 11,059 | 1,414 | 641 | 410 | 1,567 | 1,037 | 1,565 | 2,009 | 2,240 | 3,517 | 8,557 | 3,844 | 49,543 |
| IA[20] | 30,760 | 27,623 | 19,824 | 8,114 | 6,243 | 7,411 | 8,192 | 6,243 | 6,782 | 9,781 | 7,643 | 6,012 | 5,123 | 149,751 |
| KS[7] | 59,190 | 54,714 | 24,117 | 9,775 | 5,493 | 12,427 | 8,101 | 12,727 | 19,692 | 16,120 | 29,980 | 49,437 | 26,512 | 328,285 |
| KY[11] | 19,913 | 25,606 | 7,212 | 3,758 | 3,139 | 6,539 | 2,696 | 2,176 | 2,582 | 2,413 | 6,048 | 6,174 | 3,580 | 91,836 |
| LA[2] | 20,376 | 18,440 | 1,052 | 1,416 | 360 | 1,014 | 978 | 1,311 | 2,364 | 1,754 | 2,867 | 1,777 | 395 | 54,104 |
| MD[25] | 1,747 | 1,664 | 488 | 236 | 335 | 708 | 319 | N/D | N/D | N/D | N/D | N/D | N/D | 5,497 |
| MA[19] | 58 | 83 | 63 | 582 | 200 | 174 | 60 | 54 | 87 | 54 | 44 | 113 | 75 | 1,647 |
| MI[3] | 39,950 | 59,690 | 20,430 | N/D | N/D | N/D | N/D | 16,555 | 18,873 | N/D | 24,531 | 31,060 | 25,106 | 236,195 |
| MN[27] | 14,000 | 10,000 | 9,000 | 6,000 | 6,000 | 5,000 | 6,000 | 5,000 | 5,000 | 6,000 | 6,000 | 6,000 | 7,000 | 91,000 |
| MS | 20,078 | 16,632 | 7,209 | 3,969 | 2,008 | 2,218 | 2,366 | 1,649 | 2,552 | 1,809 | 3,872 | 3,378 | 3,304 | 71,044 |
| MO[31] | 82,276 | 59,323 | 16,610 | 7,726 | 8,774 | 18,887 | 14,622 | 16,007 | 21,737 | 16,900 | 24,632 | 18,828 | 5,951 | 312,273 |
| NE[35] | 17,553 | 23,498 | 7,912 | 4,831 | 3,009 | 5,436 | 4,114 | 3,692 | 8,015 | 9,683 | 18,517 | 22,839 | 19,223 | 148,322 |

157

# APPENDIX III

*Number of Animals Trapped in the United States.*

Indicates trapped data.

Indicates trapped, hunted or other data.

N/D  No data provided/available

| State | 1986–87 | 1987–88 | 1988–89 | 1989–90 | 1990–91 | 1991–92 | 1992–93 | 1993–94 | 1994–95 | 1995–96 | 1996–97 | 1997–98 | 1998–99 | Total by State 1986–99 |
|---|---|---|---|---|---|---|---|---|---|---|---|---|---|---|
| **Opossum (continued)** | | | | | | | | | | | | | | |
| NH | 0 | 0 | 0 | 0 | 0 | 0 | 0 | 0 | 0 | 35 | 33 | 32 | 100 | |
| NJ[38] | 4,557 | 6,736 | 3,231 | 1,532 | 969 | 1,091 | 1,455 | 490 | 1,052 | 918 | 1,893 | 1,565 | 1,298 | 26,787 |
| NY[40] | 43,092 | 46,116 | 25,113 | 11,827 | 8,998 | 9,585 | 7,849 | 4,254 | 5,587 | 5,557 | 10,919 | 15,999 | 11,799 | 206,695 |
| NC[41] | 3,703 | 1,635 | 208 | 380 | 145 | 233 | 109 | 372 | 256 | 215 | 534 | 146 | 59 | 7,995 |
| OH[43] | 22,544 | 26,661 | 4,945 | 2,848 | 2,319 | 5,169 | 3,504 | 2,976 | 4,750 | 4,050 | 5,451 | 6,492 | 2,666 | 94,375 |
| OK[44] | 32,729 | 7,643 | 5,191 | 1,148 | 1,451 | 1,933 | 1,197 | 950 | 2,262 | 1,649 | 3,713 | 2,671 | 469 | 63,006 |
| OR[45] | 2,620 | 2,923 | 1,219 | 750 | 754 | 1,287 | 962 | 786 | 901 | 1,053 | 1,032 | 962 | 574 | 15,823 |
| PA[46] | 210,953 | 217,552 | 105,812 | 80,660 | 36,574 | 37,177 | 27,754 | 25,807 | 29,621 | 29,688 | 48,549 | 60,717 | 56,287 | 967,151 |
| RI[47] | 171 | 166 | 62 | 32 | 35 | 25 | 82 | 39 | 57 | 64 | 55 | 73 | 123 | 984 |
| SC[48] | 2,241 | 1,301 | 1,395 | 896 | 1,171 | 2,090 | 1,058 | 1,043 | 1,136 | 2,174 | 1,973 | 1,886 | 2,256 | 20,620 |
| SD[49] | 138 | 131 | 39 | 0 | 0 | 124 | 36 | 15 | 39 | 156 | 360 | 20 | 6 | 1,064 |
| TN | 13,081 | 9,325 | 1,611 | 753 | 308 | 1,213 | 386 | 349 | 902 | 834 | 1,068 | 718 | 313 | 30,861 |
| TX[50] | 58,755 | 151,327 | 54,496 | 16,048 | 12,686 | 12,638 | 9,907 | 9,809 | 13,780 | 10,185 | 27,515 | 26,672 | 12,359 | 416,177 |
| VT [52] | N/D | N/D | N/D | N/D | N/D | 25 | 0 | 0 | 10 | 17 | 15 | N/D | N/D | 67 |
| VA[53] | 8,761 | 5,714 | N/D | 680 | 385 | 1,369 | 619 | 396 | 1,352 | 727 | 2,375 | 1,446 | 464 | 24,288 |
| WV[55] | 9,011 | 10,741 | 1,968 | 842 | 641 | 1,500 | 807 | 582 | 1,012 | 715 | 2,198 | 1,553 | 1,201 | 32,771 |
| WI[56] | 3,751 | 7,644 | 25,886 | 443 | 687 | 16,917 | 20,352 | 19,218 | 21,850 | 19,001 | 21,829 | 25,094 | 24,742 | 207,414 |
| Total | 856,361 | 911,492 | 378,140 | 178,035 | 112,235 | 168,652 | 136,846 | 147,730 | 192,578 | 163,269 | 288,244 | 328,926 | 227,365 | |

Totals from 1986 through 1999 = 4,089,872

| State | 1986–87 | 1987–88 | 1988–89 | 1989–90 | 1990–91 | 1991–92 | 1992–93 | 1993–94 | 1994–95 | 1995–96 | 1996–97 | 1997–98 | 1998–99 | Total by State 1986–99 |
|---|---|---|---|---|---|---|---|---|---|---|---|---|---|---|
| **River Otter** | | | | | | | | | | | | | | |
| AL[1] | 982 | 961 | 358 | 169 | 20 | 30 | 2 | 14 | 60 | 131 | 213 | 104 | 40 | 3,084 |
| AK[4] | 1,865 | 2,433 | 1,563 | 1,490 | 1,200 | 1,485 | 1,182 | 1,127 | 1,393 | 1,506 | 1,908 | 1,792 | 1,164 | 20,108 |
| AR[9] | 776 | 998 | 683 | 498 | 482 | 642 | 806 | 1,531 | 2,059 | 2,407 | 3,158 | 1,816 | 2,343 | 18,199 |
| CT[32] | 111 | 133 | 136 | 112 | 101 | 103 | 131 | 113 | 227 | 151 | 206 | 177 | 113 | 1,814 |
| DE[12] | 74 | 34 | 28 | 28 | 3 | 27 | 28 | 4 | 14 | 42 | 51 | 51 | 61 | 445 |
| FL[60] | 1,052 | 1,692 | 398 | 151 | 19 | 190 | 105 | 213 | 175 | 245 | 238 | 342 | 22 | 4,842 |
| GA[14] | 1,316 | 1,666 | 680 | 725 | 224 | 433 | 380 | 559 | 909 | 1,029 | 1,101 | 1,103 | 804 | 10,929 |
| ID | 0 | 0 | 0 | 0 | 22 | 34 | 25 | 29 | 32 | 36 | 35 | 45 | 31 | 289 |
| LA[2] | 5,074 | 4,021 | 1,924 | 1,365 | 1,203 | 1,779 | 1,983 | 4,063 | 6,418 | 7,555 | 5,649 | 7,200 | 2,483 | 50,717 |
| ME[23] | 1,037 | 1,035 | 676 | 753 | 558 | 759 | 887 | 908 | 1,324 | 760 | 1,237 | 876 | 836 | 11,646 |
| MD[25] | 218 | 246 | 151 | 138 | 169 | 207 | 219 | N/D | N/D | N/D | N/D | N/D | N/D | 1,348 |
| MA[19] | 94 | 181 | 114 | 124 | 129 | 128 | 149 | 151 | 165 | 171 | 147 | 13 | 15 | 1,581 |
| MI[26] | 1,431 | 1,030 | 731 | 896 | 654 | 878 | 896 | 1,251 | 1,552 | 1,137 | 1,438 | 1,323 | 1,028 | 14,245 |
| MN[30] | 777 | 1,386 | 922 | 1,294 | 888 | 855 | 1,368 | 1,459 | 2,445 | 1,435 | 2,219 | 2,145 | 1,946 | 19,139 |
| MS | 955 | 1,064 | 532 | 425 | 199 | 302 | 349 | 449 | 598 | 452 | 1,404 | 922 | 1,003 | 8,654 |

| State | 1986–87 | 1987–88 | 1988–89 | 1989–90 | 1990–91 | 1991–92 | 1992–93 | 1993–94 | 1994–95 | 1995–96 | 1996–97 | 1997–98 | 1998–99 | Total by State 1986–99 |
|---|---|---|---|---|---|---|---|---|---|---|---|---|---|---|
| | | | | | River Otter (continued) | | | | | | | | | |
| MO | 0 | 0 | 0 | 0 | 0 | 0 | 0 | 0 | 0 | 0 | 1,054 | 1,149 | 852 | 3,055 |
| MT[33] | 62 | 38 | 30 | 45 | 26 | 35 | 35 | 51 | 62 | 61 | 65 | 84 | 67 | 661 |
| NV[37] | 49 | 19 | 4 | 3 | 0 | 9 | 1 | 8 | 7 | 5 | 8 | 13 | 1 | 127 |
| NH[36] | 319 | 361 | 308 | 329 | 271 | 316 | 285 | 405 | 504 | 317 | 451 | 344 | 288 | 4,498 |
| NJ[38] | 22 | 32 | 33 | 29 | 34 | 38 | 39 | 22 | 30 | 34 | 46 | 49 | 50 | 458 |
| NY[40] | 895 | 1,003 | 818 | 991 | 736 | 873 | 889 | 1,214 | 1,707 | 722 | 1,826 | 1,035 | 640 | 13,349 |
| NC[41] | 785 | 689 | 367 | 408 | 247 | 321 | 265 | 909 | 831 | 607 | 698 | 605 | 468 | 7,200 |
| OR[45] | 450 | 471 | 262 | 313 | 244 | 306 | 272 | 440 | 476 | 370 | 503 | 446 | 388 | 4,941 |
| RI | 0 | 0 | 0 | 0 | 0 | 0 | 0 | 0 | 0 | 0 | 0 | 0 | 4 | 4 |
| SC[48] | 637 | 601 | 291 | 140 | 113 | 169 | 127 | 301 | 344 | 498 | 495 | 502 | 0 | 4,218 |
| TN | 0 | 0 | 0 | 47 | 34 | 86 | 62 | 146 | 81 | 96 | 92 | 135 | 100 | 879 |
| TX[50] | 796 | 855 | 335 | 378 | 67 | 319 | 134 | 528 | 604 | 330 | 2,532 | 1,386 | 324 | 8,588 |
| VT[52] | 174 | 195 | 129 | 124 | 105 | 125 | 140 | 150 | 207 | 136 | 232 | 196 | 161 | 2,074 |
| VA[53] | 733 | 785 | N/D | 182 | 140 | 436 | 267 | 363 | 845 | 445 | 1,162 | 839 | 196 | 6,393 |
| WA[54] | 966 | 682 | 467 | 536 | 386 | 482 | 597 | 564 | 798 | 1,358 | 703 | 771 | 656 | 8,966 |
| WI[56] | 1,588 | 1,724 | 1,127 | 1,213 | 744 | 762 | 969 | 1,928 | 2,376 | 1,517 | 2,443 | 2,704 | 1,530 | 20,625 |
| Total | 23,238 | 24,335 | 13,067 | 12,906 | 9,018 | 12,129 | 12,592 | 18,900 | 26,243 | 23,553 | 31,314 | 28,167 | 17,614 | |

Totals from 1986 through 1999 = 253,076

| State | 1986–87 | 1987–88 | 1988–89 | 1989–90 | 1990–91 | 1991–92 | 1992–93 | 1993–94 | 1994–95 | 1995–96 | 1996–97 | 1997–98 | 1998–99 | Total by State 1986–99 |
|---|---|---|---|---|---|---|---|---|---|---|---|---|---|---|
| | | | | | Raccoon | | | | | | | | | |
| AL[1] | 57,511 | 54,667 | 12,037 | 2,956 | 416 | 806 | 158 | 511 | 938 | 767 | 2,524 | 475 | 399 | 134,165 |
| AZ[8] | 876 | 834 | 241 | 190 | 67 | 84 | 49 | 74 | 24 | 0 | 57 | 49 | 114 | 2,659 |
| AR[9] | 167,458 | 138,793 | 49,041 | 22,273 | 18,939 | 28,719 | 18,110 | 23,673 | 37,123 | 52,876 | 79,340 | 47,129 | 23,352 | 706,826 |
| CA[58] | 4,846 | 3,793 | 1,745 | 1,104 | 879 | 646 | 1,100 | 786 | 355 | 1,012 | 1,057 | 983 | 459 | 18,765 |
| CO[59, 15] | 4,798 | 4,384 | 2,446 | 1,384 | 1,425 | 1,098 | 2,102 | 1,870 | 3,260 | 2,009 | 1,745 | N/D | N/D | 26,521 |
| CT[10] | 4,959 | 5,826 | 3,120 | 1,881 | 2,098 | 1,430 | 1,420 | 1,000 | 1,110 | 838 | 1,142 | 1,868 | 719 | 27,411 |
| DE[12] | 3,300 | 7,600 | 2,986 | 2,149 | 1,460 | 910 | 1,169 | 2,381 | 2,400 | 2,147 | 3,014 | 2,365 | 1,386 | 33,267 |
| FL[60] | 29,763 | 40,049 | 9,111 | 3,793 | 407 | 1,450 | 1,345 | 1,503 | 2,286 | 2,606 | 3,610 | 2,712 | 667 | 99,302 |
| GA[14] | 32,735 | 42,202 | 14,465 | 6,305 | 2,886 | 4,150 | 3,549 | 3,971 | 5,046 | 5,937 | 8,904 | 6,646 | 5,964 | 142,760 |
| ID[16] | 1,621 | 1,610 | 845 | 606 | 354 | 785 | 356 | 431 | 509 | 600 | 964 | 839 | 654 | 10,174 |
| IL[17] | 306,261 | 261,418 | 137,807 | 83,284 | 70,845 | 174,452 | 99,990 | 126,211 | 175,671 | 153,052 | 229,805 | 278,680 | 163,320 | 2,260,796 |
| IN[18] | 64,668 | 74,481 | 24,616 | 17,396 | 8,922 | 20,224 | 19,799 | 24,609 | 30,478 | 29,735 | 47,733 | 205,069 | 134,527 | 702,257 |
| IA[20] | 179,756 | 150,718 | 93,372 | 41,529 | 39,318 | 45,240 | 49,591 | 50,939 | 112,686 | 118,136 | 123,698 | 149,492 | 106,641 | 1,261,116 |
| KS[7] | 119,488 | 118,879 | 72,028 | 38,274 | 27,137 | 43,977 | 33,710 | 48,203 | 64,951 | 58,600 | 93,190 | 108,727 | 71,709 | 898,872 |
| KY[11] | 17,158 | 26,677 | 12,037 | 7,616 | 3,511 | 8,608 | 5,658 | 3,553 | 6,506 | 5,042 | 16,923 | 18,338 | 9,652 | 141,279 |
| LA[2] | 240,396 | 164,184 | 34,987 | 27,940 | 12,018 | 30,657 | 22,549 | 26,718 | 54,717 | 61,513 | 122,095 | 66,267 | 15,441 | 879,482 |
| ME[23] | 17,848 | 22,025 | 6,439 | N/D | N/D | N/D | N/D | N/D | N/D | N/D | N/D | N/D | N/D | 46,312 |
| MD[25] | 14,768 | 13,803 | 5,019 | 3,775 | 2,660 | 5,426 | 3,186 | N/D | N/D | N/D | N/D | N/D | N/D | 48,637 |

Indicates trapped data.

Indicates trapped, hunted or other data.

N/D  No data provided/available

# APPENDIX III

*Number of Animals Trapped in the United States.*

## Raccoon (continued)

| State | 1986–87 | 1987–88 | 1988–89 | 1989–90 | 1990–91 | 1991–92 | 1992–93 | 1993–94 | 1994–95 | 1995–96 | 1996–97 | 1997–98 | 1998–99 | Total by State 1986–99 |
|---|---|---|---|---|---|---|---|---|---|---|---|---|---|---|
| MA[19] | 6,163 | 5,857 | 3,431 | 4,580 | 2,846 | 2,807 | 2,150 | 1,438 | 1,471 | 640 | 998 | 559 | 368 | 33,308 |
| MI[3] | 78,780 | 96,790 | 40,420 | N/D | N/D | N/D | N/D | 45,831 | 71,670 | N/D | 93,109 | 125,968 | 79,805 | 632,373 |
| MN[27] | 95,000 | 134,000 | 74,000 | 41,000 | 34,000 | 31,000 | 34,000 | 56,000 | 59,000 | 58,000 | 74,000 | 71,000 | 71,000 | 832,000 |
| MS | 41,400 | 41,898 | 17,901 | 7,893 | 4,232 | 5,443 | 5,763 | 4,887 | 7,971 | 5,399 | 13,704 | 11,607 | 10,559 | 178,657 |
| MO[31] | 229,908 | 196,259 | 106,558 | 68,564 | 63,327 | 103,261 | 67,933 | 99,854 | 144,045 | 125,252 | 208,888 | 177,337 | 107,267 | 1,698,453 |
| MT[33] | 8,764 | 9,166 | 4,485 | 2,765 | 1,452 | 3,987 | 2,139 | 4,067 | 4,392 | 4,687 | 9,216 | 6,956 | 4,200 | 66,276 |
| NE[35] | 112,868 | 136,867 | 72,109 | 50,423 | 37,240 | 69,384 | 61,991 | 88,833 | 150,695 | 130,697 | 231,986 | 252,525 | 174,238 | 1,569,856 |
| NV[37] | 106 | 108 | 52 | 53 | 14 | 52 | 17 | 56 | 23 | 14 | 48 | 62 | 11 | 616 |
| NH[36] | 3,748 | 5,135 | 1,884 | 890 | 796 | 965 | 854 | 994 | 888 | 902 | 519 | 96 | 459 | 18,130 |
| NJ[38] | 21,404 | 29,677 | 17,169 | 10,593 | 6,946 | 6,788 | 6,618 | 4,200 | 4,679 | 3,941 | 6,907 | 7,168 | 4,437 | 130,527 |
| NM[39] | 1,712 | 886 | N/D | 487 | 871 | 543 | 533 | 1,458 | 1,137 | 158 | 144 | 188 | 33 | 8,150 |
| NY[40] | 114,314 | 125,615 | 65,015 | 27,754 | 25,172 | 29,274 | 29,975 | 22,715 | 27,135 | 17,512 | 35,485 | 40,990 | 29,339 | 590,295 |
| NC[41] | 70,525 | 63,445 | 19,633 | 18,456 | 8,515 | 9,301 | 4,648 | 9,802 | 12,491 | 10,447 | 19,354 | 10,914 | 6,375 | 263,906 |
| ND[42] | 24,303 | 24,266 | 11,456 | 4,767 | 4,516 | 6,946 | 4,543 | 4,765 | 8,668 | 7,657 | 12,579 | 15,643 | 5,052 | 135,161 |
| OH[43] | 248,240 | 227,281 | 117,975 | 88,128 | 62,090 | 139,182 | 111,965 | 107,474 | 155,811 | 126,998 | 156,593 | 186,945 | 105,014 | 1,833,696 |
| OK[44] | 67,749 | 43,399 | 22,663 | 6,452 | 2,506 | 7,938 | 4,111 | 4,641 | 9,284 | 7,690 | 23,082 | 20,948 | 7,258 | 227,721 |
| OR[45] | 8,117 | 7,068 | 2,540 | 1,174 | 1,113 | 2,172 | 988 | 1,383 | 1,448 | 1,172 | 2,509 | 5,179 | 3,868 | 38,731 |
| PA[46] | 426,625 | 443,534 | 224,514 | 155,761 | 116,443 | 130,608 | 124,404 | 118,964 | 186,551 | 120,462 | 214,958 | 194,696 | 195,110 | 2,652,630 |
| RI[47] | 253 | 331 | 120 | 42 | 78 | 74 | 306 | 294 | 342 | 347 | 232 | 158 | 230 | 2,807 |
| SC[48] | 29,505 | 32,292 | 9,472 | 2,559 | 1,707 | 2,079 | 1,142 | 1,256 | 1,207 | 1,898 | 4,708 | 2,904 | 2,108 | 92,837 |
| SD[49] | 34,038 | 35,409 | 14,976 | 6,300 | 8,451 | 14,926 | 9,187 | 14,586 | 21,409 | 23,227 | 22,645 | 30,728 | 15,739 | 251,621 |
| TN | 58,126 | 39,054 | 8,001 | 6,903 | 1,971 | 7,898 | 1,508 | 1,697 | 6,060 | 4,743 | 9,845 | 7,929 | 7,261 | 160,996 |
| TX[50] | 61,365 | 419,848 | 149,195 | 69,767 | 48,077 | 57,901 | 49,507 | 58,098 | 88,527 | 67,236 | 181,896 | 122,146 | 58,771 | 1,432,334 |
| UT[51] | 2,412 | 2,619 | 3,104 | 2,464 | 1,156 | 2,273 | 1,851 | 2,259 | 3,025 | 2,914 | 4,228 | 4,989 | 7,765 | 41,059 |
| VT[52] | 7,422 | 6,733 | 1,981 | 786 | 665 | 757 | 812 | 931 | 1,051 | 483 | 470 | 566 | 239 | 22,896 |
| VA[53] | 69,678 | 65,065 | N/D | 9,125 | 4,256 | 5,254 | 4,918 | 3,607 | 8,860 | 10,966 | 21,723 | 17,851 | 4,414 | 225,717 |
| WA[54] | 3,602 | 2,504 | 1,326 | 1,089 | 698 | 1,172 | 833 | 950 | 1,105 | 810 | 1,273 | 1,307 | 832 | 17,501 |
| WV[55] | 37,635 | 38,338 | 16,843 | 6,773 | 4,540 | 7,518 | 4,478 | 3,496 | 9,532 | 6,790 | 23,262 | 17,846 | 9,939 | 186,990 |
| WI[56] | 227,502 | 251,018 | 158,161 | 2125,83 | 138,314 | 184,219 | 228,408 | 313,224 | 320,924 | 301,157 | 215,112 | 160,830 | 398,691 | 3,110,143 |
| WY[57] | 4,565 | 5,119 | 3,800 | 2,191 | 1,569 | 1,963 | 1,243 | 1,279 | 1,202 | 432 | 1,765 | 3,489 | 1,263 | 29,880 |
| Total | 3,364,039 | 3,621,523 | 1,651,126 | 1,072,777 | 776,903 | 1,204,347 | 1,030,666 | 1,295,472 | 1,808,663 | 1,537,501 | 2,327,039 | 2,389,163 | 1,846,649 | |

Totals from 1986 through 1999 = 23,925,868

| State | 1986–87 | 1987–88 | 1988–89 | 1989–90 | 1990–91 | 1991–92 | 1992–93 | 1993–94 | 1994–95 | 1995–96 | 1996–97 | 1997–98 | 1998–99 | Total by State 1986–99 |
|---|---|---|---|---|---|---|---|---|---|---|---|---|---|---|
| **Ringtail** | | | | | | | | | | | | | | |
| AZ[8] | 3,851 | 4,475 | 1,968 | 1,091 | 174 | 403 | 258 | 372 | 157 | 12 | 30 | 16 | 8 | 12,815 |
| CO[59, 19] | 584 | 261 | 237 | 106 | 34 | 143 | 115 | 292 | 131 | 0 | 0 | N/D | N/D | 1,903 |
| NV[37] | 28 | 86 | 25 | 29 | 9 | 17 | 14 | 16 | 25 | 9 | 15 | 10 | 7 | 290 |
| NM[39] | 1,378 | 645 | N/D | 306 | 236 | 53 | 274 | 434 | 322 | 60 | 42 | 69 | 8 | 3,827 |
| OK[44] | 9 | 3 | 0 | 0 | 0 | 0 | 0 | 0 | 0 | 0 | 0 | 0 | 0 | 12 |
| TX[50] | 49,882 | 50,641 | 20,611 | 9,222 | 5,146 | 4,534 | 6,975 | 6,257 | 6,786 | 6,601 | 19,822 | 14,960 | 4,013 | 205,450 |
| UT[51] | 205 | 268 | 186 | 132 | 99 | 220 | 107 | 64 | 159 | 136 | 46 | 57 | 138 | 1,817 |
| **Total** | 55,937 | 56,379 | 23,027 | 10,886 | 5,698 | 5,370 | 7,743 | 7,435 | 7,580 | 6,818 | 19,955 | 15,111 | 4,171 | |

Totals from 1986 through 1999 = 226,113

| State | 1986–87 | 1987–88 | 1988–89 | 1989–90 | 1990–91 | 1991–92 | 1992–93 | 1993–94 | 1994–95 | 1995–96 | 1996–97 | 1997–98 | 1998–99 | Total by State 1986–99 |
|---|---|---|---|---|---|---|---|---|---|---|---|---|---|---|
| **Skunk** | | | | | | | | | | | | | | |
| AL[1] | 63 | 54 | 5 | 4 | 5 | 1 | 0 | 0 | 1 | 11 | 10 | 4 | 5 | 163 |
| AZ[8] | 2,400 | 2,537 | 1,255 | 590 | 154 | 336 | 300 | 271 | 170 | 46 | 89 | 61 | 114 | 8,323 |
| AR[9] | 175 | 104 | 49 | 10 | 6 | 10 | 0 | 40 | 56 | 119 | 93 | 59 | 5 | 726 |
| CA[58] | 3,842 | 3,515 | 2,512 | 1,402 | 1,021 | 729 | 1,021 | 758 | 406 | 1,910 | 1,127 | 148 | 1,061 | 19,452 |
| CO[59, 19] | 5,004 | 3,658 | 2,219 | 1,651 | 1,386 | 1,218 | 2,486 | 1,466 | 6,296 | 452 | 281 | N/D | N/D | 26,117 |
| CT[10] | 156 | 189 | 106 | 69 | 84 | 49 | 74 | 60 | 210 | 150 | 130 | 232 | 81 | 1,590 |
| DE[12] | N/D | N/D | 165 | 31 | 10 | 27 | 3 | 57 | 121 | 23 | 34 | 8 | 18 | 497 |
| GA[14] | 1,642 | 2,139 | 929 | 500 | 220 | 294 | 247 | 388 | 426 | 364 | 318 | 246 | 228 | 7,941 |
| ID[16] | N/D | N/D | N/D | N/D | N/D | N/D | N/D | N/D | 340 | 440 | 681 | 466 | 518 | 2,445 |
| IL[17] | 119 | 233 | 176 | 55 | 49 | 128 | 120 | 203 | 207 | 164 | 214 | 224 | 55 | 1,947 |
| IN[18] | 109 | 70 | 34 | 4 | 2 | 17 | 21 | 35 | 88 | 64 | 76 | 128 | 108 | 756 |
| IA[20] | 2,540 | 1,198 | 712 | 245 | 189 | 211 | 791 | 643 | 510 | 786 | 693 | 649 | 536 | 9,703 |
| KS[7] | 10,460 | 8,847 | 4,233 | 2,043 | 1,258 | 3,576 | 3,125 | 2,610 | 4,131 | 2,877 | 8,065 | 9,323 | 6,375 | 66,923 |
| KY[11] | 2,047 | 2,606 | 1,174 | 737 | 562 | 1,034 | 673 | 684 | 567 | 444 | 750 | 1,021 | 631 | 12,930 |
| LA[2] | 8 | 25 | N/D | N/D | N/D | N/D | N/D | N/D | N/D | N/D | N/D | N/D | N/D | 33 |
| MD[25] | 1 | 50 | 2 | 15 | 24 | 152 | 13 | N/D | N/D | N/D | N/D | N/D | N/D | 257 |
| MA[19] | 42 | 25 | 50 | 299 | 42 | 60 | 31 | 31 | 52 | 41 | 11 | 99 | 64 | 847 |
| MI[3] | 15,640 | 14,540 | 6,740 | N/D | N/D | N/D | N/D | 4,281 | 5,746 | N/D | 4,858 | 8,576 | 4,743 | 65,124 |
| MN[27] | 42,000 | 54,000 | 31,000 | 17,000 | 15,000 | 10,000 | 7,000 | 9,000 | 9,000 | 8,000 | 11,000 | 11,000 | 9,000 | 233,000 |
| MS | 1,870 | 1,832 | 1,031 | 386 | 177 | 300 | 452 | 380 | 100 | 135 | 261 | 204 | 370 | 7,498 |
| MO[31] | 362 | 317 | 153 | 78 | 48 | 103 | 166 | 209 | 334 | 275 | 278 | 260 | 105 | 2,688 |
| MT[33] | 8,378 | 7,958 | 4,743 | 1,525 | 1,384 | 1,649 | 1,548 | 1,734 | 3,219 | 1,784 | 3,382 | 2,682 | 1,567 | 41,553 |
| NE[35] | 6,159 | 6,342 | 2,540 | 1,469 | 1,814 | 2,696 | 1,277 | 2,211 | 4,113 | 2,359 | 6,753 | 10,643 | 10,238 | 58,614 |
| NV[37] | 129 | 80 | 30 | 103 | 49 | 118 | 53 | 67 | 45 | 13 | 96 | 35 | 21 | 839 |
| NH[36] | 161 | 175 | 129 | 131 | 89 | 112 | 106 | 198 | 337 | 26 | 287 | 432 | 265 | 2,448 |
| NJ[38] | 1,082 | 1,435 | 864 | 1,050 | 1,000 | 882 | 730 | 321 | 398 | 459 | 450 | 333 | 460 | 9,464 |

# APPENDIX III

*Number of Animals Trapped in the United States.*

| | Indicates trapped data. |
| | Indicates trapped, hunted or other data. |
| N/D | No data provided/ available |

| State | 1986–87 | 1987–88 | 1988–89 | 1989–90 | 1990–91 | 1991–92 | 1992–93 | 1993–94 | 1994–95 | 1995–96 | 1996–97 | 1997–98 | 1998–99 | Total by State 1986–99 |
|---|---|---|---|---|---|---|---|---|---|---|---|---|---|---|
| **Skunk (continued)** | | | | | | | | | | | | | | |
| NM[39] | 3,378 | 1,624 | N/D | 704 | 334 | 434 | 1,263 | 1,281 | 1,148 | 253 | 61 | 119 | 15 | 10,614 |
| NY[40] | 10,291 | 11,938 | 6,047 | 3,820 | 2,126 | 2,323 | 2,011 | 1,355 | 2,748 | 3,083 | 5,262 | 5,797 | 3,365 | 60,166 |
| NC[41] | 57 | 22 | 1 | 6 | 0 | 10 | 0 | 0 | 5 | 0 | 3 | 4 | 0 | 108 |
| ND[42] | 557 | 62 | 1,134 | 367 | 245 | 108 | 0 | 185 | 550 | 6,277 | 11,296 | 19,582 | 2,832 | 43,195 |
| OH[43] | 330 | 580 | 132 | 65 | 50 | 107 | 72 | 191 | 200 | 227 | 180 | 101 | 31 | 2,268 |
| OK[44] | 360 | 98 | 48 | 12 | 22 | 24 | 16 | 37 | 59 | 18 | 97 | 34 | 14 | 839 |
| OR[45] | 1,919 | 2,029 | 797 | 589 | 542 | 729 | 523 | 528 | 833 | 441 | 991 | 719 | 575 | 11,215 |
| PA[46] | 39,064 | 39,632 | 16,351 | 20,409 | 9,298 | 8,907 | 7,221 | 7,920 | 12,620 | 9,995 | 11,571 | 12,344 | 11,190 | 206,522 |
| RI[47] | 34 | 29 | 13 | 6 | 8 | 6 | 67 | 83 | 90 | 112 | 63 | 246 | 309 | 1,066 |
| SC[48] | 82 | 183 | 132 | 103 | 126 | 147 | 94 | 95 | 89 | 103 | 117 | 125 | 73 | 1,469 |
| SD[49] | 1,881 | 2,499 | 1,137 | 524 | 706 | 368 | 97 | 203 | 516 | 1,486 | 481 | 711 | 342 | 10,951 |
| TN | 124 | 79 | 3 | 11 | 0 | 0 | 1 | 2 | 18 | 11 | 33 | 8 | 7 | 297 |
| TX[50] | 65,713 | 53,595 | 23,549 | 10,834 | 5,746 | 8,780 | 11,729 | 7,487 | 7,005 | 6,579 | 15,015 | 20,809 | N/D | 236,841 |
| UT[51] | 1,851 | 2,404 | 966 | 1,289 | 645 | 1,037 | 922 | 1,465 | 1,438 | 1,756 | 1,762 | 2,890 | 3,227 | 21,613 |
| VT[52] | 48 | 32 | 41 | 8 | 17 | 26 | 34 | 22 | 19 | 10 | 16 | 21 | 5 | 299 |
| VA[53] | 5 | 54 | N/D | 17 | 1 | 2 | 3 | 16 | 58 | 75 | 74 | 98 | 12 | 415 |
| WA[54] | 455 | 529 | 200 | 193 | 0 | 0 | 0 | 146 | 204 | 79 | 225 | 127 | 164 | 2,322 |
| WV[55] | 150 | 288 | 47 | 30 | 21 | 51 | 59 | 44 | 81 | 26 | 105 | 79 | 40 | 1,021 |
| WI[56] | 279 | 436 | 12,904 | 79 | 169 | 9,559 | 8,050 | 12,290 | 11,469 | 8,100 | 9,064 | 11,430 | 8,863 | 92,692 |
| WY[57] | 5,444 | 4,763 | 2,934 | 1,301 | 1,177 | 2,636 | 1,398 | 1,216 | 1,040 | 598 | 941 | 2,756 | 1,270 | 27,474 |
| Total | 236,411 | 232,805 | 127,287 | 69,764 | 45,806 | 58,956 | 53,797 | 60,213 | 77,063 | 60,168 | 97,258 | 124,833 | 77,624 | |

Totals from 1986 through 1999 = 1,321,985

| State | 1986–87 | 1987–88 | 1988–89 | 1989–90 | 1990–91 | 1991–92 | 1992–93 | 1993–94 | 1994–95 | 1995–96 | 1996–97 | 1997–98 | 1998–99 | Total by State 1986–99 |
|---|---|---|---|---|---|---|---|---|---|---|---|---|---|---|
| **Weasel** | | | | | | | | | | | | | | |
| AL[1] | 1 | 3 | 0 | 0 | 0 | 0 | 0 | 0 | 0 | 0 | 0 | 2 | 0 | 6 |
| AR[9] | 2 | 3 | 2 | 1 | N/D | 1 | 0 | 0 | 0 | 0 | 1 | 0 | N/D | 10 |
| CA[58] | 13 | 5 | 3 | 35 | 0 | 2 | 2 | 13 | 2 | 13 | 2 | 1 | 1 | 92 |
| CO[59,11] | 160 | 75 | 316 | 218 | 115 | 66 | 64 | 109 | 447 | N/D | N/D | N/D | N/D | 1,570 |
| CT[32] | 52 | 14 | 19 | 2 | 7 | 5 | 2 | 2 | 3 | 20 | 6 | 8 | 4 | 144 |
| DE[12] | N/D | N/D | 5 | 20 | 3 | 0 | 0 | 21 | 0 | 32 | N/D | 5 | N/D | 86 |
| ID[16] | 79 | 439 | 627 | 254 | 154 | 206 | 156 | 129 | 88 | 50 | 67 | 78 | 51 | 2,378 |
| IL[17] | 39 | 37 | 10 | 4 | 5 | 1 | 2 | 3 | 20 | 15 | 6 | 24 | 9 | 175 |
| IN[18] | 81 | 49 | 6 | 2 | 5 | 4 | 7 | 11 | 22 | 11 | 3 | 17 | 5 | 223 |
| KS[7] | 21 | 23 | 5 | 4 | 0 | 0 | 2 | 146 | 9 | 2 | 40 | 101 | 107 | 460 |

| State | 1986–87 | 1987–88 | 1988–89 | 1989–90 | 1990–91 | 1991–92 | 1992–93 | 1993–94 | 1994–95 | 1995–96 | 1996–97 | 1997–98 | 1998–99 | Total by State 1986–99 |
|---|---|---|---|---|---|---|---|---|---|---|---|---|---|---|
| **Weasel (continued)** | | | | | | | | | | | | | | |
| KY[11] | 78 | 78 | 68 | 9 | 29 | 87 | 12 | 47 | 15 | 3 | 36 | 23 | 6 | 493 |
| MD[25] | N/D | N/D | 1 | N/D | N/D | 1 | 0 | 0 | N/D | N/D | N/D | N/D | N/D | 2 |
| MA[19] | 3 | 1 | 1 | 25 | 11 | 7 | 0 | 0 | 4 | 15 | 1 | 5 | 2 | 75 |
| MI[3] | 2,460 | 910 | 1,770 | N/D | N/D | N/D | N/D | 877 | 1,503 | N/D | 972 | 2,426 | 2,194 | 13,112 |
| MN[27] | 6,000 | 14,000 | 6,000 | 4,000 | 2,000 | 2,000 | 2,000 | 3,000 | 9,000 | 6,000 | 6,000 | 6,000 | 4,000 | 70,000 |
| MS | 15 | 17 | 9 | 0 | 0 | 0 | 0 | 5 | 0 | 0 | 4 | 2 | 0 | 52 |
| MO[31] | 19 | 10 | 4 | 1 | 0 | 1 | 1 | 1 | 3 | 1 | 7 | 3 | 2 | 53 |
| MT[33] | 938 | 992 | 676 | 464 | 308 | 393 | 378 | 327 | 802 | 343 | 1,094 | 381 | 246 | 7,342 |
| NE[3] | 23 | 21 | 9 | 5 | 0 | 0 | 47 | 25 | 0 | 43 | 0 | N/D | N/D | 173 |
| NV[37] | 0 | 2 | 2 | 2 | 1 | 1 | 0 | 0 | 1 | 0 | 2 | 1 | 0 | 12 |
| NH[36] | 51 | 75 | 34 | 25 | 31 | 30 | 45 | 48 | 26 | 99 | 23 | 33 | 36 | 556 |
| NJ[38] | 41 | 56 | 82 | 36 | 99 | 4 | 5 | 0 | 0 | 7 | 0 | 5 | 27 | 362 |
| NM[39] | 21 | 5 | N/D | 5 | 0 | 0 | 0 | 43 | 98 | 2 | 0 | N/D | N/D | 174 |
| NC[41] | 3 | 18 | 3 | 0 | 0 | 1 | 0 | 0 | 0 | 0 | 0 | 0 | 0 | 25 |
| ND[42] | 184 | 83 | 688 | 2 | 116 | 1 | 21 | 6 | 4 | 0 | 0 | 0 | 0 | 1,105 |
| OH[43] | 74 | 91 | 13 | 8 | 2 | 14 | 10 | 24 | 18 | 28 | 9 | 13 | 13 | 317 |
| OR[45] | 106 | 123 | 48 | 30 | 16 | 16 | 23 | 15 | 45 | 14 | 22 | 22 | 6 | 486 |
| PA[46] | N/D | N/D | N/D | N/D | 798 | 481 | 343 | 526 | 723 | 687 | 589 | 1,172 | 662 | 5,981 |
| RI[47] | 8 | 12 | 2 | 0 | 0 | 3 | 4 | 2 | 0 | 2 | 0 | 0 | 0 | 33 |
| SC | 3 | 0 | 1 | 0 | 0 | 0 | 0 | 1 | 0 | 0 | 0 | N/D | N/D | 5 |
| SD[49] | 13 | 24 | 27 | 1 | 2 | 6 | 0 | 3 | 13 | 29 | 10 | 8 | 6 | 142 |
| TN | 12 | 4 | 6 | 1 | 1 | 2 | 1 | 4 | 4 | 0 | 1 | 0 | 1 | 37 |
| TX | N/D | N/D | N/D | N/D | N/D | N/D | N/D | N/D | N/D | 178 | 635 | 0 | N/D | 813 |
| UT[51] | 123 | 212 | 91 | 33 | 31 | 19 | 28 | 31 | 13 | 299 | 13 | 28 | 33 | 954 |
| VT[52] | 24 | 25 | 11 | 5 | 2 | 2 | 14 | 8 | 8 | 3 | 3 | 9 | 0 | 114 |
| VA[53] | 9 | 12 | N/D | 0 | 0 | 0 | 0 | 0 | 2 | 0 | 3 | 2 | N/D | 28 |
| WA[54] | 169 | 83 | 98 | 63 | 36 | 65 | 78 | 2 | 78 | 49 | 49 | 49 | 47 | 866 |
| WV[55] | 25 | 13 | 12 | 4 | 3 | 6 | 4 | 0 | 4 | 6 | 27 | 23 | 0 | 127 |
| WI[56] | 293 | 190 | 391 | 177 | 11 | 372 | 448 | 3,750 | 11,368 | 1,922 | 399 | 850 | 467 | 20,638 |
| WY[57] | 109 | 346 | 255 | 121 | 77 | 66 | 57 | 156 | 22 | 1 | 11 | 453 | 14 | 1,688 |
| Total | 11,252 | 18,051 | 11,295 | 5,557 | 3,866 | 3,863 | 3,754 | 9,335 | 24,345 | 9,874 | 10,035 | 11,744 | 7,941 | |
| | | | | | | | | | | | Totals from 1986 through 1999 = 130,909 | | | |
| **Gray Wolf** | | | | | | | | | | | | | | |
| AK[4, 6] | 801 | 1,101 | 860 | 1,082 | 1,089 | 1,162 | 1,043 | 1,600 | 1,483 | 1,251 | 1,448 | 1,229 | 1,495 | 15,644 |
| Total | 801 | 1,101 | 860 | 1,082 | 1,089 | 1,162 | 1,043 | 1,600 | 1,483 | 1,251 | 1,448 | 1,229 | 1,495 | |
| | | | | | | | | | | | Totals from 1986 through 1999 = 15,644 | | | |

| | Indicates trapped data. | | | | | | | | | | | | |
|---|---|---|---|---|---|---|---|---|---|---|---|---|---|

**APPENDIX III**

*Number of Animals Trapped in the United States.*

Key:
- ☐ Indicates trapped data.
- ▨ Indicates trapped, hunted or other data.
- N/D No data provided/available

| State | 1986–87 | 1987–88 | 1988–89 | 1989–90 | 1990–91 | 1991–92 | 1992–93 | 1993–94 | 1994–95 | 1995–96 | 1996–97 | 1997–98 | 1998–99 | Total by State 1986–99 |
|---|---|---|---|---|---|---|---|---|---|---|---|---|---|---|
| **Wolverine** | | | | | | | | | | | | | | |
| AK[4] | 636 | 570 | 464 | 493 | 528 | 591 | 381 | 496 | 629 | 389 | 549 | 589 | 496 | 6,911 |
| MT[33] | 10 | 8 | 9 | 10 | 6 | 9 | 6 | 9 | 9 | 12 | 12 | 15 | 9 | 124 |
| Total | 646 | 578 | 473 | 503 | 534 | 600 | 387 | 505 | 638 | 401 | 661 | 604 | 505 | |

Totals from 1986 through 1999 = 7,035

### Note 1: Alabama

Data were tabulated from mandatory fur dealer reports.

### Note 2: Louisiana

Trappers are not required to submit a report of annual take. Data derived from survey of randomly selected sample of fur dealers.

### Note 3: Michigan

Data derived from questionnaires sent to a randomly selected sample of trappers. Numbers given in this table are estimates of trapped animals only (figures do not include hunted animals). The data were not collected or species were not trapped for those years that are blank. For badger, fisher, river otter, and bobcat for years 1989–90 through 1992–93 and 1995–96, the data are from registered harvest reports.

### Note 4: Alaska

Data obtained from mandatory fur dealer reports and pelt sealing (of the 16 furbearer species trapped in Alaska, 5 require sealing statewide: beaver, lynx, river otter, wolf, and wolverine). Alaska does not maintain records on mammals legally trapped, except for those that are required to be sealed. Species trapped but not recorded are reflected as N/D. Data on arctic fox provided by the Alaska Department of Fish and Game.

### Note 5: Alaska

Marten are required to be sealed in specific Management Units. Marten sealing is required in Regions I and II (GMUs 1–5, 7, 13E, 14–16) only.

### Note 6: Alaska

No distinction made between different wolf sub-species trapped (reported only as "wolf" in fur dealer reports). Arctic fox and red fox data were not separated for the 1992–93, 1993–94, and 1994–95 seasons so the data recorded for those years under each species reflect the total number for both.

### Note 7: Kansas

Data derived from questionnaires sent to a randomly selected sample of trappers. Figures include both hunted and trapped animals. In the 1996–97 season, 73% of total bobcats killed (figure shown in chart) were trapped; the remaining 27% were either hunted or the kill method was unknown. 94% of all swift foxes killed in the 1996–97 season were trapped; the remaining 6% were shot or "salvaged."

### Note 8: Arizona

Data are collected from mandatory trapper and fur dealer reports. Trappers are required to report take on prescribed forms. Failure to do so is a misdemeanor violation. Arizona Fish and Game (AZFG) does not separate fox species trapped in the state; both gray and kit foxes are legally trapped. AZFG told API that approximately 90% of all trapped foxes are gray and 10% are kit. API used these percentages in estimating numbers of each species trapped.

### Note 9: Arkansas

Data are obtained from "fur report booklets." Fur dealers are supplied these booklets and instructed to complete and return them within 30 days following the close of the furbearing season. The 1994–95 season was calculated from the percent change from the 1995–96 season.

### Note 10: Connecticut

Totals estimated from questionnaires sent to a randomly selected sample of trappers. The number includes trapped and may include hunted and vehicle-killed animals. Pelt tagging is required of all trapped beaver, river otter, red fox, gray fox, wild mink, and coyote.

### Note 11: Kentucky

Data shown are Kentucky Department of Fish and Wildlife Resources' estimates of the total trapped catch, derived from licensed trapper surveys and mandatory fur dealer reports, with the exception of the bobcat total, which is obtained from actual tagging data.

### Note 12: Delaware

Data are from voluntary mail surveys sent to trappers and fur dealers (except for otter and beaver, which must be checked and tagged by the state.)

### Note 13: Kentucky

Data obtained from mandatory fur dealer reports and from survey of randomly selected sample of trappers (with the exception of the bobcat total, which is obtained from actual tagging data). The 1995–96 data are the total number of trapped bobcats that were tagged in the Eastern Bobcat Harvest Zone or LBL.

### Note 14: Georgia

Data derived from mandatory trapper and fur dealer reports.

### Note 15: Hawaii

There is no commercial or recreational trapping allowed in Hawaii. Wild pigs are trapped with snares in the name of "habitat management."

### Note 16: Idaho

Trapping totals based on mandatory trapping reports.

### Note 17: Illinois

Trapping totals derived from mandatory fur dealer reports and from survey of randomly selected sample of trappers.

### Note 18: Indiana

Trappers are not required to report their annual take. Indiana bases its furbearer hunting and trapping kill estimates upon stratified random mail surveys and mandatory annual fur dealer reports. Trapping estimates are not obtained on an annual basis. Indiana has not sampled its trapping license holders since 1989. The estimated trapped figure is derived from the total number of animals hunted and trapped, with the estimate based on a letter received by API from Indiana's Department of Natural Resources dated April 16, 1997.

### Note 19: Colorado/Massachusetts

During the November 5, 1996, general election, voters outlawed leghold traps in Colorado and banned padded leghold traps in Massachusetts, which had previously outlawed unpadded traps.

### Note 20: Iowa

Data obtained from mandatory annual fur dealer reports and include both hunted and trapped animals. Data on red fox, raccoon, and coyote were separated between trapped and hunted until 1993–94. In the 1994–95 season, Iowa began selling a general fur-harvester license and stopped separating trapped/hunted data.

### Note 23: Maine

Pelts of all furbearers, except weasel, raccoon, muskrat, skunk, and opossum, must be tagged by an agent of the Maine Department of Inland Fisheries and Wildlife. Maine stopped tracking numbers of weasel, raccoon, muskrat, skunk, and opossum trapped beginning in the 1989–90 season.

### Note 24: Multi State

The data shown include trapped and hunted animals.

### Note 25: Maryland

The data estimate represent minimums due to under-reporting and/or poor or totally absent trapping survey processes. Maryland relies on mandatory annual fur dealer reports for determining trap kill estimates but admits that these statistics do not accurately reflect total annual take. Beginning in the 1993–94 season, Maryland stopped producing reported and/or estimated trapping harvest data. Instead, a "furbearer population trends" document is produced that is not an accurate reflection of numbers of animals trapped in the state.

### Note 26: Michigan

Data based on survey of randomly selected sample of trappers. Numbers given in this table are estimated trapped-only kill numbers (does not include hunted animals).

### Note 27: Minnesota

Minnesota's estimates of trapper harvests are from survey of randomly selected sample of trappers and mandatory annual fur dealer reports. The numbers given were rounded to the nearest 1000.

### Note 28: Minnesota

Minnesota's registered harvest for bobcat includes animals taken by hunting. The numbers provided by the Minnesota Department of Natural Resources are rounded to the nearest 1000 — 1000 represents any number between 500 and 1000; < 1000 is any number between 1 and 499(< 500). Therefore, 501 would be rounded to 1000 and 1001 would be rounded to 2000, etc.

### Note 29: Minnesota

Minnesota's count of less than 500 spotted skunks is not included in the total.

### Note 30: Minnesota

Minnesota's registered kill of bobcat includes animals taken by hunting. River otter, fisher, and marten are registered kill numbers versus estimated totals.

### Note 31: Missouri

The fur take estimates are based on mandatory recording of fur purchases by licensed fur buyers and fur dealers, on forms provided by the Missouri

Department of Conservation. This provides a minimum kill figure for both hunted and trapped furbearers and does not include the number of unsold pelts or damaged pelts. Bobcat kill information was compiled from mandatory pelt registration records.

**Note 32: Connecticut**

Total estimated from questionnaires sent to random sample of trappers. The number reflects animals that were trapped only.

**Note 33: Montana**

Furbearer trapping and hunting kill data are compiled annually. The annual kill of marten, fisher, wolverine, lynx, bobcat, and otter is monitored through a statewide pelt tagging and harvest registration system. Kill data on other trapped species (muskrat, mink, weasel, skunk, coyote, fox, raccoon, badger) and additional information on tagged furbearers were collected through a trapping and furbearer harvest survey questionnaire mailed to a randomly selected sample of license holders. The Montana Fish, Parks & Wildlife Department has failed to generate any trap kill data on species that do not require tags, such as beaver, since 1995.

**Note 34: Montana, Washington**

These states do not differentiate between fox species. Refer to red fox for totals.

**Note 35: Nebraska**

Nebraska's trapping totals are obtained from an annual mail survey sent in the spring to a percentage of the individuals purchasing "fur harvest" (trapping) permits. Response rate is very low (19% in 1997) and expanded estimates are therefore most likely not very accurate. Bobcat kill is actual count from tagging records.

**Note 36: New Hampshire**

The trapping license year runs July 1 to June 30. The mandatory trapper reports are due on April 15 annually. The numbers reported between 1986 and 1993 are based on sealing records (except muskrat, skunk, and weasel) and include trapped, hunted, and miscellaneous kills. The trap kill summaries since 1993 are based solely on mandatory trapper reports. Fur buyers are also required to submit annual reports of pelts purchased.

**Note 37: Nevada**

Trap kill data are derived from questionnaires sent to all trapping license holders each year and pelt sealing data. The returned questionnaire sample is expanded to reflect trap kill figures of all licensed trappers (and therefore is not highly accurate).

**Note 38: New Jersey**

New Jersey does not register or license its raw fur

dealers or require them to keep records on the type or volume of animals trapped in the state. The trapper survey is the only tool presently available to estimate the volume of furbearing animals killed. Written questionnaires are mailed annually to a sample of trappers and a sample of hunters. Response to the survey is voluntary. Beaver and otter are brought to check stations and sealed.

**Note 39: New Mexico**

Kill figures may include both hunted and trapped animals. Data from 1986–1995 are projected kill figures taken from the New Mexico Cooperative Fish and Wildlife Service's publication "Ecological-Based Management Evaluation For Sustainable Harvest and Use of New Mexico Furbearer Resources." Beginning in the 1995–96 season, the NM Department of Fish and Game (DFG) began disseminating only reported trap kill numbers obtained from a random survey of trappers, which does not accurately reflect total annual take. Data from 1988–89 season are missing because DFG has no data for this season.

**Note 40: New York**

Pelt sealing is only required for beaver, coyote, fisher, bobcat, marten, and river otter. All trappers and hunters must report the number of pelts they obtain from these species. For other species reported, New York conducts a random telephone survey of trappers in February or March in order to compile estimated statistics of trapped and hunted animals.

**Note 41: North Carolina**

The reported furbearer kill total reflects only the number of pelts sold to licensed fur dealers in North Carolina by licensed hunters and trappers. North Carolina does not have estimates of the numbers of furbearers taken, only fur dealer reports, which may not accurately reflect total take of species trapped and hunted for fur.

**Note 42: North Dakota**

All fur buyers within the state are required to submit to the Game and Fish Department an annual report of all furs purchased before their current license will be renewed. The 1994–95 and 1996–97 season statistics represent only those furs that were sold to North Dakota fur buyers and include trapped and hunted furbearers. The 1995–1996 statistics estimates reflect only trapped species, with the numbers obtained from mailed questionnaires sent to a sample of individuals who indicated they would buy a furbearer stamp when they purchased their general license.

**Note 43: Ohio**

The reported furbearer kill count includes a list of furs received by fur dealers direct from hunters and trappers. The information is not adequate to estimate the percentage of Ohio furs sold to dealers outside the state or the total number of animals killed for their fur. Badger data for the 1995–96 and 1996–97 were not included in the data provided by the department.

## Note 44: Oklahoma

The furbearer kill data originate from various sources. Fur dealers are required to submit reports of all pelts purchased in state from hunters and trappers. Trappers are not required to report total numbers of animals trapped annually except for bobcat, which must be tagged. The season on ring-tailed cat was closed after 1988.

## Note 45: Oregon

Any person hunting or trapping furbearers or unprotected mammals is required to fill out and return a "harvest" report form by April 15. Failure to do so will deny the license holder the opportunity to purchase a hunting or fur takers license for the following furbearer season. Each person desiring to kill bobcat or river otter must secure a bobcat or river otter record card prior to hunting or trapping these species.

## Note 46: Pennsylvania

Estimates given are from game take surveys prior to the 1990–91 seasons. Post-1990, total kill estimates of furbearer species were determined from questionnaires mailed to a random sample of purchasers of trapping and hunting licenses. Beaver pelts must be tagged by trappers. Fur dealers are required to submit annual reports of pelts purchased.

## Note 47: Rhode Island

The furbearer trap kill statistics are collected from a mandatory catch card that licensed trappers are required to mail in. If trappers do not mail in their card they will be denied a license in subsequent years. Information on pelts taken by fur dealers is obtained from fur auctions that occur bi-annually in the state.

## Note 48: South Carolina

Data from 1994–95 and 1995–96 are trap kill numbers only. All other years include trapped, hunted, and other kill methods. Furbearing animals killed for commercial purposes must be tagged at the time the fur is removed from the carcass or, in the case of whole animals, at the time it is stored or before it is sold. Any person taking furbearing animals for commercial purposes must file an annual report of his/her total kill by April 15 of each year. Fur buyers must keep a daily register of furs purchased on forms provided by the Department of Natural Resources and must submit these forms on a monthly basis.

## Note 49: South Dakota

Furbearer kill numbers are derived from fur dealer reports submitted annually.

## Note 50: Texas

Texas requires a report by April 30 by holders of retail fur buyer and wholesale fur dealer licenses. Prior to purchase, sale, or transport outside Texas, bobcat pelts taken in Texas must be permanently tagged. Some trapped species were either not tracked some years or the "sample was inadequate to provide reliable estimates," according to the Texas Parks and Wildlife Department.

## Note 51: Utah

Utah obtains kill data for bobcats and marten through tagging. For other furbearers, data were determined through a voluntary "fur harvest" questionnaire, which was mailed to holders of a fur harvest license.

## Note 52: Vermont

Furbearer kill reports are produced annually. Trapper reports were optional until 1997. Currently, data originate from mandatory trapper/hunter reports, mandatory fur dealer reports, and pelt-sealing. Trappers are required to report and turn in the carcasses of bobcat, beaver, otter, and fisher for biological examination. All other species are reported on a mandatory trapper mail survey form. The kill numbers exclude out-of-state pelt sales by trappers. Prior to the 1991–92 season the number of opossum trapped was not recorded.

## Note 53: Virginia

Virginia produces a furbearer status or summary report annually. Most furbearer data are derived from fur buyer reports (trappers are not required to submit records of animals trapped). Tagging is required of bobcat and river otter. No data exist on numbers of animals trapped during the 1988–89 season because the Virginia Department of Game and Inland Fisheries reported that the data were "lost."

## Note 54: Washington

Data regarding bobcat and coyote kill totals reflect both trapped and hunted animals. Trapping and hunting reports are published annually. Total furbearer kill summaries are produced based on mandatory return of trapper catch reports and by mandatory pelt sealing records for bobcat and river otter.

## Note 55: West Virginia

Data taken from mandatory fur dealer reports.

## Note 56: Wisconsin

The data from 1986 through 1989 are based on surveys of hunters and trappers and include both hunted and trapped animals. Years 1991–92 and 1994–1996 are based on a survey of trappers and include only trapped animals. Bobcats, fishers, and otters must be registered/tagged by Wisconsin Department of Natural Resources personnel.

### Note 57: Wyoming

Furbearer kill data are compiled by the Wyoming Game and Fish Department from responses to a voluntary trapper survey report. A few trappers with limited quota permits are required to report to local game wardens. Fur dealers are required to submit a report of pelts purchased with the trapper's license number to the local game warden.

### Note 58: California

(Note: In November 1998, California voters passed an initiative banning the use of body-gripping traps for commercial/recreational trapping statewide. See Chapter 7.)

Data obtained from mandatory trapper and fur dealer reports. All licensed trappers are required to report their season's total kill by the end of trapping year (July) or they will be denied a trapping license for the next season. Likewise, licensed fur dealers are required to report the number of furs of each species killed in California that they purchased.

### Note 59: Colorado

Trap kill statistics are generated via a random mail survey and are estimates that reflect trends, not actual numbers of animals trapped. Passage of Amendment 14 in 1996 outlawed commercial/recreational trapping with body-gripping traps. Amendment 14, however, allowed for landowners to request a 30-day trapping permit from the CDOW. According to Lynn Stevens of the CDOW, the agency only started receiving reliable data on the numbers of animals killed through the 30-day trapping permit process beginning in the 2001 season.

### Note 60: Florida

Furbearer kill estimates originate from fur dealer report forms. Trappers and hunters are not required to report their take. A number of trappers ship or transport their pelts out of state for sale and therefore are not included in purchases reported by fur dealers.

# Annotated Bibliography
# of Trap Research

(Items are arranged chronologically within each section.)

*Christopher M. Papouchis*

## Leghold Traps

Gilbert, F. F., and N. Gofton. 1982. Terminal dives in mink, muskrat and beaver. *Physiology & Behavior* 28:835–840.

Behavioral responses and length of time to unconsciousness, clinical death, and loss of cardiac function were examined for mink, muskrat, and beaver held underwater by leghold traps in controlled laboratory conditions. To monitor heart rate and EEG, live-trapped wild animals were surgically implanted with transmitters and allowed to recuperate for at least 24 hours before the start of the study. Nos. 3 and 4 Victor double longspring leghold traps were used for beaver and Nos. 1½ and 2 (mink only) were used for mink or muskrat. Floating log sets with No. 1½ Victor leghold traps were also used with some mink and muskrats, as well as a submarine trap for muskrats. Mink fell into the water when trapped, more as a result of struggling than diving to escape. Mink struggled "violent[ly]" for an average of 2.02 min. Nine of 13 mink (69%) experienced "wet" drowning (took water into their lungs). Muskrat dove into the water as soon as they were trapped and struggled with the trap for an average of 3.58 min. Four of the 16 muskrats (25%) suffered from lacerations and abrasions and one had a fractured humerus. Five others trapped in floating log or submarine sets took much longer to cease struggling and lose their EEG than did the platform-trapped animals. Nine muskrats (38%) died by "wet" drowning. The 20 beaver struggled for more than 8 minutes on average (range 5–13 minutes). Average time to loss of EEG was about 9.5 min and loss of cardiac function about 16 min. Five beavers (25%) drowned after 20 minutes. Given the stated criteria for "humane traps" of 3 minutes to loss of consciousness, the researchers concluded drowning traps are as humane as Conibear traps for mink and muskrat, although muskrat took an average of > 3.5 minutes to cease struggling and over 4 minutes for loss of brain waves. Moreover, mink struggled frantically prior to loss of consciousness, indicating extreme trauma. The researchers admitted that drowning leghold traps were probably not humane for beaver.

**Key words:** trap injuries, leghold trap, drowning sets, beaver, muskrat, mink

Tullar, B. F. 1984. Evaluation of a padded leg-hold trap for capturing foxes and raccoons. *NY Fish and Game Journal* 31:97–103.

The New York Department of Environmental Conservation compared the capture efficiency and the injuries caused by padded and unpadded Victor No. 1½ leghold traps at the request of the Woodstream Corp. The spring force of both traps was reduced from the commercial standard of 70 lbs. to 40 lbs. in an attempt to reduce injuries. A Woodstream representative trapped while the author recorded and analyzed the data. Traps were fitted with a 10-inch heavy wire chain with a small extension spring. Red and gray foxes were targeted, but raccoons were added as target animals after a significant number were caught. Commercial fox bait, lure, and urine were used. Traps were visited daily. Captured animals were shot and the department's lab examined (presumably necropsied) them for foot damage only. Only 15 fox and 24 raccoons were examined. Padded traps caused significantly less damage to foxes (P ≤ 0.01) with the greatest difference being in lacerations, which were observed in 85% and 25% of foxes caught in unpadded and padded traps, respectively. Less damage was also observed in raccoons caught in padded traps compared to those caught in unpadded traps, but at a lower significance level (P < 0.10). Six animals (3 foxes and 3 raccoons) had scores > 100 (compound fracture or worse) in unpadded traps. Four of the 14 raccoons (29%) caught in unpadded traps and examined had mutilated their trapped foot. Since only foot damage was examined, the overall degree of injury was likely understated. The presence of the Woodstream representative may have biased the results by increasing performance over studies where a representative was not in attendance.

Key words: trap injuries, capture efficiency, leghold trap, padded jaws, red fox, gray fox, raccoon

Turkowski, F. J., A. R. Armistead, and S. B. Linhart. 1984. Selectivity and effectiveness of pan tension devices for coyote foothold traps. *Journal of Wildlife Management* 48:700–708.

Selectivity and capture rates of three pan tension devices (shear-pin, leafspring, and steel tape) mounted on unpadded No. 3 Victor NM double longspring leghold traps were evaluated against the same traps without pan tension devices. Pan tension devices modify the trap so that smaller, lighter animals are less likely to spring them. Soil type and moisture affect the operation of some of these devices. Conditions varied in the 5 western states (CA, NM, OR, TX, UT) studied in 1980, and in two states (CA, TX) in 1981, all during spring, summer, and autumn. Two or more "recommended" ADC personnel performed tests. The 1980 tests yielded 9,866 trap nights culminating in 374 coyote and 875 designated non-target species visits (determined by tracks left in the trap area). The shear-pin, leaf spring, and standard trap excluded 91%, 90%, and 30% of all non-target species, respectively. There was a significant decline in capture rates for coyotes caught in traps using the pan tension devices. For all soil types combined, capture rates were 70%, 67%, and 93% for the shear-pin, leaf spring, and standard traps, respectively. Selectivity and efficiency were reduced in wet areas with clay or alkali soils. The researchers concluded that the decreased non-target captures should compensate for lower coyote capture rates since traps remain available for coyotes.

Key words: trap selectivity, capture efficiency, pan tension device, leghold trap, coyote, non-target species

Kuehn. D. W., T. K. Fuller, L. D. Mech, J. P. William, S. H. Fritts, and W. E. Berg. 1986. Trap-related injuries to gray wolves in Minnesota. *Journal of Wildlife Management* 50:90–91.

Wolves trapped in northern Minnesota for radio-telemetry studies and livestock depredation control were assessed for capture-related injuries. From 1968 to 1985, a total of 375 adult and 179 juveniles were trapped using 4 types of Newhouse double longspring leghold traps: No. 4 (smooth jaws not offset), No. 4 OS (smooth jaws offset 0.2 cm), No. 14 (toothed jaw offset 0.7 cm), and No. 14 OS (custom-made toothed jaws offset 1.8 cm). Injuries were classified as: Class I, no visible injuries or slight swelling; Class II, cut(s) < 2.5 cm long in aggregate; Class III, cuts > 2.5 cm long and/or one fractured or dislocated phalanx or metacarpal; Class IV, ≥ 2 injured phalanges or metacarpals and

/or injured carpal(s), radius, or ulna. Edema was not recorded. More adults had Class III and IV injuries than did juveniles when captured in the No. 4 or No. 14 trap. The No. 14 OS trap caused no Class III or IV injuries to adults or juveniles, although sample sizes were much smaller than for other traps (adult *n* = 21; juvenile *n* = 15). Dentition damage was documented for 202 (54%) adults and 104 (58%) juveniles. Most tooth injuries were minor. The authors suggested the use of the No. 14 OS jaws with a 1.8 cm offset since they appeared to cause fewer injuries than the other traps tested.

Key words: trap injuries, leghold trap, toothed jaws, offset jaws, gray wolf

Linhart, S. B., G. J. Dasch, C. B. Male, and R. M. Engeman. 1986. Efficiency of unpadded and padded steel foothold traps for capturing coyotes. *Wildlife Society Bulletin* 14:212–218.

Capture efficiency of leghold traps for trapping coyotes was compared. Four types of double coil-spring leghold traps were used: unpadded Victor No. 3 NM (offset malleable jaws); unpadded Victor No. 3 NR (offset stamped jaws); unpadded Victor No. 3 OS (offset stamped jaws); padded Victor No. 3 NR (offset stamped jaws); and padded Victor No. 3 Soft Catch (stamped jaws). Researchers lab tested trap closure speeds in different soil types, and field tested capture efficiency. In field studies, 6 experienced Animal Damage Control trappers were provided with an equal number of padded No. 3 Victor NR and No. 3 Victor Soft Catch leghold traps, each fitted with a 15 cm chain center mounted to a swivel and a 4 cm long coil-spring attached to the middle of the chain. These traps were compared to No. 3 Victor NM or No. 4 Newhouse leghold traps that had 91 cm kinkless chain swivel mounted to one spring. Traps were placed in triplicate (Soft Catch, Victor NM and unpadded trap) along trapper selected trap lines and checked daily. Trappers logged 153 days of trapping and captured 111 coyotes. The padded traps had slower closure speeds and lower capture rates than unpadded traps (padded capture rate of ~50%, unpadded capture rate of 73%). The researchers concluded that padded traps captured and held coyotes in moderate (not frozen) conditions.

Key words: capture efficiency, leghold trap, padded jaws, offset jaws, coyote

Olsen, G. H., S. B. Linhart, R. A. Holmes, G. J. Dasch, and C. B. Male. 1986. Injuries to coyotes caught in padded and unpadded steel foothold traps. *Wildlife Society Bulletin* 14:219–223.

Injuries sustained by coyotes were compared among four leghold traps: unpadded No. 3 Victor double longspring with 91 cm kinkless center-mounted chain; padded No. 3 Victor double longspring with same chain as the unpadded trap; padded No. 3 Victor double longspring, with a 15 cm center-mounted chain and shock-absorbing coil; padded No. 3 Victor double coil-spring with a 15 cm center mounted chain with shock absorbing coil. Traplines were set in south Texas and eastern Colorado during fall and winter 1983–84 as in routine depredation control and checked daily, although animals were left in traps for 48 hours to simulate legal requirements. Trapping continued until 20 coyotes were captured in each trap type. Trapped legs, and randomly chosen untrapped legs, were removed and frozen for necropsy. To determine potential injury to non-target species, 10 kit foxes were also trapped in unpadded No. 3 Victor NR or padded No. 3 Soft Catch traps. Mean injury scores to coyotes captured in the 3 padded traps were 48–71% lower than those caught in the unpadded trap, with no significant difference observed among the padded traps. Padded traps did cause severe injuries, however, including joint injuries, fractures, and severe lacerations. For example, padded traps caused fractures in ≥ 15% of captured coyotes and 1 compound fracture was observed in both the Soft Catch and the padded No. 3 Victor with 15 cm chain. Unpadded traps caused fractures in 90% of coyotes caught. Two of 4 kit foxes caught in the Soft Catch trap had simple or compound fractures while 4 of 6 captured in the unpadded Victor trap had complete or near complete amputation. The researchers suggested that while padded traps do not eliminate injuries, they may be useful in population studies, radio-collaring, or the relocation of problem animals.

Key words: trap injuries, leghold trap, padded jaws, coyote, kit fox, non-target species

Linhart, S. B., F. S. Blom, G. J. Dasch, and R. M. Engeman. 1988. Field evaluation of padded jaw coyote traps: effectiveness and foot injury. *Proceedings of the Vertebrate Pest Conference* 13:226–229.

Capture efficiency and injuries to coyotes in south Texas caught in padded No. 3 Victor Soft Catch and unpadded No. 3 Victor double longspring leghold traps were compared. Two studies were conducted: one to determine efficiency and one to assess injuries. These studies (1986–87) augmented data from a 1984–85 study reported in Olsen et al. (1986). The injury study used 7 varieties of leghold traps: 2 padded Soft Catch double coil-spring traps with different size springs and 15 cm center mounted chains; 2 unpadded double longspring traps with pads added and variable chain lengths (15 and 90 cm); and 3 unpadded double longspring traps, 1 with stamped and 2 with malleable jaws

and variable chain lengths (15 and 90 cm). Traps were checked daily, but trapped animals were not removed for 48 hours to simulate local law. Trapping continued until 20 coyotes had been captured in each trap type. Trapped animals were shot and both front legs removed for later necropsy. Leg injuries were scored using the Olsen injury scale. Only mean injury scores were reported. Padded traps had significantly lower injury scores than unpadded traps. Moreover, the Soft Catch had lower injury scores than the padded longspring traps. Longer chain length reduced injury in the padded trap, but may have led to increased injury in the unpadded trap. The capture efficiency study used six trappers. Four traps (two padded Soft Catch traps, an unpadded trap with a pad added, and an unpadded trap) were alternated on each trap line. These data were also compared to the 1984–85 study and trap types. Padded traps were significantly less efficient than unpadded traps. The authors suggest that padded traps may be useful in coyote depredation trapping situations where "valued fox or raccoon hunting dogs" could be accidentally caught and injured in standard steel-jaw leghold traps.

Key words: trap injuries, capture efficiency, leghold trap, padded jaw, coyote

Olsen, G. H., R. G. Linscombe, V. L. Wright, and R. A. Holmes. 1988. Reducing injuries to terrestrial furbearers by using padded foothold traps. *Wildlife Society Bulletin* 16:303–307.

The leg injuries sustained by bobcats, coyotes, red and gray foxes, and raccoons caught in padded and standard leghold traps were compared. Traps tested were the unpadded Nos. 1½ and 3 Victor double coil-spring traps and two padded Soft Catch leghold traps corresponding in size to the unpadded Victor traps. No. 1½ traps were used to capture raccoons, red foxes, gray foxes, and eastern bobcats. No. 3 traps were used to capture coyotes and western bobcats. The Victor traps were modified for a center-mounted chain and the No. 3 trap's angular jaws were replaced with rounded jaws. State furbearer biologists supervised selected trappers (experience not mentioned) who alternated padded and standard traps along their trap lines. No trap check time is noted. Captured animals were killed (method not cited) and their limbs were removed at least 15 cm above point of the trap strike and frozen. Injuries were scored using the modified Olsen injury scale. The No. 1½ padded traps reduced the frequency of serious injuries sustained by gray foxes and red foxes. The gray foxes were more likely than the red foxes to receive serious injury in padded traps because of their smaller size. Raccoons trapped with No. 1½ padded traps in the Southeast displayed slightly less severe injuries from the padded trap. However, because unpadded traps caused less damage to the larger raccoons in the Northeast, the difference between unpadded and padded traps was not significant in that region. In both the Southeast and Northeast, over 50% of all raccoons received numerous serious or severe injuries from both trap types and the researchers noted, "more work is needed to further improve padded traps for raccoons." There was no reduction in injuries to bobcats (*Lynx rufus*) trapped in No. 1½ Soft Catch traps, although the sample size was small (*n* = 21). However, bobcats caught with No. 3 Soft Catch traps sustained less severe injuries than those captured in the unpadded traps. Coyotes sustained fewer serious injuries in the No. 3 padded traps than in steel-jaw leghold traps. Overall, the results suggested that padded traps can reduce, but not eliminate, serious limb injuries received by coyotes, red and gray foxes, bobcats, and raccoons. The padded traps still caused a number of serious and severe injuries to most of the species studied, especially raccoons.

**Key words:** trap injuries, leghold trap, padded jaws, coyote, bobcat, red fox, gray fox, raccoon

**Linscombe, R. G. and V. L. Wright. 1988. Efficiency of padded foothold traps for capturing territorial furbearers.** *Wildlife Society Bulletin* 16:307–309.

The capture efficiency of two unpadded (Nos. 1½ and 3 Victor) and two padded (Nos. 1½ and 3 Soft Catch) double coil-spring leghold traps were compared. Unpadded traps were modified by center-mounting the anchor chain and replacing the square jaws with rounded jaws on the No. 3 traps. Furbearer biologists selected 51 trappers in the states studied (see below) and each trapper was given 12 Soft Catch and 12 standard traps, which they alternated along traplines. Trapping procedures varied among trappers. Data were pooled among states with no statistical differences. Region 1 included Georgia, Louisiana, Minnesota, Mississippi, New York, and part of Texas. Region 2 included Arizona, Kansas, and part of Texas. Region 3 was Idaho. Region 1 trappers alternated the No. 1 standard and Soft Catch traps for capture of bobcats, red foxes, gray foxes, and raccoons. Region 2 and 3 trappers used the No. 3 standard and Soft Catch traps for bobcat and coyote. The number of visits to padded or unpadded traps was similar, except in Region 3 where standard traps had 58% of visits, indicating either trap site selection was not comparable or padded traps were more easily detectable. Without being triggered by an animal, the padded traps sprung more frequently than their unpadded counterparts, though the difference was only about 0.5%, and spontaneous releases were less than 1.5% for all traps. The number of potential captures was similar for

padded and unpadded traps in Regions 1 and 2. In both regions, the padded traps caught fewer animals, and had more misses and escapes than the unpadded traps. In Regions 1 and 2, fewer bobcats and raccoons were caught in the No. 1½ Soft Catch trap than in the No. 1½ unpadded trap, although when raccoons were specifically targeted, there was no difference between trap types. In the 2 northern states, standard traps caught more red fox than the padded traps, while no difference was observed in the southern states. When No. 3 traps were used in Region 2, the number of bobcat captures was similar. However, because of more missed animals and more escapes, No. 3 padded traps caught fewer coyotes than standard traps. In Region 3, padded traps also caught fewer coyotes than unpadded traps. The researchers suggested that padded traps might catch about 66% of the coyotes that would be caught by unpadded traps. However, they noted that the results assumed experienced trappers would set padded and unpadded traps with equal expertise. Since the trappers in the study had more experience with standard traps, the authors expected capture efficiency would increase as trappers gained experience with padded traps. Additionally, a defect in the pads may have increased the likelihood of escapes. (Manufacturer has corrected this defect.)

**Key words:** capture efficiency, leghold trap, padded jaws, coyote, bobcat, red fox, gray fox, raccoon

**Kreeger, T. J., P. J. White, U. S. Seal, and J. R. Tester. 1990. Pathological responses of red foxes to foothold traps.** *Journal of Wildlife Management* 54:147–160.

This three-year study analyzed the behavioral, physiological, endocrine, biochemical, and pathological responses of red foxes to capture in leghold traps. Captive raised foxes were surgically implanted with heart rate and body temperature radio transmitters and allowed to recover for two weeks before being moved to a 4.05 ha observation pen. After a 1–2 week acclimation period, either a No. 1½ Soft Catch or standard No. 1½ leghold trap was placed in the pen, baited, and then monitored with a video recorder. Captured foxes were held for 2 (*n* = 6) or 8 (*n* = 5) hours in the padded trap or 8 hours (*n* = 10) in the unpadded traps. Wild foxes were also captured in padded (*n* = 12) and unpadded (*n* = 9) traps for variable periods. Twenty-three nontrapped, free-ranging foxes were used as controls and were observed, then shot or euthanized while sleeping. Mean time spent resisting the trap did not differ significantly for foxes captured in padded and unpadded traps over the 8-hour period. Trapped foxes had higher levels of adrenocorticotropin, B-endorphin, and cortisol and lower levels of thyroxine and insulin compared to control foxes (P < 0.05). Foxes captured in unpadded traps had higher cortisol levels, but lower B-endorphin values, than those caught in padded traps (P < 0.05). Capture in unpadded traps also yielded higher counts in other hormones (P < 0.05). Limb injury scores [using Tullar's (1984) injury scale] for foxes caught in unpadded trap were higher than those caught in padded traps (P < 0.02). However, padded traps did not eliminate injuries or trauma. Overall, the researchers concluded that padded traps "caused less trauma to red foxes than unpadded traps."

Key words: trap injuries, leghold trap, padded jaws, red fox

Phillips, R. L, F. S. Blom, G. J. Dasch, and J. W. Guthrie. 1992. Field evaluation of three types of coyote traps. *Proceedings of the Vertebrate Pest Conference* 15:393–395.

The capture efficiency, selectivity, and extent of injury to coyotes by the padded No. 3 Soft Catch leghold, unpadded No. 3 Victor NM leghold, and unpadded No. 4 Newhouse longspring leghold traps were compared. Both the Victor and Newhouse had offset jaws and were attached to a 1 m kinkless chain. The Soft Catch had padded jaws and a 15 cm chain with coil-spring attachment. Three trappers (> 10 yrs. experience each) were provided with 12 traps of each type and set them out along unimproved ranch roads in Texas. Trappers checked the traps daily and recorded visible foot injuries. Injury categories were unique to this study: slight injuries = swollen feet, small punctures and small cuts < 0.5cm; moderate or severe injuries = cuts > 0.5cm, cuts exposing tendons or bones, cut tendons, or cut bones. Sixty coyotes were caught and held, 20 in each trap. Capture rates among the 3 traps were similar, with the padded Soft Catch achieving a higher percentage (95%) than described in previous studies. The Soft Catch caused the least severe injuries (50% with slight injuries, none with moderate to severe), followed by the Newhouse (45% with moderate to severe injuries), and finally the Victor (80% moderate to severe). One skunk was caught in the Newhouse and one rabbit in the Soft Catch. The involvement of a Woodstream representative and the use of trappers to classify injuries creates a strong potential for bias.

Key words: trap injuries, capture efficiency, trap selectivity, leghold trap, padded jaw, offset jaws, coyote, non-target species

Linhart, S. B. and G. J. Dasch. 1992. Improved performance of padded jaw traps for capturing coyotes. *Wildlife Society Bulletin* 20:63–66.

The fourth generation padded No. 3 Victor Soft

Catch leghold trap was compared against an unpadded No. 3 Victor double longspring and an unpadded No. 3 Victor double coil-spring (both with offset jaws) for efficiency in trapping coyotes. Two trappers (> 15 yrs. experience) were issued an equal number of all three and were supervised by a trapping specialist from the Woodstream Corp. Although traps were checked daily, captured coyotes were left in the trap for 48 hours to simulate Alberta's trap-check law. Sixty-three coyotes were captured and 58 held (5 pulled out). Capture rates did not differ significantly among trap types. The authors note that the Soft Catch capture rate (79%) was higher than previously recorded. No record was made of type of injury or severity, or the incidental capture of non-target species. The presence of the Woodstream representative may have biased the results by increasing performance over studies where a representative was not in attendance.

Key words: capture efficiency, leghold trap, padded jaws, offset jaws, coyotes

Proulx, G., D. K. Onderka, A. J. Kolenosky, P. J. Cole, R. K. Drescher, and M. J. Badry. 1993. Injuries and behavior of raccoons (*Procyon lotor*) captured in the Soft Catch™ and the EGG™ traps in simulated natural environments. *Journal of Wildlife Diseases* 29:447–452.

The padded No. 1½ Soft Catch leghold trap was tested against the EGG trap (an encapsulated leghold trap designed to reduce self-mutilation in raccoons) for humaneness in a simulated natural environment. A trapping device was considered "humane" if it held 9 of 9 raccoons without serious injury (< 50 points on the Onderka scoring system). Traps were checked 12 and 24 hours after initial capture. The Soft Catch was considered a "humane" trap in the 12-hour segment because all 9 raccoons had injury scores < 50. However, 7 of the 9 raccoons (78%) had notable injuries, 2 of which involved joint luxation or metacarpal subluxation. The 12-hour evaluation of the EGG trap was also determined "humane," although 8 out of 9 (89%) had notable injuries and 3 were rated in a class of injury that included tendon maceration. During the first 12 hours, all of the raccoons in both traps spent an average of 7 hours either fighting their surroundings or fighting the trap. The Soft Catch trap was not considered "humane" at 24 hours since all 9 raccoons were injured and 1 had severely chewed its paws. At 24 hours, all 9 raccoons captured in the EGG traps had evidence of injury, 4 in a class that included tendon maceration. The EGG trap was considered "humane" in the 24-hour period, however, because all raccoons had scores < 50. The investigators noted that the controlled and protected conditions of an enclosure may underestimate the injuries sustained by raccoons captured in field trap lines because of behavioral differences and vulnerability to predation by other animals while in the trap.

Key words: trap injuries, leghold trap, padded jaws, EGG trap, raccoon

Houben, J. M., M. Holland, S. W. Jack, and C. R. Boyle. 1993. An evaluation of laminated offset jawed traps for reducing injuries to coyotes. *Proceedings Great Plains Wildlife Damage Control Conference* 11:148–153.

The capture efficiency and injuries to coyotes caused by padded No. 3 Victor Soft Catch and unpadded No. 3 Northwoods coil-spring leghold traps were compared. The Soft Catch trap used a 15 cm center-mounted chain with attached coil-spring and was refitted with heavier coil-springs, which increased pressure from 50 lbs. to 70 lbs. The Northwoods trap had offset and laminated jaws with a 45 cm chain with coil-spring attachment and two additional coil-springs, bringing pressure up to 90 lbs. All traps were staked with a double-stake connector to the end-chain swivel. Traps were set in Mississippi as part of regular depredation control work and checked daily. Experience of trappers is not cited. Coyotes were euthanized (method not mentioned) and the trapped and opposite legs were amputated above the elbow and frozen for necropsy. The Olsen scoring system was used to determine severity of injuries. Sample sizes were small as the legs of only 10 coyotes were examined from each trap type. No significant difference was observed in mean injury scores between traps. Four of the 10 coyotes caught in the Soft Catch had small cuts and bruises while 2 coyotes chewed their feet during capture, 1 severely. No self-mutilation was noted for coyotes in Northwoods traps. The most severe injury caused by the Northwoods was ligament maceration. Ninety percent of coyotes captured in both types of trap had cumulative scores ≤ 15 points. The authors concluded that the modified Northwoods trap reduced limb injury when compared to other unpadded traps, a finding they attributed to the laminated, offset jaws and increased spring tension. Moreover, they believed that increasing the spring tension of the Soft Catch trap did not result in added injury.

Key words: trap injuries, capture efficiency, leghold traps, padded jaws, offset jaws, laminated jaws, coyote

Kern, J. W., L. L. McDonald, D. D. Strickland, and E. Williams. 1994. Field evaluation and comparison of four foothold traps for terrestrial furbearers in Wyoming. Western EcoSystems Technology, Cheyenne, Wyoming.

Four types of leghold traps were evaluated for injuries they inflicted on "target" species (red fox, coyotes, badgers, and raccoons) and for capture efficiency, capture rate, and selectivity. Traps used were the regular and laminated No. 1½ Victor steel-jaw leghold, the padded No. 1½ Soft Catch, and the Butera offset jaw leghold. The three unpadded traps were staked in place and covered with sifted dirt, while the padded trap was set at a 5-degree angle to help target the animal's foot as recommended by the manufacturer. Four trappers received 24 randomly selected traps and maintained their trap line for 30 days, until each trapper caught 80 red fox, or until a total of 250 red fox were captured. Traps were checked daily "in most cases," although animals suspected of being held for longer than one night were analyzed separately. Nontarget species were released "when appropriate." Each captured red fox, coyote, badger, or raccoon was euthanized immediately (method not noted). A wildlife pathologist necropsied the limbs and head of each animal and scored injuries using both the Olsen scale and the draft ISO standard. A total of 243 red fox, 25 coyote, 24 badger, and 21 raccoon were trapped. Median Olsen scores for red foxes were highest for the standard trap (40), followed by the offset jaw (25) and laminated traps (17.5), and finally the padded trap (10). Using the draft ISO standard, more than 80% of trapped red fox had scores < 75 (the ISO criterion for an acceptable trap) for all traps except the standard No. 1½ Victor trap. The median scores for all trap types were similar for badger, coyote, and raccoon. Of the 460 animals trapped in the study, 62 (13%) were non-target captures. "Non-targets" included jackrabbits, cottontail rabbits, feral cats, bobcats, porcupines, dogs, and a mule deer. Most rabbits were predated while in the trap. The researchers concluded that the sample sizes of trapped coyotes, badgers, and raccoons were not large enough for accurate evaluation of trap types against the ISO draft standard. However, "high injury scores in raccoons were associated with self mutilation in the padded jaw trap and standard [leghold] trap."

Key words: trap injuries, capture efficiency, capture rate, trap selectivity, leghold trap, offset jaws, padded jaws, red fox, coyote, raccoon, badger, non-target species

Serfass, T. L., R. P. Brooks, T. J. Swimley, L. M. Rymon, and A. H. Hayden. 1996. Considerations for capturing, handling, and translocating river otters. *Wildlife Society Bulletin* 24:25–31.

This study reported on techniques used by the Pennsylvania River Otter Reintroduction Project (PRORP) and compares the efficiency and trap injuries related with the use of No. 1½ Soft Catch and No. 11 Victor double longspring leghold traps.

Researchers used Soft Catch traps, while private trappers and commercial suppliers used the Victor traps. The Soft Catch trap was modified by replacing one factory spring with a No. 2 spring to increase retention of trapped otters. Traps were anchored with a 0.5–1.25 cm chain to two steel plates positioned offshore and perpendicular to the shoreline. To prevent injuries and accidental drowning, swivels were attached to the chain at 30 cm intervals and the radius of the trap chain was cleared of branches, underwater roots, and other debris. Traps were set in September and monitored through mid-November and checked daily between 7 am and 12 pm. Captured otters were sedated using ketamine hydrochloride and thoroughly examined. Otters captured by the PRORP were examined subsequent to capture and during a physical examination prior to placement in holding facilities. Those obtained from private trappers and commercial suppliers were examined only in the latter event. Injuries to incisors, canines, and trapped appendages were recorded. Dental injuries were defined as tooth breakage; canines were also rated depending on the amount of tooth remaining above the gumline. Otters received from suppliers and private trappers could only be evaluated for severe injuries by comparing frequency of amputations since minor injuries had healed prior to acquisition by the PRORP. Modified Soft Catch traps captured 29 otters in 1,749 trap nights (60.3 nights/otter); 22 were suspected to have escaped (57% capture rate). Frequency of canine injuries sustained by otters caught in Soft Catch (59%) and No. 11 Victor traps (64%) was similar, but were significantly less than otters provided by other sources (96%). Severity of canine injuries showed a similar pattern. Among adults, only 1 otter (3.7%) caught in Soft Catch traps required amputation of a digit, compared to 12 (70.6%) and 9 (37.5%) captured in Victor traps and obtained from other sources (private trappers and commercial suppliers, using various leghold traps), respectively. The researchers concluded that the modified Soft Catch traps were an effective alternative to Hancock live traps (often used for live trapping otters). They recommend against the use of standard unpadded foothold traps for capturing river otter.

**Key words:** trap injuries, capture efficiency, leghold trap, padded jaws, Hancock trap, river otter

Phillips, R. L. and K. S. Gruver. 1996. Performance of the Paws-I-Trip™ pan tension device on 3 types of traps. *Wildlife Society Bulletin* 24:119–122.

The Paws-I-Trip (PIT) pan tension device was tested to determine its ability to exclude nontarget species from capture efforts for coyote. PITs were installed on 3 types of traps: the padded No. 3 Soft Catch double coil-spring, unpadded No 3. Victor NM (3NM) double longspring, and unpadded No. 4 Newhouse double longspring. Fifteen USDA Animal Damage Control (ADC) specialists in eight western states were each given 36 PIT kits to modify their own traps. Soft Catch traps were used in California, Newhouses in Oklahoma and Texas, and 3NMs in Idaho, Montana, Nevada, North Dakota, and Oregon. Pan tension was set between 1.4–18.8 kg. Participants recorded species captured, animal tracks on the pan, the species springing the trap, and soil type and condition from May 1993 to August 1994. Designated non-target species included swift, kit and gray foxes, skunks, opossums, cottontail rabbits, armadillos, rodents, and small birds. Other species with weights similar to coyotes were also expected to be captured, including raccoons, bobcats, porcupines, and red foxes. A total of 771 coyotes and 22 designated nontarget animals were caught in 902 coyote and 826 nontarget visits. Mean exclusion rates for the Soft Catch, 3NM, and Newhouse traps were 99.1%, 98.1%, and 91%, respectively. Capture rates of coyotes for the same traps were 81.8%, 91%, and 87.2%, respectively, and similar to previous studies not using exclusion devices. The difference in capture rates between the Soft Catch and unpadded traps was likely due to a difference in pan tension setting. An inverse relationship between exclusion and capture efficiency was observed: devices set at higher tensions to exclude smaller nontarget species will reduce capture of lighter coyotes. The researchers concluded, however, that the PIT pan tension devices "effectively reduced non-target captures without adversely affecting performance of the traps for capturing coyotes."

**Key words:** capture efficiency, trap selectivity, leghold trap, pan tension device, padded jaws, coyote, non-target species

Phillips, R. L. and C. Mullis. 1996. Expanded field testing of the No. 3 Victor Soft Catch® trap. *Wildlife Society Bulletin* 24:128–131.

Capture efficiency of padded No. 3 Soft Catch leghold traps for trapping coyotes was compared to the No. 4 Newhouse, the No. 3 Victor NM, and the Sterling MJ600 unpadded traps. Fifteen USDA Animal Damage Control trappers in seven western states (Oregon, Montana, Wyoming, California, Nevada, New Mexico, and Oklahoma) captured 412 coyotes on trap lines set along unimproved ranch roads. Pairs of traps (one padded and one unpadded) were set and checked daily. Trappers recorded the number of coyotes caught, traps sprung, coyotes caught but pulled out, and position of trap jaws on the limb. Capture efficiency ranged from 83–100% and did not differ significantly among the trap types. Locations of the trap jaws were 68% above foot pads, 19% across the pads, and 14% by the toes. The Soft Catch had 18% of captures by the toes, significantly more than the Sterling MJ600. No interpretation of this finding is offered. The researchers concluded that the Soft Catch was "as effective as other unpadded traps used for capturing coyotes under a variety of trapping conditions in the western United States."

Key words: capture efficiency, leghold trap, padded jaws, coyote

Phillips, R. L., K. S. Gruver, and E. S. Williams. 1996. Leg injuries to coyotes captured in three types of foothold traps. *Wildlife Society Bulletin* 24:260–263.

The authors compared leg injuries sustained by coyotes caught in three traps: the unpadded Sterling MJ600 with 4 coil-springs and offset jaws, the unpadded No. 3 Northwoods with laminated, offset jaws and additional modifications, and the padded No. 3½ EZ Grip double longspring. Traps were set by nine experienced trappers in California, Colorado, Idaho, and Texas from October 1993 to June 1995 and were checked daily. Captured coyotes were euthanized (method not cited) and trapped legs were removed near the elbow or knee joint and frozen. A pathologist necropsied the legs, identifying and scoring injuries based on a modified Olsen (1996) injury scale. A total of 192 coyote legs were examined: 68 from Sterling, 59 from Northwoods, and 65 from EZ Grip captures. Both unpadded traps had a mean injury score greater than 50 (Sterling = 103.3, Northwoods = 79.3) while the padded EZ Grip trap had a mean score of 29.0. The padded EZ Grip was considered less injurious than the two unpadded traps, although it still caused several significant injuries, including bone fractures, major periosteal abrasions, and self-mutilation. The researchers concluded that "padded traps are the most significant trap modification to substantially reduce foot injuries to captured coyotes."

Key words: trap injuries, leghold trap, padded jaws, offset jaws, laminated jaws, coyote

Gruver, K. S., R. L. Phillips, and E. S. Williams. 1996. Leg injuries to coyotes captured in standard and modified Soft Catch® traps. *Proceedings of the Vertebrate Pest Conference* 17:91–93.

Leg injuries of coyotes captured in standard padded No. 3 Soft Catch leghold traps were compared with those captured in No. 3 Soft Catch traps with two additional coil-springs that provided a 70% increase in clamping force. In conjunction with livestock predator control programs, ADC specialists captured 53 and 60 coyotes in the standard and modified traps, respectively. All traps were anchored to a stake with a center-mounted 36 cm kinkless chain fitted with an inline shock spring and were checked daily. Coyotes were euthanized (method not indicated) and the trapped leg was removed near the elbow or knee joint and frozen. Injuries were identified and scored based on a trauma scale developed by the International Organization for Standardization (ISO) process. The authors examined legs from 53 standard and 60 modified Soft Catch captures. Edema or hemorrhage was apparent in 96% of the legs, with no significant difference observed between the two trap types. The standard Soft Catch caused more frequent lacerations (83% vs. 73%) and more frequent "serious injuries" (scoring 25 points or higher), including severed ligaments, joint dislocations, and bone fractures. The standard Soft Catch was also responsible for three "severe" 100-point injuries, including a major joint dislocation, a compound fracture, and a major severed tendon, while the modified trap caused no "severe" injuries. While median injury scores were similar for both traps, the standard Soft Catch had a higher mean injury score. The researchers postulated that the increased clamping power of the modified Soft Catch reduced movement of the trapped leg and therefore reduced the possibility of more severe injuries. The modified Soft Catch still caused significant injuries, however, including fractures, luxations, and major lacerations.

Key words: trap injuries, leghold trap, padded jaws, coyote

Hubert, G. F. Jr., L. L. Hungerford, G. Proulx, R. D. Bluett, and L. Bowman. 1996. Evaluation of two restraining traps to capture raccoons. *Wildlife Society Bulletin* 24:699–708.

The EGG trap and the unpadded No. 1 Victor coil-spring leghold trap were compared for capture efficiency and trap-related injuries. The study was conducted during the 1992 trapping season using five experienced trappers working five trap lines. Technical supervision was intended to eliminate trapper bias; however, trappers made all decisions regarding trapping sites and set design or destroying or releasing trapped animals. Each trapper was supplied with 12 of each type of trap. Traps were checked daily and captured raccoons were euthanized by gunshot and placed in plastic bags and frozen. A modified Onderka injury scale was used to assess injuries. A total of 102 raccoons were examined: 10 were found dead in the traps, 1 had been killed by a predator, and 9 died of hypothermia. Overall, mean limb injury scores were lower than total body scores. Higher injury scores were observed for the Victor trap. However, both traps had mean injury scores exceeding 50 points (serious injury). Mean total body and trapped limb injury scores, respectively, were 68 and 52 for the EGG trap and 116 and 96 for the Victor trap. Self-mutilation injuries were noted in 25% of raccoons captured in the Victor trap, but only 3% of the animals caught in the EGG trap. The mean injury score for these animals was 244 (over 100 is defined as severe). The EGG trap had a higher capture efficiency than the Victor trap. Non-target captures included 12 opossums, 1 cat, 1 dog, and 1 mink. The dog and cat were released "unharmed." The researchers concluded that the EGG trap should be promoted "as an attractive restraining device for raccoons."

Key words: trap injuries, capture efficiency, leghold trap, EGG trap, raccoon, non-target species

Hubert, G. F., L. L. Hungerford, and R. D. Bluett. 1997. Injuries to coyotes captured in modified foothold traps. *Wildlife Society Bulletin* 25:858–863.

Injuries to coyotes captured in unpadded No. 3 Bridger coil-spring leghold traps were compared to those captured in the No. 3 Bridger modified with 0.48 cm offset and laminated jaws and two additional coil-springs for increased clamping force. Twenty-four leghold traps of each type were placed in pairs on three traplines in Illinois during the legal furbearer-trapping season in the winter of 1993–94. Four trappers, each with > 15 yrs. experience, were accompanied by a technician to reduce device-specific bias and ensure accurate record-keeping. Traplines were checked daily, beginning in early morning. Captured coyotes were euthanized by gunshot to the head, then placed in plastic bags and frozen. Injuries were scored as described by Onderka. Unlike most studies, the entire body was examined for injuries and subsequently three additional injury types were included: avulsed (ripped off) nail, permanent tooth fracture exposing pulp cavity, and damage to periosteum (bone covering containing blood vessels and nerves). The inclusion of the whole body examination provides a more thorough and accurate depiction of the extent of injuries caused by trapping. A total of 48 coyotes were examined: 19 captured in the standard leghold and 29 in the modified leghold trap. Overall leg injury scores were ~15% lower than the whole-body scores, highlighting the importance of considering the entire body when assessing the extent and severity of injuries. Permanent tooth fractures were noted in 11% of standard and 17% of modified captures, with no significant statistical difference observed. Severe injuries (≥ 125 points) were recorded for 7 (37%) and 5 (17%) coyotes captured in the standard and modified traps, respectively. Whole-body and trapped-limb-only scores were higher for the standard leghold trap, although the differences were not statistically significant. The researchers concluded that modifying unpadded traps was unlikely to reduce injuries as much as padded traps.

Key words: trap injuries, leghold trap, offset jaws, laminated jaws, coyote

Hubert, G. F. Jr., G. K. Wollenberg, L. L. Hungerford, and R. D. Bluett. 1999. Evaluation of injuries to Virginia opossums captured in the EGG™ trap. *Wildlife Society Bulletin* 27:301–305.

Injuries to opossums captured in EGG traps in central Illinois during the 1996–97 trapping season were evaluated. A selected trapper set all traps along streambanks or adjacent to animal trails in upland or wooded areas. All sets were baited with fish, staked solidly, and checked daily beginning in the morning. Captured opossums were killed by .22-caliber rimfire firearm shot to the head. The animal was frozen and later subject to a whole-body necropsy (see Onderka et al. 1990). A total of 40 opossums were assessed for trap-related injuries and trap-related injuries were scored as per Hubert et al. (1996). All animals had some level of edema (1–5 points), nearly half had lacerations ≤ 2 cm long (5 points), and one-fourth had permanent tooth fractures (10 points). Fractures (100–200 points) were noted in 15% of opossums, and the most severe injury was a luxated elbow joint (200 points). The mean injury score was 47 (range 1–223). Thirty opossums (75%) had injury scores < 50. Smaller opossums received the only severe injuries. The researchers concluded that the EGG trap causes less severe injuries than unpadded No. 2 coil-spring leghold traps examined in previous studies, and recommended further field testing.

Key words: trap injuries, leghold trap, EGG trap, Virginia opossum

Warburton, B. N. Gregory, and M. Bunce. 1999. Stress response of Australian Brushtail Possums captured in foothold and cage traps. Pp. 53–66 *in* G. Proulx, ed. *Mammal trapping*. Alpha Wildlife Research & Management Ltd., Sherwood Park, Alberta.

Physiological responses of Australian brushtail possums to capture in Victor No. 1 Soft Catch leghold traps, Lanes-Ace leghold trap (unpadded, serrated-jawed), and wire-mesh cage traps was evaluated. Trapping occurred between November 1995 and October 1996 at Goose Bay, New Zealand. Time of capture was determined by radio-transmitters that switched on when the trap was sprung. Captured possums were killed by gunshot. The response of the possum to the observer/shooter was observed and any animal that showed an obvious adverse response to the observer or that were not cleanly shot were excluded from the sample. Blood was sampled either 30 minutes or 8 hours after capture. Physiological responses were determined by comparing concentrations of serum enzymes, electrolytes, and hormones, and ultimate muscle pH in trapped possums to that from non-trapped control possums. Cortisol levels in cage trapped possums were not significantly higher than the control animals but were significantly less than those captured in leghold traps. Serum enzymes associated with muscle damage and/or exercise showed significant increases at 8 hours post-capture in leghold traps. No difference in serum hormone or chemistry response was observed between leghold trap types. The researchers concluded that possums showed a lesser physiological response to capture in cage traps than to capture in leghold traps.

Key words: trap injuries, leghold trap, padded jaws, cage trap, Australian brushtail possum

Seddon, P. J., Y. V. Heezik, and R. F. Maloney. 1999. Short- and medium-term evaluation of foot hold trap injuries in two species of fox in Saudi Arabia. Pp. 67–77 in G. Proulx, ed. Mammal Trapping. Alpha Wildlife Research & Management Ltd., Sherwood Park, Alberta.

This study sought to determine short- and longer-term impacts of foothold trapping on fox survival. No. 3 Victor Soft Catch traps were used to trap two species of small desert fox in Saudi Arabia — the Arabian red fox and the smaller Ruppell's fox. Traps were checked daily at dawn and closed, then reopened at dusk. Any animal caught would have been captured for no more than 12 hours. A total of 47 foxes were trapped: 28 red and 19 Ruppell's. Capture rate was 89% for both species combined (tracks of both species are difficult to distinguish from each other). Injuries were assessed for 80 trapped limbs: 51 red and 29 Ruppell's. Injuries were classified as per Van Ballenberghe (1984): Class I, slight foot and/or leg edema with no lacerations, broken bones, or dislocated joints; Class II, moderate to severe edema, skin lacerations longer than 2.5 cm with visible damage to underlying tissue, and /or fracture of a toe bone; Class III, skin lacerations longer than 2.5 cm with visible damage to underlying tissues with intact tendons, and bone breakage limited to one phalanx or metacarpal; Class IV, any combination of deep, wide lacerations, severed tendons, broken metacarpals or metatarsals, broken radius or ulna, tibia, or fibula, and joint dislocations. Class IV injuries were observed in 18% of red fox and 10% of Ruppell's. Fractures were above the point of trap impact, suggesting that struggle after capture was responsible. In two cases, foxes were held in cages for up to 24 hours after capture using leghold traps and a marked increase in edematous swelling occurred, resulting in temporary lameness that would have

led to reclassification of the original injury from Class I to Class II. Even short-term lameness in foxes has the potential to reduce survival through increased risk of predation and lowered fitness. No. 3 Victor Soft Catch traps caused fewer severe immediate injuries for Ruppell's foxes (90% of animals had only Class I or II injuries) than to the larger red foxes (68% Class I or II) because Ruppell's foxes struggled more in traps. Fifty-eight percent of Ruppell's foxes previously caught in cage traps were confirmed alive after 6 months and 36% after 12 months. Subsequent cage trapping of Ruppell's foxes found that only 8% of foxes caught previously in leghold traps were recaptured after 6 months and none after 12, indicating that capture in a leghold trap may lower likelihood of survival during a period of 6 months after trapping.

Key words: trap injuries, capture efficiency, survivorship, leghold trap, padded jaws, Arabian red fox, Ruppell's fox

# Neck and Body Snares

Guthery, F. S. and S. L. Beasom. 1978. Effectiveness and selectivity of neck snares in predator control. Journal of Wildlife Management 42:457–459.

This short communication reports on a predator elimination project in south Texas in which leghold traps, snares, and M-44s were laid out along a 27 km route within a 15.5 km$^2$ area. Traps were checked daily, except when it rained. A total of 20,436 snare-days were recorded, with a total capture of 65 coyotes, 9 bobcat, 7 badger, 4 raccoon, 1 striped skunk, 1 gray fox, and a number of non-target species, including 12 collared peccaries. Snares were intermediate in capture efficiency (3.6 captures/1,000 device days), between leghold traps (8.9 captures/1,000 device days) and M-44s (1.4 captures/1,000 device days). Non-predatory (non-target) species made up 38% of all captures. Of the 65 total coyotes snared, 59% were neck catches, 20% flank, 11% both front leg and neck, and 10% foot. Of all captured coyotes, 52% were dead the morning after being snared. Snares were at least 10 times more selective than leghold traps when "target" species were defined as coyotes and bobcats and 12 times more selective when all predators were considered targets.

Key words: capture efficiency, trap selectivity, neck/body snare, leghold trap, M-44, coyote, bobcat, badger, raccoon, skunk, gray fox, non-target species

Proulx, G. and M. W. Barrett. 1990. Assessment of power snares to effectively kill red fox. Wildlife Society Bulletin 18:27–30.

The ability of King, Mosher, and Olecko power snares to quickly kill red fox was tested in a simulated natural environment. The King and Mosher snares were modified to maximize constricting pressure on the animal's neck. Researchers defined "humane death" as irreversible unconsciousness within 5 minutes. A new snare was used for each animal. In kill tests, incidents of neck-only placements were made by 0 of 4 King, 2 of 5 Mosher, and 6 of 7 Olecko power snare captures. Eight of the 16 foxes (50%) were euthanized because of prolonged consciousness. Of the remaining 8, 4 showed evidence of consciousness for more than 5 but less than 6 minutes. Time to loss of consciousness was lowest for the King snare. The researchers concluded: "Power snares developed to kill large furbearers appear to have limited application as we search for humane trapping methods." The potential danger of these devices to non-target animals and people was also cited as reason for their limited usefulness.

Key words: trap injuries, power snare, red fox

Proulx, G., A. J. Kolenosky, M. J. Badry, P. J. Cole, and R. K. Drescher. 1994. Snowshoe hare snare system to minimize capture of marten. *Wildlife Society Bulletin* 22:639–643.

The use of snares in trapping showshoe hares is common in Newfoundland. Capture of non-target species, however, including the threatened American marten, is frequent. The authors developed and tested a snare in a simulated natural environment that would allow martens to escape while maintaining capture efficiency of snowshoe hare. The tested design allowed all the marten ($n = 9$) to escape the snare by pulling out the anchor ($n = 8$) or breaking the wire ($n = 1$). The mean duration of struggle was 23.3 min. in the snare. All the nooses fell off their necks within 72 hours and none of the martens were visibly injured. Nine of 9 snowshoe hares (100%) caught in the snare died in an average of 18 minutes and struggled for 2.5 minutes. The researchers determined this snare design would allow martens to escape without a reduction in capture efficiency of snowshoe hares. They noted, however, that in their judgment, snares are not humane devices for trapping snowshoe hares because of the prolonged time until death.

Key words: body snare, capture efficiency, snowshoe hare, marten, non-target species

Phillips, R. L. 1996. Evaluation of 3 types of snares for capturing coyotes. *Wildlife Society Bulletin* 24:107–110.

Capture rate and selectivity of three types of snares, the Gregerson, Kelley, and a Denver Wildlife Research Center (DWRC) prototype, were evaluated. These breakaway snares are intended to capture coyotes, but release non-target animals exerting sufficient force against the snare cable or lock. All three snares required at least 118 kg or 260 pounds of force to escape, whereas coyotes and deer fawns exert force of less than 34 kg or 75 pounds. Field tests were conducted from 1992 to 1994 using nine USDA Animal Damage Control specialists and three South Dakota Game and Fish extension specialists, all experienced with setting snares. The researcher assumed all trappers were equally capable. The duration of capture or the length of time between snare checks was not controlled. It was assumed that variations in trapping technique were unimportant. In all, 374 coyotes were captured: 89% by the neck, 7% by the body, and 4% by the leg. Of the coyotes snared by the neck with the Kelley locks, 94% were dead when snare lines were inspected versus 71% and 68% for the Gregerson and DWRC locks, respectively. Trap check times are not reported and it is therefore unknown how long animals struggled in the traps. Non-target captures included 91 deer and 6 domestic cows or calves, totaling 26%, 20%, and 11% of all DWRC, Gregerson, and Kelley captures, respectively. Fifty-six percent of the deer were unable to escape and all but four of these died. All cattle escaped. The authors concluded that efforts to snare coyotes should not be conducted in areas frequented by deer or livestock.

Key words: capture efficiency, trap selectivity, breakaway snare, coyote, non-target species

## Kill Traps

Proulx, G., S. R. Cook, and M. W. Barrett. 1989. Assessment and preliminary development of the rotating-jaw Conibear 120™ trap to effectively kill marten (*Martes americana*). *Canadian Journal of Zoology* 67:1074–1079.

In an effort to maximize the killing ability of Conibear traps for marten, four trigger mechanisms for the Conibear 120 (C120) were tested for their accuracy in positioning animals before release of the trap jaws, critical to causing unconsciousness within the prescribed "humane" time frame (defined as rendering unconscious within three minutes). In a pre-selection test, the pitchfork shaped trigger allowed the C120 to render 5 of 6 animals unconscious within three minutes. Subsequently, the C120 with pitchfork trigger was tested against the C120 Mark IV, a more powerful version of the C120. Two C120 Mark IVs were examined, one with a metal bar welded to the bottom jaw and one with the bar welded to the upper jaw. In kill tests, the C120 failed to induce unconsciousness within five minutes in 2 of 6 animals. The C120 Mark IV with bar welded to the lower jaw failed to cause unconsciousness in under three minutes in 5 of 6 marten; 2 were conscious for longer than five minutes. The C120 Mark IV with bar welded to the upper jaw produced unconsciousness in 5 of 6 marten within three minutes. One marten did not lose unconsciousness within five minutes and was euthanized. By protocol, the C120 Mark IV with bar welded to the upper jaw was deemed a potentially "humane" trap for marten. However, the investigators noted that the behavior of study animals was likely to differ from their wild counterparts; the study animals may have been less wary of the trapping mechanisms. In addition, it was evident that the trap must hit within a region behind the ears and above the C1 cervical vertebrae to render unconsciousness within the designated time frame. That area was deemed by the investigators to be too small to be practical. The commercially available C120 was determined to be unlikely to humanely kill marten under practical conditions. Even with the modifications, the investigators concluded that the Conibear 120 needed further improvements and study.

Key words: trap injuries, Conibear 120 trap, Conibear 120 Mark IV trap, marten

Proulx, G. M. W. Barrett, and S. R. Cook. 1989. The C120 Magnum: an effective quick-kill trap for marten. *Wildlife Society Bulletin* 17:294–298.

After the Conibear 120 (C120) and C120 Mark IV failed to meet criteria established by the Canadian General Standards Board for acceptance as potentially "humane" kill traps for marten (5 of 6 animals rendered unconscious in ≤ 3 minutes) the authors designed the more powerful, experimental C120 Magnum. The C120 Magnum uses a C120 frame with two C220 springs, a flat metal bar welded to each striking bar, and a 4-pronged trigger. In testing, the striking and clamping forces of the C120 Magnum were twice that of the C120 and 1/3 greater than the C120 Mark IV. In kill tests on marten, 13 of 14 trials resulted in the death of the marten; 1 animal was euthanized when it did not lose consciousness within 5 minutes due to a technical failure. For the 13 "successful" trials, the average time to loss of consciousness and heartbeat were estimated at < 68 (± 8.2) seconds and 203 (± 18.4) seconds, respectively. The researchers concluded that the C120 Magnum was the first killing trap to meet the standards of the Canadian General Standards Board for kill-type traps.

Key words: Conibear 120 Magnum trap, marten

Barrett, M. W. G. Proulx, D. Hobson, D. Nelson, and J. W. Nolan. 1989. Field evaluation of the C120 Magnum trap for marten. *Wildlife Society Bulletin* 17:299–306.

This paper studied the C120 Magnum to see if field tests would yield results similar to previous controlled tests (see Proulx *et al.* 1989), and to compare the trap's capture efficiency, strike locations, and trauma to marten against other trapping devices currently in use. Tests ran from November through December 1986 on two remote traplines in northern Alberta. Traplines were selected for prior success in marten capture and willingness of trappers to participate in the test. The C120 Magnums, placed in elevated box sets, were tested against an equal number of C120, C126, C160, and Nos. 3 and 4 leghold traps that were placed in running pole and low box sets. Trap lines were checked every 3–4 days. The C120 Magnum and standard traps caught a total of 55 marten in 3,888 and 3,862 trap nights, respectively. The head and neck of marten were struck more frequently by C120 Magnum captures (87% of strikes) than by the other Conibear captures (18%). The C120 Magnum failed to kill 3 captured marten (5% of captures) compared to 5 of 30 marten (17%) found in the standard Conibear traps. A total of 131 non-target animals were caught in the C120 Magnums (70% of all captures), mostly flying squirrels, ermine, red squirrels, and gray jays. One saw-whet owl was also captured. Standard traps captured 54 non-target animals (50% of captures) including ermine, fishers, muskrats, red squirrels, flying squirrels, and gray jays. The researchers stated that even if strikes were optimal, standard Conibear traps would likely not induce rapid unconsciousness due to lower impact momentum and clamping force. However, they recommend the C120 Magnum as a quick-killing device for capturing marten.

Key words: Conibear trap, leghold trap, marten, non-target species

Proulx, G. M. W. Barrett, and S. R. Cook. 1990. The C120 Magnum with pan trigger: A humane trap for mink (*Mustela vison*). *Journal of Wildlife Diseases* 26:511–517.

The authors developed a trigger system for the Conibear 120 Magnum trap that would cause consistent double strikes to the head-neck and thorax region of mink to ensure rapid death. The device was tested on mink in a simulated natural environment to determine whether it would meet the Canadian General Standards Board (CGSB) guidelines for "humane" killing traps (five of six animals rendered unconscious ≤ 3 minutes). Although similar to the C120 Magnum used by Proulx *et al.* (1989), these traps used four clamping bars instead of two to reinforce the frame. Double strikes were sought because such strikes to the head-neck and thorax region of mink had been previously shown to produce consistent and rapid unconsciousness. In approach tests mink were allowed to approach traps wired open so they would not fire and video monitoring was used to project where the trap would have struck the animal. Using a 66x69 mm pan trigger, all approach tests resulted in double strikes to the head-neck and thorax region. In subsequent kill tests, six of six mink were killed with an estimated average time to loss of consciousness and heartbeat of < 72 (± 24) seconds and 158 (± 48) seconds, respectively. The researchers concluded that the C120 Magnum was the first mink kill trap to meet the requirements of the CGSB for killing traps.

Key words: Conibear 120 Magnum trap, mink

**Proulx, G. and M. W. Barrett. 1991. Evaluation of the Bionic trap to quickly kill mink (*Mustela vison*) in simulated natural environments. *Journal of Wildlife Diseases* 27:276–280.**

The Bionic trap was assessed for its ability to consistently strike mink in the head or neck and to cause irreversible unconsciousness in ≤ 3 minutes. In a simulated natural environment (see Proulx et al. 1989), the Bionic trap was set on the ground and wired to a tree. Beaver meat bait was used as an attractant. Initially, a 10 cm cone was used to guide the animal into position. However, early simulations showed that this was ineffective and therefore the opening was reduced and the bait repositioned. In kill tests using a 6 cm cone, the Bionic trap killed 9 of 9 mink when bait was placed at the back of the cone to limit a mink's ability to escape. The average time to loss of consciousness and heartbeat were estimated at < 60 (± 26) seconds and 340 (± 55) seconds, respectively. The researchers concluded that the Bionic trap can be expected to render > 79% of captured mink unconscious in ≤ 3 minutes (P < 0.05). Because of numerous trap manipulations required to obtain the desired results, the researchers noted that the trap's "construction is complex and involves several moving pieces. Therefore, some redesigning will be necessary to increase its longevity, reduce its manufacture costs and facilitate trapper acceptance."

Key words: Bionic trap, mink

**Proulx, G., A. J. Kolenosky, M. J. Badry, P. J. Cole, and R. K. Drescher. 1993. Assessment of the Sauvageau 2001-8 trap to effectively kill arctic fox. *Wildlife Society Bulletin* 21:132–135.**

The Sauvageau 2001-8 kill-type trap was evaluated under simulated natural conditions to determine its potential to quickly kill arctic fox. The trap, equipped with an extra striking bar on one of the frames and an offset trigger made of 2 short prongs shaped in a 5 x 11.8 cm rectangle, was placed in a portable 3-sided wire mesh cubby positioned on a post so the bottom of the trap was 22 cm above the ground. The trigger prongs were wrapped with a cloth dipped in fish oil for bait. In preselection tests, the trap rendered 5 of 5 arctic foxes irreversibly unconscious in ≤ 3 minutes. In kill tests, 9 of 9 foxes were rendered unconscious in ≤ 3 minutes with an average time to loss of unconsciousness and heartbeat of < 73.4 and 213.6 seconds, respectively. Skull fractures and damage to the central nervous system were present in all tests. The authors intended to follow up with a field study (see Proulx *et al.* 1994).

Key words: trap injuries, Sauvageau 2001-8 trap, arctic fox

**Proulx, G. and M. W. Barrett. 1993. Evaluation of the Bionic trap to quickly kill fisher (*Martes pennanti*) in simulated natural environments. *Journal of Wildlife Diseases* 29:310–316.**

The Bionic trap was assessed for its ability to consistently strike fisher in the head or neck and to cause irreversible unconsciousness in ≤ 3 minutes. In a simulated natural environment (see Proulx et al. 1989), the Bionic trap was set on the ground or on the trunk of a tree. Beaver meat or dog food was used as an attractant. In kill tests using the 10 cm cone, the Bionic trap killed 9 of 9 fisher when cocked at eight notches. The average time to loss of consciousness and heartbeat were estimated at < 55 seconds and 305 (± 8) seconds, respectively. The researchers concluded that the Bionic trap can be expected to render > 70% of captured fisher unconscious in ≤ 3 minutes (P < 0.05), thus meeting the researchers guidelines for a "humane" trap. Field testing was recommended.

Key words: Bionic trap, fisher

**Proulx, G. and M. W. Barrett. 1993. Evaluation of mechanically improved Conibear 220 traps to quickly kill fisher (*Martes pennanti*) in simulated natural environments. *Journal of Wildlife Diseases* 29:317–323.**

The potential of modified Conibear 220 traps to "humanely" kill fisher was tested. "Humane killing" was defined as a device with the potential, at a 95% confidence level, to render ≥ 70% of "target" animals irreversibly unconscious in ≤ 3 minutes. Tested traps included a standard Conibear 220, the standard C220 frame using 19 cm long Conibear 280 springs, and the standard C220 frame with stronger Conibear 330 springs. A simulated natural environment was used. The C220 and C220/280 failed preliminary tests and were excluded from "kill" tests. The Conibear 220/330 caused unconsciousness in ≤ 3 min. in only 1 of 4 fishers. The authors concluded that the Conibear 220 is not a humane trap for fisher, even with the tested modifications, and suggested other potential modifications to improve this trap.

Key words: trap injuries, Conibear trap, fisher

Proulx, G. M., A. J. Kolensosky, and P. J. Cole. 1993. Assessment of the Kania® trap to humanely kill red squirrels (*Tamiasciurus hudsonicus*) in enclosures. *Journal of Wildlife Diseases* 29:324–329.

The Kania trap, a narrow mouse-type trap with a striking bar powered by a coil-spring, was assessed for its ability to consistently strike squirrels in the head and neck region and to cause irreversible unconsciousness in $\leq 3$ min. In approach tests of the original trap, 5 of 6 squirrels were positioned correctly for head and neck strikes. However, only one kill test of the original trap was conducted because of the squirrels' rapid movements at the time the trap fired. During the next set of approach tests, the trap and its set were "modified to bring the animals to a full stop at firing time." In 9 of 9 kill tests, squirrels were rendered irreversibly unconscious in $\leq 65$ seconds and heartbeats ceased in $\leq 91$ seconds. The researchers concluded that the Kania trap can be expected to render $\geq 70\%$ red squirrels irreversibly unconscious in $\leq 3$ minutes ($P < 0.05$), and therefore warranted capture efficiency tests on traplines.

Key words: Kania trap, red squirrel

Proulx, G. and M. W. Barrett. 1993. Field testing the C120 Magnum for mink. *Wildlife Society Bulletin* 21:421–426.

The C120 Magnum was field tested to: 1) evaluate its ability to properly strike and effectively kill mink; 2) compare it to existing mink traps; and 3) compare it to C120 and C120 Magnum traps (in enclosure tests) with regard to strike locations and trauma. The C120 Magnums tested had 4 clamping bars and were equipped with a 66 x 69 mm metal pan trigger designed to promote consistent double strikes to the head-neck and thorax regions. Traps were placed in a wooden ground cubby box anchored to the ground and with the back end closed with wire mesh. Trappers recommended by area fur managers operated two traplines, one in British Columbia (BC), the other in Newfoundland (NF). In BC, the standard trap used for comparison was a C120 with custom wooden pan trigger placed in a ground cubby. The NF trapline used No. 1 and 1½ longspring, No. 1 and 1½ coil-spring, No. 1½ jump spring, and the No. 1½ Soft Catch legholds as the standard traps. These leghold traps were placed just below the surface of the water in drowning sets. Trappers selected trap sites, alternating the C120 and C120 Magnum on the BC trapline, and randomly selecting traps on the NF trapline. Traplines were visited every 3–4 days. On the BC trapline, the C120 Magnum and C120 captured a similar number of mink (15 vs. 18) and non-target species

(42 vs. 35), mostly ermine and marten. On the NF trapline, the C120 Magnum and the leghold traps caught a similar number of mink, but the C120 Magnum caught fewer non-target animals (39 vs. 68). The C120 Magnum double struck 29 of 30 mink in the head-neck and thorax regions. The C120 struck 16 of 18 mink and leghold traps captured all mink by a limb. All mink on both traplines were dead when found. Autopsies suggested, however, that the C120 may not consistently suffocate trapped mink within the acceptable time frame as previously supposed. The researchers recommended the C120 Magnum, but not the C120, as an efficient, "humane" killing trap for mink.

Key words: Conibear trap, C120 Magnum trap, leghold trap, mink, non-target species

Proulx, G. and R. K. Drescher. 1994. Assessment of rotating-jaw traps to humanely kill raccoons (*Procyon lotor*). *Journal of Wildlife Diseases* 30:335–339.

The Conibear 280, Sauvageau 2001-8, and mechanically improved models of these traps failed to render raccoons that had been chemically immobilized irreversibly unconscious in $\leq 3$ minutes in lab tests. The researchers concluded that it is unlikely these traps, as well as the less powerful Conibear 220, have the potential to humanely kill raccoons and are unsuitable for this use and recommended "use of live-holding devices for capture of raccoons."

Key words: Conibear trap, Sauvageau 2001-8 trap, raccoon

Naylor, B. J. and M. Novak. 1994. Catch efficiency and selectivity of various traps and sets used for capturing American martens. *Wildlife Society Bulletin* 22:489–496.

To determine methods of increasing selectivity of Conibear traps, the authors compared capture efficiency and selectivity between 1) Conibear 120s placed in various set types, 2) C120s and a version of the Conibear 120 Magnum, and 3) C120s and wire cage live traps used by trappers harvesting martens. Sixteen traplines in northern Ontario, Canada, were used for this study. Trappers selected trap sites, but traps were set according to a random schedule. Full-time field coordinators accompanied trappers to ensure compliance with protocol and consistency in data collection. A total of 581 furbearers (408 martens, 107 ermines, 39 red squirrels, 18 minks, 9 striped skunks) and 432 non-target animals (382 flying squirrels, 26 gray jays, 18 snowshoe hares, 1 ruffed grouse, 1 boreal owl, 1 unidentified hawk) were caught. C120s set in wooden boxes had the highest target capture efficiency. C120s in wire boxes caught fewer nontarget animals/100 trap nights (TN), but also fewer martens/100 TN. These two sets caught a similar number of animals/furbearers. Ground sets were more selective than those in trees with a similar capture efficiency. Marten caught in ground sets were > 3 times more likely to incur pelt damage from scavenging mice. Open trap sets on a running pole had the lowest catch efficiency and selectivity. C120s and live traps had similar selectivity, but live traps were less efficient. The researchers were unable to offer recommendations on a trap or set design to optimize selectivity.

Key words: Conibear traps, live trap, capture efficiency, trap selectivity, marten, non-target species

Proulx, G., J. A. Kolenosky, P. J. Cole, and R. K. Drescher. 1995. A humane killing trap for lynx (*Felis lynx*): the Conibear 330 with clamping bars. *Journal of Wildlife Diseases* 31:57–61.

The Conibear 330 (C330) and a C330 with clamping bars welded to the opposite jaws were tested in a simulated natural environment to determine if they met the standards for "humane killing" of lynx. Humane killing was defined as a device with the potential to render ≥ 70% of target animals irreversibly unconscious in ≤ 3 minutes (P = 0.05). However, the investigators considered redefining and prolonging the "humane killing" time to 5 minutes if neither of the traps performed to the shorter time, which they did not. The standard Conibear 330 failed to meet the "humane killing" criterion since 3 of the 9 (33%) animals tested were conscious for longer than 3 minutes and had to be euthanized. The modified C330 rendered 8 lynx struck in the neck and 1 struck in the shoulders irreversibly unconscious in < 3 minutes. Five of 9 lynx (56%) displayed evidence of trauma, including cervical fracture and dislocation or pulmonary emphysema. The researchers concluded that the modified Conibear 330 could be considered a "humane killing" trap for lynx under the 5 min. killing-time criterion, while the standard Conibear 330 was not. Researchers suggested protocols for future studies.

Key words: trap injuries, Conibear trap, lynx

Proulx, G. 1999. The Bionic: an effective marten trap. Pp. 79–87 *in* G. Proulx, ed. *Mammal Trapping*. Alpha Wildlife Research & Management Ltd., Sherwood Park, Alberta.

The Bionic trap was field-tested for its ability to quickly kill American marten on a trapline in British Columbia, Canada, in fall 1996. The Bionic trap was wired to a horizontal pole, set at four notches, and baited with beaver meat. The Challenger, a planar trap (i.e., a trap where the spring forms the killing bar and closes in the same plane), was used as the control trap and was wired to vertical trunks and baited with beaver meat. The trapper who had been selected for her proven experience trapping marten selected trap sites. A bionic and control trap were set ≤ 30 m from each other at each site. Trap visits varied due to weather and accessibility. Trap placement on the animal, bleeding, oral or anal discharge, and pelt damage were recorded for each trapped animal. Skinned carcasses were frozen and then necropsied by a veterinary pathologist. The study covered a total of 574 trap nights. The Bionic traps caught 12 marten and 1 short-tailed weasel, while the Challengers caught 18 marten, 3 short-tailed weasels, 1 red squirrel, 1 northern flying squirrel, and 2 gray jays. All 12 martens captured in Bionic traps had lesions associated with strikes between the eyes and the back of the skull, and sustained multiple skull fractures with damage to the central nervous system. The researchers concluded that the Bionic trap could be expected, at a 95% confidence level, to render ≥ 70% of martens captured on traplines unconscious in ≤ 3 min.

Key words: Bionic trap, Challenger trap, marten, non-target captures

## Live Traps

White, P. J., T. J. Kreeger, U. S. Seal, and J. R. Tester. 1991. Pathological responses of red foxes to capture in box traps. *Journal of Wildlife Management* 55:75–80.

The physiological responses of red foxes caught in box traps were compared with those observed in Kreeger et al. (1990), who compared responses of untrapped (control) foxes and those caught in padded and unpadded leghold traps. Ten red fox pups were captured in the wild and raised in captivity. At 7–10 months of age they were paired male and female and had heart rate and body temperature transmitters surgically implanted. After a two-week recovery they were released into a 4.05 ha enclosure. One week later, a Tomahawk Model 109 box trap was baited and set in the enclosure. When a fox was trapped, a video camera recorded their behavior and heart rate (HR), and body temperature (BT) was monitored. After 8 hours in the trap, the animals were killed by a rifle or pistol shot to the head. Blood was collected and necropsies performed. Cortisol levels of foxes captured in box traps were significantly correlated to heart rate and time spent active in the traps. No limb injuries or edema were noted. Mean HR, BT, and length of time spent attempting to escape did not differ among foxes trapped in box or leghold traps. Levels of cortisol and several other hormones were lower in foxes caught in box traps than those caught in unpadded or padded foothold traps. The authors concluded that box traps caused less trauma than padded or unpadded foothold traps and that limb restraint contributes to trauma in leg trapped foxes.

Key words: trap injuries, box trap, leghold trap, padded jaws, red foxes

Copeland, J. P., E. Cesar, J. M. Peek, C. E. Harris, C. D. Long, and D. L. Hunter. 1995. A live trap for wolverine and other forest carnivores. *Wildlife Society Bulletin* 23:535–538.

Log live-traps are used by researchers to study wolverine, lynx, bobcat, red fox, American marten, fisher, American badger, and striped skunk. This study focused on wolverine. The trap was made on-site out of logs and other available natural materials and a trigger was added later to activate the system. Trap design and setup are described. Trap transmitter signals were monitored daily and traps were visited every four days. Twelve individual wolverines were trapped a total of 37 times during the winters of 1992–93 and 1993–94 in Idaho. Most tried to escape by chewing their way through logs and out of the trap. Three succeeded in chewing holes large enough to escape. No injuries were observed in any animal caught by the traps. The log trap, although labor intensive for construction and maintenance, appears to be a highly useful, efficient, selective, and humane tool for researchers.

Key words: trap injuries, live trap, wolverine

Sweitzer, R. A., B. J. Gonzales, I. A. Gardner, D. Van Vuren, J. D. Waithman, and W. M. Boyce. 1997. A modified panel trap and immobilization technique for capturing multiple wild pig. *Wildlife Society Bulletin* 25:699–705.

The authors developed a portable modified steel mesh panel trap to reduce capture-related injuries to wild pigs caught in simple square panel traps. Box traps are made with wood slats or fencing. Panel traps are square or rectangular, with prefabricated steel-mesh panels wired together and supported by steel fence posts. The modified trap included the use of a gated entrance with a runway leading to an expanded corral section. Nylon netting was used to line the inside of the trap. Immobilization drugs administered with blow darts were used in lieu of physical restraint. An average of 2.5 pigs per trap night were captured. Of 212 individual pigs involved in 343 captures there were a total of 11 injuries (5%). Injuries consisted of 8 cuts and 3 broken teeth. Some of the lacerations were likely from other pigs caught in the trap. All 6 wild pigs captured in the unmodified square panel trap sustained injuries. No mortalities occurred as a result of trapping. The modified trap design was

efficient at capturing groups of pigs in one trap. The trap modifications and use of chemical immobilants appeared to reduce capture stress and the number of injuries compared to the unmodified square panel trap.

Key words: trap injuries, live trap, wild pig

## Trap Comparison Studies

Beasom, S. L. 1974. Selectivity of predator control techniques in south Texas. *Journal of Wildlife Management* 38:837–844.

The complete, lethal removal of predators, mainly aimed at coyotes, bobcats, and other small predatory furbearers, was attempted on 5,400 acres of brushland, grassland, and pasture in Texas over two years. The author and a professional hunter implemented control techniques, which included M-44s, hunting, strychnine tablets, and Nos. 3 and 4 Oneida steel-jaw leghold traps. The effort consisted of 12,833 M-44 days, 250 hunting hours, 4,000 strychnine egg and 8,000 strychnine meat baits, and 27,446 steel trap days. M-44s and hunting were the most selective methods and killed only targeted animals, although accidental mortality caused by the M-44s could not be ruled out. The high selectivity demonstrated by M-44s was likely due to the absence of other vulnerable species, including wolves, bears, wolverines, and domestic dogs. Strychnine egg and meat baits were far less selective and were responsible for killing numerous raptors, mammals, and reptiles. Leghold traps were more efficient for capturing bobcats, while coyotes were taken more efficiently by M-44s. Leghold traps were highly non-selective (56% of captures were non-target species) and caught more individuals and species of animals than any other method.

Key words: trap selectivity, capture efficiency, leghold trap, coyote, bobcat, furbearer, non-target species.

Palmisano, A. W. and H. H. Dupuie. 1975. An evaluation of steel traps for taking fur animals in coastal Louisiana. Louisiana Cooperative Wildlife Unit. Louisiana State University. Baton Rouge, Louisiana. 12 pp.

The Conibear 220 and Nos. 1½ and 2 Victor double longspring leghold trap were compared for capture efficiency in trapping nutria, raccoons, and muskrats on the Rockefeller Wildlife Refuge in southwestern Louisiana from 1972–1974. Authors performed the trapping, randomly choosing trap types, but trap sites were selected in advance. Traps were checked daily. Undersized animals were released and other animals, if alive, were killed with a blow to the skull. A total of 2,514 trap nights were recorded. More nutria were caught with the No. 2 leghold (4.8 nutria/100 trap nights) than with the Conibear 220 (2.4/100 TN). No difference was observed between leghold traps. The leghold trap captured more raccoons ($n = 27$) than the Conibear ($n = 2$) in the same number of trap nights. During the 1973 season, the Conibear was more successful in taking muskrats (5.3/100 TN) than the leghold trap (1.5/100 TN) in flooded marshes. Non-target animals captured included 33 clapper rails, 1 night heron, 1 mottled duck, 1 robin, 1 boat-tailed grackle, 2 mink, and 4 opossum. The leghold traps caught more birds than the Conibear in 1973, while the situation was reversed in 1974. Both mink and 1 opossum were caught in the Conibear. Five of 62 animals (8%) were found alive in the Conibear, compared to 84.2% in the leghold traps. In summary, the leghold was more efficient in capturing nutria and raccoons, but not muskrats. Although not analyzed by the authors, both traps captured a number of non-target species (from 6–25% of captures).

**Key words:** capture efficiency, Conibear trap, leghold trap, nutria, muskrat, raccoon, non-target species

Linscombe, G. 1976. An evaluation of the No. 2 Victor® and Conibear 220™ traps in coastal Louisiana. *Proceedings of the Annual Conference of the Southeastern Association of Fish & Wildlife Agencies* 30:560–568.

The No. 2 Victor steel-jawed leghold and Conibear 220 traps were compared for efficiency in several fresh and brackish (salt) marsh habitats along the Louisiana coast. The nine study areas used were primarily in federal and state wildlife refuges and management areas as well as two privately owned tracts. A total of 23 trappers (experience not cited) alternated trap types in their trap lines. Refuge personnel maintained close contact with the trappers and some trappers were eliminated after the data were collected due to improper procedure. A total of 10,671 and 7,567 trap nights were recorded for the No. 2 Victor and C220 trap, respectively. The No. 2 Victor caught significantly more nutria than the C220, but not more muskrat. The Victor also caught more raccoon in brackish marshes. Sample sizes for mink and river otter were too small for comparison; however, all 9 river otter captured were taken by the C220. The C220 failed to kill 9.7% of adult and 10.7% of juvenile nutria, 17.86% of adult muskrat, 25% of adult raccoon, 14.29% of adult mink, and 11.11% of adult otter. A large number of nontarget animals were caught, including 57 mammals and 127 birds, mainly cottontails and rabbits, opossums, rails, coots, and ducks. Non-target mammal capture rate per 100 trap nights was 0.23 for the Victor and 0.38 for the C220; however, this difference was not tested sta-

tistically. Overall, no significant differences were observed in non-target bird catches between trap types, although in brackish marsh the C220 captured more birds than the Victor did. The researchers concluded that the C220 was most effective active animal trails along bayous and canals. The Conibear did not allow for releasing undersized nutria; only 11% of immature nutria were alive in Conibear vs. 70% in leghold. Finally, they note that the Conibear would not be a more efficient replacement for leghold traps in coastal Louisiana.

**Key words:** capture efficiency, trap selectivity, leghold trap, Conibear trap, nutria, raccoon, mink, river otter, non-target species

Berchielli, L. T. and B. F. Tullar. 1980. Comparison of a leg snare with a standard leg-gripping trap. *NY Fish and Game Journal* 27:63–71.

The Ezyonem leg snare was compared with a No. 1½ double coil-spring leghold trap with regards to capture efficiency and trapping-related injuries. Primary target species were red fox, gray fox, and raccoon. Secondary targets were opossum and skunk. Trap sites were determined by a preliminary search for animal signs and traps were laid out in pairs (1 leghold and 1 snare). A total of 66 set locations were used, some maintained for as many as 29 nights. Traps were checked daily, in the morning and at midday. Most captured animals were restrained for study and released, but skunks were shot. Injuries were recorded as none, minor lacerations, moderate lacerations, fractures, and chewing. Teeth were not examined because of the difficulty in checking restrained animals. A total of 87 and 6 animals were caught in leghold traps and snares, respectively. Capture efficiency of the leghold trap was 85.3% compared to only 13.6% for the snare. The leg snare was found to be less efficient than the leghold trap for all target species except skunks. The leghold traps caused 26 minor and 2 moderate skin lacerations, 15 fractures, and 17 incidences of chewed feet or toes. Of the 6 snare captures, 3 had minor lacerations and 1 raccoon had chewed its foot. Six non-target animals were caught in the leghold trap and none in the snare. The researchers concluded that the leg snare was less efficient and did not appear to be more humane than the leghold trap. Since only 6 animals were caught with leg snares, however, these conclusions may be inaccurate.

**Key words:** trap injuries, capture efficiency, trap selectivity, snare, leghold trap, red fox, gray fox, raccoon, non-target species

Novak, M. 1981. The foot-snare and the leg-hold traps: a comparison. *Proceedings Worldwide Furbearer Conference* 3:1671–1685.

The Novak leg snare was compared with the No. 2 coil-spring and No. 4 longspring leghold traps for injuries, capture efficiency, and escape rates. Two experienced trappers independently tested the traps on southern Ontario agricultural land, checking them daily. Foxes and, occasionally, coyotes were targeted. Trappers categorized injuries using six categories ranging from no injury to "wring offs" (amputation of a limb). Four categories of swelling were recorded from none noticeable to non-weight-bearing. In total, 184 animals were captured in leg snares and 71 in leghold traps. Among the non-target species captured were 12 dogs, 7 cats, 8 sheep, 1 turkey vulture, 7 porcupine, and 11 groundhogs. When only fox and coyote were considered target species, non-target capture rates were 53% and 76% for the leg snare and leghold trap, respectively. The red fox capture rate was 89% for the leg snares and 85% for the legholds. Of animals caught in leg snares, 2% had either no marks or only rubbed skin/nicks on their legs. In contrast, 52% of animals caught in leg holds had more severe injuries, including 3 "wring-offs" and 14 with chewed feet. The author hypothesized that the light weight and flexibility of the leg snare prevented excessive or continuous pain. The author concluded that the leg snare captures targeted furbearers as efficiently as the leghold but with greatly reduced injuries.

**Key words:** capture efficiency, trap injuries, trap selectivity, leghold trap, leg snare, coyote, red fox, gray fox, non-target species

Waller, D. J. 1981. **Effectiveness of kill-type traps versus leg-hold traps utilizing dirt-hole sets.** *Proceedings of the Annual Conference of the Southeastern Association of Fish & Wildlife Agencies* 35:256–260.

The Conibear 220 and No. 2 Blake and Lamb double coil-spring leghold trap were compared for capture rate and humaneness. Traps were alternated at 0.32 km intervals along wooded roads in six study areas in Georgia. The author, who checked traps daily, performed all trapping. A total of 448 trap nights were conducted for each trap type, resulting in 49 captures in the leghold traps and 14 in the Conibear traps. No target species were designated, so all captured animals were considered targets. The leghold trap had a higher capture rate for total animals, opossum, and raccoons. There was no difference in capture rate for gray foxes, rabbits, and feral dogs. Sample sizes of bobcat, red fox, skunk, red squirrel, and feral cat were too small for analysis. The Conibear appeared to instantly kill only 1 (a feral dog) of the 14 animals captured (7.1%). Two dogs, 1 raccoon, and 2 opossums were caught by the leg (37.5%); the other 8 animals were captured by the head or neck (64.3%). All 6 gray fox were caught by the

head or neck. Seven of the 14 animals (50%) were found alive in the Conibear, 5 of which were leg captures. The other animals showed signs of struggle before death and likely suffocated. The author suggested that leghold traps were more effective because of the visibility of Conibear traps at the trap site. He also noted "Conibears generally did not kill captured animals instantly and only 64.3% of the animals were captured by the neck or head."

**Key words:** trap injuries, capture efficiency, leghold trap, Conibear trap

Englund, J. 1982. **A comparison of injuries to leg-hold trapped and foot-snared red foxes.** *Journal of Wildlife Management* 46:1113–1117

This study compared dental and leg injuries sustained by red foxes captured in Nos. 2 and 3 double longspring leghold traps; the same leghold traps covered with 2–3 mm thick plastic tubing on the jaws, chain, and pole; and a leg snare made of plastic-sheathed wire. Trapping occurred during winter in northern Sweden without bait or scent. Although Swedish law requires traps to be checked twice daily, the investigator admitted that the participating trappers may have disregarded the law although he speculated that few, if any, foxes remained in the traps over 24 hours. The number of trap sets and trap days were not reported. Trappers supplied skulls and legs along with information on the capture, sex, weight, trap type, and visible trap injuries resulting from chewing on trapped appendages. Molars and premolars were examined and classified in four groups from no damage to severe dental injuries. Toes, feet, and leg injuries were also assessed. Minor injuries were defined as those not expected to be life-threatening and included fractured, dislocated, and luxated digits, superficial lacerations, and abrasions caused by rubbing. Very minor injuries were not recorded. Major injuries were those considered life-threatening and included fractured, dislocated, or luxated bones or joints of the leg or shoulder. Researchers examined 1,651 red foxes. Of these, 1,374 (83%) were taken in unmodified leghold traps, 154 (9.5%) in plastic covered traps, and 123 (7.5%) in leg snares. Severe dental injuries were found in 19% of juveniles and 58% of adult foxes caught in the unmodified leghold traps. Foxes trapped in the plastic-coated leghold trap had half as many severe dental injuries. Only 2 foxes caught in the leg snares had severe dental injuries. Thirty percent of foxes caught in the unmodified leghold traps had broken bones. A higher percentage (although not statistically significant) of fractures occurred in the plastic covered traps. Only 3 of 117 leg-snared foxes (2.5%) had fractures. The investigator concluded covering parts of the leghold traps with plastic could reduce the severity and frequency of dental injuries, but not injuries to feet and legs. Leg snares also caused fewer limb injuries than either leghold trap. These results refer only to capture of red foxes caught in winter with below-freezing temperatures.

Key words: trap injuries, leghold trap, leg snare, red fox

Bortolotti, G. R. 1984. Trap and poison mortality of golden and bald eagles. *Journal of Wildlife Management* 48:1173–1179.

The causes of mortality of 143 golden eagles and 172 bald eagles were obtained from labels of museum study skins. Trapping or poison were responsible for 71% of known types of golden eagle mortalities and 33% of known bald eagle mortalities, which represented 19% and 4% of total samples of golden and bald eagles, respectively. Female golden eagles were trapped or poisoned nearly six times as often as males. Spatial segregation between the sexes may partially account for the differences in capture rates. Strychnine was responsible for all ($n = 4$) of the bald eagle and 7 of 11 golden eagle deaths associated with poison incidental to poisonings of gray wolves, coyotes, and foxes. Traps set for predators and furbearers killed 16 (42%) and 5 (14%) golden and bald eagles whose cause of death was known.

Key words: trap selectivity, leghold trap, leg snare, golden eagle, bald eagle, non-target species

Van Ballenberghe, V. 1984. Injuries to wolves sustained during live-capture. *Journal of Wildlife Management* 48:1425–1429.

This is a retrospective report of injuries and mortalities sustained by 126 wolves during live-capture programs in Minnesota 1969–1971 and Alaska 1975–1976. Wolves were captured in Minnesota with steel leghold traps (No. 3 or 4 double longspring or No. 14 double longspring with teeth and offset jaws), steel cable leg snares (spring-activated Aldrich), and steel cable neck snares. Traps and snares were checked daily. Trapped wolves were assigned to one of four injury categories: Class I, slight foot and/or leg edema with no lacerations, broken bones, or dislocated joints; Class II, moderate to severe edema, skin lacerations longer than 2.5 cm with visible damage to underlying tissue and/or fracture of a toe bone; Class III, skin lacerations longer than 2.5 cm with visible damage to underlying tissues with intact tendons, and bone breakage limited to one phalanx or metacarpal; Class IV, any combination of deep, wide lacerations, severed tendons, broken metacarpals or metatarsals, broken radius or ulna, tibia or fibula, and joint dislocations. Trapped wolves were also examined for tooth, lip, and gum

injuries, which result when struggling animals chew on traps. A total of 106 wolves were trapped: 93 in steel traps, 12 in leg snares, and 1 in a neck snare. Certain individuals were caught more than once for a total of 124 captures. Of these, 44 captures involved pups (2–6 months). Of all trapped wolves, 41% received Class III or IV injuries; 11% were potentially life-threatening. Of 14 wolves trapped in the toothed leghold traps, 3 had Class IV injuries, "demonstrating that such injuries are possible even if the foot is held from slipping between the jaws." Pups received fewer severe injuries in steel-jaw leghold traps. Tooth, lip, and gum injuries, often accompanied by severe edema, occurred in 50 of 109 adults (46%) captured in steel-jaw leghold traps. No Class III or IV injuries occurred in leg snares, but the 1 wolf trapped in a neck snare died. The use of neck snares was discontinued. The researchers concluded: "Steel traps, as used in this study, produced a high rate of severe injuries even when checked daily." In addition, reduced fitness and shortened life span from the capture-caused injuries was raised as a serious consideration. Long-term effects of broken teeth, missing feet, severed tendons, or poorly healed bones are likely serious handicaps for predators.

Key words: trap injuries, leghold trap, neck snare, leg snare, offset jaws, toothed jaws, gray wolf

Stocek, R. F and D. J. Cartwright. 1985. Birds as nontarget catches in the New Brunswick furbearer harvest. *Wildlife Society Bulletin* 13:314–317.

Researchers surveyed 2,836 fur trappers (31% of active trappers) in New Brunswick in the early 1980s to determine the frequency and composition of non-target bird catches and to relate them to trap type and furbearer harvest. Trappers surveyed used Conibears, snares (type not specified), and leghold traps to capture a wide variety of furbearer species. Approximately 24% of trappers reported catching birds each year, for a total of 2,006 birds during the three trapping seasons studied (3.3% of reported captures). Corvids (jays, crows, ravens) were caught more than any other group of birds. Phasianidae (grouse and pheasants) were the second most reported group. Raptors (hawks, eagles, owls) were captured by 5% of trappers surveyed. Sixty-seven percent of raptors caught were trapped in leghold traps. Other species trapped are also discussed. An estimated 2,128 birds were caught each year during the study period. Leghold traps were responsible for the majority of non-target losses (72% in 1982–1983). The researchers noted, "The impact of incidental trapping on raptor populations, with low population densities and recruitment rates, may warrant concern."

Key words: trap selectivity, leghold trap, Conibear trap, snare, raptors, birds, non–target species

Skinner, D. L. and A. W. Todd. 1990. Evaluating efficiency of footholding devices for coyote capture. *Wildlife Society Bulletin* 18:166–175.

The performance of leg-holding devices for capturing coyotes was evaluated in Alberta, Canada, during two trapping seasons from 1985 to 1987. Devices tested were the Novak and Fremont leg snares, an unpadded No. 3 Victor double coil-spring leghold trap with 24 cm end mounted chain with swivel, and a padded No. 3 Victor Soft Catch with a 15 cm center mounted chain with 4 cm coil-spring for shock resistance. The six trappers were experienced with standard foothold devices but inexperienced with modified footholds such as the padded trap and with leg snares. Traps were set for 30,060 trap nights during the study in six study areas (3 forested, 3 agricultural). Coyotes approached 552 trap sets and avoided 202 of them; 90 coyotes were captured. Trapped coyotes escaped more often from unpadded traps and Fremont leg snares than from other devices. Capture efficiency was three times greater for leghold traps than for leg snares (4.3 vs. 1.5/1,000 trap nights) but there was no difference among the different types of leghold traps or leg snares. Overall, the capture rate for leghold traps was higher than for leg snares. The investigators explained this difference as inexperience with the devices on the part of the trappers. In addition, trappers tended to select different types of trap sets for different devices, which may also have biased the sampling. Trapping efficiency doubled from the first to second season as trappers become more proficient with the various devices. There were 65 non-target animals captured, including 19 furbearers, although no breakdown by trap type is provided. The remaining 46 included 14 porcupines, 13 snowshoe hares, 10 birds of 4 species, 5 deer, 3 domestic dogs, and 1 domestic cat. The authors concluded that "the padded trap is as efficient as the unpadded trap for the capture of coyotes," and that the leg snares "may require further optimization, although their poor performance may have resulted in part from the trappers' inexperience with them."

Key words: capture efficiency, leg snare, leghold trap, padded jaws, coyote, non-target species

Onderka, D. K., D. L. Skinner, and A. W. Todd. 1990. Injuries to coyotes and other species caused by four models of footholding devices. *Wildlife Society Bulletin* 16:303–307.

The unpadded No. 3 Victor double coil-spring leghold trap, padded No 3. Victor Soft Catch leghold trap, and two models of leg snares (Novak and Fremont) were studied during two trapping seasons in Alberta, Canada, predominantly in winter with subfreezing temperatures. Traps were checked daily. Captured animals were necropsied and the type and severity of injuries was recorded. The trapped limb was specifically examined for evidence of partial or complete freezing. A total of 82 coyotes were examined: 34 in unpadded, 28 in padded, 10 in Fremont snare, and 10 in Novak snare traps. Mean damage scores were 64.9, 21.6, 5.9, and 59.4 for the unpadded leghold, padded leghold, Fremont snare, and Novak snare, respectively. The maximum damage score for the unpadded trap was 22 times that of the Fremont snare, 2.5 times higher than the Novak snare, and 1.4 times higher than the padded trap. Fractures were observed in 48% and 50% of coyotes caught in the unpadded trap and the Novak leg snare, respectively. Partial or complete freezing of a limb occurred in 53% of 57 coyotes trapped overnight in subfreezing weather and was encountered in all four devices. Fifty-two other animals were incidentally trapped, including porcupine, snowshoe hare, lynx, red fox, birds, dogs, a cat, and deer. No breakdown of non-target captures by trap type is included. Three of 5 foxes caught in unpadded traps had fractures, as did 2 of 10 porcupines. Foxes caught in padded traps received only minor injuries, as did raccoons caught in Fremont snares. All the snowshoe hares trapped in padded and unpadded traps were found dead "with severely macerated legs." Birds were found dead in traps (no breakdown provided), with injuries to legs, wings, and chest. All 5 deer were caught in Fremont snares and had injuries associated with struggle, including muscle bruising. The researchers concluded that the Fremont leg snare appeared to significantly reduce injuries compared to the other traps tested, which they stated may be a result of the reduced constriction pressure produced by the larger diameter snare cable. Padded leghold traps reduced, but did not eliminate, injuries to captured species.

Key words: trap injuries, leghold trap, leg snare, padded jaws, coyote, non-target species

Proulx, G., I. M. Pawlina, D. K. Onderka, M. J. Badry, and K. Seidel. 1994. Field evaluation of the number 1½ steel-jawed leghold and the Sauvageau 2001-8 traps to humanely capture arctic fox. *Wildlife Society Bulletin* 22:179–183.

This study had three objectives: 1) examine the ability of the Sauvageau 2001-8 trap to humanely kill arctic fox; 2) determine the degree of injuries caused by the No. 1½ steel-jawed leghold trap, and 3) compare the capture efficiency of both traps. Trappers (experience not noted) selected trap sites and randomly selected trap type on two traplines in Canada's Northwest Territories. Average trap check time was 1.4 days for Trapline 1 and 8 days for Trapline 2. Animals found alive were killed with a blow to the head and then frozen. Necropsies were performed and injuries scored using the Onderka scoring system. The leghold trap captured more arctic fox than the Sauvageau on Trapline 1 while no difference was observed on Trapline 2. The Sauvageau trap struck a fox's head in 88.7% of 62 arctic fox captured; 11.3% were hit in the neck. No fox were found alive. Necropsies of 60 animals found 86.7% had received major traumatic lesions involving mostly the nervous system. Leghold traps captured 155 arctic foxes, 150 of which were available for necropsy. No evidence of self-mutilation was observed. Of 96 arctic foxes captured on Trapline 1, 82% (78) had minor injuries (< 15 score), 8% (8) had serious injuries (50–124 score) and 6% (6) had severe injuries (> 125 score). Of 53 arctic foxes captured on Trapline 2, 49% (26) had minor injuries, 23% (12) had serious injuries, and 17% (9) had severe injuries. The greater degree of injuries on Trapline 2 was associated with the longer trap check time. The researchers considered the Sauvageau 2001-8 trap and the No. 1½ leghold trap (when examined daily) to be humane. To reduce the degree of suffering by trapped animals, they recommended the use of the Sauvageau trap over the leghold trap when traplines are remote and cannot be regularly checked.

**Key words:** trap injuries, capture efficiency, leghold trap, Sauvageau 2001-8 trap, arctic fox

Mowat, G., B. G. Slough, and R. Rivard. 1994. A comparison of three live capturing devices for lynx: capture efficiency and injuries. *Wildlife Society Bulletin* 22: 644–650.

The padded No. 3 Soft Catch leghold trap, Fremont leg snare, and 110A and 209.5 Tomahawk box traps were compared for capture efficiency and trap injuries for trapping lynx. Traps were set in southwest Yukon from December to April 1986–1993 and were checked daily. Experience of trappers was not cited. Technicians changed over the course of the study and may not have randomly selected traps, which weakens the results. Captured animals were chemically immobilized, visually inspected for injuries, and released within 2 hours. Minor injuries were defined as not life-threatening (fractured, dislocated and luxated digits, superficial lacerations and abrasions). Major injuries were defined as life-threatening (fractured, dislocated, and luxated joints and bones of the leg or shoulder). Categorization of injuries by trappers likely led to underestimation of severity. A total of 22,686 trap nights were logged over four trapping seasons for the three trap types. Leg snares were approached more often than the other trap types, probably because they were used more often. Non-target captures included 6 red fox, 1 mink, 6 wolverine, 1 moose calf, 52 snowshoe hares, 26 gray jays, 1 bald eagle, and 1 domestic dog. All

injuries to non-target species were reported as minor. Two hundred five lynx captures were recorded (135 new captures and 70 recaptures). Capture efficiency was statistically similar among traps, although the researchers note that the leg snare may have been more efficient than the box traps. Of 23 lynx caught in padded leghold traps, 22% had minor injuries, 39% had frozen toes or feet, and 4% had edema (swelling). Of 19 lynx caught in box traps, 32% had minor injuries, and there were no recorded cases of freezing or edema. Initially, leg snares caused the most serious injuries with 15% of 54 lynx sustaining serious injuries and 50% exhibiting edema. Further modifications (placement in areas with little or no brush and using larger trees [>30 cm diameter] as anchors to reduce entanglement) reduced this injury rate to below that of box traps and padded leghold traps. The authors recommend the modified Fremont leg snare for trapping lynx in winter. Leghold and box traps were rejected because of the high incidence of freezing and inefficiency, respectively.

**Key words:** trap injuries, capture efficiency, leghold trap, leg snare, box trap, padded jaw, lynx, non-target species

Blundell, G. M., J. W. Kern, R. T. Bowyer, and L. K. Duffy. 1999. Capturing river otters: a comparison of Hancock and leg-hold traps. *Wildlife Society Bulletin* 27:184–192.

During research on river otters in Alaska, the authors compared capture success and injury rate for river otters live-captured in Hancock and No. 11 Sleepy Creek double longspring leghold traps. Differences in capture efficiency, rate of escape, rate of trap malfunction, and utility was tested. Trap type was selected based on topography, substrate, and width of otter trails at latrines and traps were set on land without lure or bait. Some leghold traps were anchored using stakes tipped with double-swivels to allow the trap to rotate 360 degrees around the stake. Anchor chains were ≤ 70 cm with swivels attached to the trap, anchor point, and along the chain. Hancock traps were anchored to a tree without swivels because captured otters would be contained within the trap. All traps had trans-mitters that indicated when they were sprung and signals were checked 2–3 times/day. Captured otters were immobilized with Telazol and examined on-site for injuries, especially to teeth or appendages. A total of 39 individual river otters were captured, 29 in leghold traps and 10 in Hancock. Leghold traps also incidentally caught 4 mink and 2 porcupines without serious injury. No difference in capture efficiency was observed. Trauma scores (using draft ISO standards) were not statistically different between leghold and Hancock traps. However, otters caught in Hancock traps had significantly more serious injuries to teeth than leghold traps. The authors also compared the Sleepy Creek trap with data gathered by Serfass et al. (1996) on the No. 1½ Soft Catch and found the Sleepy Creek had a lower escape rate, lower dental injury rate, and similar appendage injury rate. The Sleepy Creek No. 11 leghold trap was recommended to live-capture and handle river otters.

**Key words:** trap injuries, leghold trap, Hancock trap, river otter, non-target species

# APPENDIX V

*Results of 1997 survey by the U.S. Fish and Wildlife Service regarding trapping programs in the National Wildlife Refuge System from 1992 to 1996. (See p. 208 for chart key.)*

| State(s) | National Wildlife Refuge Unit Name | Acreage | Number Trapping Programs | Primary Purpose(s) | Target Species | Threatened & Endangered Species Inhabiting Refuge Unit | Cost in $ Thousands | Live Enclosure | Steel-Jaw Leghold | Kill-Type | Kill Snares | Other Body-Hold Devices | Refuge-Specific Regs. | Refuge-Specific Trap Check Times |
|---|---|---|---|---|---|---|---|---|---|---|---|---|---|---|
| AK | Alaska Maritime NWR | 351,340 | 1 | B | 28,30 | 2, 35, 36, 41, 42, 47, 51, 55, 64, 68, 71, 73 | 130 | X | X | X | X |  | N | None |
| AK | Alaska Maritime NWR-Adak st. |  | 1 | K | 30 |  | NR |  | X |  |  |  | Y | None |
| AK | Alaska Peninsula NWR | 3,500,085 | 2 | H,K | 15, 23, 24, 26, 27, 28, 31, 32, 35, 40 | 36 | 1 | X | X | X | X |  | N | None |
| AK | Arctic NWR | 19,575,711 | 3 | H, I, K | 14, 15, 16, 23, 24, 26, 27, 28, 30, 32, 35, 40 | 35, 36, 42 | 19 | X | X | X | X | X | N | None |
| AK | Becharof NWR | 12,170,750 | 2 | H, K | 15, 23, 24, 26, 27, 28, 31, 32, 40 | 36 | 1 | X | X | X | X |  | N | None |
| AK | Innoko NWR | 385,160 | 2 | H, K | 15, 17, 24, 26, 27, 28, 32, 35 |  | 10 | X | X | X | X | X | N | None |
| AK | Izembek NWR | 303,094 | 2 | H, K | 17, 24, 26, 28, 32, 40 | 36, 51, 64 | NR | X | X | X |  | X | Y | See Note 6 |
| AK | Kanuti NWR | 1,430,002 | 3 | H, K | 14, 15, 17, 23, 24, 26, 27, 28, 32, 35, 40 |  | 15 | X | X | X | X | X | N | None |
| AK | Kenai NWR | 1,906,214 | 5 | H, K | 14, 15, 17, 23, 24, 26, 27, 31, 32, 35, 40 |  | 36 | X | X | X | X |  | Y | Every 4 Days |
| AK | Kodiak NWR | 1,878,016 | 1 | K | 15, 23, 24, 28 | 36, 47, 51, 55, 64, 71 | NR |  | X | X | X | X | N | Yes |
| AK | Koyukuk/ Nowinta Refuge Complex | 5,110,000 | 2 | I, K | 14, 15, 23, 24, 26, 27, 28, 32, 35, 40 | 6, 30 | 4 | X | X | X | X | X | N | None |

| State(s) | National Wildlife Refuge Unit Name | Acreage | Number Trapping Programs | Primary Purpose(s) | Target Species | Threatened & Endangered Species Inhabiting Refuge Unit | Cost in $ Thousands | Live Enclosure | Steel-Jaw Leghold | Kill-Type | Kill Snares | Other Body-Hold Devices | Refuge-Specific Regs. | Refuge-Specific Trap Check Times |
|---|---|---|---|---|---|---|---|---|---|---|---|---|---|---|
| AK | Selawik NWR | 2,150,000 | 1 | K | 14, 15, 16, 17, 23, 24, 26, 27, 28, 30, 31, 32, 35 | 36 | NR | | X | X | X | X | N | None |
| AK | Tetlin NWR | 700,054 | 2 | I, K | 35 | 30 | 40 | X | X | X | X | X | N | None |
| AK | Togiak NWR | 4,097,431 | 5 | D, E, H, K | 14, 15, 16, 17, 23, 24, 26, 27, 28, 20, 31, 32, 35, 40 | 35, 36, 64 | 71 | X | X | X | X | X | N | None |
| AK | Yukon Delta NWR | 19,131,646 | 3 | A, I, K | 14, 15, 16, 17, 23, 24, 26, 27, 28, 30, 31, 32, 35, 40 | 35, 36 | 2 | X | X | X | X | X | N | None |
| AK | Yukon Flats NWR | 8,630,000 | 3 | H, K | 14, 15, 16, 17, 23, 24, 26, 27, 28, 32, 35, 38, 40 | 30 | 11 | X | X | X | X | X | N | None |
| AL | Choctaw NWR | 4,218 | 2 | A, D | 3, 19 | 6, 39 | 2 | X | | | | | N | 2X daily |
| AL | Wheeler NWR | 34,247 | 1 | G | 14, 15 | 6, 30, 50 | 5 | | | X | X | | N | None |
| AL, GA | Eufaula NWR | 7,953 | 1 | E | 15 | 6, 30, 39 | 1 | | | X | X | | N | NS |
| AR | Big Lake NWR | 11,036 | 1 | G | 12, 14, 15 | 6 | 1 | | | X | | | Y | None |
| AR | Cache River NWR | 43,817 | 1 | G | 15 | 6 | 1 | | | X | X | | Y | None |
| AR | Felsenthal NWR | 64,902 | 2 | C, K | 12, 14, 15, 18, 19, 24, 26, 31 | 6, 32 | 75 | | X | X | | | Y | Daily |
| AR | Holla Bend NWR | 6,428 | 1 | G | 15 | 6 | NR | | | | | X | N | Every 24 Hours |
| AR | Overflow NWR | 12,118 | 1 | C | 12, 14, 15, 18, 19, 24, 26, 31 | 6, 25 | 60 | | X | X | | | Y | Daily |
| AR | White River NWR | 1,547,861 | 1 | G | 12, 15 | 6 | 1 | | | X | X | | N | Every 24 Hours |
| AZ | Buenos Aires NWR | 116,961 | 3 | C, I, K | 20, 29, 31, 34, 40 | 9, 26, 30 | NR | X | X | | | | N | None |
| AZ | Kofa NWR | 666,480 | 2 | C, H | 40 | 30 | 4 | X | | | | | N | None |
| AZ | San Bernardino/Leslie Canyon NWR | 5,133 | 2 | D, H | 2, 17 | 9 | NR | X | | | | | Y | Every A.M. |

| State(s) | National Wildlife Refuge Unit Name | Acreage | Number Trapping Programs | Primary Purpose(s) | Target Species | Threatened & Endangered Species Inhabiting Refuge Unit | Cost in $ Thousands | Live Enclosure | Steel-Jaw Leghold | Kill-Type | Kill Snares | Other Body-Hold Devices | Refuge-Specific Regs. | Refuge-Specific Trap Check Times |
|---|---|---|---|---|---|---|---|---|---|---|---|---|---|---|
| AZ, CA | Imperial NWR | | 3 | D, H | 5, 6, 16, 17, 33, 34, 40 | 6, 8, 11, 30, 34, 39, 78 | 7 | X | | | | | N | None |
| AZ, CA | Havasu NWR | 7,235 | 1 | H | 17 | 6, 8, 11, 30, 34, 78 | 1 | X | | | | X | N | None |
| CA | Bitter Creek NWR | 14,057 | 1 | H | 17 | 10, 70 | 5 | X | | | | | N | None |
| CA | Colusa NWR | 4,507 | 2 | E, L | 10, 13, 14, 15, 17 | 2, 6, 30 | 1 | | | X | X | X | N | None |
| CA | Delevan NWR | 5,797 | 3 | D, E, L | 2, 10, 13, 15, 17 | 2, 6, 30 | 2 | X | | X | | X | N | None |
| CA | Don Edwards San Francisco Bay NWR | 21,524 | 1 | B | 2, 10, 19, 20, 28 | 8, 11, 25, 30, 37, 69 | 50 | X | X | | | | N | Daily |
| CA | Humboldt Bay NWR | 2,113 | 3 | D, H, I | 2, 17 | 2, 30, 37 | 3 | X | | | | | N | Every A.M. |
| CA | Kern NWR | 10,618 | 1 | H | 17 | 6, 30, 70, 77 | 4 | X | | | | | N | None |
| CA | Modoc NWR | 6,696 | 1 | D | 1, 2 | 6, 30 | 1 | X | X | X | | | Y | See Note 9 |
| CA | Pixley NWR | 6,389 | 1 | I | 17 | 2, 6, 30, 70, 74, 77 | 5 | X | | | | | N | None |
| CA | Sacramento NWR | 10,783 | 2 | G, L | 10, 13, 15, 16 | 2, 6, 30 | 1 | | | X | | X | N | None |
| CA | Sacramento River NWR | 8,171 | 1 | G | 15 | 6, 30 | 1 | | | X | | | N | None |
| CA | Salinas River NWR | 367 | 1 | B | 2, 10, 20, 28 | 8, 6, 37 | 20 | X | X | | | | N | Daily |
| CA | Seal Beach | 911 | 1 | B | 1, 2, 18, 19, 20, 28 | 8, 11, 25, 30, 37 | 6 | X | X | | | | Y | Yes, NS |
| CA | Sutter NWR | 2,590 | 2 | E, L | 10, 13, 14, 15, 17 | 2, 6, 30 | 2 | | | X | X | X | N | None |
| CA | Sweetwater Marsh NWR | 316 | 1 | B | 1, 2, 16, 18, 19, 20, 40 | 11, 24, 25, 37 | NR | X | | | | | Y | Yes, NS |
| CA | Tijuana Slough NWR | 1,022 | 2 | B, H | 1, 2, 10, 16, 17, 18, 19, 20, 23, 28, 31 | 8, 11, 25, 25, 37 | 17 | X | X | | | | Y | Yes, NS |

| STATE(s) | National Wildlife Refuge Unit Name | Acreage | Number Trapping Programs | Primary Purpose(s) | Target Species | Threatened & Endangered Species Inhabiting Refuge Unit | Cost in $ Thousands | Live Enclosure | Steel-Jaw Leghold | Kill-Type | Kill Snares | Other Body-Hold Devices | Refuge-Specific Regs. | Refuge-Specific Trap Check Times |
|---|---|---|---|---|---|---|---|---|---|---|---|---|---|---|
| CA | Tule Lake | 39,117 | 1 | E | 14 | | 1 | | X | X | | | Y | Every 24 Hours |
| CA, OR | Lower Klamath NWR | 40,294 | 1 | E | 14 | 6, 30 | 1 | | X | X | | | Y | Every 24 Hours |
| CO | Alamosa/Monte Vista NWR | 11,246 | 2 | A, E | 15, 19, 20, 23, 40 | 6, 30 | 5 | X | X | X | | | N | See Note 1 |
| CO | Arapaho NWR Complex | 23,268 | 4 | A, E, H, L | 14, 15, 17, 21, 23, 25, 26, 28, 31 | 6, 30 | 3 | X | X | X | | X | Y | Every 24 Hours |
| CO | Browns Park NWR | 13,455 | 3 | A, H, I | 19, 20, 28, 40 | 6, 30 | 4 | X | | X | | | N | None |
| CO | Rocky Mountain Arsenal NWR | 17,000 | 1 | I | 25 | 6 | NR | X | X | | | | N | None |
| CT | Stewart B. McKinney NWR | 773 | 1 | A | 19 | 33 | 2 | X | | | | | N | Daily |
| DE | Bombay Hook NWR | 16,996 | 3 | C, E, G | 14, 15, 19 | 6, 30 | 3 | X | | X | | | Y | Every 24 Hours |
| DE | Prime Hook NWR | 970 | 1 | G | 14, 19 | 6, 30, 44 | 1 | X | | X | | | N | Every 24 Hours |
| FL | Archie Carr NWR | 39 | 2 | B, H | 19, 40 | 81, 82, 84, 85 | NR | X | | | | | Y | Daily |
| FL | Arthur R. Marshall Loxahatchee NWR | 145,787 | 1 | H | 10, 17, 18, 19, 20, 21, 23, 26 | 4, 6, 12, 30, 39, 49, 79 | 1 | X | | | | | N | 3X daily |
| FL | Cedar Keys NWR | 832 | 1 | A | 19 | 6, 30, 31 | 1 | X | | | | | N | None |
| FL | Crocodile Lake NWR | 6,686 | 1 | H | 17 | 6, 30, 39, 60, 75, 79 | NR | X | | | | | N | None |
| FL | Florida Panther NWR | 26,529 | 1 | I | 17 | 6, 12, 30, 32, 39, 49, 61, 76 | NR | | | | | X | N | None |
| FL | Hobe Sound NWR | 980 | 1 | B | 18, 19, 20, 21, 40 | 6, 13, 30, 31, 39, 79, 81, 84, 85 | 1 | X | | | | | N | Every A.M. |
| FL | Lake Woodruff NWR | 21,559 | 1 | H | 19 | 6, 12, 13, 39, 49, 79 | 1 | X | | | | | N | 2X daily |

| STATE(s) | National Wildlife Refuge Unit Name | Acreage | Number Trapping Programs | Primary Purpose(s) | Target Species | Threatened & Endangered Species Inhabiting Refuge Unit | Cost in $ Thousands | Live Enclosure | Steel-Jaw Leghold | Kill-Type | Kill Snares | Other Body-Hold Devices | Refuge-Specific Regs. | Refuge-Specific Trap Check Times |
|---|---|---|---|---|---|---|---|---|---|---|---|---|---|---|
| FL | Lower Suwannee NWR | 50,838 | 1 | E | 15 | 6, 13, 30, 31, 39, 48, 79, 81, 83, 85 | 1 | | | X | | | N | None |
| FL | Merritt Island NWR | 139,155 | 2 | B, D | 3, 19 | 6, 13, 30, 31, 33, 39, 48, 72, 76, 79, 81, 82, 83, 84, 85 | 17 | X | | | | | Y | Daily |
| FL | National Key Deer Refuge | 8,542 | 2 | H | 17, 40 | 6, 30, 39, 59, 63, 67, 79 | NR | X | | | | | N | None |
| FL | St. Vincent NWR | 12,490 | 3 | B, C, H | 19, 40 | 6, 30, 31, 39, 79, 85 | 5 | X | X | | | | N | None |
| GA | Blackbeard Island NWR | 5,618 | 1 | B | 19 | 6, 30, 31, 39, 48, 85 | 2 | X | | | | | N | Every A.M. |
| GA | Bond Swamp NWR | 5,490 | 1 | I | 3 | 6, 39 | NR | X | | | | | N | Yes, NS |
| GA | Harris Neck NWR | 2,762 | 1 | D | 3 | 6, 30, 39, 48 | 2 | X | | | | | N | Daily |
| GA | Piedmont NWR | 34,967 | 2 | G, I | 15, 40 | 6, 32 | 1 | X | | X | | | N | Yes, NS |
| GA | Wassaw Island NWR | 10,070 | 1 | B | 19 | 6, 30, 31, 39, 85 | 2 | X | | | | | N | Every A.M. |
| GU | Guam NWR | 23,274 | 1 | I | 17 | | NR | | | | | X | N | See Note 5 |
| HI | Hakalau Forest NWR | 32,730 | 4 | B, G, I, L | 2, 3, 10, 11, 40 | 1, 18, 19, 20, 21, 29 | 3 | X | | | X | X | N | None |
| HI | Hanalei NWR | 917 | 1 | B | 1, 2, 10, 40 | 16, 17, 19, 22 | 25 | X | | | | | N | None |
| HI | James Campbell NWR | 164 | 1 | B | 1, 2, 10, 11, 17 | 16, 17, 19, 22 | 10 | X | | | | | N | Every 48 hours |
| HI | Kakahaia NWR | 45 | 1 | B | 1, 2, 10, 11, 17 | 16, 17, 19, 22 | 10 | X | | | | | N | Every 48 hours |
| HI | Kealia Pond NWR | 692 | 1 | B | 2, 10, 11, 17 | 17, 22 | 15 | X | | | | | N | Every 24 hours |
| HI | Kilauea Point NWR | 200 | 1 | B | 1, 2, 10, 40 | 54 | 20 | X | | | | | N | None |

| State(s) | National Wildlife Refuge Unit Name | Acreage | Number Trapping Programs | Primary Purpose(s) | Target Species | Threatened & Endangered Species Inhabiting Refuge Unit | Cost in $ Thousands | Live Enclosure | Steel-Jaw Leghold | Kill-Type | Kill Snares | Other Body Hold Devices | Refuge-Specific Regs. | Refuge-Specific Trap Check Times |
|---|---|---|---|---|---|---|---|---|---|---|---|---|---|---|
| HI | Pearl Harbor NWR | 61 | 1 | B | 1, 2, 10, 11, 17 | 17, 19, 22 | 10 | X | | | | | N | Every 48 hours |
| IA | Iowa WMD | 13,774 | 1 | K | 14, 18, 19, 20, 26, 28, 29 | | NR | | X | X | X | | N S | NS |
| IA | Union Slough NWR | 2,916 | 2 | A, G | 2, 14, 15, 18, 19, 20, 26, 28, 29 | 6 | 16 | X | | X | | | NS | NS |
| IA | Walnut Creek NWR - Prairie Learning Center | | 1 | H | 40 | 56 | 1 | X | | | | | NS | NS |
| IA, NE | DeSoto NWR | 3,503 | 1 | I | NS | 6, 25, 30, 31 | NS | X | | | | | NS | NS |
| IA, WI, MN | Upper Miss. River Wildlife & Fish Refuge McGregor Dist. | 51,026 | 2 | A, K | 14, 15, 19, 24, 26, 28, 31 | 6, 30 | 2 | | X | X | | | NS | |
| ID | Grays Lake NWR | 16,739 | 1 | I | 40 | 6, 30, 38 | 3 | X | X | | | | N | 2X daily |
| ID | Kootenai NWR | 2,774 | 3 | A, E, G | 15, 19 | 6, 30 | 1 | X | | X | | | N | Every 24 hours |
| ID | Oxford Slough WPA | | 1 | K | 14, 26, 28, 31 | 30 | NR | | X | X | | | N | Every 72 hours |
| ID, OR | Deer Flat NWR | 162 | 1 | D | 1, 2 | 6 | NR | X | | | | | N | None |
| IL | Crab Orchard NWR | 43,662 | 3 | E, I, K | 14, 15, 18, 19, 20, 21, 26, 28, 29, 31 | 6 | NR | X | X | X | | | NS | NS |
| IL | Cypress Creek NWR | 13,558 | 1 | G | 15 | 6, 25, 50, 56, 86 | 1 | | | X | | | NS | NS |
| IL, IA | Mark Twain NWR, Wapello District | 18,854 | 3 | E, I, L | 14, 15, 17, 18, 19, 20 | 6, 30, 56 | 1 | X | | X | | X | NS | NS |
| IL, MO | Mark Twain NWR, Annada District | | 1 | E | 15 | | 1 | | | X | | | Y | Daily |
| IN | Muscatatuck NWR | 7,802 | 2 | E, L | 14, 15, 17 | 6, 30, 56, 86 | NR | | X | X | | X | NS | NS |
| KS | Flint Hills NWR | 117 | 1 | E | 15 | 6, 30 | NR | | | X | | | Y | Daily |
| KS | Kirwin NWR | 10,778 | 1 | I | 40 | 6, 25, 30, 38 | NR | | | | | X | N | Yes, NS |
| KS | Quivira NWR | 21,820 | 1 | C | 17 | 6, 25, 30, 31, 38 | NR | X | | | | | N | None |
| LA | Bayou Sauvage NWR | 22,331 | 1 | D | 3 | 6, 8, 30, 31, 62 | NR | X | | | | | Y | None |

| STATE(s) | National Wildlife Refuge Unit Name | Acreage | Number Trapping Programs | Primary Purpose(s) | Target Species | Threatened & Endangered Species Inhabiting Refuge Unit | Cost in $ Thousands | Live Enclosure | Steel-Jaw Leghold | Kill-Type | Kill Snares | Other Body-Hold Devices | Refuge-Specific Regs. | Refuge-Specific Trap Check Times |
|---|---|---|---|---|---|---|---|---|---|---|---|---|---|---|
| LA | Cameron Frairie NWR | 13,169 | 1 | G | 12, 14, 19, 26, 31 | 30 | 1 | | X | | | | N | Daily |
| LA | Catahoula NWR | 9,621 | 2 | D, G | 3, 15, 40 | 6 | 4 | X | X | X | X | | N | None |
| LA | D'Arbonne NWR | 6,545 | 1 | G | 12, 15, 18, 19, 24, 26, 28, 29, 31 | 6, 32 | NR | | X | X | X | | Y | Daily |
| LA | Sabine NWR | 17,420 | 2 | G, I | 12, 14, 31, 33 | 30 | 35 | | X | X | X | X | Y | Every 24 hours |
| LA | Tensas River NWR | 64,008 | 1 | I | 38 | 62 | 10 | X | | X | X | | N | See Note 11 |
| LA | Upper Ouachita NWR | 33,947 | 1 | G | 12, 14, 15, 18, 24, 26, 29, 31, 34 | 6, 32 | NR | | X | X | X | | Y | Daily |
| LA, MS | Bogue Chitto NWR | 6,808 | 1 | K | 19, 26 | 6, 30, 80, 87 | 1 | | X | | | | Y | None |
| MA | Parker River NWR | 4,652 | 2 | B, H | 18, 19, 20, 28 | 6, 30, 31 | 2 | X | X | | | | Y | 2X daily |
| MD | Blackwater NWR | 22,906 | 5 | G, H, I, L | 12, 14, 17, 18, 19, 20, 28, 40 | 6, 30, 44 | 22 | X | X | X | | X | Y | Every 24 hours |
| MD | Eastern Neck NWR | 2,286 | 2 | G, H | 17, 19 | 6, 30, 44 | 5 | X | | | | | N | 2X daily |
| ME | Carlton Pond Waterfowl Prod. Area | | 1 | K | 14, 15 | 6 | NR | | | | | | N | None |
| ME | Moosehorn NWR | 24,519 | 5 | A, E, H, L | 14, 15, 17, 19, 20, 23, 26, 28, 31, 38 | 6, 30 | 3 | X | X | X | | | Y | Yes, NS |
| ME | Petit Manan NWR | 3,953 | 1 | H | 17 | 6, 30, 33 | NR | X | | | | | N | None |
| ME | Rachel Carson NWR | 4,629 | 1 | B | 19, 20 | 6, 30, 31, 33 | NR | X | | | | | N | Every A.M. |
| ME | Sunkhaze Meadows NWR | 10,190 | 1 | I | 17 | 6, 30 | NR | X | | | | X | N | None |
| MI | Seney NWR | 95,206 | 1 | E | 14, 15, 19, 20, 26 | 6, 52 | 500 | | X | X | | | NS | NS |
| MI | Shiawassee NWR | | 2 | A, E | 19 | 6, 30 | 1 | X | X | X | | | Y | Daily |

| State(s) | National Wildlife Refuge Unit Name | Acreage | Number Trapping Programs | Primary Purpose(s) | Target Species | Threatened & Endangered Species Inhabiting Refuge Unit | Cost in $ Thousands | Live Enclosure | Steel-Jaw Leghold | Kill-Type | Kill Snares | Other Body-Hold Devices | Refuge-Specific Regs. | Refuge-Specific Trap Check Times |
|---|---|---|---|---|---|---|---|---|---|---|---|---|---|---|
| MN | Agassiz NWR | 61,501 | 5 | A, E, F, G, I | 14, 15, 19, 20, 24, 26, 28, 32, 40 | 6, 30, 52 | 19 | X | X | X | | X | Y | Every 24 hours |
| MN | Big Stone NWR | 11,520 | 3 | A, E, K | 14, 15, 16, 19, 20, 26, 28 | 6 | 5 | X | X | X | X | | Y | Yes, NS |
| MN | Fergus Falls WMD | 64,364 | 3 | A, E, K | 14, 15, 19, 20, 23, 25, 26, 28, 29, 31 | 6, 30, 31, 52 | 16 | X | X | X | X | | NS | NS |
| MN | Litchfield WMD | 4,022 | 2 | A, K | 14, 15, 16, 17, 18, 19, 20, 23, 24, 25, 26, 27, 28, 29, 31 | 52 | 7 | X | X | X | | | NS | NS |
| MN | Morris WMD | 7,064 | 2 | E, K | 14, 15, 17, 19, 20, 26, 28, 31, 40 | 6, 30, 31 | 2 | | X | X | | | N | Every 24 hours |
| MN | Sherburne NWR | 29,606 | 3 | A, E | 14, 15, 19, 26 | 6, 30 | 2 | | X | X | | | NS | NS |
| MN | Tamarac NWR | 35,191 | 1 | K | 14, 15, 19, 24, 25, 26, 28, 31 | 6, 52 | NR | | X | X | X | | NS | NS |
| MN | Windom WMD | 11,571 | 1 | K | 14, 15, 19, 20, 26, 28, 29, 31 | | NR | | | | | | NS | NS |
| MN, IA, WI, IL | Upper Mississippi River Wildlife & Fish Refuge | 33,540 | 3 | A, K | 14, 15, 18, 19, 20, 23, 24, 26, 28, 31, 40 | 6, 30 | 9 | X | X | X | | | NS | NS |
| MO | Clarence Cannon NWR | 3,750 | 1 | E | 15 | | 1 | | | X | | | Y | Every 24 hours |
| MO | Mingo NWR | 21,746 | 1 | E | 15 | 6, 30 | NR | | X | X | | | NS | NS |
| MS | Dahomey NWR | 9,166 | 1 | E | 15 | | 1 | | X | X | X | | N | None |
| MS | Hillside NWR | 18,078 | 1 | G | 15 | 6, 25, 30, 39 | NR | | X | X | X | | N | Daily |
| MS | Mississippi Sandhill Crane NWR | 19,713 | 1 | B | 1, 3, 18, 19, 28, 29, 31, 34 | 6, 27, 30, 32, 80 | 7 | X | X | | X | | Y | Yes, NS |
| MS | Mississippi WMD | | 1 | E | 15 | | 1 | | | X | X | | N | None |
| MS | Morgan Brake NWR | 7,372 | 1 | G | 15, 19 | 6, 30 | NR | | X | X | X | | N | Daily |
| MS | Noxubee NWR | 46,874 | 1 | E | 12, 14, 15, 19 | 6, 32 | 6 | X | X | X | X | X | N | None |
| MS | Panther Swamp NWR | 65,242 | 1 | K | 15 | 6, 30, 39, 62 | NR | | X | X | X | | N | Daily |

| STATE(S) | NATIONAL WILDLIFE REFUGE UNIT NAME | ACREAGE | NUMBER TRAPPING PROGRAMS | PRIMARY PURPOSE(S) | TARGET SPECIES | THREATENED & ENDANGERED SPECIES INHABITING REFUGE UNIT | COST IN $ THOUSANDS | LIVE ENCLOSURE | STEEL-JAW LEGHOLD | KILL-TYPE | KILL SNARES | OTHER BODY-HOLD DEVICES | REFUGE-SPECIFIC REGS. | REFUGE-SPECIFIC TRAP CHECK TIMES |
|---|---|---|---|---|---|---|---|---|---|---|---|---|---|---|
| MS | St. Catherine Creek NWR | 24,611 | 2 | D, E | 3, 12, 15 | 6, 25, 30, 39, 62 | 2 | X | X | X | X | | Y | Daily |
| MS | Tallahatchie NWR | 4,839 | 1 | E | 15 | | 1 | | | X | X | | N | None |
| MS | Yazoo NWR | 12,940 | 1 | G | 12, 15, 19 | 6, 25, 30, 39, 62 | NR | | X | X | X | | N | Daily |
| MT | Benton Lake NWR | 12,459 | 2 | A, L | 17, 19, 20 | 6, 30, 31 | 3 | X | | X | | X | N | See Note 2 |
| MT | Benton Lake WMD | | 1 | K | 14, 15, 19, 20, 23 25, 26, 28, 31, 34 | 6, 30, 53 | NR | | | | | | N | None |
| MT | Bowdoin NWR | 15,872 | 4 | A, B, D, L | 2, 17, 19, 20 | 6, 30, 31 | 3 | X | | X | | | Y | Daily |
| MT | Bowdoin WMD | 60,576 | 1 | A | 19, 20 | 6, 30 | 1 | | | X | | | Y | None |
| MT | Charles M Russell WMD | 904,509 | 1 | K | 14, 15, 19, 20, 28, 31 | 6, 25, 30, 31 | NR | | X | X | | | N | Every 48 hours |
| MT | Lee Metcalf NWR | 2,793 | 3 | G, I, L | 15, 17 | 6, 30 | NR | X | | X | | X | N | Yes, NS |
| MT | Medicine Lake NWR | 31,484 | 4 | A, B, C, E | 14, 15, 19, 20, 25, 26, 28, 31 | 6, 30, 31, 38 | 2 | X | X | X | | | Y | Every 24 hours |
| MT | National B son Range | 18,524 | 5 | C, H, L, M | 17, 31, 40 | 6, 30 | 46 | X | X | | X | X | N | Daily |
| MT | Northeast Montana NWR | | 2 | A, B | 19, 20, 25, 26, 28, 31 | | 1 | | | X | | | Y | Every 48 hours |
| MT | NW Montana WMD | | 4 | A, E, I | 14, 17, 20, 26, 31 | | 1 | X | X | X | | | N | Daily |
| MT | Pablo NWR | 2,542 | 1 | I | 20 | 6, 30 | NR | X | | | | | N | Daily |
| NC | Alligator River NWR | 156,125 | 3 | C, I, K | 12, 14, 15, 18, 19 24, 26, 27, 28, 29 31, 34, 38, 40 | 6, 30, 32, 66 | 230 | X | X | X | | X | Y | Daily |
| NC | Pee Dee NWR | 8,439 | 1 | E | 15 | 32 | 1 | | | X | | | N | 2X daily |
| NC | Pocosin Lakes NWR | 108,654 | 2 | E, H | 12, 14, 15, 33 | 6, 30, 66 | 1 | | X | X | | | Y | Daily |

| State(s) | National Wildlife Refuge Unit Name | Acreage | Number Trapping Programs | Primary Purpose(s) | Target Species | Threatened & Endangered Species Inhabiting Refuge Unit | Cost in $ Thousands | Live Enclosure | Steel-Jaw Leghold | Kill-Type | Kill Snares | Other Body-Hold Devices | Refuge-Specific Regs. | Refuge-Specific Trap Check Times |
|---|---|---|---|---|---|---|---|---|---|---|---|---|---|---|
| NC | Swanquarter NWR | 16,411 | 1 | I | 40 | 6 | NR | | | | | | N | See Note 10 |
| NC | Mattamuskeet NWR | 50,180 | 2 | C, I | 24, 40 | 6, 30 | NR | | X | | | | N | See Note 8 |
| NC, VA | Mackay Island NWR | 7,150 | 2 | A, E | 12, 14, 19 | 6, 30 | 8 | | | X | | | N | Daily |
| ND | Appert Lake NWR | 908 | 1 | K | 2, 14, 15, 19, 20, 25, 26, 28, 31 | 6, 30 | 1 | | X | X | | | Y | Every 24 hours |
| ND | Arrowwood NWR | 15,934 | 3 | A, C, G | 15, 16, 19, 20, 25, 26, 28 | 6, 30, 31 | 3 | X | X | X | X | | Y | Daily |
| ND | Arrowwood WMD | 25,203 | 2 | A, K | 14, 15, 19, 20, 23, 25, 26, 28, 31 | 6, 30, 31, 38 | 1 | | X | X | | | Y | Every 48 hours |
| ND | Audubon NWR | 14,739 | 4 | A, D, E, I | 1, 2, 14, 15, 19, 20, 23, 25, 26, 28, 31 | 6, 25, 30, 31, 38 | 3 | X | X | X | X | | Y | Every 24 hours |
| ND | Audubon WMD | 117,956 | 2 | A, K | 14, 15, 19, 20, 23, 25, 26, 28, 31 | 6, 25, 30, 31, 38 | 1 | | X | X | X | | Y | Every 48 hours |
| ND | Brumda NWR | 1,977 | 1 | K | 14, 15, 19, 20, 25, 26, 28, 31 | 6, 30 | NR | | X | X | X | | N | None |
| ND | Chase Lake NWR | 4,385 | 1 | A | 16, 19, 20, 25, 26, 28 | 6, 30, 31, 38 | 3 | | | X | | | Y | Every 2 or 3 days |
| ND | Chase Lake Prairie Project/WMD | 96,188 | 3 | A, I, K | 14, 15, 16, 19, 20, 25, 26, 28, 31 | 6, 30, 31, 38 | 17 | | X | X | X | | N | See Note 3 |
| ND | Crosby WMD | 89,922 | 2 | A, K | 14, 15, 19, 20, 23, 25, 26, 28, 31 | 30, 31, 38 | 1 | | X | X | | | N | None |
| ND | Des Lacs NWR | 19,547 | 2 | A, E | 15, 16, 19, 20, 23, 26 | 6 | 1 | | | X | | | Y | Every 24 hours |
| ND | Devils Lake WMD | 202,088 | 3 | A, E, K | 14, 15, 19, 20, 25, 26, 28, 31 | 6, 30, 31, 38 | NR | | X | X | X | | N | None |
| ND | Florence Lake NWR | 1,888 | 1 | K | 3, 14, 15, 19, 20, 23, 25, 26, 28, 31 | 6, 30 | 1 | | X | X | | | Y | Every 24 hours |
| ND | Hobart NWR | 2,077 | 1 | K | 14, 15, 19, 26, 28, 31 | 6, 30 | NR | | X | X | | | Y | Daily |

| State(s) | National Wildlife Refuge Unit Name | Acreage | Number Trapping Programs | Primary Purpose(s) | Target Species | Threatened & Endangered Species Inhabiting Refuge Unit | Cost in $ Thousands | Live Enclosure | Steel-Jaw Leghold | Kill-Type | Kill Snares | Other Body-Hold Devices | Refuge-Specific Regs. | Refuge-Specific Trap Check Times |
|---|---|---|---|---|---|---|---|---|---|---|---|---|---|---|
| ND | J. Clark Salyer NWR | 59,383 | 3 | A, E, K | 14, 15, 19, 20, 25, 26, 28 | 6, 30, 31 | 7 | | X | X | | | Y | Every 24 hours |
| ND | J. Clark Salyer WMD | 158,180 | 2 | A, K | 14, 15, 19, 20, 25, 26, 28, 31 | 6, 30, 31, 38 | 2 | | X | X | X | X | N | None |
| ND | Johnson Lake NWR | 6,052 | 1 | A | 14, 15, 19, 20, 25, 28, 31 | | NR | | X | X | | | Y | Daily |
| ND | Kellys Slough NWR | 1,270 | 1 | A | 2, 19, 20, 25, 28 | | 2 | | X | X | X | | N | Every 48 hours |
| ND | Kulm WMD | 155,432 | 2 | A, K | 14, 15, 16, 19, 20, 23, 25, 26, 28, 31 | 6, 30, 31, 38 | 2 | X | X | X | X | | N | None |
| ND | Lake Alice NWR | 11,355 | 2 | A, E | 15, 19, 20, 25, 26, 28, 31 | 6, 30, 31 | 5 | | X | X | X | | N | Every 48 hours |
| ND | Lake Ardoch NWR | 2,696 | 1 | K | 14, 15, 19, 20, 25, 26, 28, 31 | | NR | | X | X | X | | N | None |
| ND | Lake Elsie NWR | 635 | 1 | K | 14, 15, 19, 20, 26, 28, 31 | | NR | | X | X | | | N | None |
| ND | Lake Ilo NWR | | 2 | A, D | 2, 19, 20, 23, 25, 26, 28 | 6, 30, 31, 38 | 1 | | X | X | | | Y | Every 24 hours |
| ND | Lake Nettie NWR | 3,055 | 2 | A, G | 1, 2, 14, 15, 19, 20, 23, 25, 26, 28, 31 | 6, 25, 30, 31, 38 | 1 | | X | X | | | Y | Every 24 hours |
| ND | Long Lake NWR | 22,499 | 2 | A, K | 1, 2, 14, 15, 16, 19, 20, 25, 26, 28, 31 | 6, 25, 30, 31, 38 | 14 | X | X | X | | | Y | See Note 7 |
| ND | Long Lake WMD | 123,674 | 2 | A, K | 2, 14, 15, 16, 19, 20, 21, 23, 25, 26, 27, 28, 30, 31 | 6, 25, 30, 31, 38 | 20 | X | X | X | X | | N | None |
| ND | Lords Lake NWR | 1,915 | 1 | K | 14, 19, 26, 28, 31 | 6, 30, 38 | NR | | X | X | | | N | None |
| ND | Lostwood WMD | 26,904 | 3 | A, B, K | 14, 15, 16, 19, 20, 23, 25, 26, 27, 28, 31 | 31 | 3 | | X | X | X | | Y | None |
| ND | Pleasant Lake NWR | 898 | 1 | K | 14, 15, 19, 20, 25, 26, 28, 31 | | NS | | X | X | X | | N | None |

| State(s) | National Wildlife Refuge Unit Name | Acreage | Number Trapping Programs | Primary Purpose(s) | Target Species | Threatened & Endangered Species Inhabiting Refuge Unit | Cost in $ Thousands | Live Enclosure | Steel-Jaw Leghold | Kill-Type | Kill Snares | Other Body-Hold Devices | Refuge-Specific Regs. | Refuge-Specific Trap Check Times |
|---|---|---|---|---|---|---|---|---|---|---|---|---|---|---|
| ND | Rock Lake NWR | 5,506 | 1 | K | 14, 15, 19, 20, 25, 26, 28, 31 | 6, 30 | NR | | X | X | X | | N | None |
| ND | School Section Lake NWR | 297 | 1 | K | 14, 15, 19, 26, 28, 31 | 6, 30, 38 | NR | | X | X | | | N | None |
| ND | Silver Lake NWR | 3,348 | 1 | K | 14, 15, 19, 20, 25, 26, 28, 31 | 6 | NR | | X | X | X | | N | None |
| ND | Slade NWR | 33,000 | 1 | K | 2, 14, 15, 19, 20, 23, 25, 26, 28, 31 | 6, 30 | 1 | | X | X | | | Y | Every 24 hours |
| ND | Snyder Lake NWR | 1,550 | 1 | K | 14, 15, 19, 20, 25, 26, 28, 31 | 6, 30 | NR | | X | X | X | | N | None |
| ND | Springwater NWR | 640 | 1 | K | 2, 14, 15, 19, 20, 25, 26, 28, 31 | 6, 30 | 1 | | X | X | | | N | Every 24 hours |
| ND | Stoney Slough NWR | 880 | 1 | K | 14, 15, 19, 26, 28, 31 | 6, 30 | NR | | X | X | | | Y | Daily |
| ND | Storm Lake NWR | 686 | 1 | K | 14, 15, 19, 20, 23, 25, 26, 28 | 6, 30 | NR | | X | X | | | Y | Yes, NS |
| ND | Stump Lake NWR | 27 | 1 | A | 19, 20, 28 | | NR | | | X | | | N | None |
| ND | Sullys Hill National Game Preserve | 1,675 | 1 | E | 15 | 6 | NR | | | X | | | Y | None |
| ND | Tewaukon NWR | 8,364 | 5 | A, I, K | 2, 15, 16, 17, 19, 20, 23, 26, 28 | 6, 30 | 8 | X | X | X | | X | Y | Every 24 hours |
| ND | Tewaukon WMD | 49,324 | 1 | K | 14, 15, 19, 20, 23, 25, 26, 28, 31 | 6, 30 | NR | | X | X | X | X | N | None |
| ND | Tomahawk NWR | 440 | 1 | K | 14, 15, 19, 26, 28, 31 | 6, 30 | NR | | X | X | | | Y | Daily |
| ND | Upper Souris NWR | 32,302 | 3 | A, C, E | 14, 15, 19, 20, 23, 25, 26, 28 | 6, 30, 31, 38 | 2 | X | X | X | | | Y | Every 24 hours |
| ND | Valley City WMD | 59,755 | 1 | K | 14, 15, 19, 26, 28, 31 | 6 | NR | | X | X | X | | N | None |
| ND | White Lake NWR | 1,040 | 1 | A | 2, 14, 15, 19, 20, 23, 25, 26, 28, 31 | 6 | NR | | X | | | | Y | Every 24 hours |
| ND | Willow Lake NWR | 2,620 | 1 | K | 14, 15, 19, 26, 28, 31 | 6, 30, 31, 38 | NR | | X | X | | | N | None |

202

| STATE(s) | National Wildlife Refuge Unit Name | Acreage | Number Trapping Programs | Primary Purpose(s) | Target Species | Threatened & Endangered Species Inhabiting Refuge Unit | Cost in $ Thousands | Live Enclosure | Steel-Jaw Leghold | Kill-Type | Kill Snares | Other Body-Hold Devices | Refuge-Specific Regs. | Refuge-Specific Trap Check Times |
|---|---|---|---|---|---|---|---|---|---|---|---|---|---|---|
| NE | Fort Niobrara NWR | 19,133 | 1 | I | 19 | 6, 30, 38 | 50 | X | | | | | N | None |
| NE | Rainwater Basin WMD | 2,401 | 1 | K | NS | 6, 25, 30, 31, 38 | NS | | | | | | N | None |
| NE | Valentine NWR | 71,517 | 2 | A, K | 14, 18, 19, 20, 23, 25, 26, 31 | 6, 38 | NR | | X | X | X | | N | Yes, NS |
| NH | Great Bay NWR | 1,083 | 2 | D, I | 2, 17 | 6, 30 | NR | X | | | | | N | None |
| NJ | Edwin B. Forsythe NWR | 43,080 | 2 | B, C | 1, 2, 10, 14, 18, 19, 20, 28 | 6, 30, 31 | 5 | X | | X | | X | Y | Every 24 hours |
| NJ | Great Swamp NWR | 7,415 | 3 | A, H | 14, 15, 17, 19, 27, 28 | 6, 30 | 3 | X | | | | | Y | Daily |
| NJ | Supwana Meadows NWR | 2,857 | 1 | G | 14 | | 1 | | | X | | | N | Every 24 hours |
| NJ, NY | Wallkill River NWR | 3,227 | 2 | H, L | 10, 17 | 6, 30 | 1 | | | | | X | N | None |
| NM | Bosque del Apache NWR | 57,191 | 3 | E, H | 15, 17, 40 | 6, 30, 34, 38 | NR | X | X | X | | | Y | None |
| NM | Maxwell NWR | 3,699 | 1 | L | 17 | 6, 30, 34 | 1 | | | | | X | N | None |
| NM | San Andres NWR | 57,215 | 2 | H, I | 17, 36, 40 | 6, 30 | 2 | X | | | | X | N | Yes, NS |
| NM | Sevilleta NWR | 229,674 | 1 | I | 40 | 6, 30, 34, 38 | NR | | | | | X | N | Every 24 hours |
| NV | Ash Meadows NWR | 13,268 | 4 | D, H, I, L | 5, 17, 40 | 30 | 3 | X | | | | X | N | None |
| NV | Desert NWR | 1,588,819 | 2 | C, H | 17, 40 | 78 | 7 | X | | | | X | N | None |
| NV | Pahranagat NWR | 5,383 | 1 | H | 17 | 6 | 2 | X | | | | | N | None |
| NV | Ruby Lake NWR | 57,631 | 3 | G, I, L | 2, 15, 17, 20 | 6, 30 | 1 | X | | X | | | N | Every 24 hours |
| NV | Stillwater NWR | 82,926 | 1 | H | 16, 17 | 6, 30 | 1 | X | | X | | | Y | Yes, NS |
| NY | Iroquois NWR | 10,822 | 2 | A, G | 14, 15, 19, 20, 26, 28, 29, 31, 40 | 6 | 1 | | X | X | | | Y | Every 24 hours |

| State(s) | National Wildlife Refuge Unit Name | Acreage | Number Trapping Programs | Primary Purpose(s) | Target Species | Threatened & Endangered Species Inhabiting Refuge Unit | Cost in $ Thousands | Live Enclosure | Steel-Jaw Leghold | Kill-Type | Kill Snares | Other Body-Hold Devices | Refuge-Specific Regs. | Refuge-Specific Trap Check Times |
|---|---|---|---|---|---|---|---|---|---|---|---|---|---|---|
| NY | Long Island NWR Complex | | 1 | I | 10, 17, 18, 19, 20, 23, 26, 28 | | NR | X | X | | | | N | Yes, NS |
| NY | Montezuma NWR | 7,136 | 1 | G | 14, 15, 18, 19, 26, 28 | 6, 30 | NR | X | X | X | | | Y | Every 24 hours |
| OH | Cedar Point NWR | 2,450 | 1 | G | 14, 18, 19, 20, 26, 28 | 6, 30 | 1 | | X | X | | | NS | NS |
| OH | Ottawa NWR | 5,793 | 1 | G | 14, 18, 19, 20, 26, 28 | 6, 30 | 1 | | X | X | | | NS | NS |
| OK | Little River NWR | 12,029 | 2 | E, H | 15, 40 | 6, 25, 30 | 1 | X | | X | | | Y | Daily |
| OK | Salt Plains NWR | 32,057 | 3 | A, E, L | 15, 19, 20 | 6, 25, 30, 38 | 1 | X | | X | | | N | Daily |
| OK | Sequoyah NWR | 20,800 | 2 | G, I | 15, 17 | 6, 25, 30 | 2 | X | | | X | X | N | None |
| OK | Wichita Mountains Wildlife Refuge | 5,902 | 2 | B, D | 3, 19 | 6, 7 | 9 | X | | | | | N | Every 24 hours |
| OR | Hart Mountain National Antelope Refuge | 262,907 | 3 | C, D, L | 5, 6, 17, 40 | 6, 30 | 11 | X | | | | X | N | None |
| OR | Lewis and Clark NWR | 41,034 | 2 | G, I | 12, 26 | 6, 30, 43 | NR | | X | | | | Y | Every 24 hours |
| OR | Malheur NWR | 185,876 | 2 | A, E | 14, 15, 19, 26, 31 | 6, 30 | 19 | X | X | X | X | | N | Every 48 hours |
| OR | Upper Klamath NWR | 14,966 | 1 | E | 14 | 6 | NR | | X | | | | Y | Every 24 hours |
| OR, NV | Sheldon NWR | 627 | 2 | D, L | 5, 6, 17 | 6 | 15 | X | | | | X | N | None |
| OR, WA | Umatilla NWR | 16,300 | 1 | G | 17 | 6, 36 | NR | | | | | X | Y | None |
| PR | Cabo Rojo NWR | 387 | 1 | I | 11 | 40 | 1 | X | | | | | N | 2X daily |
| RI | Trustom Pond NWR | 642 | 1 | B | 2, 18, 19, 20, 23, 26, 28, 31 | | 1 | X | X | X | | | N | None |
| SC | Cape Romain NWR | 65,225 | 1 | B | 19 | 5, 6, 30, 31, 39, 66, 85 | 1 | X | X | | | | N | Every A.M. |
| SC | Carolina Sandhills NWR | 45,348 | 2 | B, E | 15, 40 | 6, 32, 46 | 12 | X | | X | | | N | None |
| SD | Huron WMD | 133,663 | 1 | K | 14, 15, 18, 19, 20, 23, 25, 26, 28, 31 | | NR | X | X | X | X | | N | Every 48 hours |

| State(s) | National Wildlife Refuge Unit Name | Acreage | Number Trapping Programs | Primary Purpose(s) | Target Species | Threatened & Endangered Species Inhabiting Refuge Unit | Cost in $ Thousands | Live Enclosure | Steel-Jaw Leghold | Kill-Type | Kill Snares | Other Body-Hold Devices | Refuge-Specific Regs. | Refuge-Specific Trap Check Times |
|---|---|---|---|---|---|---|---|---|---|---|---|---|---|---|
| SD | Lacreek NWR | 16,855 | 2 | A, E | 1, 2, 14, 15, 19, 20, 23, 26, 28, 31 | 6, 30, 38 | 1 | | X | X | X | | Y | Every 24 hours |
| SD | Lake Andes NWR | 939 | 1 | A | 2, 18, 19, 20, 26, 28 | 6, 30, 38 | 1 | X | | X | | | N | Every 48 hours |
| SD | Lake Andes WMD | 63,033 | 1 | I | 40 | 6, 30, 38 | NR | X | | | | X | N | Every 48 hours |
| SD | Madison WMD | 110,184 | 1 | K | 14, 15, 16, 18, 19, 20, 23, 25, 26, 28, 31, 34 | | NR | X | X | X | X | X | Y | Every 48 hours |
| SD | Sand Lake NWR | 21,820 | 5 | A, C, I, K | 2, 14, 15, 16, 17, 19, 20, 23, 25, 26, 28, 31, 40 | | 4 | X | X | X | X | X | Y | Every 24 hours |
| SD | Sand Lake WMD | 484,528 | 1 | K | 14, 15, 19, 20, 25, 26, 28, 31 | | NR | | X | X | X | | N | Every 48 hours |
| SD | Waubay NWR | 4,740 | 2 | A, L | 17, 19, 20 | 6, 30 | NR | | | X | | X | N | None |
| SD | Waubay WMD | | 2 | E, K | 14, 15, 19, 20, 23, 26, 28, 31 | 6, 30 | NR | X | X | X | X | X | N | Every 48 hours |
| SD, NE | Karl E. Mundt NWR | 1,044 | 1 | G | 15 | 6, 30 | 1 | | | X | | | N | Every 48 hours |
| TN | Hatchie NWR | 11,556 | 1 | E | 15 | 6 | 4 | | | | | X | N | None |
| TN | Lower Hatchie NWR | 9,035 | 1 | E | 15 | 6, 25 | 1 | | | X | X | | Y | Daily |
| TN | Tennessee NWR | 51,359 | 1 | E | 14, 15, 19, 29, 31 | 6, 30, 46 | 4 | X | X | X | | X | N | None |
| TX | Anahuac NWR | 34,296 | 2 | D, E | 3, 10, 17 | 6, 30, 31, 39 | NR | X | | | | X | N | None |
| TX | Aransas/Matagorda Is. NWR Complex | 114,397 | 4 | D, I, L | 3, 17, 19, 34, 37, 40 | 3, 6, 8, 31, 38, 39, 81, 82, 83, 84, 85 | 13 | X | | | | | N | None |
| TX | Attwater Prairie Chicken NWR | 8,007 | 1 | B | 18, 19, 20, 34 | 3, 6, 30 | 5 | X | | X | | | N | Every A.M. |
| TX | Balcones Canyonlands NWR | 15,360 | 1 | D | 3 | 7, 14 | 5 | X | | X | X | | N | Daily |
| TX | Brazoria NWR | 43,905 | 1 | I | 40 | 6, 30, 31, 39 | NR | X | | | | | N | None |

| State(s) | National Wildlife Refuge Unit Name | Acreage | Number Trapping Programs | Primary Purpose(s) | Target Species | Threatened & Endangered Species Inhabiting Refuge Unit | Cost in $ Thousands | Live Enclosure | Steel-Jaw Leghold | Kill-Type | Kill Snares | Other Body-Hold Devices | Refuge-Specific Regs. | Refuge-Specific Trap Check Times |
|---|---|---|---|---|---|---|---|---|---|---|---|---|---|---|
| TX | Buffalo Lake NWR | 7,664 | 2 | I, L | 17, 40 | 6, 25 | NR | X | | | | X | Y | Daily |
| TX | Hagerman NWR | 11,320 | 1 | E | 15 | 6, 25, 31 | 1 | | | X | | | N | None |
| TX | Laguna Atascosa NWR | 45,187 | 3 | H, I, L | 17, 34, 37 | 6, 8, 9, 28, 30, 31, 39, 57, 58, 65, 85 | 9 | X | | | | X | Y | Daily |
| TX | San Bernard NWR | 28,095 | 2 | A, D | 3, 19 | 6, 8, 30, 31, 39 | 1 | X | | | | | N | None |
| TX | Santa Ana NWR | 2,088 | 2 | D, I | 3, 37 | 6, 7, 8, 14, 28, 30, 31, 39, 57, 58, 65 | 3 | X | | | | | N | Every A.M. |
| UM | Johnston Island NWR | 100 | 1 | L | 17 | | NR | | | | | X | N | None |
| UM | Midway Atoll NWR | 90,097 | 1 | A | 10, 17 | | 2 | X | | | | X | N | None |
| UT | Bear River Migratory Bird Refuge | 73,645 | 1 | I | 19, 20 | 6, 30 | 1 | X | | | | | N | Daily |
| UT | Fish Springs NWR | 17,992 | 3 | E, H | 14, 17, 40 | 6, 30 | 1 | X | | X | | X | Y | Yes, NS |
| UT | Ouray NWR | 12,138 | 2 | A, E | 15, 19, 20, 28, 31 | 6, 30, 38 | 1 | | X | X | X | | N | Every 48 hours |
| VA | Marumsco NWR | 63 | 1 | E | 15 | 6, 30 | NR | | | X | | | N | None |
| VA | Mason Neck NWR | 2,276 | 1 | D | 1, 2 | 6, 30 | 1 | X | | | | | N | None |
| VA, MD | Chincoteague NWR | 13,596 | 6 | B, D, E, H, I | 2, 10, 18, 19, 28, 40 | 6, 30, 31, 44, 85 | 2 | X | X | X | X | | N | Every A.M. |
| VA, NC | Great Dismal Swamp NWR | 82,197 | 3 | C, H, I | 33, 38, 40 | 6, 45 | 506 | X | | | | X | N | None |
| VI | Sandy Point NWR | 327 | 1 | I | 11 | 81, 82, 84 | 1 | X | | | | | Y | 2X daily |
| VT | Missisquoi NWR | 6,346 | 2 | A, E | 14, 15, 19 | 6 | NR | | X | X | | | Y | Every 24 hours |
| WA | Columbia NWR | 29,597 | 4 | A, E, G, L | 15, 17, 19, 26, 31 | 6, 30 | 3 | X | X | X | X | X | N | See Note 4 |
| WA | Little Pend Oreille NWR | 39,999 | 3 | H, K, L | 14, 15, 17, 23, 34 | 6 | 5 | X | X | | | X | N | Every 24 hours |
| WA | Nisqually NWR | 2,925 | 1 | I | 17, 40 | 6, 30 | 1 | X | | | | | N | 2X daily |

| STATE(s) | NATIONAL WILDLIFE REFUGE UNIT NAME | ACREAGE | NUMBER TRAPPING PROGRAMS | PRIMARY PURPOSE(s) | TARGET SPECIES | THREATENED & ENDANGERED SPECIES INHABITING REFUGE UNIT | COST IN $ THOUSANDS | LIVE ENCLOSURE | STEEL-JAW LEGHOLD | KILL-TYPE | KILL SNARES | OTHER BODY-HOLD DEVICES | REFUGE-SPECIFIC REGS. | REFUGE-SPECIFIC TRAP CHECK TIMES |
|---|---|---|---|---|---|---|---|---|---|---|---|---|---|---|
| WA | Ridgefield NWR | 5,218 | 1 | L | 40 | 2, 6, 30 | NR | X | | | | X | N | None |
| WA | Saddle Mountain NWR | 30,810 | 2 | H, I | 17 | 6, 30 | NR | X | | | | | N | None |
| WA | Steigerwald Lake NWR | 955 | 1 | E | 15 | | NR | | X | | | X | N | None |
| WA | Turnbull NWR | 17,882 | 2 | H, I | 40 | 6 | 16 | X | | | | X | N | Every A. M. |
| WA, OR | Julia Butler Hansen Refuge | 2,750 | 1 | G | 12 | 6, 43 | NR | | X | | | | Y | Every 24 hours |
| WI | Horicon NWR | 21,176 | 1 | E | 14, 18, 19, 20, 23, 26, 28, 29 | 6, 30 | 2 | | X | X | | | NS | NS |
| WI | Leopold WMD | | 1 | E | 14, 19, 23, 24, 26, 28, 29, 31 | 6, 30, 52 | NR | | X | X | | | NS | NS |
| WI | Necedah NWR | 43,696 | 3 | C, E, H | 14, 15, 17, 18, 19, 20, 23, 26 | 6 | 32 | X | X | X | X | X | NS | NS |
| WI | St. Croix WMD | 5,931 | 1 | K | 14, 15, 18, 19, 24, 26, 28 | 6, 23, 30, 52 | NR | | X | | | | NS | NS |
| WI | Trempealeau NWR | 5,754 | 1 | K | 14, 15, 18, 19, 20, 26 | 6, 30 | 4 | X | X | X | | | NS | NS |
| WY | Seedskadee NWR | 23,332 | 4 | A, E, H, L | 1, 2, 15, 19, 20, 26 | 6 | 203 | X | X | X | | X | Y | Every 24 hours |

# Notes for Appendix V

**National Wildlife Refuge Unit Name**

NWR = National Wildlife Refuge

WMD = Wetland Management District

**Primary Purpose(s):**

A = Predator control for migratory bird protection

B = Predator control for threatened and endangered species protection

C = Population management

D = Feral animal control

E = Facilities protection

F = Disease control

G = Habitat management or protection

H = Surveys or monitoring

I = Research

K = Recreation/commerce/subsistence

L = Public health and safety

M = Other

* Felsenthal NWR (AR): Program K is indicated as used in part 1 of the survey, but not in part 2.

^ Upper Mississippi River Wildlife & Fish Refuge, McGregor District (IA, WI, MN): Program A is indicated as used in part 1 of the survey, but not in part 2.

**Target Species:**

1 = feral dog

2 = feral cat

3 = feral pig

4 = feral goat

5 = feral horse

6 = feral burro

7 = other feral animals (general)

8 = nilgai antelope

9 = exotic sheep

10 = norway and/or black rat

11 = mongoose

12 = nutria

13 = other exotics (general)

14 = muskrat

15 = beaver

16 = ground squirrels (general)

17 = other rodents (general)

18 = opossum

19 = raccoon

20 = striped skunk

21 = spotted skunk

22 = hog-nosed skunk

23 = weasels (general)

24 = river otter

25 = badger

26 = mink

27 = other mustelids (general)

28 = red fox

29 = gray fox

30 = arctic fox

31 = coyote

32 = gray/timber wolf

33 = other canids (general)

34 = bobcat

35 = lynx

36 = cougar

37 = other felids (general)

38 = black bear

39 = grizzly bear

40 = other

**Threatened & Endangered Species Inhabiting Refuge Unit**

*Birds*

1 = Akiapolaau

2 = Aleutian Canada Goose

3 = Attwater's Greater Prairie Chicken

4 = Audubon's Crested Caracara

5 = Bachman's Warbler

6 = Bald Eagle

7 = Black-capped Vireo

8 = Brown Pelican

9 = Cactus Ferruginous Pygmy Owl

10 = California Condor

11 = Clapper Rail (light-footed)

12 = Everglade Sail Kite

13 = Florida Scrub Jay

14 = Golden-checked Warbler

15 = Hawaiian Akepa

16 = Hawaiian Common Moorhen

17 = Hawaiian Coot

18 = Hawaiian Creeper

19 = Hawaiian Duck

20 = Hawaiian Goose

21 = Hawaiian Hawk

22 = Hawaiian Stilt
23 = Kirtland's Warbler
24 = Least Bells Vireo
25 = Least Tern
26 = Masked Bobwhite
27 = Mississippi Sandhill Crane
28 = Northern Aplomando Falcon
29 = 'O'u (honeycreeper)
30 = Peregrine Falcon
31 = Piping Plover
32 = Red Cockaded Woodpecker
33 = Roseate Tern
34 = Southwestern Willow Flycatcher
35 = Spectacled Eider
36 = Steller's Eider
37 = Western Snowy Plover
38 = Whooping Crane
39 = Woodstork
40 = Yellow-shouldered Black Bird

*Mammals*

41 = Blue Whale
42 = Bowhead Whale
43 = Colombian White-tailed Deer
44 = Delmarva Peninsula Fox Squirrel
45 = Dismal Swamp Southeastern Shrew
46 = Eastern Cougar (probably extinct)
47 = Finback whale
48 = Florida Manatee
49 = Florida Panther
50 = Gray Bat
51 = Gray Whale
52 = Gray Wolf
53 = Grizzly Bear
54 = Hawaiian Monk Seal
55 = Humpback Whale
56 = Indiana Bat
57 = Jaguar
58 = Jaguarundi
59 = Key Deer
60 = Key Largo Cotton Mouse
61 = Key Largo Wood Rat
62 = Louisiana Black Bear
63 = Lower Keys Rabbit
64 = Northern Steller Sea Lion
65 = Ocelot

66 = Red Wolf
67 = Rice Rat
68 = Right Whale
69 = Salt Marsh Harvest Mouse
70 = San Joaquin Kit Fox
71 = Sei Whale
72 = Southeastern Beach Mouse
73 = Sperm Whale
74 = Tipton Kangaroo Rat

*Reptiles*

75 = American Crocodile
76 = Atlantic Salt Marsh Snake
77 = Blunt-nosed Leopard Lizard
78 = Desert Tortoise
79 = Eastern Indigo Snake
80 = Gopher Tortoise
81 = Green Sea Turtle
82 = Hawksbill Sea Turtle
83 = Kemp Ridley's Sea Turtle
84 = Leather Back Sea Turtle
85 = Loggerhead Sea Turtle
86 = Northern Copperbelly Water Snake
87 = Ringed Sawback Turtle

**Cost in Thousands**

NR = Not reported

A number of refuge managers failed to indicate the dollar amount spent to administer trapping programs. Thus, one can assume that the total amount spent to administer trapping programs on the NWRS was greater than the $2,823,000 indicated.

**Refuge Specific Regulations**

NS = Refuge failed to specify whether or not refuge-specific trap check time requirements exist.

**Refuge-specific trap check time:**

NS = Refuge failed to specify whether or not refuge-specific trap check time requirements exist.

Yes = Refuge indicated the existence of refuge-specific trap check time requirements, but failed to include specific details about the requirements.

**Notes**

1. Traps are checked every 48 hours for water sets, and every 24 hours for all others.

2. Live traps are checked daily, while Conibear traps are checked at least twice weekly.

3. Conibear traps and snares are checked every 2 or 3 days, and leghold traps are checked daily.

4. Snares and live enclosure traps are checked daily. Check time requirements for other traps are not specified.

5. Traps are checked "During one evening and the following morning / Total time required to set and pick up traps was 24 hours."

6. Traps or snares that hold and do not immediately kill animals are checked daily. Time check requirements are not specified for other traps.

7. Refuge requires trap checks every 24 hours for trappers who are issued permits. There are no trap check requirements for kill-type traps used by staff.

8. Pitfall traps used to catch shrews are checked at least every 48 hours, starting 5 days after installation. Other trap check times are not specified.

9. Refuge requires that leghold traps are checked at least every 18 hours and that Conibear and live enclosure traps are checked at least every 24 hours.

10. Pitfall traps used to catch shrews are checked at least every 48 hours, starting 5 days after installation. Other trap check times are not specified.

11. Conibear traps are checked every other day. Check time requirements are not specified for other types of traps.

# Glossary of Terms

*(For thorough descriptions of trap types
and modifications, see Chapter Three.)*

**Anchor Chain:** A chain used to connect a trap to either a stationary object or a **drag.**

**Bailey Trap:** A live-holding/**restraining trap** resembling a wire mesh clamshell joined by spring-powered hinges. Generally used to trap beaver.

**Bionic Trap:** A mousetrap-style **kill trap** generally used to trap medium-sized furbearers, including mink and marten.

**Box/Cage Trap:** A **restraining trap** designed in the form of a box made in any shape or size and of any material such as metal, wire, wood, or netting.

**Capture Efficiency:** The capability of a trap to capture target animals within a specified period of time and typically expressed as number of captures/number of trap nights (where trap nights = number of traps x nights set). Studies sometimes use capture efficiency and capture rate interchangeably.

**Capture Rate:** The capability of a trap to capture target animals expressed as number of target animals captured/potential captures (where potential captures equals all animals captured + sprung traps without capture + temporary captures + any unsprung traps with footprints on the trap pan). Studies sometimes use capture efficiency and capture rate interchangeably.

**Colony Trap:** A cage or box trap set in water to capture and drown multiple animals.

**Conibear Trap:** The most commonly used kill trap, designed to strike the head-neck or thorax region of an animal. There are many types and modifications of Conibear traps, including the C120 Magnum, C120 Mark IV, and the Sauvageau series.

**Deadfall Trap:** A **kill trap** consisting of a baited trigger attached to a heavy object, such as a rock or tree limb, that falls on and kills the animal pulling on the trigger.

**Drag:** A device that is attached to a trap and used to allow a trapped animal a certain degree of movement while ensuring that the animal cannot travel far from the trap set site. Generally, a drag consists of metal prongs that will tangle in brush, rocks or fences.

**EGG Trap:** A **leghold trap** encased in an egg-shaped plastic cover to prevent self-mutilation by captured raccoons.

**Floating Log Set:** One or more leghold traps placed on a secured floating log or plank. The trap chains are stapled to the bottom of the float and the traps are baited and concealed. When a muskrat or other aquatic animal is caught, it dives off the float and the weight of the trap holds the animal underwater until it drowns.

**Hancock Trap:** A live-holding/**restraining trap** resembling a wire mesh trunk and comprised of two open sections, joined together by spring-powered hinges. Generally used to trap beaver, otter, and other terrestrial animals.

**Kania Trap:** A mousetrap-style **kill trap** generally used for trapping small furbearers such as squirrels and mink.

**Kill Trap:** A trap designed and set with the intention of killing an animal. Types include **Conibear,** C120 Magnum, C120 Mark IV, Sauvageau, Bionic, Kania, neck/body **snare,** and **deadfall.**

**Laminated Jaws:** Jaws of a standard leghold trap modified with the addition of round steel rods.

**Leghold (Foothold) Trap:** A **restraining trap** that targets the leg or foot of an animal. There are many types of leghold traps.

**Log Trap:** A **box trap** made of wood and other materials secured on the spot and designed to trap lynx, wolverine, bobcat, fox, and other forest carnivores.

**Non-Target Species:** Species other than the one for which the trap has been set.

**Offset Jaws:** Jaws of a **leghold trap** modified to create a gap when closed (size varies, but usually less than $\frac{1}{4}$").

**Padded Jaws:** Jaws of a **leghold trap** with rubber padding (sometimes also called a "Soft Catch" leghold trap).

**Pan Trigger:** A flat pan attached to a **leghold trap** or **leg snare** that triggers the trap when stepped on by an animal.

**Pan-Tension Device:** A weight-sensitive device that replaces the standard pan trigger of a leghold trap and is designed to exclude small non-target species.

**Pole Set:** Pole sets generally consist of leghold traps (sometimes snares or Conibear traps are used) set above the ground and attached to a pole, log, or tree branch. When an animal becomes trapped, it will dangle in the air, unable to gnaw or twist its caught appendage free of the trap, thereby preventing a loss for the trapper. Pole sets are legal in most states.

**Restraining Trap:** A trap designed and set with the intention of live-capturing an animal. Types include **leghold trap, box trap, log, pitfall,** and **foot/leg snares.**

**Slide Set:** Designed to drown an animal, a slide set consists of a trap (generally a leghold trap) set on land or in very shallow water that is attached to a wire, which is staked to a stick or pole. When the animal is trapped, a weight connected to the wire pulls the trapped animal underwater, ostensibly drowning the animal.

**Snare:** A simple trapping device generally consisting of a light wire cable looped through a locking device, designed to tighten as the animal pulls against it. Snares are categorized as "neck," "body" or "leg/foot." Snares can be **restraining** or **killing** devices, depending upon how they are set and whether "stop-locks" are used. Snares can also be "manual" (killing or restraining force supplied by animal) or "power" (killing force supplied by spring-activated mechanism).

**Stake:** A pole, stick, or fence post used to secure a set trap. Stakes are used to limit movement of the trapped animal, but leave the restrained animal exposed to the elements and to predators.

**Submersion Set:** A set in which a trap or snare is used to restrain or kill an animal underwater.

**Swivel:** A simple device which can be attached to an **anchor chain** of a **leghold trap** or **snare** to prevent the chain from becoming twisted while an animal struggles in the trap.

**Target Species:** Species for which a trap has been set with the intent to capture.

**Trap Injuries:** The injuries sustained by an animal resulting from capture in a trap.

**Trapline:** An area where a trapper sets his traps, which may cover many acres or miles of land, making frequent trap checks difficult, especially in inclement weather. Trappers may have multiple active traplines during the trapping season.

**Trap Selectivity:** A measure of a trap's ability to minimize the capture of **non-target** animals, expressed as the number of **target** animals captured divided by the total number of all animals captured, including non-target animals.

# Photograph and
# Illustration Credits

# Index